A Concise Survey of Music Philos

MW00804026

A Concise Survey of Music Philosophy helps music students choose a philosophy that will guide them throughout their careers. The book is divided into three sections: central issues that any music philosophy ought to consider (e.g., beauty, emotion, and aesthetics); secondly, significant philosophical positions, exploring what major thinkers have had to say on the subject; and finally, opportunities for students to consider the ramifications of these ideas for themselves. Throughout the book, students are encouraged to make choices that will inform a philosophy of music and music education with which they are most comfortable to align.

Frequently, music philosophy courses are taught in such a way that the teacher, as well as the textbook used, promotes a particular viewpoint. *A Concise Survey of Music Philosophy* presents the most current, prevalent philosophies for consideration. Students think through different issues and consider practical applications.

There are numerous musical examples, each with links from the author's home website to online video performances. Examples are largely from the Western classical canon, but also jazz, popular, and world music styles. In the last two chapters, students apply their views to practical situations and learn the differences between philosophy and advocacy.

Donald A. Hodges was Covington Distinguished Professor and Director of the Music Research Institute of Music Education at the University of North Carolina, Greensboro, and author of *Music in the Human Experience* (Routledge 2011). He has taught university courses in Music for more than forty-two years.

A Concise Survey of Music Philosophy

Donald A. Hodges

Routledge
Taylor & Francis Group

NEW YORK AND LONDON

First published 2017
by Routledge
711 Third Avenue, New York, NY 10017

and by Routledge
2 Park Square, Milton Park, Abingdon, Oxon, OX14 4RN

Routledge is an imprint of the Taylor & Francis Group, an informa business

Library of Congress Cataloging-in-Publication Data
Names: Hodges, Donald A., author.
Title: A concise survey of music philosophy / Donald A. Hodges.
Description: New York, NY ; Abingdon, Oxon : Routledge, 2016. | "2016 |
    Includes bibliographical references and index.
Identifiers: LCCN 2016012664 (print) | LCCN 2016013609 (ebook) |
    ISBN 9781138954526 (hardback) | ISBN 9781138954519 (paperback) |
    ISBN 9781317356479 ()
Subjects: LCSH: Music—Philosophy and aesthetics.
Classification: LCC ML3800. H713 2016 (print) | LCC ML3800 (ebook) |
    DDC 780.1—dc23
LC record available at http://lccn.loc.gov/2016012664

ISBN: 978-1-138-95452-6 (hbk)
ISBN: 978-1-138-95451-9 (pbk)
ISBN: 978-1-315-66689-1 (ebk)

Typeset in Sabon
by Apex CoVantage, LLC

Editor: Constance Ditzel
Editorial Assistant: Peter Sheehy
Production Editor: Katie Hemmings
Marketing Manager: Jessica Plummer
Copy Editor: Apex CoVantage, LLC
Proofreader: Apex CoVantage, LLC
Cover Design: Mathew Willis

Contents

List of Illustrations   xiii
List of Musical Examples   xv
Preface   xxvii

SECTION I
Beginning the Journey   1

1   The Plan and Purpose of This Book   3
What Is Philosophy? 4
Why Do I Need to Have a Philosophy of Music? 5
Section I: Beginning the Journey 7
Section II: A Review of Major Music Philosophies 9
Section III: Making It Your Own 10
Summary and Thought Questions 11
Notes 12

2   Science and Religion   14
Science 14
    Examples of Scientific and Philosophical Interactions 14
    Music Psychology and Music Philosophy 16
Religion 17
    Philosophy of Religion 18
    Philosophy, Religion, and Music 19
Summary and Thought Questions 21
Notes 22

3   Knowledge and Education   24
Knowledge 24
    Key Ideas in Epistemology 24
    Musical Knowledge 26

Education 29
  Educational Philosophy 30
  Social Justice and Culturally Responsive Teaching 33
Summary and Thought Questions 34
Notes 35

4   **Beauty**   39
Questions about Beauty in Art 39
  Question 1: *What Is Beauty? 39*
  Question 2: *Is Beauty in the Eye (Ear) of the Beholder, or Is It
    Inherent in an Art Object (e.g., a Statue, a Musical Composition,
    etc.) Independent of Human Perception? 41*
  Question 3: *Does Every Opinion about What Is Beautiful Art Carry Equal
    Weight? 41*
  Question 4: *Can You Identify Objective Properties in Beautiful
    Art? 42*
  Question 5: *Do Subjective Judgments Play a Role in Determining
    Beauty in Art? 42*
  Question 6: *Are There Connections between Beauty in Art and Truth,
    Goodness, Morals, or Similar Terms? 42*
  Question 7: *Can Art Considered Ugly by One Standard Be Considered
    Beautiful in Another Context? 43*
Beauty in Music 46
Research on Beauty in Music 48
Summary and Thought Questions 49
Notes 49

5   **Emotion**   53
What Is an Emotion? 54
What Have Philosophers Thought about Musical Emotions? 55
*Does Psychological Research Support or Contradict Various Philosophical
  Views? 56*
What Role Will Musical Emotions Play in Your Philosophy? 58
Summary and Thought Questions 59
Notes 60

6   **Aesthetics**   62
What Is Art? What Is Music? 62
What Does the Word 'Aesthetic' Mean? 64
What Is an Aesthetic Experience? 65
What Are Aesthetic Values? 66
What Can We Gain from Art? 67
Who Determines Aesthetic Values? 69

Experimental Aesthetics 70
    The Golden Mean 72
    Berlyne's Arousal Theory 72
    Preference for Prototype Theory 72
    Chills as an Indicator of Aesthetic Response 73
    Juslin's BRECVEMA Model 74
    Neuroaesthetics 74
Summary and Thought Questions 75
Notes 76

7 **A Philosophical Framework**   81
What Is the Basis for Determining Musical Meaning and Value? 81
What Kind of Music Has Aesthetic Value? 93
    Does Popular Music Have Aesthetic Value? 93
    A Special Case of 'School' Music 95
    World Music 98
Summary and Thought Questions 100
Notes 101

SECTION II
A Review of Major Music Philosophies   105

8 **Contributions to Music Philosophy from the Ancient Greeks**   107
Music in Ancient Greece 107
Philosophical Ideas 108
    Music as Mathematics 108
    Music as an Imitation of Harmonious Balance 109
    Music as an Influence on Human Behavior 110
    Aristotle's Contributions 111
Summary and Thought Questions 112
Notes 113

9 **From Classical Antiquity to the Renaissance**   115
Neoplatonism 115
    Music in Ancient Rome 115
    Plotinus 116
    Music in the Early Church 117
    St. Augustine 117
Music Philosophy in the Middle Ages and Renaissance 118
    Boethius 118
    Thomas Aquinas 119
    Martin Luther 120

Summary and Thought Questions 121
Notes 122

10 Rationalism, Empiricism, and Idealism   125
Rationalism 126
Empiricism 127
Idealism 128
   Immanuel Kant 128
   Friedrich Schiller 129
   Georg Wilhelm Friedrich Hegel 130
   Arthur Schopenhauer 131
Musical Examples 132
Summary and Thought Questions 133
Notes 135

11 Formalism   138
Eduard Hanslick 138
Edmund Gurney 140
Clive Bell 141
Leonard Meyer 142
An Evaluation of Formalism 144
Musical Examples 145
Music Psychology Research 146
Summary and Thought Questions 147
Notes 148

12 Expressionism   152
Leo Tolstoy 153
Benedetto Croce 154
R. G. Collingwood 154
Deryck Cooke 155
Peter Kivy 156
Stephen Davies 157
Jenefer Robinson 157
Musical Examples 158
Research on Musical Emotions 160
Summary and Thought Questions 163
Notes 165

13 Symbolism   169
Susanne Langer 169
Nelson Goodman 170

Monroe Beardsley 171
Jean-Jacques Nattiez 172
Music from a Symbolist Perspective 172
Summary and Thought Questions 176
Notes 176

14 Phenomenology   180
Musical Experiences 180
Edmund Husserl 181
Maurice Merleau-Ponty 181
Mikel Dufrenne 182
Thomas Clifton 182
David Burrows 183
Eleanor Stubley 183
Mark Johnson 184
Summary and Thought Questions 184
Notes 185

15 Pragmatism   187
Charles Sanders Peirce 187
William James 188
John Dewey 188
A Utilitarian View 191
Summary and Thought Questions 191
Notes 192

16 Social Philosophy   194
Theodor Adorno 194
Jacques Attali 196
Music in a Social Context 197
Summary and Thought Questions 198
Notes 199

17 Praxialism   201
Phillip Alperson 202
David Elliott 203
Alperson Revisited 205
Thomas Regelski 206
Musical Examples 206
Summary and Thought Questions 207
Notes 207

18 Feminism   210

   Women in Music History 210
      Hildegard von Bingen 210
      Maria Anna Mozart 211
      Fanny Mendelssohn Hensl 211
      Clara Wieck Schumann 211
      Alma Schindler Mahler 212
      Nadia Boulanger 212
   A Musical Example 214
   Feminist Philosophies of Music 217
      Heide Göttner-Abendroth 217
      Susan McClary 219
      Marcia Citron 220
   Summary and Thought Questions 221
   Notes 222

19 Postmodernism   226

   Postmodernism in Music 227
   Postmodernism as a Music Philosophy 228
   Possible Solution? 231
   Summary and Thought Questions 233
   Notes 234

SECTION III
Making It Your Own   237

20 Articulating a Philosophy of Music   239
   Exercises 240
   Notes 248

21 Applying Your Philosophy   249
   Chapter 8: Contributions to Music Philosophy from the Ancient Greeks 249
   Chapter 9: From Classical Antiquity to the Renaissance 249
   Chapter 10: Rationalism, Empiricism, and Idealism 250
   Chapter 11: Formalism 250
   Chapter 12: Expressionism 250
   Chapter 13: Symbolism 251
   Chapter 14: Phenomenology 251
   Chapter 15: Pragmatism 252
   Chapter 16: Social Philosophy 252
   Chapter 17: Praxialism 252

Chapter 18: Feminism 253
Chapter 19: Postmodernism 253
Notes 254

22 Advocacy   255
What Is Advocacy? 255
Why Is Advocacy Necessary? 255
What Not to Do 256
Strategies and Resources for Music Advocacy 259
  Prevention Not Cure 260
  Economic Rationales in Music Advocacy 260
Additional Resources 261
Summary and Thought Questions 261
Final Comments 262
Notes 263

Bibliography   265
Index   291

Illustrations

Figures

Chapter 4 Beauty

4.1	Michelangelo's *David*.	40
4.2	"Beautiful" hands.	43
4.3	"Ugly" hands.	43
4.4	Sculpted face.	44
4.5	Michelangelo's *Bandini Pietà*.	45

Chapter 6 Aesthetics

6.1	Maximum pleasure is based upon an optional level of arousal potential.	73

Chapter 7 A Philosophical Framework

7.1	Fugue No. 11 in F Major from *The Well-Tempered Clavier*, BWV 846.	82
7.2	Excerpt from 'On the Trail,' from *Grand Canyon Suite* by Ferde Grofé.	82
7.3	Opening measures of 'Dies Irae' (Day of Wrath) from Mozart's *Requiem in d minor*, K. 626.	83
7.4	Schubert's Octet in F Major, Op. 166 (D. 803), opening of second movement.	84
7.5	Music and musical experiences of any kind.	85
7.6	Formalism: The focus is on the music or musical experience and the meaning and value come from intellectual appreciation.	86
7.7	'Take Five' by Paul Desmond.	86
7.8	Referentialism: The focus is on what the music refers to outside itself.	87
7.9	Absolute expressionism: Anything external to the music, such as lyrics, programmatic titles, and so on, are expressed in musical elements.	88
7.10	The love theme from Tchaikovsky's *Romeo and Juliet Fantasy Overture*.	88
7.11	The beginning of the main theme of Fantaisie and Variations on *The Carnival of Venice* as arranged by Arban and revised by Goldman; only the solo trumpet part is shown.	89
7.12	Opening measures of George Gershwin's *An American in Paris*; reduced piano score.	89

Chapter 11 Formalism

11.1 Opening melody in the second movement of Haydn's Symphony No. 94.   143

Chapter 13 Symbolism

13.1 The last five measures of *Also sprach Zarathustra* by Richard Strauss.   174
13.2 The trumpet figure representing 'The Perennial Question of Existence' from
      Charles Ives's *The Unanswered Question.*   175

Chapter 22 Advocacy

22.1 SAT scores among students with more than four years of study in English,
      mathematics, foreign language, or art/music.   259

Tables

Chapter 7 A Philosophical Framework

7.1 Dichotomy 1.   81
7.2 Dichotomy 2.   84
7.3 Simplified chart of music philosophies.   84

Chapter 18 Feminism

18.1 Outline of Robert Schumann's *Frauenliebe und -leben.*   215

Musical Examples

This listing includes specific musical works mentioned in the text. In addition, numerous musical experiences such as singing in a church choir or playing in a garage band are also discussed. In the text, musical examples listed below are indicated with the icon ♫. Superscript numbers in this list indicate the endnote for the example. Here, and in the endnotes at the ends of each chapter, is a link to a YouTube recording for each example. You may also go to this URL—https://sites.google.com/a/uncg.edu/https-sites-google-com-site-concisesurveyofmusphil/home—to click on active links to the recordings. Because YouTube links change frequently, you may find a broken link; however, it should be relatively easy to find another recording.

Chapter 2 Science and Religion

[48]Duke Ellington: 'In the Beginning God' from *Sacred Concerts*, performed by Duke Ellington: https://www.youtube.com/watch?v=8jFa-4b2FTk.

[49]Duke Ellington: 'Something 'bout Believing' from *Sacred Concerts*, performed by Duke Ellington: https://www.youtube.com/watch?v=R_ty0XVhxQY.

[50]Duke Ellington: 'Father Forgive' from *Sacred Concerts*, performed by combined choirs conducted by Randall Keith Horton: http://www.youtube.com/watch?v=weI3UKMn2Sg.

[56]Johannes Brahms: *Requiem*, performed by Herbert Blomstedt conducting the Denmark Radio Symphony Orchestra: http://www.youtube.com/watch?v=dJelOS-fjrY.

[57]Ernest Bloch: *Schelomo*, performed by Mstislav Rostropovich, cellist; Leonard Bernstein, conductor; and the Orchestre Nacional de France: http://www.youtube.com/watch?v=vlUQyEh_q4k.

[58]John Coltrane: 'Dear Lord,' performed by John Coltrane: http://www.youtube.com/watch?v=FpoyOwKJ1A0.

[61]George Frideric Handel: *Messiah*, performed by the Academy of Ancient Music and Choir of King's College, Cambridge, conducted by Stephen Cleobury: https://www.youtube.com/watch?v=AZTZRtRFkvk.

Chapter 3 Knowledge and Education

[13]Claude Debussy: *La Mer*, performed by Valery Gergiev and the London Symphony Orchestra: http://www.youtube.com/watch?v=hlR9rDJMEiQ.

Chapter 4 Beauty

[20]Wolfgang Mozart: 'Sull'aria' from *The Marriage of Figaro*, sung by Kiri te Kanawa and Mirella Freni: http://www.youtube.com/watch?v=goYSEpSsX3o.

[21]Leo Delibes: 'Flower Duet' from *Lakme*, duet sung by Anna Nerebko and Elina Garanca: http://www.youtube.com/watch?v=M9NK-EbUAao.

[22]Georges Bizet: 'Au fond du temple saint' from *The Pearl Fishers*, sung by Dmitri Hvorostovsky and Jonas Kaufmann: http://www.youtube.com/watch?v=p2MwnHpLV48.

[23]Erich Korngold: 'Marietta's Lied' from *Die tote Stadt*, performed by Leontyne Price: http://www.youtube.com/watch?v=vh_8Sos4szY.

[24]Richard Strauss: 'Beim schlafengehn' from *Four Last Songs*, sung by Kiri te Kanawa: http://www.youtube.com/watch?v=3XP2chJ6Ujc.

[25]Reynaldo Hahn: *L'Enamourée*, sung by Anna Netrebko: http://www.youtube.com/watch?v=kUZPljVpWak .

[26]Heitor Villa-Lobos: 'Aria' (Cantilena) from *Bachianas brasileiras* No. 5, sung by Anna Moffo: http://www.youtube.com/watch?v=anxdAcilnsM.

[27]María Grever: *Júrame*, performed by Ramón Vargas, tenor, and Alun Francis conducting the Orquesta Filharmónca de la UNAM (National Autonomous University of Mexico): https://www.youtube.com/watch?v=8JbbWpknygM.

[28]Felix Mendelssohn: 'Lift Thine Eyes' from *Elijah*, sung by Choristers of Canterbury Cathedral: http://www.youtube.com/watch?v=BT7rFMrrkYU.

[29]Morton Lauridsen: *O Magnum Mysterium*, sung by King's College Choir: http://www.youtube.com/watch?v=Q7ch7uottHU.

[30]François Couperin: *Les Barricades Mystérieuses*, performed by Scott Ross on harpsichord: http://www.youtube.com/watch?v=sf-LMHrslHw.

[31]J. S. Bach: 'Aria' from *Goldberg Variations*, performed by Glenn Gould, piano: https://www.youtube.com/watch?v=Gv94m_S3QDo.

[32]Wolfgang Mozart: Piano Concerto No. 23, 2nd movement, K. 488, played by Vladimir Horowitz: http://www.youtube.com/watch?v=9LqdfjZYEVE.

[33]Ludwig van Beethoven: Piano Sonata No. 31, in A Flat, Op. 110, 1st movement, played by Hélène Grimaud: http://www.youtube.com/watch?v=lPpy5YrhMp4.

[34]Frédéric Chopin: Nocturne, Op. 9, No. 1, performed by Arthur Rubinstein: https://www.youtube.com/watch?v=WnFs85pLmj4.

[35]Johannes Brahms: Intermezzo, Op. 118, No. 2 in A Major, performed by Arthur Rubinstein: http://www.youtube.com/watch?v=cqBzK5tKFVc.

[36]Clara Schumann: Romance Op. 11 No. 1 in e flat minor, performed by Tomer Lev: https://www.youtube.com/watch?v=1L3WPzNr-og.

[37]Edvard Grieg: 'Melodie' from *Lyric Pieces*, Book II, Op. 38–3, performed by Walter Gieseking: http://www.youtube.com/watch?v=yK8EjfG_dH4.

[38]Howard Hanson: *Fantasy Variations on a Theme of Youth*, Op. 40, performed by Carol Rosenberger, piano, and the New York Chamber Symphony, Gerard Schwarz, conductor: https://www.youtube.com/watch?v=M4J6B6fUzis.

[39]John Adams: *China Gates*, performed by Fraser Graham: http://www.youtube.com/watch?v=sV0JFg0xlF0.

[40]J. S. Bach: Double Violin Concerto in d minor, BWV 1043, 2nd movement, performed by Isaac Stern and Itzhak Perlman, with the New York Philharmonic, conducted by Zubin Mehta: http://www.youtube.com/watch?v=axFUvA_he-o.

[41]Wolfgang Mozart: Clarinet Concerto in A Major, K. 622, 2nd movement, performed by Karl Leister and the Berlin Philharmonic, conducted by Herbert von Karajan: http://www.youtube.com/watch?v=zsvgIW2YMWA.

[42]Ludwig van Beethoven: Symphony No. 2 in D Major, Op. 21, 2nd movement, performed by Bernard Haitink conducting the Royal Concertgebouw Orchestra: http://www.youtube.com/watch?v=YmNxqMxZoRk.

[43]Johannes Brahms: Piano Quartet in c minor, Op. 60, 3rd movement, performed by Sara Okamoto, piano; Stefano Succi, violin; Wolfgang Tluck; viola; Ulrich Horn, cello: http://www.youtube.com/watch?v=UCIo1LP4G_8.

[44]Edward Elgar: 'Nimrod' from *Enigma Variations*, performed by Daniel Barenboim conducting the Chicago Symphony: http://www.youtube.com/watch?v=sUgoBb8m1eE.

[45]Gustav Mahler: Symphony No. 5, 4th movement (Adagietto), performed by Daniel Barenboim conducting the Chicago Symphony Orchestra: https://www.youtube.com/watch?v=VWPACef2_eY.

[46]Sergei Rachmaninoff: Piano Concerto No. 2 in c minor, Op. 18, performed by Evgeny Kissin, pianist, and Andrew Davis conducting the BBC Symphony Orchestra: http://www.youtube.com/watch?v=DgYhcM5TB_c.

[47]Percy Grainger: 'Horkstow Grange' from *Lincolnshire Posy*, performed by the United States Marine Band, conducted by Col. Michael J. Colburn: https://www.youtube.com/watch?v=G2q8oxHUaMI.

[48]Eric Whitacre: 'October,' performed by the United States Navy Band, conducted by Russell Gross: http://www.youtube.com/watch?v=WZaYOGYdI4w.

[49]Michael Kamen: Brass Quintet, performed by The Canadian Brass: http://www.youtube.com/watch?v=HjBT8ElQ7Pw.

[50]Vernon Duke: 'Autumn in New York,' performed by Ella Fitzgerald and Louie Armstrong: http://www.youtube.com/watch?v=5oZL8TnMBN8.

[51]Walter Gross: 'Tenderly,' performed by Miles Davis: https://www.youtube.com/watch?v=ISnrLn4LnZs.

[52]Ennio Morricone: 'Gabriel's Oboe' from *The Mission*, performed by the London Philharmonic Orchestra conducted by Ennio Morricone: https://www.youtube.com/watch?v=Ixby9BzJfEo Listen also to Yo-Yo Ma's version of 'Gabriel's Oboe,' with the Roma Sinfoneitta Orchestra, conducted by Ennio Morricone: https://www.youtube.com/watch?v=XISBJ-MJ0HI.

[53]John Barry: *Dances with Wolves* (theme), performed by the London Symphony conducted by John Williams: https://www.youtube.com/watch?v=EuaDf0L11E4.

[54]Anne Murray: 'Could I Have This Dance': https://www.youtube.com/watch?v=iE3z-6XO2Ds.

[55]Beautiful World (Phil Sawyer): 'In Existence': https://www.youtube.com/watch?v=gIt-B5dujCI.

[56]Goldfrapp: 'Dreaming': http://www.youtube.com/watch?v=OxdC-FhTPfQ.

[57]Dead Can Dance: 'Yulunga': https://www.youtube.com/watch?v=sJqUbb-WuPQ.

[58]Daniel Licht: 'Blood Theme' from *Dexter*: https://www.youtube.com/watch?v=e2xxizpHuoo.

[59]David Arkenstone & Kostia: 'The Cello's Song': http://www.youtube.com/watch?v=GUv9AH6JkpQ.

Chapter 5 Emotion

[8]Ludwig van Beethoven: Cello Sonata No. 3 in A Major, Op. 69, performed by Yo-Yo Ma, cello, and Emmanuel Ax, piano: https://www.youtube.com/watch?v=X9pivx91mVk.

[17]J. S. Bach: *Well-Tempered Clavier, Book I*, BWV 846-893, performed by Maurizio Pollini, piano: https://www.youtube.com/watch?v=8Ks9Q8AF4Do ; *Book II*, BWV 870-893, performed by Glenn Gould, piano: https://www.youtube.com/watch?v=99UmaWyNlDI.

Chapter 6 Aesthetics

[42]Ludwig van Beethoven: Symphony No. 9 in d minor, Op. 125, performed by Leonard Bernstein conducting the Vienna Philharmonic Orchestra: http://www.youtube.com/watch?v=3MnGfhJCK_g.

[43]Franz Schubert: C Major Quintet, Op. 163, D. 956, performed by Isaac Stern, Alexander Schenider, Milton Katims, Pable Casals, and Paul Tortilier: http://www.youtube.com/watch?v=S3tmFhrOgNk.

[45]Ludwig van Beethoven: Piano Sonata No. 30 in E Major, Op. 109, performed by Daniel Barenboim: https://www.youtube.com/watch?v=qqSetFrR-Xo.

[48]Johannes Brahms: *Four Serious Songs*, Op. 121, performed by Dietrich Fischer-Dieskau, baritone, and Gerald Moore, piano: https://www.youtube.com/watch?v=knHeiIjzvYU.

[49]Richard Strauss: *Four Last Songs*, performed by Renée Fleming, soprano, and the Lucerne Festival Orchestra conducted by Claudio Abbado: https://www.youtube.com/watch?v=z5xFL-iFh0Q.

[72]Giacomo Puccini: *La Bohème*, performed by Carlos Kleiber conducting at La Scala, with Luciano Pavarotti and Ileana Cotrubas: http://www.youtube.com/watch?v=kHAS7r8Pd0k.

[73]Franz Haydn: Symphony No. 104 in D Major, H 1/104, performed by Mariss Jansons conducting the Bavarian Radio Symphony Orchestra: https://www.youtube.com/watch?v=zRfGwzHCSSU.

[88]Edward Elgar: *Pomp and Circumstance*, March No. 1, Op. 39, performed by Jiří Bělohlávek conducting the BBC Symphony Orchestra and Chorus: http://www.youtube.com/watch?v=Vvgl_2JRIUs.

Chapter 7 A Philosophical Framework

[2]J. S. Bach: Fugue No. 11 from *The Well-Tempered Clavier, Book 1*, performed by Wanda Landowska: https://www.youtube.com/watch?v=-ay0ihqjT4o.

[3]Ferde Grofé: 'On the Trail' from *The Grand Canyon Suite*, performed by Leonard Bernstein conducting the New York Philharmonic Orchestra, John Corigliano, Sr., violin: http://www.youtube.com/watch?v=bVKVB0MImOg.

[4]J. S. Bach–Leopold Stokowski: Toccata and Fugue in d minor, BWV 565, arranged by Leopold Stokowski as it appeared in Walt Disney's *Fantasia*: http://www.youtube.com/watch?v=z4MQ7GzE6HY.

[6]Richard Strauss: *Don Quixote*, Op. 35, performed by the NHK Philharmonic, Wolfgang Sawallisch, conductor; Mischa Maisky, cellist: http://www.youtube.com/watch?v=dJNEuvfeshg.

[7]Dolly Parton: *Coat of Many Colors*, performed by Dolly Parton: https://www.youtube.com/watch?v=9zLsAf6SCwY.

[8]Wolfgang Mozart: 'Dies Irae' from *Requiem in d minor*, K. 626, performed by John Eliot Gardner conducting the English Baroque Soloists and Monteverdi Choir: http://www.youtube.com/watch?v=DFq-HHA0k2E.

[9]Franz Schubert: Octet in F Major, Op. 166, 2nd movement, D. 803, performed by Janine Jansen, violin; Julia-Maria Kretz, violin; Maxim Rysanov, viola; Jens Peter Maintz, cello; Stacey Watton, contrabass; Chen Halevi, clarinet; Sergio Azzolini, bassoon; Radovan Vlatkovic, horn: http://www.youtube.com/watch?v=g5flFNalapk.

[11]Paul Desmond: *Take Five*, performed by The Dave Brubeck Quartet: http://www.youtube.com/watch?v=PQLMFNC2Awo.

[13]Alan Jackson: 'Where Were You When the World Stopped Turning?', performed by Alan Jackson: http://www.youtube.com/watch?v=fvj6zdWLUuk.

[15]Pytor Tchaikovsky: *Romeo and Juliet Fantasy Overture*, performed by Valery Gergiev conducting the London Symphony Orchestra: https://www.youtube.com/watch?v=ZxOtYNf-eWE.

[16]Jean Arban–Edwin Goldman: Fantaisie and Variations on *The Carnival of Venice*, performed by Ronald Romm: https://www.youtube.com/watch?v=F0rTi3i1zOw.

[17]George Gershwin: *An American in Paris*, performed by Lorin Maazel conducting the New York Philharmonic: http://www.youtube.com/watch?v=BUfI6v6SwL4.

[30]Pyotr Tchaikovsky: *1812 Overture*, performed by Eugene Ormandy conducting the Philadelphia Orchestra with the Mormon Tabernacle Choir: http://www.youtube.com/watch?v=r3ZMpv9CnZk.

[54]Music from ancient India: https://www.youtube.com/watch?v=BoAoqT55Wos.

[55]Javanese gamelan music: https://www.youtube.com/watch?v=wwjXwEO8_NU.

[56]Traditional Chinese music: https://www.youtube.com/watch?v=6SMgRkhwHg0.

[57]Music from Korea: https://www.youtube.com/watch?v=XwrnoWaJb2g.

[59]From Zimbabwe, *Sarangarike*, performed by Frank Mgomba: https://www.youtube.com/watch?v=Tdw5IoqUOhs.

Chapter 8 Contributions to Music Philosophy from the Ancient Greeks

[5]Kithara played by Sean Folsom: http://www.youtube.com/watch?v=tOqCwIV9ztU.

[7]Chelys-lyre played by Paul Butler: http://www.youtube.com/watch?v=7KcETZ7OImA&list=PLZM9yT8vav_IqixwPTzjbW2bKh19au7hb.

[10]Aulos played by Sean Folsom: http://www.youtube.com/watch?v=KCZBPtjwZMo.

[19]Monochord played by Sean Folsom: http://www.youtube.com/watch?v=KCZBPtjwZMo.

[23]Music in the Lydian mode composed and performed by Michael Levy: http://www.youtube.com/watch?v=xBZ7Ogb8EJ4.

[26]Music in the Dorian mode composed and performed by Michael Levy: http://www.youtube.com/watch?v=JNBfy1tjJXk.

Chapter 9 From Classical Antiquity to the Renaissance

[21]Ambrose: *Deus, creator omnium*, performed by Schola Gregoriana Mediolanensis: http://www.youtube.com/watch?v=7B2AY3avN8Q.

[53]Martin Luther: *A Mighty Fortress Is Our God*, performed by the Roger Wagner Chorale: http://www.youtube.com/watch?v=ADamVJaXZMg.

[54]J. S. Bach: *Ein Feste Burg is Unser Gott*, BWV 80, performed by Phillipe Hereweghe conducting La Chapelle Royale and Collegium Vocale: https://www.youtube.com/watch?v=x0zBmcckFoM.

Chapter 10 Rationalism, Empiricism, and Idealism

[31]Ludwig van Beethoven: Symphony No. 9 in d minor, Op. 125, 4th movement, performed by Leonard Bernstein and the Vienna Philharmonic Orchestra: https://www.youtube.com/watch?v=QDViACDYxnQ.

[56]Guillaume Dufay: *Nuper rosarum flores*, performed by the Hilliard Ensemble. https://www.youtube.com/watch?v=EOWHvIZzXPI.

[60]Giovanni Gabrielli: *In Ecclesiis*, performed by the Choir of King's College, Cambridge, and the Philip Jones Brass Ensemble: https://www.youtube.com/watch?v=q2BOBnAD1Es.

Chapter 11 Formalism

[8]J. S. Bach: *St. Matthew Passion*, BWV 244, performed by Ton Koopman conducting the Amsterdam Baroque Orchestra: https://www.youtube.com/watch?v=ZgA6twxoLRM.

[10]Ludwig van Beethoven: *Missa Solemnis*, Mass in D Major, Op. 123, performed by Kurt Masur conducting the Leipzig Gewandhaus Orchestra: http://www.youtube.com/watch?v=njCCxCQa9sI.

[11]Ludwig van Beethoven: Symphony No. 9 in d minor, Op. 125, performed by Leonard Bernstein conducting the Vienna Philharmonic: http://www.youtube.com/watch?v=3MnGfhJCK_g.

[16]Johannes Brahms: Symphony No. 2 in D Major, Op. 73, performed by Carlos Kleiber conducting the Vienna Philharmonic: https://www.youtube.com/watch?v=XHmkl7GM_es.

[19]Richard Strauss: *Don Juan*, Op. 20, performed by Fritz Reiner conducting the Chicago Symphony Orchestra: http://www.youtube.com/watch?v=obEYUa_U8sc.

[22]Anton Bruckner: Symphony No. 8 in c minor, performed by Herbert van Karajan conducting the Vienna Philharmonic: https://www.youtube.com/watch?v=iU-lNkqbUbI.

[24]Richard Wagner: *Tristan and Isolde* (end of Act 3, *Liebestod*), performed by Daniel Barenboim, conductor, with Siegfried Jerusalem and Waltraud Meier at Bayreuth: http://www.youtube.com/watch?v=OAEkTK6aKUM.

[25]Richard Wagner: *Tannhäuser*, performed by Sir Colin Davis, conductor, at Bayreuth: http://www.youtube.com/watch?v=8du71AE0h6o.

[26]Richard Wagner: *Lohengrin*, performed by Andris Nelsons, conductor, at Bayreuth: http://www.youtube.com/watch?v=VXwSV0sjYzg.

[29]Richard Wagner: Overture to *Die Meistersinger von Nürnberg*, performed by Christian Thielemann conducting the Vienna Philharmonic: http://www.youtube.com/watch?v=uyypHlrZsgg.

[35]Richard Wagner: *Parsifal*, performed by Herbert von Karajan conducting the Berlin Philharmonic: https://www.youtube.com/watch?v=p1BFR5UfXe0.

[55]Isaac Watts (text) and Lowell Mason (music, arr. of Handel): *Joy to the World*, performed by Faith Hill: http://www.youtube.com/watch?v=x-8i_N-thek.

[57]Franz Haydn: Second movement of Symphony No. 94 in G Major, *Surprise*, Hob.1.94, performed by Leslie Jones conducting the Little Orchestra of London: http://www.youtube.com/watch?v=mNwMXj0Y1_Y.

[58]Bedrich Smetana: *Die Moldau* (or *Vltava*), performed by Nikolaus Harnencourt conducting the Chamber Orchestra of Europe: http://www.youtube.com/watch?v=h3_EsIKarl8.

[65]John Cage: *4'33"*, performed by William Marx: http://www.youtube.com/watch?v=JTEFKFiXSx4.

[69]Richard Strauss: 'Dance of the Seven Veils' from *Salome*, performed by Karita Mattila, with James Conlon conducting the l'Orchestra de l'Opéra National Paris: https://www.youtube.com/watch?v=owdJmtuMSIw.

[70]Richard Strauss: 'Dance of the Seven Veils' from *Salome*, performed by Erich Leinsdorf conducting the London Symphony Orchestra: http://www.youtube.com/watch?v=C14LfoE8G14.

[71]Arcangelo Corelli: Violin Sonata No. 12 in d minor, *La Folia*, performed by Henryk Szeryng, violin, and Huguette Dreyfus, harpsichord: http://www.youtube.com/watch?v=XS-Nqzprais.

[72]J. S. Bach: *Goldberg Variations*, BWV 988, performed by Glenn Gould, piano: https://www.youtube.com/watch?v=Ah392lnFHxM.

[73]Ludwig van Beethoven: *Diabelli Variations*, Op. 120, performed by Rudolf Serkin, piano: http://www.youtube.com/watch?v=PebmYKm-BE4.

[74]Johannes Brahms: *Variations on a Theme by Haydn*, Op. 56, performed by Ricardo Muti conducting the Philadelphia Orchestra: http://www.youtube.com/watch?v=SJO4aXoKptM.

[75]Sergei Rachmaninoff: *Rhapsody on a Theme by Paganini*, performed by Daniil Trifonov, piano, and Zubin Mehta conducting the Israel Philharmonic Orchestra: http://www.youtube.com/watch?v=AAu6BRWL8p8.

[76]Charles Ives: *Variations on America*, performed by Timothy Foley conducting the United States Marine Band: http://www.youtube.com/watch?v=hs0VjhNWqn8.

[77]Arnold Schoenberg: *Theme and Variations for Wind Band*, Op. 43a, performed by Gunther Schuller conducting the United States Marine Band: http://www.youtube.com/watch?v=JEVZwr8GP1s.

[78]Thelonious Monk: ''Round Midnight,' performed by Thelonious Monk, Dizzy Gillespie, and the Giants of Jazz: http://www.youtube.com/watch?v=VUVuX3lLrdg.

Chapter 12 Expressionism

[3]Henry Purcell: 'Dido's Lament' from *Dido and Aeneas*, performed by Janet Baker, with Charles Mackerras and the Glyndebourne Opera: http://www.youtube.com/watch?v=D_50zj7J50U.

[11]Frédéric Chopin: Nocturne in E Flat Major, Op. 9, No. 2, performed by Arthur Rubinstein: http://www.youtube.com/watch?v=YGRO05WcNDk.

[14]Ludwig van Beethoven: Symphony No. 9 in d minor, Op. 125, performed by Leonard Bernstein conducting the Vienna Philharmonic Orchestra: http://www.youtube.com/watch?v=3MnGfhJCK_g.

[43]Ludwig van Beethoven: *Missa Solemnis* in D Major, Op. 123, performed by Leonard Bernstein conducting the Hilversum Radio Chorus and the Vienna Philharmonic: https://www.youtube.com/watch?v=06PPhF2tX1g.

[62]Franz Schubert: *Wanderer Fantasy*, D.760, performed by Alfred Brendel: https://www.youtube.com/watch?v=7WIVTKXb8RI.

[64]Johannes Brahms: Intermezzo, Op. 117, No. 2, performed by Vladimir Horowitz: http://www.youtube.com/watch?v=RooR3nsYWzw.

[72]Giacomo Puccini: 'Un bel di' from *Madama Butterfly*, performed by Renata Tebaldi: http://www.youtube.com/watch?v=1woH96ROG-c.

[73]Giacomo Puccini: 'Con onor muore' from *Madama Butterfly*, performed by Renata Scotto: http://www.youtube.com/watch?v=vi4n2YbQPd8.

[74]Felix Mendelssohn: 'It Is Enough' from *Elijah*, performed by Dietrich Fischer-Diskau, baritone, with Rafael Frühbeck de Burgos conducting the New Philharmonia Orchestra: http://www.youtube.com/watch?v=tEkClendR3s.

[75]Elton John and Bernie Taupin: 'Candle in the Wind,' performed by Elton John: http://www.youtube.com/watch?v=A8gO0Z818j4.

[77]Pussy Riot: 'Punk Prayer,' performed by Pussy Riot: http://www.youtube.com/watch?v=ALS92big4TY.

[79]Modest Mussorgsky: *Pictures at an Exhibition*, performed by Evgeny Kissin: http://www.youtube.com/watch?v=g8ei1NF0oic.

[80]Modest Mussorgsky: *Pictures at an Exhibition*, orchestrated by Maurice Ravel, performed by Georg Solti conducting the Chicago Symphony Orchestra: https://www.youtube.com/watch?v=DXy50exHjes.

[81]Ludwig van Beethoven: Rondo alla ingharese quasi un capriccio in G Major, *Rage Over a Lost Penny*, Op. 129, performed by Alexander Brailowsky, piano: https://www.youtube.com/watch?v=_6k_CrWBqBA.

[83]Arnold Schoenberg: *Theme and Variations for Wind Band*, Op. 43a, performed by Gunther Schuller conducting the United States Marine Band: http://www.youtube.com/watch?v=JEVZwr8GP1s.

[87]Claude Debussy: 'Reflections in the Water' from *Images, Book I*, performed by Arturo Michelangeli: http://www.youtube.com/watch?v=LLbpQl1cCl8.

[88]Felix Mendelssohn: Scherzo from *Midsummer Night's Dream*, Op. 21, performed by Valery Gergiev conducting the Mariinsky Theatre Orchestra: http://www.youtube.com/watch?v=hHTV3GFyHfM.

[89]Franz Liszt–Ferruccio Busoni arrangement of Niccolò Paganini: *Etude* No. 2 in E Flat Major, performed by Vladimir Horowitz: http://www.youtube.com/watch?v=-Nfdve3huIA.

[90]Pyotr Tchaikovsky: Symphony No. 6 in b minor, *Pathetique*, performed by Herbert von Karajan conducting the Vienna Philharmonic: http://www.youtube.com/watch?v=wHAfvUFtCIY.

[91]Richard Wagner: Prelude to Act III from *Lohengrin*, performed by Mariss Jansons conducting the Berlin Philharmonic: https://www.youtube.com/watch?v=qy2k_xnE2XQ.

[99]Frédéric Chopin: *Prelude*, Op., No. 4, performed by Martha Argerich: http://www.youtube.com/watch?v=Tovh6JjaQ1A.

[114]Ernst Bloch: 'Prayer' from *From Jewish Life*, No. 1, performed by Amit Peled, cello, and Stefan Petrov, piano: http://www.youtube.com/watch?v=rTso0wYH4f4.

Chapter 13 Symbolism

[25]J. S. Bach: French Suites, BWV 812–817, performed by Andras Schiff, piano: https://www.youtube.com/watch?v=0sDleZkIK-w.

[29]Ludwig van Beethoven: Piano Sonata in A Major, Op. 101, performed by Daniel Barenboim: https://www.youtube.com/watch?v=yn2CbJls2_A.

[31]Ludwig van Beethoven: Symphony No. 5 in c minor, Op. 67, performed by Christian Thielemann, conducting the Vienna Philharmonic: http://www.youtube.com/watch?v=-VVXqNt4qU0.

[42]Bruce Springsteen: 'Born in the USA,' performed by Bruce Springsteen: http://www.youtube.com/watch?v=lZD4ezDbbu4.

[43]Guiseppe Verdi: 'Dies Irae' from *Messa da Requiem*, performed by Robert Shaw conducting the Atlanta Symphony Orchestra and Chorus: https://www.youtube.com/watch?v=_jBLyIQvNf0.

[44]Lewis Allan: 'Strange Fruit,' performed by Billie Holiday: http://www.youtube.com/watch?v=h4ZyuULy9zs.

[46]James Sanderson, music; Albert Gamse, text (based on words from Sir Walter Scott's *The Lady of the Lake*): *Hail to the Chief*, performed by the United States Army Herald Trumpets: http://www.youtube.com/watch?v=JW8AJds1CzI.

[47]'Taps,' performed by buglers from the United States Army Band. https://www.youtube.com/watch?v=Bfe4TxvUOiw.

[48]Camille Saint-Saëns: *Carnival of the Animals*, performed by Andrea Licata, conducting the Royal Philharmonic Orchestra, with pianists Vivian Troon and Roderick Elms: https://www.youtube.com/watch?v=5LOFhsksAYw.

[49]Hector Berlioz: *Symphony Fantastique*, Op. 14, performed by Rafael Frühbeck de Burgos conducting the Denmark Radio Symphony Orchestra: http://www.youtube.com/watch?v=W9CYLAuKdtU.

[50]Hector Berlioz: *idée fixe* as it first appears in the *Symphonie Fantastique* as explained by Leonard Bernstein, conductor, and Julius Baker, flautist: http://www.youtube.com/watch?v=Mvh1gpdxCv0.

[50]John Williams: 'Raiders March' from *Raiders of the Lost Ark*, performed by John Williams conducting the Los Angeles Philharmonic Orchestra: http://www.youtube.com/watch?v=oKdhEWM6n_o.

[52]Gioachino Rossini: *William Tell Overture*, performed by Leonard Slatkin conducting the Detroit Symphony Orchestra: http://www.youtube.com/watch?v=7TJbH0hBNyA.

[53]Paul Dukas: 'The Sorcerer's Apprentice,' performed by Leopold Stowkoski conducting the Philadelphia Orchestra in the Walt Disney movie *Fantasia*: https://www.youtube.com/watch?v=Gkj2QeogAsU.

[54]Richard Strauss: *Don Juan*, Op. 20, performed by Fritz Reiner conducting the Chicago Symphony Orchestra: http://www.youtube.com/watch?v=obEYUa_U8sc.

[55]Richard Strauss: *Death and Transfiguration*, Op. 24, performed by George Szell conducting the Cleveland Orchestra: https://www.youtube.com/watch?v=4K3E1wZWSn0.

[56]Richard Strauss: *Till Eulenspiegel's Merry Pranks*, Op. 28, performed by Georg Solti conducting the Chicago Symphony Orchestra: http://www.youtube.com/watch?v=vKFKf07lIDw.

[57]Richard Strauss: *Also sprach Zarathustra*, Op. 30, performed by Gustavo Dudamel conducting the Vienna Philharmonic Orchestra: https://www.youtube.com/watch?v=ETveS23djXM.

[58]Richard Strauss: *Don Quixote*, Op. 34, performed by Daniel Barenboim conducting the Chicago Symphony Orchestra: http://www.youtube.com/watch?v=IdbMOkzOYaI.

[59]Richard Strauss: *Ein Heldenleben*, Op. 40, performed by Richard Strauss conducting the Bavarian State Orchestra: http://www.youtube.com/watch?v=dC6t5SdQc0I.

[60]Richard Strauss: *Sinfonia Domestica*, Op. 53, performed by Rudolf Kempe conducting the Staatskapelle Dresden: http://www.youtube.com/watch?v=ANmiGCLWA_w.

[61]Richard Strauss: *An Alpine Symphony*, Op. 64, performed by Bernard Kaitink conducting the Vienna Philharmonic Orchestra: http://www.youtube.com/watch?v=FQhpWsRhQGs.

[67]Charles Ives: *The Unanswered Question*, performed by Leonard Bernstein conducting the New York Philharmonic Orchestra: https://www.youtube.com/watch?v=vXD4tIp59L0.

Chapter 16 Social Philosophy

[2]Béla Bartók: *Mikrokosmos*, performed by Béla Bartók: http://www.youtube.com/watch?v=DPZX4YAcFKI.

[4]Igor Stravinksy: *Pulcinella Suite*, performed by the Netherlands Radio Chamber Orchestra conducted by Jaap van Zweden: https://www.youtube.com/watch?v=VwongNsp1RA.

[5]Igor Stravinsky: *Symphony of Psalms*, performed by Lukas Foss conducting the Milwaukee Symphony and the Wisconsin Conservatory Symphony Chorus: http://www.youtube.com/watch?v=LUGyAtcEFy8.

[16]‘We Shall Overcome,’ sung by Mahalia Jackson: http://www.youtube.com/watch?v=TmR1YvfIGng.

[18]Dmitri Shostakovich: Symphony No. 10, performed by Gustavo Dudamel conducting an El Sistema Orchestra from Venezuela: https://www.youtube.com/watch?v=XKXQzs6Y5BY.

[30]Jan Sibelius: *Finlandia*, performed by Vasily Petrenko conducting the Royal Liverpool Orchestra: http://www.youtube.com/watch?v=L6P3cIJHWjw.

Chapter 17 Praxialism

[11]Frank Ticheli: *An American Elegy*, performed by Eugene Corporan conducting the North Texas Wind Symphony: https://www.youtube.com/watch?v=YIIKdBYfmlo.

Chapter 18 Feminism

[5]Hildegard von Bingen: *11000 Virgins*, Chants for St. Ursula, performed by Anonymous 4: http://www.youtube.com/watch?v=n9uMd1ap51A.

[13]Fanny Mendelssohn: ‘Italien’ from *Twelve Songs*, Op. 8, No. 3, performed by Akiko Ogawa, alto, and Hiroaki Yamada, piano: http://www.youtube.com/watch?v=OSA029AGsY8.

[17]Clara Schumann: Piano Trio in g minor, Op. 17, performed by the Galos Piano Trio: https://www.youtube.com/watch?v=C5dBOpy0_zg.

[22]Alma Mahler: *Lieder*, performed by Hiroaki Yamada (alto) and Hiroaki Yamada, piano: http://www.youtube.com/watch?v=M9CYlOU_SJU.

[23]Nadia Boulanger: *Trois pieces*, performed by Dora Kuzmin, cello, and Petra Gilming, piano: http://www.youtube.com/watch?v=YfcUkVbyy9M.

[27]Igor Stravinsky: *Dumbarton Oaks Concerto*, performed by Igor Stravinsky conducting the Orchestra della Radiotelevisione della Svizzera Italiana: https://www.youtube.com/watch?v=C-8fr2QRFGI.

[39]Joan Tower: *Fanfares for the Uncommon Woman*, performed by Octavio Mas-Arocas conducting the Interlochen Arts Academy Orchestra: http://www.youtube.com/watch?v=hm8EZj5skY8.

[40]Pauline Oliveros: 'Bottoms Up 1' from *Reverberations: Tape and Electronic Music*: http://www.youtube.com/watch?v=UbKMdszoY_Y.

[41]Tania León: *Inura*, performed by Tania León, conducting Son Sonora Voices, Son Sonora Ensemble, and DanceBrazil Percussion: http://www.youtube.com/watch?v=gFN05rFPxTA.

[43]Robert Schumann: *Frauenliebe und -Leben*, Op. 42, performed by Jessye Norman, soprano, and Irwin Gage, piano: https://www.youtube.com/watch?v=1KEgm9DV70o.

[46]Robert Schumann: *Myrthen*, Op. 25, performed by Mitsuko Shirai, soprano, and Harmut Höll, piano: https://www.youtube.com/watch?v=MpfnWGH1xRY.

[62]Sergei Rachmaninov: *Vocalise*, Op. 34, No. 14, performed by Kiri Te Kanawa, soprano, at the Royal Opera House in Covent Garden, Stephen Barlow conducting: http://www.youtube.com/watch?v=fW630zFA93Y.

[85]Wolfgang Mozart: 'Porgi amor' from *The Marriage of Figaro*, performed by Renee Fleming at the Metropolitan Opera: http://www.youtube.com/watch?v=NToJ2phG7Qk.

[86]Wolfgang Mozart: 'Dove sono' from *The Marriage of Figaro*, performed by Leontyne Price at the Metropolican Opera: http://www.youtube.com/watch?v=WXEENQoiy_s.

[87]Wolfgang Mozart: 'Madamina, il catalogo è questo' from *Don Giovanni*, performed by Ferrucio Furlanetto at the Metropolitan Opera, conducted by James Levine: https://www.youtube.com/watch?v=INF9r5jju0A.

[90]Georges Bizet: 'Habañera' from *Carmen*, performed by Grace Bumbry in a movie version directed by Herbert von Karajan: http://www.youtube.com/watch?v=Qs0E2CufQ7c.

[92]Wolfgang Mozart: Piano Concerto in G Major, K. 453, 2nd movement, performed by Leonard Bernstein, pianist and conductor with the Vienna Philharmonic: http://www.youtube.com/watch?v=itiY352hgjM.

[101]Cécile Chaminade: Piano Sonata in c minor, Op. 21, performed by Peter Basil Murdock-Saint: https://www.youtube.com/watch?v=Tg3Sa7oppis.

Chapter 19 Postmodernism

[11]John Cage: *4'33"*, performed by William Marx: http://www.youtube.com/watch?v=JTEFKFiXSx4.

[13]John Cage: *0'00"*, performed by Haco: https://www.youtube.com/watch?v=6I1gfOlNNo4.

[17]John Cage: *Organ2/ASLSP*, performed by Christoph Bossert, organ: https://www.youtube.com/watch?v=ZYnEWbL6yao.

[29]Ludwig van Beethoven: *An die Ferne Geliebte*, Op. 98, performed by Dietrich Fischer-Dieskau, voice, and Gerald Moore, piano: https://youtu.be/KOk7EWYbyqk.

[30]Britney Spears: 'I'm a Slave 4 U,' performed by Britney Spears: https://youtu.be/Mzybwwf2HoQ.

[31]Britney Spears: 'Baby One More Time,' performed by Britney Spears: https://youtube/C-u5WLJ9Yk4.

[40]Gustav Mahler: Symphony No. 8, performed by Leonard Bernstein conducting the Vienna Philharmonic Orchestra: https://www.youtube.com/watch?v=NSYEOLwVfU8.

[43]Sergei Prokofiev: Sonata No. 7 in B Flat Major, Op. 33, performed by Sviatoslav Richter: https://www.youtube.com/watch?v=NNb1qYqWP0E.

[44]Wolfgang Mozart: *The Magic Flute*, performed by Riccardo Muti conducting the Vienna Philharmonic at the 2006 Salzburg Festival: https://www.youtube.com/watch?v=w9zwQNib-h4.

[45]Felix Mendelssohn: *Elijah*, performed by Ann Howard Jones, conductor, and the Boston University Chorus and Orchestra: https://www.youtube.com/watch?v=iBMTzryAnrk.

[46]'Ride On King Jesus,' performed by the In HIS Presence Gospel Choir: https://youtu.be/etGrFu6dyAE.

Chapter 20 Articulating a Philosophy of Music

[2]Dolly Parton: 'Two Doors Down,' performed by Dolly Parton: https://youtu.be/9w3WHYFohCM.

[3]Richard Strauss: 'Im Abendrot' (At Sunset) from *Vier Letzte Liederi* (*Four Last Songs*), performed by Kiri Te Kanawa, soprano, and Georg Solti conducting the BBC Philharmonic Orchestra: https://www.youtube.com/watch?v=co61XmUu-tc.

Chapter 22 Advocacy

[13]Wolfgang Mozart: Sonata for Two Pianos in D Major, K. 448, performed by Murray Perahia and Radu Lupu: https://www.youtube.com/watch?v=v58mf-PB8as.

Preface

For the past 42 years, music philosophy has been part of my teaching assignment, in both complete courses and units in courses for undergraduate and graduate students. Sometimes these courses (or units) have been comprised of music education students, but more often they have included music majors of all types, and occasionally non-music majors. Throughout these experiences of teaching music philosophy, I have used a variety of textbooks. While these were admirable books for many reasons, I gradually became convinced that I would like a book that had certain features. Finding none that matched exactly what I was looking for, I decided to write one myself. This project has taken many years, and along the way I have used drafts—initially of selected chapters and eventually of the entire book—as the textbook in my classes at the University of North Carolina at Greensboro. My colleague and friend, Peter Webster, has also used a draft version in several of his classes at the University of Southern California. Students in these classes provided invaluable feedback that led to numerous adjustments. The features that distinguish this book include breadth, conciseness, clarity, musical examples, insights from research, student empowerment, and applications to musical careers.

Breadth

An important feature of this book is that it presents a broad range of philosophical views and approaches. Numerous philosophers have written books to explain and promote their own beliefs about music and one aim of the book is to present readers with a comprehensive overview of this body of literature.

Books written to promote a singular view are often powerfully persuasive. Students who are given only one book with a singular philosophical view as a textbook may be overwhelmed. They may lack the background and experience to read such a book critically and, in fact, may feel that it is their primary task to echo important ideas as if they represented their own beliefs. This situation can be exacerbated when the teacher has also adopted this view and uses the textbook as a means of inculcating this music philosophy among the students. Imagine, for example, that in two different music education classes, one teacher uses Bennett Reimer's *A Philosophy of Music Education* and another uses David Elliott's *Music Matters*. Suppose, too, that each teacher is a strong advocate of the position represented in the book he or she chose. Students in these two classes would get very different orientations, and may even be unaware that there are many other possibilities as well.

My approach in this book is to present students with the opportunity to learn about a wide variety of philosophical viewpoints. This is a different approach than presentation of a single view, not necessarily a better one. The goal is to help students think through important issues and consider practical applications. I encourage them to ask the question, "If I believe *X*, what will be the effect on my own musical life (i.e., as a listener, performer, teacher, composer, etc.)?" In the short-term, considering multiple viewpoints may lead to some confusion and uncertainty, but in the long-term it more often than not leads to a stronger, more confidently-held set of beliefs about the nature, meaning, and value of music.

Conciseness

The music philosophy literature is voluminous and it is unreasonable to expect that students would be able to read even a moderate sampling of it. In addition to providing a broad overview, another feature of this book is its conciseness. It is not a simple matter to reduce the writings of a major philosopher into a manageable size, but I constantly strove to consider just how much a middle school band director or prospective university music theory teacher needed to know about, say, Hegel's or Schopenhauer's thoughts on music. Of course, the danger is in leaving out important concepts or lacking clarity because of missing details. However, I have quoted more liberally in this book than I normally do, so that students would have the opportunity to read core statements in the authors' own words. Also, students are encouraged to read original sources whenever they come across ideas that spark their curiosity or that introduce them to critical concepts about which they wish to know more.

Clarity

Some philosophical writings are notoriously difficult to understand and students often struggle to make sense of certain passages. My aim has been to explain complex ideas in clear language or to provide illustrations without 'dumbing down' important concepts. Of course, in so doing, it is possible that I have altered or even misconstrued the original. However, my intent has been to stay as true as possible to the original ideas.

Musical Examples

I always encourage students to utilize specific musical examples as they discuss various philosophical issues. These examples are not limited to 'works' *per se*, but can and should include musical experiences, such as teaching a private lesson, performing in a community band, improvising alone in a practice room, singing in a church choir, and so on. Accordingly, I have included numerous examples sprinkled throughout the book. Regarding specific musical works, 199 of them are identified in the text with the superscript icon ♪. The endnote for each composition so marked contains a YouTube link to a recording. A master list of musical works is provided in the front matter. Also, by going to this URL—https://sites.google.com/a/uncg.edu/https-sites-google-com-site-concisesurveyofmusphil/home—the reader can click on a link to each recording. Because YouTube links change frequently, this is an imperfect system. However, it may provide encouragement for students to listen to works that are unfamiliar. Even when a link is broken, the student can readily find another recording of the same work.

Musical examples, supplemented by many musical engagements discussed in the text, cover a wide variety of genres, including:

- Jazz artists: Louis Armstrong, Dave Brubeck, John Coltrane, Miles Davis, Duke Ellington, Ella Fitzgerald, Dizzy Gillespie, Billie Holiday, and Thelonius Monk.
- Female composers: Hildegard von Bingen, Nadia Boulanger, Cécile Chaminade, Maria Grever, Tania León, Alma Mahler, Fanny Mendelssohn, Pauline Oliveros, Clara Schumann, and Joan Tower.
- World music: from China, India, Java, Korea, and Zimbabwe.
- Wind band literature: Percy Grainger, Arnold Schoenberg, Frank Ticheli, and Eric Whitacre; movie music: John Barry, Ennio Morricone, and John Williams; country music: Alan Jackson, Anne Murray, and Dolly Parton; gospel music: In HIS Presence Gospel Choir and Mahalia Jackson; and contemporary styles: David Arkenstone & Kostia, Dead Can Dance, Goldfrapp, Elton John, Daniel Licht, Pussy Riot, Britney Spears, Bruce Springsteen, and Beautiful World (Phil Sawyer).
- In Chapter 7: A Philosophical Framework, there are discussions about popular music, 'school' music (especially literature for the wind band), and world music. In Chapter 19: Postmodernism, there is a discussion of Robert Walker's comparison of Beethoven (*To the Distant Beloved*) with Britney Spears ('I'm a Slave 4 U' and 'Baby One More Time'). And so on.

Even with this variety, the bulk of the examples are comprised of Western classical music, ranging from Guillaume Dufay to John Cage. The reason for this imbalance is that, generally speaking, it was not until the second half of the 20th century that philosophers considered and wrote about styles other than Western classical art music. At every point, however, students are encouraged to identify their own examples, again to include musical experiences in addition to specific works.

Insights from Research

Whenever applicable, music research findings are presented to inform students' thinking about various topics. As indicated in the extended discussion of science and philosophy in Chapter 2, there are a variety of opinions about the role of science in philosophical thinking. Simplistically, one can choose to incorporate or disregard research findings when developing a philosophy. The discussion of research on conceptions of beauty in Chapter 4 provides a good example. Several philosophers are quoted as saying that beauty is no longer an important concept in aesthetics. Yet, several research studies indicate that beauty is still uppermost in the minds of many music listeners. To which one philosopher might say "never mind what people say, philosophically beauty is not a core component of the aesthetic experience," while another might use research findings to bolster her philosophical view that beauty is a core concept of musical aesthetics. No attempt is made to lead readers in one direction or another; rather, students are guided to think through these issues and resolve them according to their own views.

Student Empowerment

For me, the most important feature of the book and of my teaching approach is encouraging students to find their own voice. As I explain, for younger, less experienced students, the best approach may be to identify a viewpoint, among the many presented, that most resonates with their own ideas. In this case, the students' language in expressing their philosophies may be highly imitative of the original. Students with more experience may choose to base their philosophical statement on the ideas of a published philosopher, but may decide to alter some of the language or modify some of the ideas to fit their own conceptions more closely. Finally, some—ideally those with more extensive experience in philosophy, such as some doctoral students—may want to strike out on their own, creating a personalized philosophy that represents their deepest held beliefs about the nature, value, and meaning of music. No matter where a student falls on a continuum from novice to emerging expert, an adopted philosophy should be true to his or her own conception of music. Encouraging student ownership of a music philosophy is a primary goal of this book.

Applications to Musical Careers

In this book I make a distinction between a philosophy of music and a philosophy of music education or any other application. The approach is to have students make determinations about the nature, value, and meaning of music and then apply it to specific circumstances, such as teaching music in a school, teaching private studio lessons, working with music therapy clients, and so on. In that case, there may be some distinctions between a philosophy of music and a philosophy of music education (or other), but they should be highly consistent and related to one another. Having a well-articulated philosophy will be of minimal value if it does not influence one's musical life and career. No matter whether one is teaching, performing, composing, listening, working with therapy clients, or examining music from a theoretical-analytic approach, one's choices, decisions, attitudes, and actions should be a reflection of a distinctive philosophical view.

Actually, the process is not a one-way street. That is, one does not have to express a philosophy and then begin to apply it. Rather, often it is helpful for the students to think deeply about how they listen, teach, perform, and so on, and also to draw insights from their daily engagements with music, moving back and forth from a philosophy to the application of it. Students are encouraged not to leave their philosophy sitting 'on the shelf,' but to put it into regular practice.

These, then, are the features I endeavored to incorporate into my book. A final comment concerns my decision to leave my own views out. One reviewer called me to task on this, saying that it was 'odd' to ask students to commit to a philosophical statement when I was not willing to do so. I understand this concern, but I have also seen, repeatedly, how some students will automatically adjust their own views in light of a professor's or author's stance. Some, of course, are not affected, but there are always those who see something in print as the 'correct' view. Occasionally, a student will even veer toward an oppositional view, just to proclaim autonomy. Either way, an authoritarian view can inhibit student growth in independent thinking.

Of course, a professor—or in this case author—has an important role to play in guiding students. However, rather than tell students their emerging philosophical views are right or wrong, I have found it more effective to help them clarify their thinking and their use of language, identifying faulty logic or contradictions, pointing out gaps (i.e., missing ideas and concepts), and encouraging them to provide musical illustrations and make appropriate applications.

Articulating a well-reasoned philosophy of music is not an easy thing. It takes a great deal of practice in writing and speaking. I encourage students to do this in three ways: a formal written statement, a formal verbal presentation, and an informal discussion of philosophical views in which there is give and take. It is a process, and ideally one that continues throughout one's career. It is my hope that this book will be helpful as the student moves along this important journey.

I would like to thank the dozens of students who have provided important feedback on draft versions. Their suggestions ranged from identifying a missing comma to recognition that a particular passage was lacking in clarity. I incorporated many of their ideas. As mentioned, Peter Webster has been a sounding board, providing much cogent advice. I am appreciative of all his help. Finally, I would like to dedicate this book to my wife, Diana Allan. She has given me a great deal of helpful editorial advice, but more importantly, she has been a source of constant and steady love and support. I am very grateful for her unfailing encouragement.

Section I

Beginning the Journey

1 The Plan and Purpose of This Book

Musicians are used to *doing*. We enjoy such things as rehearsing, performing, improvising, composing, conducting, and teaching. We may pause now and then to think about *what* we are doing or *how* we are doing it, but far less often do we slow down or stop to think about *why* we do what we do. I became more keenly aware of this stereotypical description of musical life during an oral exam of a graduate student. This student was already a member of a major symphony orchestra. His degree recital was masterful, and in both his written and oral examinations he answered questions about repertoire and pedagogy with ease and at a very high level. Yet, when I asked him near the end of the exam why all of *this* was important, what meaning did it have, he did not have an answer and moreover thought the question slightly ridiculous.

Of course, not every musician is this way. Many have considered why a career in music has meaning and what contributions they can make to society through their music. Even for a significant number of these, perhaps, a notion of the nature, meaning, and value of music—a philosophy of music, if you will—remains implicit rather than explicit. That is, many musicians may have ambiguous, generalized thoughts somewhere in the back of their minds and could mumble some reasonable sounding phrases if called upon to justify their musical existence. However, some have not committed to the struggle of stating in clear and unambiguous language, in both written and verbal forms, exactly what it is they believe about music. Even those who have fashioned a formal statement of musical beliefs can always revise and extend their thinking, because to be of real value, a philosophy needs to grow and change along with the person.

There are two primary purposes of this book. The first is to provide a broad but concise overview of what some of the greatest minds in history have had to say about the nature, meaning, and value of music. The second primary purpose of this book is to help you articulate a philosophy of music that will serve as a guiding star throughout your career. In some cases, especially for those who have had limited exposure to music philosophy, you may wish to align yourself closely with a philosopher with whose ideas you are most in agreement. In other cases, you may wish to make slight amendments to a given philosophical position to make it conform more closely to your particular circumstances. Finally, among those who have had considerable exposure to philosophy in general and to music philosophy specifically, you may wish to create your own philosophy; this may be based upon others' ideas but be more reflective of your own personality and experiences. Although, as stated previously, your philosophy is likely to change over time, especially if you continue to read and think, it is important to come as close as you can to a statement that reflects your current set of beliefs.

The process by which we will achieve the two primary purposes of this book is threefold: first, we will investigate some central issues that any music philosopher ought to consider; next, we will review significant philosophical positions to find out what major thinkers have had to say on the subject; and finally, we will consider the ramifications of these ideas for your particular circumstances. The three sections of the book represent these three aspects, and at the end of this chapter we will provide more details. In the meantime, let us start more broadly.

What Is Philosophy?

According to A. R. Lacey, to ask "what is philosophy?" is to ask a philosophical question.[1] In other words, there is no agreed-upon definition. The word philosophy in the original Greek means 'love of wisdom,' but it has come "to stand for knowledge in general about man and the universe."[2] While admitting that any definition of philosophy is controversial, Lord Quinton said that the shortest, most acceptable definition might be that it is "thinking about thinking."[3] This *thinking*, however, is of a particular kind. Mere opinion about something does not constitute a philosophy. Rather, philosophy involves systematic, logical thought that commonly seeks answers to questions in one or more of the following areas:

> "Rightly defined philosophy is simply the love of wisdom."
>
> (Cicero)

Metaphysics, or theory of existence, is concerned with the nature of the universe. What is ultimate reality? What is time? Can things exist outside of space-time?

Epistemology deals with the theory of knowledge, determining truths of reason versus truths of fact, and distinguishing what is acquired directly from what is acquired by inference. What is knowledge? What is truth? How can we determine what is true?

Ethics, sometimes called moral philosophy, is concerned with the conduct of life. What does it mean to live a moral life? Is there any advantage to living a moral life? What is the 'good life'?

Political Philosophy is an extension of ethics into the social realm. What is good government? Is an individual under an obligation to follow a governmental rule or decree if he disagrees with it? Does government exist for its own sake?

Aesthetics, although sometimes called the study of beauty, is more fully concerned with the nature, value, and meaning of art. What is art (music)? What is great art (music)? What is the meaning of art (music)? Can art (music) reveal truth or help us to lead a moral life?

Other conceptions of philosophy include *Ontology*, the nature of being, and *Logic*, which establishes the principles of valid reasoning.[4] However, the structure of philosophy is another area of disagreement, as some would include ontology under the umbrella of metaphysics and logic as a subdivision of epistemology.[5] Although the bulk of our deliberations about music philosophy in this book would fit most clearly under aesthetics, they are not constrained to this branch of philosophy. For example, a discussion of Plato's notion that music can influence a person's moral character represents an overlap of aesthetics and ethics, and Theodor Adorno's ideas about the role of music in social progress come at the juncture of aesthetics and political philosophy.

Many, including philosophers themselves, see philosophy as a complex and complicated discipline, even "'brain-breakingly' difficult."[6] British philosopher C.E.M. Joad said, "Philosophy is an exceedingly difficult subject and cannot with the best will in the world be made into an easy one."[7] Why, then, should we spend so much time on something that can be so perplexing and even frustrating? What is the value of philosophy, after all?

> "Making itself intelligible is suicide for philosophy."
> (Martin Heidegger)

In response, we might say simply, as Will Durant did, "only philosophy can give us wisdom."[8] If we wish to search for truth, if we wish, more particularly, to be as clear-minded and certain as possible about the meaning of music and of our purpose as musicians, we must turn to philosophy. Only by struggling with the *big* and *important* questions of art will we ever arrive at a settled assurance of just how significant, vital, and even imperative creating, performing, and teaching music is for us. Only by articulating a philosophy of music will your career and your passion stand on a firm foundation. Buffeting winds in the form of self-doubt, criticism, failure, and uncertainty will assail us all from time-to-time, but those who have a clearly stated philosophy will be standing on solid rock.

Why Do I Need to Have a Philosophy of Music?

To continue the previous discussion, some musicians may wonder why they need a philosophy of music at all. To begin with, a philosophy serves as a professional career guide. Return for a moment to the vignette presented in the opening paragraph. The symphony student knew what to do and how to do it; he did not know why he did it. Perhaps he performed music because he felt compelled or driven to; perhaps he did it simply because he loved to do it. Perhaps he did it because he felt he had no alternatives, that is, that he had no other marketable skills.

A philosophy of music cannot tell you how to perform or compose or conduct or teach, but it can help you understand why it is important for you to do so. Imagine three college students having a conversation over a cup of coffee. One is a premedical student. She speaks passionately about her studies and is enthusiastic about some day being able to heal people. Another is a hydrology major. He has a strong desire to live and work in a third world country, helping local citizens develop and maintain adequate sources of clean water. The third student is a bassoon major. She looks forward to her hours in the practice room as they prepare her for a career as a performer and teacher. One would hardly need to ask the premedical or hydrology major why their career choices are important. One can well imagine, however, that some would be curious about the decision to spend a lifetime playing and teaching the bassoon. Why is that important? What does this contribute to society?

Suppose we revisit these three students 40 years after graduation and suppose that all three realized their aspirations. The physician can look back at a lifetime of helping patients deal with illness and pain. The hydrologist can reminisce about his years of helping people improve the quality of their lives by having access to disease-free water. And the bassoonist? The point is not to suggest that the bassoonist's life is inferior to the others in any way. In fact, the bassoonist could point out that if the issue is quality of life, the creation of beauty is a significant contribution. Merely living a healthy life may not be enough if it is lived in ugliness. After all, when we speak of 'quality of life,' to what are we referring? This is where we arrive at philosophy.

The purpose of having a philosophy of music is not only so that you can convince others that what you are doing is important; primarily it is to convince yourself. That seems odd, does it not, that you would have to convince yourself that what you spend hours doing every day is important?

If you are one of the lucky few who has not doubted yourself, consider yourself fortunate. Most of us have moments or even phases of our lives when we imagine that everything we are, everything we do, everything we think and feel, is a charade. We long to believe that our lives have meaning and purpose. To the extent that there is much more to life than a career, our philosophy of life must be all encompassing and involve much more than music. I once heard a cello professor at a prestigious conservatory say that there is more to music than playing the cello and there is more to life than music. However, for many of us, our identities are wrapped up in our musicianship. Music is not just a career; it is who we are. If we lose our musical identity through a failed jury, audition, or interview, or an injury that compromises performance, we feel bereft and may face an identity crisis.

Another primary reason for articulating a philosophy of music is that it helps us make choices. Having a firm and clear philosophical view guides our actions. We will have much more to say on this matter in Section III, but for the moment consider three university piano faculty members (or three middle school band directors, three opera singers, etc.). One piano professor is committed to philosophy X, another to philosophy Y, and the third to no philosophical view in particular. Further, suppose philosophies X and Y are diametrically opposed to each other, and that the adherents of philosophies X and Y make musical choices and decisions based on their respective beliefs. First, note that the antithetical views of X and Y do not indicate that either or both are flawed.[9] Both could represent reasonable positions. Then, consider that regardless of whether you agree with position X or Y, at least you know that the proponents are making decisions from a particular viewpoint. The third teacher is not making repertoire and pedagogical choices, along with other important decisions, in light of a particular viewpoint. He or she may be making choices on a rather haphazard or arbitrary basis.

> "One's philosophy is not best expressed in words; it is expressed in the choices one makes . . . and the choices we make are ultimately our responsibility."
>
> (Eleanor Roosevelt)

A final reason for having a firm grasp of philosophical issues has to do with how we influence others. Although the term *music education* is often construed in the limited sense of teaching music in K–12 settings, let us use it in the broadest sense. Whenever any of us as conductors, performers, teachers, or therapists influences others through music, we will consider that to be music education. In that spirit, consider this quote from Bennett Reimer, a music education philosopher:

> Until our concerns pervade all dimensions of music education, . . . philosophy will be regarded as being largely irrelevant to the realities of teaching and learning music, as it tends to be regarded now by many if not most music teachers.[10]

This statement should influence not only what we do when conducting middle school bands and high school choirs, but also when we direct an opera production, teach private clarinet lessons, use music in a therapy session with a child who has autism, speak to the symphony board, or do anything related to our professional craft as musicians. Your philosophy needs to permeate every aspect of your musical life. It should make a difference.

One goal I have in writing this book is to promote and criticize each viewpoint presented in such a way that by the end of the book you have no idea which philosophical view is my own. By analogy, think of a television sports announcer, whose job is to call the game impartially. He should critique each team's performance equally and fairly. Even though he may have a favorite team, his bias should not be apparent. To further explain this approach, let us examine the three major sections of the book.

Section I: Beginning the Journey

Following this introduction, Chapters 2 through 7 present selected topics that have engaged philosophers for centuries. Science, religion, knowledge, and education are topics that occupy prominent places in philosophy in general. Beauty, emotion, and aesthetics are topics that have a special relevance for music philosophy. Each of these chapters is intended to provide an introduction and to prepare you to consider these issues more deeply as they reoccur periodically in Section II, when the particular views of various philosophers are discussed. At this juncture, you are encouraged to begin thinking deeply about your own perspective while retaining an open mind. If you begin Section II with some ideas about each of these issues without being rigidly entrenched, you may clarify, modify, or completely alter your thinking as you read the particular views of great thinkers. Thus, when you arrive at the time to develop an explicit statement of your philosophy in Section III, you will have engaged in thoughtful reflection on the key ideas that should be considered in any philosophy of music.

Chapter 2 includes a discussion of science and religion. First, we will investigate the special relationship that philosophy and science have with each other. This is a pertinent topic for our purposes because there is a body of scientific literature, nominally grouped under the heading of music psychology, that informs our understanding of the musical experience. As you solidify your own philosophical thinking, you may wish to incorporate these findings or intentionally exclude them—one could make a good argument for either approach.

Next, we consider religion, another topic with a long-standing connection to philosophy and of particular relevance for music philosophy. Your music philosophy could have a strong foundation based in faith or not. One issue to note, which we will discuss in this chapter, is that those who teach or work in a public setting such as a state university or public school will need to find an appropriate way of presenting a faith-based philosophy. In short, while it is inappropriate to make open declarations of faith in a public school classroom, for example, this does not preclude an individual from having a philosophy grounded in religion.

We will cover knowledge and education in Chapter 3. Knowledge is central to the consideration of music's meaning because some philosophers have contended that music is a special kind of knowledge. If you decide that music does represent a unique way of knowing—a proposition with which many philosophers would disagree—you must then decide what kind of knowledge music provides. What can one know through music? One notion frequently put forward, for example, is that music provides insights into the human condition. You will want to consider the extent to which music is a form of knowledge and if so, what information or understanding it provides.

All cultures and societies are concerned with education. While informal learning is critically important, formal education, or schooling, is perhaps more strongly connected to philosophy. Adopting differing philosophical views has consequences for what is taught, how, and why. In music, we can consider both music education in the sense of K–12 schools and a host of music teaching learning experiences outside schools (e.g., private lessons, university studio teaching, and so on). Thus, while developing an educational philosophy may be more critical for some, it likely has a bearing for all.

Many philosophers have thought deeply about the concept of beauty. In Chapter 4, we will consider a number of important questions. What is beauty? Is beauty inherent in the music itself or does it reside in our perceptions of it? Can ugliness be considered beautiful in certain circumstances? How prominently does beauty come into play when you think about music you know well or are in the process of learning or performing? It will be important for you to determine how central the concept of beauty is to your philosophy of music.

Chapter 5 deals with emotion, a topic that seemingly lies at the core of the human musical experience. However, when it comes to philosophy, nothing is ever as easy or as evident as it seems. Great thinkers have struggled mightily with the notion of emotions in music. Since the music itself is emotionless—a non-living entity cannot feel—is it the case that we perceive an emotion expressed in the music without undergoing it, or do we actually experience a specific emotion? Alternatively, perhaps music represents emotions in the sense that they show us symbolically how emotions go. The role emotions play in your philosophy of music is one of critical importance.

Chapter 6 deals with aesthetics. This is a confusing term to many who have not spent much time learning or thinking about it. The first definition for 'aesthetic' given in the *Merriam-Webster Dictionary* is "of, or relating to, or dealing with aesthetics or the beautiful."[11] This definition may suffice for most people; however, for philosophers the matter is not quite so simple. Regardless of how you end up conceiving of the term aesthetics, it is something you will need to ponder as you develop your own philosophy. The word *aesthetic* does not have to appear in your formal statement, but if omitted, it should be left out intentionally, not from neglect.

> "What is the use of aesthetics if they can neither teach how to produce beauty nor how to appreciate it in good taste? . . . Even if aesthetics are not the mathematics of beauty, they are the proof of the calculation."
>
> (Franz Grillparzer)

Section I concludes with Chapter 7: A Philosophical Framework. Here, we will review a general structure that will help you organize the many competing theories that follow in Section II. To simplify matters, most, but certainly not all, music philosophies can be divided into two categories, Absolutism and Referentialism. Absolutists believe that the primary value of music comes from the music itself, while referentialists believe that it comes from external things to which the music refers. A further schism exists between Formalists, who hold that the meaning of music is primarily intellectual, and Expressionists, who find meaning in the expressiveness of music. As indicated, there are many whose ideas do not fit within this framework. Phenomenologists, for example, find value in the bodily experience of music.

The second section of Chapter 7 concerns the different styles and genres of music. Because this book focuses mainly on Western philosophies, the music discussed is primarily Western. Not only that, the focus for many philosophers, whether stated or implied, is on art music. With few exceptions, it is not until the 20th century that philosophers widened their horizons to include other genres such as folk or popular music or non-Western styles generally referred to as World Music. The purpose of this chapter is to help you think through relevant issues to make choices about how exclusive or inclusive your music philosophy will be. In general, the intent of Chapter 7 is to present the *smörgåsbord* of choices that will come in Section II in order to help you put a mental structure in place.

Overall, Section I represents what David Ausubel called an advance organizer.[12] That is, you will encounter many of the critical ideas and central concepts that form important aspects of recognized music philosophies in preparation for a more detailed examination in Section II. Ideally, these introductory chapters will stimulate your thinking and you are encouraged to pursue a middle course at this point. If you are rigid in your thinking, too certain of what you believe—in short, close-minded—you will be immune to the thoughts of some of the greatest thinkers in world history. On the other hand, if you do not begin to ponder your own position on these topics, you may be swayed too easily by the ideas of these imposing figures.

Section II: A Review of Major Music Philosophies

Browse the philosophy section in any library or bookstore and you will see numerous volumes dedicated to the works of such famous names as Plato, Aristotle, Descartes, Kant, Hegel, Hume, Schiller, Schopenhauer, Kierkegaard, Langer, and on and on. You will also find philosophical compendia that are more than a thousand pages long. Face it, philosophy has a massive literature. The first restriction in this book is that it makes no claim to be comprehensive. That would be impractical, if not impossible, and is probably unnecessary anyway. A second restriction is that, generally speaking, the presentation of various philosophers' ideas is focused on those topics that inform an understanding of the nature, meaning, and value of music. Most philosophers wrote on a great number of topics that provide few insights into the musical experience. You will not be reading too much about those ideas in this book.

> "Music produces a kind of pleasure which human nature cannot do without."
>
> (Confucius)

A third restriction is that discussions of particular philosophies are concise summaries. Readers are encouraged to consult sources indicated for further details. Finally, the coverage in this book is restricted primarily to Western philosophers and Western music. This should not be taken as an indication that there is less value in non-Western sources. Obviously, philosophers such as Lao-Tzu or Confucius made significant contributions and some of them wrote about music. However, for the particular purposes of this book, the focus is on Western thought. Furthermore, I took a cue from others. If, for example, experts such as Monroe Beardsley, in his review of aesthetics,[13] and Bertrand Russell, in his survey of philosophy,[14] restricted their coverage to Western scholars, it seemed advisable that I should do the same. Those whose philosophy is more focused on World Music may wish to consult additional sources.[15]

In Chapter 7, you will read an overview of the various philosophers presented in Section II, Chapters 8–19. Here, I simply list the various topics, along with associated philosophers:

- Chapter 8: Contributions to Music Philosophy from the Ancient Greeks—Pythagoras, Plato, Aristotle.
- Chapter 9: From Classical Antiquity to the Renaissance—Plotinus, St. Augustine, Boethius, Thomas Aquinas, Martin Luther.
- Chapter 10: Rationalism, Empiricism, and Idealism. Rationalism—Descartes, Spinoza, Leibniz; Empiricism—Hobbes, Locke, Berkeley, Hume, Rousseau; Idealism—Kant, Schiller, Hegel, Schopenhauer.
- Chapter 11: Formalism—Hanslick, Gurney, Bell, Meyer.
- Chapter 12: Expressionism—Tolstoy, Croce, Collingwood, Cooke, Kivy, Davies, Robinson.

- Chapter 13: Symbolism—Langer, Goodman, Beardsley, Nattiez.
- Chapter 14: Phenomenology—Husserl, Merleau-Ponty, Dufrenne, Clifton, Burrows, Stubley, Johnson.
- Chapter 15: Pragmatism—Peirce, James, Dewey.
- Chapter 16: Social Philosophy—Adorno, Attali.
- Chapter 17: Praxialism—Freire, Sparshott, Small, Alperson, Elliott, Regelski.
- Chapter 18: Feminism—Göttner-Abendroth, Cusick, McClary, Citron.
- Chapter 19: Postmodernism—Nietzsche, Derrida, Lyotard, Rorty.

Although this list may seem daunting at this juncture, it really will be informative for you to have at least a basic introduction to and understanding of the ideas of some of the greatest thinkers in Western history. As you can tell simply by the various chapter titles, there is considerable discrepancy. In fact, even within a particular philosophical label (e.g., idealism) there are significant differences among various philosophers. As important as it is for you to have this basic background, even more important is for you to arrive at a settled position in your own mind about what you believe. As an educated musician, it is important for you to know what Plato and others thought and wrote about the value of music. However, simply parroting someone else's ideas without thinking through the numerous relevant issues will lead you to a weak position. Conversely, making up your own philosophy in the absence of any sense of what the giants of intellectual thought wrote about music hardly seems like a good way to proceed.

Section III: Making It Your Own

In Section III we will take the general descriptions from Section I and the more focused discussions in Section II and help you craft your own statement. We will do this in three steps. Step one is taken in Chapter 20: Articulating a Philosophy of Music. As you read the first two sections of the book you will likely begin to formulate your own ideas in agreement, disagreement, or some modification of the positions presented. In Chapter 20, we will walk through a number of exercises that will help you refine and clarify your thoughts. It will be important for you to develop your philosophy in both written and spoken form. Each mode of presentation has certain advantages and by working back and forth from writing to speaking, each can inform the other.

One thing we have not mentioned that will be a critically important part of the process is to include musical examples. Throughout Section II, I have attempted to place each of the various philosophical views into a musical context by means of numerous examples. I encourage you to think of specific musical examples throughout your reading of this book. These ought to include compositions that are part of your personal repertoire; for example, singers should think of arias, lieder, and other vocal/choral repertoire with which they are familiar. Oboists and hornists should identify sonatas, concertos, and orchestral excerpts from their own repertoire, and so on. You will also want to identify and consider repertoire outside your personal sphere of performance or study. Pianists may want to include opera, string quartets, or wind band music, for example. Depending on your position, you may wish to include music or activities from genres other than Western art music, such as popular music, jazz, or even non-Western music. Some philosophers are more disposed toward the creation and performance of music than on the contemplation of works of art *per se*. Thus, musical examples also can and should include scenarios such as a jam session, a high school choir rehearsal, or a music therapy session.

Another thing you may wish to do, and in fact are encouraged to do, is to read beyond what is contained in this book. As indicated previously, the philosophical literature is voluminous. One suggestion to narrow the possibilities is to try reading some of the original work of one or more philosophers whose ideas you find attractive. Original sources are provided in the footnotes to each chapter, along with many commentaries on philosophy, aesthetics, music philosophy, and other topics of interest.

Once you have a good draft of your philosophy well under way, step two is to think about the implications of your philosophy. A philosophy will do you no good if it does not influence the practice of your craft. At this point, you can begin moving back and forth from the philosophy statement itself to the application. Each will inform the other and help you to clarify specific thoughts and issues. Throughout this process, keep musical examples—either specific compositions or specific activities or experiences (e.g., performing on a recital or rehearsing in a practice room)—at the forefront of your reflections. Chapter 21: Applying Your Philosophy provides some brief vignettes that are intended to serve as examples. Each time you read one of the chapters in Section II (Chapters 8–19), you may want to flip back to Chapter 21 to read the example. Then you can begin to modify this example to fit your own circumstances.

Once you have a music philosophy clearly articulated and have begun to apply it in your daily profession, step three is to think about how you would lobby on behalf of music if called upon to do so. Chapter 22: Advocacy concerns a practical issue that you may face on more than one occasion throughout your career. For example, suppose civic leaders have asked you to speak to them about why the community should support a symphony orchestra or an opera company. Or, imagine that the school board is facing a budget crisis and is considering the elimination of music programs. How would you respond? As we will see, a philosophy and an advocacy position can, and probably should, be related, but they are not the same thing.

Summary and Thought Questions

In summary, the purposes of this book are to introduce you to major ideas in the history of music philosophy and to help you develop your philosophy of music, whether that is a restatement of an existing philosophy, an amended version of someone else's ideas, or a unique view. In Section I, we will investigate a number of core issues that you will want to consider in preparation for articulating your philosophy. The intent is to help you to begin thinking deeply about these topics without becoming entrenched in a mindset. In Section II, we will consider what some of the greatest philosophers have to say about the nature, meaning, and value of music. Even if you have ideas of your own already or are prone to dismiss unusual or unfamiliar ideas precipitously, I encourage you to read each discussion with an open mind and to consider each idea carefully before you decide to agree or disagree with it. In Section III, you will write a formal statement of your philosophy, apply it to particular aspects of your chosen career path, and learn about distinctions between philosophy and advocacy. Here are some thoughts and questions to help you get started:

1. As you ponder what the value of having a philosophy might be, consider the words of C.S. Lewis who said, "Friendship is unnecessary, like philosophy, like art. . . . It has no survival value; rather it is one of those things that give value to survival."[16] What do you think he meant by this? Do you agree that a music philosophy or that music itself has no survival value? In

what ways do you think having a music philosophy might help you survive? You might also wish to consider how art in general and music specifically help us survive.

2. Several strong statements spoke to the difficulty of developing a philosophy. If you are tempted along the way to quit, you may wish to print out this statement of Jacob Riis and read it every day. In thinking about his efforts to lead a city to make important societal changes, he said,

> When it didn't seem to help, I would go and look at a stone-cutter hammering away at his rock perhaps a hundred times without as much as a crack showing in it. Yet at the hundred and first blow it would split in two, and I knew it was not that blow that did it, but all that had gone before together.[17]

Does the idea of creating an explicit philosophical statement, in both written and oral form, sound exciting or daunting? Are you eager to get started or dreading the prospect?

> "I think we ought always to entertain our opinions with some measure of doubt. I shouldn't wish people dogmatically to believe any philosophy, not even mine."
>
> (Bertrand Russell)

3. Plato quotes Socrates as saying, "The unexamined life is not worth living."[18] Think about this statement in two regards. First, in what ways have you benefitted from examining your own life? Second, what difference do you think it would make whether you did or did not examine the role that music plays in your life?
4. In a previous sidebar quote, Eleanor Roosevelt spoke about making choices. What kinds of musical choices do you think you can or should make under the guidance of an explicit philosophy?
5. Finally, let us consider Bertrand Russell's answer to the question, "Has the study of philosophy any value?" When he compared science with philosophy, he found that science arrives at definite answers while philosophical inquiry leads only to uncertainty. However, it is that uncertainty that forms the most important value of philosophy. First, although philosophy does not lead to a certain answer, it does lead to "many possibilities which enlarge our thoughts and free them from the tyranny of custom."[19] Second, philosophy leads us to contemplate great and important questions and as we do so, "the mind also is rendered great, and becomes capable of that union with the universe which constitutes its highest goal."[20] In other words, we develop a broadened perspective rather than a parochial, overly personalized view. How would you articulate the role philosophy has had in your life so far? Can you speculate how a well-defined philosophy of music might impact your musical life and career?

In closing this section, let Russell's words be encouraging. When you find yourself uncertain about your philosophy in general, specific aspects of it, or how it will apply to your musical career, take heart. That uncertainty is a sign that you are on the right track. When you step outside yourself and examine this enterprise we call *music* with a wide lens, when you consider your place in this musical universe, you will be engaging in something of infinite value. Be patient and trust that the process is worth it.

Notes

1 A. Lacey, *A Dictionary of Philosophy* (London: Routledge, 1986).
2 Ibid., 176.

3 Anthony Quinton, "Philosophy," in *The Oxford Companion to Philosophy*, ed. Ted Honderich (Oxford: Oxford University Press, 1995), 666.

4 George Davidson, *Introduction to Philosophy: The World's Great Thinkers*, ed. Philip Stokes (London: Arcturus Publishing, 2011).

5 William Sahakian and Mabel Sahakian, *Ideas of the Great Philosophers* (New York: Fall River Press, 2005).

6 Davidson, *Introduction*, 5.

7 Cyril Joad, *Guide to Philosophy* (Toronto: General Publishing Co., 1936/1957), 10.

8 Will Durant, *The Story of Philosophy* (New York: Simon and Schuster, 1953), 3.

9 L. Jonathan Cohen, "Philosophy and Science," in *The Oxford Companion to Philosophy*, ed. Ted Honderich (Oxford: Oxford University Press, 1995), 674–78.

10 Bennett Reimer, "Once More with Feeling: Reconciling Discrepant Accounts of Musical Affect," *Philosophy of Music Education Review* 12, no. 1 (2004): 15.

11 *Merriam-Webster Dictionary*, 2015. http://www.merriam-webster.com/dictionary/aesthetics.

12 David Ausubel, "The Use of Advance Organizers in the Learning and Retention of Meaningful Verbal Material," *Journal of Educational Psychology* 51, no. 1 (1960): 267–72.

13 Monroe Beardsley, *Aesthetics from Classical Greece to the Present* (Tuscaloosa, AL: The University of Alabama Press, 1966).

14 Bertrand Russell, *Wisdom of the West* (London: Rathbone Books, 1959).

15 Deborah Bradley, "Good for What, Good for Whom? Decolonizing Music Education Philosophies," in *The Oxford Handbook of Philosophy in Music Education*, ed. Wayne Bowman and Anna Lucía Frega (New York: Oxford University Press, 2012), 409–33. Peter Manuel and Stephen Blum, "Classical Aesthetic Traditions of India, China, and the Middle East," in *The Routledge Companion to Philosophy and Music*, ed. Theodore Gracyk and Andrew Kania (New York: Routledge, 2011), 245–56.

16 C. S. Lewis, *The Four Loves* (New York: Harcourt, Brace, 1960), 71.

17 Jacob Riis, *The Making of an American*. The Project Gutenberg EBook #6125, 1901/2004, 130–31. http://www.gutenberg.org/cache/epub/6125/pg6125.html.

18 Plato, *Apology*, trans. Benjamin Jowett. The Project Gutenberg Ebook #1656, p. 90. http://www.gutenberg.org/ebooks/1656.

19 Bertrand Russell, *The Problems of Philosophy* (Oxford: Oxford University Press, 1912), 157.

20 Ibid., 161.

2   Science and Religion

Science and religion have long been intertwined with philosophy and have engaged philosophers for centuries. They are germane to the development of music philosophy for at least four reasons: (1) Science and religion are representative of the kinds of matters that occupy the thoughts of philosophers. They serve as exemplars of philosophical thinking. (2) In reviewing these topics in a broad, general way, we will introduce many of the philosophers whose ideas we will discuss more thoroughly in Section II. (3) By starting to think about issues related to science and religion now, you will be preparing yourself to engage at a deeper level as we get further into more detailed discussions of the same questions later in the book. (4) Both of these topics have a direct relationship to music. In developing your own ideas, you will be free to adopt a position along a range of possibilities; however, your philosophy will be much stronger because you have made thoughtful choices based on some degree of familiarity with the nuances of various positions on each of these topics. You will choose the degree to which you incorporate or disregard scientific findings about music and you will decide whether and to what degree your philosophy has a faith basis.

Science

The history of Western thought, particularly with regard to science and philosophy, is one of mutual influences in a series of waxing and waning interactions. That is, at various times or circumstances, science and philosophy have exerted strong influences on each other or have maintained a more distant relationship.[1] The purpose of this brief section is not to present a chronological account of these two vast fields. Nor is it to consider the philosophy of science, a vital field in its own right. Rather, the purpose is threefold: first, to provide examples of ways science and philosophy interact, second, to help you begin to choose a path for the development of your own philosophy, and third, to set up some of the discussions in the ensuing chapters of Section I in which current scientific understandings of selected philosophical matters are presented.

Examples of Scientific and Philosophical Interactions

In the 6th century BC, Pythagoras conducted a series of experiments that had significant consequences for both science and philosophy. Although there is some controversy over whether Pythagoras himself actually conducted the experiments,[2] historically most writers have attributed the mathematical theorems and acoustical experiments that bear his name to Pythagoras. With details forthcoming in Chapter 8, however, it is enough to note now that nearly from the very beginnings, science and philosophy have been intertwined inextricably.

Across the ensuing centuries, many individuals whose philosophical contributions we will be reading also made significant contributions to science or mathematics,[3] including, for example:

Boethius (475–526?), who translated important books on arithmetic, geometry, and astronomy.
René Descartes (1596–1650), who demonstrated how to solve geometrical problems using algebraic equations (Cartesian geometry), developed a new conception of physical matter, and published on a number of topics such as optics and meteorology.
Immanuel Kant (1724–1804), who published a number of scientific and mathematical treatises.
David Hume (1711–1776), who based his 'science of man' project on Newtonian natural philosophy, in which he likened habits of the mind to gravity in the natural world and principles of association to the laws of motion.[4]

In a moment we will see that scientific and philosophical interactions continue into the 21st century. In the meantime, however, it is important to recognize that prior to 1879, neither philosophy nor psychology existed as separate academic disciplines in the way we know them today.[5] Many great thinkers worked fluidly among the disciplines of mathematics, science, and philosophy.

> "Science is what you know, philosophy is what you don't know."
>
> (Bertrand Russell)

There is a considerable body of literature on the philosophy of science, as for example Alexander Rosenberg's *Philosophy of Science: A Contemporary Introduction* (2012), J. A. Cover and Martin Curd's *Philosophy of Science: The Central Issues* (1998), or Paul Churchland's *Neurophilosophy at Work* (2007).[6] In contrast, and more surprising perhaps, is the notion Hans Reichenbach expressed in *The Rise of Scientific Philosophy*.[7] In this book, the author distinguishes between what he calls speculative philosophy and scientific philosophy. He derides the former as weak and vague. "Scientific philosophy, in contrast, leaves the explanation of the universe entirely to the scientist."[8] Similarly, he finds fault with speculative philosophy's attempt to establish morality by reason alone and claims, "Scientific philosophy has abandoned completely the plan of advancing moral rules."[9]

Although there are some who identify with scientific philosophy,[10] most philosophers would be inclined to see the difference between the two disciplines as expressed in this statement: "Science is concerned with what we *can* do and philosophy is concerned with what we *should* do."[11] In other words, there are differences in the kinds of questions that science and philosophy can ask and answer. Or, even when they ask the same questions, they arrive at answers in different ways. According to Will Durant, "Science gives us knowledge, but only philosophy can give us wisdom."[12] Scientists can study the universe and seek to determine its origins, but when philosophers ask questions about the meaning of the universe, they do so from a different perspective.

More recent relationships between philosophy and science range from Ludwig Wittgenstein's view that cognitive science has nothing to offer the understanding of art to the view that science is in the process of eliminating the need for philosophy.[13] For example, Stephen Hawking and Leonard Mlodinow wrote that "philosophy is dead. Philosophy has not kept up with modern developments in science, particularly physics."[14]

Rather than conjoining or polarizing the two disciplines, for our purposes it is more important to consider whether or how science can influence philosophy and in particular, how science might inform the development of your philosophy of music. In a book section called "Modern

Science Has Implications for Philosophy," Rosenberg provided several examples of how scientific discoveries can influence philosophical thought.[15] For example, Newtonian physics has altered thinking about free will. Newton demonstrated that there were deterministic laws governing the motion of all objects in the universe. Because human bodies have mass, including our decision-making brains, perhaps our sense of free will is an illusion. Several books have explored this idea, such as *The Volitional Brain: Towards a Neuroscience of Free Will*.[16] In a recent experiment,[17] neuroscientists recorded neuronal activity in the supplementary motor area, a region of the brain that prepares motor systems for action more than a second before participants reported a decision to move a finger. In other words, preconscious brain activity preceded conscious, voluntary behavior.

> Taken together, these findings lend support to the view that the experience of will emerges as the culmination of premotor activity (probably in combination with networks in parietal cortex) starting several hundreds of ms [milliseconds] before awareness. The scientific, philosophical, and societal implications of these findings remain open for debate.[18]

Before you despair at the disappearance of free will, take note of several counter claims. William Klemm identified 12 categories of flawed conclusions that scholars use to support the notion that free will is an illusion.[19] According to Daniel Dennett, "the compatibility of free will and science (deterministic or indeterministic—it makes no difference) is not as inconceivable as it once seemed."[20] Neuroscientist Michael Gazzaniga summed it up nicely when he said, "We are personally responsible agents and are to be held accountable for our actions, even though we live in a determined universe."[21] Regardless of one's stance, the point for our current purposes is the way in which science and philosophy can interact.

Music Psychology and Music Philosophy

Music psychology is an umbrella term that includes the scientific study of musical phenomena. A widely diverse field, it includes such disciplines and topics as:

Biology: hearing, the brain, the body in musical performance, and bodily responses to music.
Physics: acoustics, ergonomics, and biomechanics of musical instruments.
Anthropology and Ethnomusicology: music around the world and across time.
Sociology: music in society, including social interactions, business and economics, politics, religion, the military, youth culture, and the entertainment and media industries.
Psychology: psychoacoustics, perception and cognition of music, emotional responses to music, musical personality, special musicians (e.g., prodigies, musical savants, Williams Syndrome musicians, etc.), the development of musicality, performance anxiety, musical aptitude, and music teaching and learning.

Philosophy can influence both the way experiments in music psychology are conducted and the way that findings from those experiments are interpreted.[22] Equally, scientific experiences can provide a background for music philosophy. Indeed, "philosophical analyses must be consistent with the facts, or with interpretations of what these are. But philosophical analyses must go beyond the facts in resolving the problems, paradoxes and inconsistencies they can seem to generate."[23]

Charles Nussbaum provided an example of interactions between music and science in the Preface to his book, *The Musical Representation: Meaning, Ontology, and Emotion.* "I began to think of music less as a topic for traditional philosophical aesthetics and more as one for cognitive psychology, philosophy of mind, and philosophical semiotic."[24] He explained that the book would "proceed not only

> "If I were not a physicist, I would probably be a musician. I often think in music. I live my daydreams in music. I see my life in terms of music."
>
> (Albert Einstein)

from biology, psychology, and philosophy to music but will occasionally jog back from music to biology, psychology, and philosophy."[25] David Huron took a similar position when he stated, "Only time will tell whether we are witnessing the passing of the aesthetics baton from philosophy to empirical science."[26]

In the ensuing chapters, we will review some of the contributions music psychology has made to our understanding of beauty, emotion, and aesthetics. As you read those chapters, carefully consider whether you wish to develop your philosophy independent of scientific explorations of music or whether your philosophy will be informed by current understandings.

Religion

Most philosophy of music books omit the topic of religion. Indeed, to the extent that individuals of differing faiths or no faith might be offended or feel disenfranchised, that may be a wise course. However, there are at least two reasons why the topic is included in this book. First, it is very apparent from years of teaching music philosophy that many students are interested in the issue. Particularly for those who do have a strong faith, trying to create a secular philosophy of music may leave them feeling confused or dissatisfied.

Second, there is a great deal of religion in philosophy and a great deal of philosophy in religion. Nearly every great thinker has turned his thoughts to religion at some point, as expressed in Sir Francis Bacon's maxim, "A little philosophy inclineth man's mind to atheism, but depth in philosophy bringeth men's minds about to religion."[27] Likewise, many religious thinkers have utilized rational thought in defense of their beliefs. The chief difference between religion and philosophy is the difference between faith and reason. Pondering the meaning of life, one person chooses to believe or not in God, while another one uses logic to determine that there is or is not a God. Leaving religion out of philosophy removes a very large segment from the discussion. That would be nearly the same thing as removing sacred music from a music history course.

> "As far as possible, join faith to reason."
> (Boethius)

I sincerely hope that all readers—from those with a strong faith to those with no faith—will read the ensuing section with patience and open-mindedness. There is no intent to offend or to influence one's private beliefs in any direction. Rather, the intent is to represent with fairness and accuracy a major theme in philosophy that has historically had implications for music philosophy.

> "Religions do a useful thing: they narrow God to the limits of man. Philosophy replies by doing a necessary thing: it elevates man to the plane of God."
>
> (Victor Hugo)

Philosophy of Religion

Although Plato, Aristotle, and other ancient philosophers invoked the term *god* and wrote about other theological concepts, they were not referring to a monotheistic God as found in the Judeo-Christian tradition. However, many of their ideas have been highly influential in the history of Western religious thought. Thomas Aquinas (1225–1274), for example, labored to reconcile Aristotle's philosophy with the Christian faith. In *Summa Theologica*, he used logical arguments to produce proofs of the existence of God, which he called the Five Ways. However, as much as he desired to rely on reason to substantiate his religious views, Aquinas also recognized its limitations. "There are, therefore, some points of intelligibility in God, accessible to human reason, and other points that altogether transcend the power of human reason."[28] In this, he agreed with St. Augustine's (354–430) much earlier statement. Augustine wrote about the importance of belief and revelation from scripture, "since we are too weak by unaided reason to find out truth."[29]

St. Anselm (1033–1109) also used logical arguments to prove the existence of God. When challenged by his students to produce a rationale for the existence of God, St. Anselm (1078) responded with his 'ontological argument':

> Therefore, O Lord, you are not only that than which a greater cannot be conceived, but you are a being greater than can be conceived. For, since it can be conceived that there is such a being, if you are not this very being, a greater than you can be conceived. But this is impossible.[30]

In other words, "something than which nothing greater can be thought of must be something that exists."[31] This argument has been defended by Descartes,[32] among others, and criticized by Kant,[33] among others.

A more recent, and perhaps more poetic statement that is very similar came from Jorge Luis Borges:

> I close my eyes and see a flock of birds. The vision lasts a second, or perhaps less; I am not sure how many birds I saw. Was the number of birds definite or indefinite? The problem involves the existence of God. If God exists, the number is definite, because God knows how many birds I saw. If God does not exist, the number is indefinite, because no one can have counted. In this case I saw fewer than ten birds (let us say) and more than one, but did not see nine, eight, seven, six, five, four, three, or two birds. I saw a number between ten and one, which was not nine, eight, seven, six, five, etc. That integer—not-nine, not-eight, not-seven, not-six, not-five, etc.—is inconceivable. *Ergo*, God exists.[34]

> "The heart has its reasons, which reason does not know."
>
> (Blaise Pascal)

Philosophical rationales for the existence of God range from the early Christian writers to Friedrich Nietzsche, who is famous for stating, "God is dead! God remains dead! And we have killed him!"[35] Though the arguments have changed over time, the debates still hotly rage.

One modern arena for the philosophical debate over the existence of God is in a rationale for the universe itself. Can science account for the universe through the Big Bang Theory, or other cosmological theories, without resorting to God, or does the precision and complexity of the universe make a case for a Creator? Modern cosmology has led different philosophers and scientists to opposite conclusions on the matter. Some scientists no longer see a need for God, and some religious philosophers reject scientific claims. On the other hand, "many scientists are deeply religious people, and many religious thinkers accept the authority of science without compromising their religious faith."[36]

As Cottingham stated, "At the very least, philosophers and scientists are having to confront the question of whether there may be something about the universe that is itself favourable to the emergence of life and intelligence."[37] Consider two recent examples. Frank Wilczek, a Nobel Prize winning physicist, wrote a book concerned with a single question: Is beauty inherent in the world? In seeking to answer this question, he considered the role of God. Noted neuroscientist David Eagleman has declared himself to be a 'possibilian,' meaning that he is open to exploring possibilities beyond traditional religious dogma and atheism. Regardless of how they ultimately answer the question, both have found abundant evidence of symmetry, harmony, balance, proportion, economy, and beauty in nature.[38]

Philosophy of religion is concerned with many different questions other than the existence of God. Is there an afterlife? Can miracles occur? Why do pain and evil exist? What is the meaning and purpose of life? One can seek answers to these questions through faith or reason or some combination of both. In *Critique of Pure Reason*, Kant took a middle road when he wrote, "For it is perfectly permissible to employ, in the presence of reason, the language of a firmly rooted faith, even after we have been obliged to renounce all pretensions to knowledge."[39] Philosophers George Santayana and Paul Tillich were arranged on either side of this position. For Santayana, "The Life of Reason is the seat of all ultimate values."[40] Tillich, in stating that "Faith is not an act of any of his [man's] rational functions,"[41] was saying that faith transcended reason.

> "I find it as difficult to understand a scientist who does not acknowledge the presence of a superior rationality behind the existence of the universe as it is to comprehend a theologian who would deny the advances of science."
> (Wernher von Braun)

Beyond the connection between philosophy and religion, there is an obvious connection between religion and music. Martin Luther put it succinctly when he said, "Music is next to theology."[42] Further, he connected philosophy, religion, and music in a triangular relationship.

> I would certainly like to praise music with all my heart as the excellent gift of God which it is and to commend it to everyone. . . . [However, a]s much as I want to commend it, my praise is bound to be wanting and inadequate. For who can comprehend it all? . . . Philosophers have labored to explain the marvelous instrument of the human voice [in context, he is referring to singing]. Philosophers for all their labor cannot find the explanation; and baffled they end in perplexity; for none of them has yet been able to define or demonstrate the original components of the human voice. . . . They marvel, but they do not understand.[43]

It is this triangular relationship to which we turn now.

Philosophy, Religion, and Music

Throughout the discussions to come in Section II, we will encounter several philosophers who base their philosophy of music on a religious foundation. You may certainly choose to do so or may decide to reject such an approach. Either way, you are encouraged to balance your faith or

> "Music is my religion."
>
> (Jimi Hendrix)

lack thereof with reason. That is, as we have seen in this brief survey, famous thinkers ranging from St. Augustine to Borges have struggled to find the appropriate balance of reason and faith. While various thinkers found themselves more or less in favor of rationality, no one took the position that illogical thinking was the way to an appropriate answer.

Musicians have had no difficulty in expressing their religious views through music. As legendary jazz artist Duke Ellington put it, "Every man prays in his own language, and there is no language that God does not understand."[44] The massive amount of sacred music in all genres, from masses, motets, oratorios, and cantatas to hymns, praise choruses, gospel songs, and Christian rock, attests to this fact. Because of its prevalence, we need only give a few confirming examples here. Speaking of Bach, Albert Schweitzer said, "The S.D.G. (*Soli Deo Gloria*, "to God alone be praise") and the J.J. (*Jesu juva*, "Help me, Jesus!") with which he garnishes his scores, are for him no formulas, but the Credo that runs through all his work."[45] Brahms quoted scripture passages from the New Testament at great length, and stated, "Beethoven declared that his ideas came from God, and I can say the same."[46] Duke Ellington presented three Sacred Concerts between 1965 and 1973, utilizing his own band, gospel singers, choruses, and dancers.[47] He wrote music with titles such as 'In the Beginning God,'[48] ♫ 'Something 'bout Believing,'[49] ♫ and 'Father Forgive.'[50] ♫ He called the first Sacred Concert "the most important thing I've done."[51]

> "If I should ever die, God forbid, let this be my epitaph: THE ONLY PROOF HE NEEDED FOR THE EXISTENCE OF GOD WAS MUSIC."
>
> (Kurt Vonnegut)

Country music has an obvious and deep connection with faith. "Seemingly particular to the South, the spiritual side of country music actually extends much more broadly to the nation."[52] Contemporary Christian music provides adolescents with a means of expressing their faith with rock music traditions.

> With its angelic waifs, strutting arena rockers, choreographed girl groups, guitar-strumming folkies, flannel-encased grunge acts, posturing rappers, and wordy singer-songwriters, contemporary Christian music provides the evangelical audience with the same ethereal voices, the same driving guitars, and the same chunky rhythms that can be found anywhere on the radio dial—but with one important difference: rather than challenging predominant evangelical values, this music affirms them.[53]

Regarding rap music, Noel Erskine said, "In rap theology, God takes sides and identifies with rappers in their attempt to confront violence with counterviolence."[54]

Performers and listeners, too, may find faith experiences in music. Contrarily, even in the midst of performing or listening to Brahms's *Requiem*,[55] ♫ Bloch's *Schelomo*,[56] ♫ where the solo cello represents the voice of King Solomon, or Coltrane's 'Dear Lord,'[57] ♫ a result of his conversion experience following years of drug and alcohol abuse,[58] one can engage in a musical experience devoid of a spiritual connotation. Bernard Shaw, who said, "Among the pious I am a scoffer: among the musical I am religious,"[59] nevertheless found great pleasure in listening to *Messiah*.[60] ♫ "My favorite oratorio is *Messiah*, with which I have spent many of the hours which others give to Shakespeare, or Scott, or Dickens."[61]

As a reminder, the point of this section is neither to proselytize nor to offend. Rather, it is to acknowledge strong historical connections among philosophy, religion, and music. It is to recognize that philosophers on both sides of the divide have dealt seriously and in depth with these issues. Whether you choose to undergird your music philosophy with a faith basis or not, this is an issue that demands the same rigor in systematic, logical thinking as all the other aspects.

As a final point in this section, I want to reiterate a point raised in the first chapter. That is, if you do have a faith-based music philosophy and choose to practice your craft in a public arena such as a public school or state university, you will need to find a way to share your philosophy in a non-religious manner. Separation of church and state requires that you handle this matter with tact, fairness, and sensitivity.

> "Souls which seek one another across the sufferings of life only find one another—such is my belief—in prayer and in music."
>
> (Franz Liszt)

Summary and Thought Questions

Science and religion are certainly not the only topics that philosophers ponder. However, they do have a bearing on our pursuit of developing a philosophy of music. Although the complexity of interrelationships among these four terms—science, religion, music, and philosophy—can be a little daunting, an important concept is that you should not be developing your thoughts about the value and meaning of music in a vacuum. In the next four chapters, we will be reading and thinking about five additional terms that have strong philosophical and musical interconnections—knowledge, education, beauty, emotion, and aesthetics. As you move through them, continually weave the strands from this chapter into the new threads that create an ever-richer tapestry. Before we move onto the next chapter, spend some time pondering these questions:

1. Journals such as *Music Perception, The Psychology of Music,* or *Musicæ Scientiæ* are filled with scientific investigations about the phenomenon of music. Do these publications have anything to do with a philosophical view of music, and if so, what?
2. Are there some aspects of music philosophy that seem to be more amenable to experimentation than others? If so, what might those be? What aspects of music philosophy seem to be immune from scientific investigation?
3. For some, deciding whether a music philosophy will have a faith basis will be a very quick and clear decision; emphatically it will or will not. Others may struggle more with such a decision. How is it for you? If you are studying this book in a group or class setting, you may wish to keep your deliberations private. In a safe and accepting environment, however, it might be enlightening to share your views with others.
4. If you do decide that your music philosophy will be faith based, you may face a second challenge. Sharing your faith in a public setting, for example as a university professor at a state supported institution or as a public school teacher, is inappropriate. Therefore, you will have to negotiate the disparity between a publicly expressed view and a privately held belief. This does not necessarily mean there is a conflict between the two, rather that the language used must be appropriate to the context. If your philosophy has a strong faith basis, will you be comfortable in keeping that aspect private when it is deemed inappropriate?

Notes

1   L. Jonathan Cohen, "Philosophy and Science," in *The Oxford Companion to Philosophy*, ed. Ted Honderich (Oxford: Oxford University Press, 1995), 674–78.

2   Carl Huffman, "Pythagoras," in *The Stanford Encyclopedia of Philosophy* (2011 edition), ed. Edward Zalta. http://plato.stanford.edu/archives/fall2011/entries/pythagoras/.

3   Edward Zalta, ed. *Stanford Encyclopedia of Philosophy* (2015 edition). http://plato.stanford.edu/.

4   Eric Schliesser, "Hume's Newtonianism and Anti-Newtonianism," in *The Stanford Encyclopedia of Philosophy* (2008 edition), ed. Edward Zalta. http://plato.stanford.edu/archives/win2008/entries/hume-newton/.

5   Edward Reed, *From Soul to Mind: The Emergence of Psychology, from Erasmus Darwin to William James* (New Haven, CT: Yale University Press, 1997).

6   Alex Rosenberg, *Philosophy of Science: A Contemporary Introduction, 3rd ed.* (New York: Routledge, 2012). Marin Curd and J. A. Cover, *Philosophy of Science: The Central Issues* (New York: W.W. Norton, 1998). Paul Churchland, *Neurophilosophy at Work* (Cambridge: Cambridge University Press, 2007).

7   Hans Reichenbach, *The Rise of Scientific Philosophy* (Berkeley: University of California Press, 1951).

8   Ibid., 303.

9   Ibid., 304.

10 Luis Manuel Ledo-Regal, "What Is Scientific Philosophy?" *Scientific Philosophy* (May 15, 2008). http://scientific-philosophy.blogspot.com/.

11 Ben Dupré, *50 Philosophy Ideas You Really Need to Know* (London: Quercus, 2007), 3.

12 Will Durant, *The Story of Philosophy* (New York: Simon and Schuster, 1953), xxvii.

13 Gregory Currie, "Aesthetics and Cognitive Science," in *The Oxford Handbook of Aesthetics*, ed. Jerrold Levinson (Oxford UK: Oxford University Press, 2003), 706–21.

14 Stephen Hawking and Leonard Mlodinow, *The Grand Design* (New York: Random House, 2010), 5.

15 Rosenberg, *Philosophy of Science*.

16 Benjamin Libet, Anthony Freeman, and Keith Sutherland, eds. *The Volitional Brain: Towards a Neuroscience of Free Will* (Exeter, UK: Imprint Academic, 2004).

17 Itzhak Fried, Roy Mukamel, and Gabriel Kreiman, "Internally Generated Preactivation of Single Neurons in Human Medial Frontal Cortex Predicts Volition," *Neuron* 69, no. 3 (2011): 548–62.

18 Ibid., 557.

19 W. Klemm, "Free Will Debates: Simple Experiments Are Not So Simple," *Advances in Cognitive Psychology* 6, no. 6 (2010): 47–65.

20 Daniel Dennett, *Freedom Evolves* (New York: Penguin Books, 2003), 306.

21 Micahel Gazzaniga, *Who's in Charge? Free Will and the Science of the Brain* (New York: HarperCollins, 2011), 2.

22 Donald Hodges, *Music in the Human Experience: An Introduction to Music Psychology* (New York: Routledge, 2011).

23 Stephen Davies, "Emotions Expressed and Aroused by Music: Philosophical Perspectives," in *Oxford Handbook of Music and Emotion: Theory, Research, Applications*, ed. Patrik Juslin and John Sloboda (Oxford: Oxford University Press, 2010), 17.

24 Charles Nussbaum, *The Musical Representation: Meaning, Ontology, and Emotion* (Cambridge, MA: MIT Press, 2007), xi.

25 Ibid., xii.

26 David Huron, "Aesthetics," in *The Oxford Handbook of Music Psychology*, ed. Susan Hallam, Ian Cross, and Michael Thaut (Oxford, UK: Oxford University Press, 2011), 157.

27 Francis Bacon quoted in George Santayana, *The Life of Reason* (Amherst, NY: Prometheus Books, 1905/1998), 179.

28 Thomas Aquinas, *Summa contra Gentiles*, Book I, trans. Joseph Rickaby (1264). http://www2.nd.edu/Departments/Maritain/etext/gc1_3.htm.

29 St. Augustine, *Confessions*, Book Six, Chapter V.8, trans. Albert Outler, 398/1994. http://www.fordham.edu/halsall/basis/confessions-bod.asp.

30 St. Anselm, *Proslogion (Discourse on the Existence of God)*, Chapter XV, trans. Sidney Deane (1078). http://www.fordham.edu/halsall/basis/anselm-proslogium.asp#CHAPTER%20XV.

31 Philip Stokes, *Philosophy: The World's Greatest Thinkers* (London: Arcturus, 2007), 7.

32 John Cottingham, "Faith," in *Western Philosophy*, ed. David Papineau (New York: Metro Books, 2009), 108–31.

33 Stokes, *Philosophy*.

34 Jorge Borges, *The Aleph and Other Stories* (New York: Penguin Books, 2004), 148.

35 Friedrich Nietzsche, *The Gay Science*, trans. Josefine Nauckhoff (Cambridge: Cambridge University Press, 1882/2001), 120.

36 Robert Solomon, *Introduction to Philosophy, 8th ed.* (New York: Oxford University Press, 2005), 124.

37 Cottingham, "Faith," 111.

38 Frank Wilczek, *A Beautiful Question: Finding Nature's Deep Design* (New York: Penguin Press, 2015). David Eagleman, *The Brain: The Story of You* (New York: Pantheon Books, 2015). David Eagleman, *Incognito: The Secret Lives of the Brain* (New York: Pantheon Books, 2011).

39 Immanuel Kant, *Critique of Pure* Reason, Section II, trans. J. Meiklejohn (1981). http://philosophy.eserver. org/kant/critique-of-pure-reason.txt.

40 Santayana, *The Life of Reason*, xx.

41 Paul Tillich, *Dynamics of Faith* (New York: HarperCollins, 1957/2001), 7.

42 Robin Leaver, "Luther on Music," in *The Pastoral Luther: Essays on Martin Luther's Practical Theology*, ed. Timothy Wengert (Grand Rapids, MI: Wm. B. Eerdmans, 2009), 271.

43 Martin Luther, *Instructions for the Visitors of Parish Pastors in Electoral Saxony* (1525, LIII, 321ff), quoted in David Whitwell, *Ancient Views on Music and Religion* (Austin, TX: Whitwell Publishing, 2013), 185–86.

44 Duke Ellington quoted in Mark Tucker, *The Duke Ellington Reader* (Oxford, UK: Oxford University Press, 1993), 372.

45 Albert Schweitzer, *J.S. Bach*, trans. Ernest Newman (London: Adam and Charles Black, 1923), 166–67.

46 Johannes Brahms quoted in Arthur Abell, *Talks with Great Composers* (New York: Philosophical Library, 1955), 2.

47 Janna Steed, *Duke Ellington: A Spiritual Biography* (New York: Crossroad Publishing Co., 1999).

48 Duke Ellington, 'In the Beginning God' from *Sacred Concerts*, performed by Duke Ellington, https://www. youtube.com/watch?v=8jFa-4b2FTk.

49 Duke Ellington, 'Something 'bout Believing' from *Sacred Concerts*, performed by Duke Ellington, https:// www.youtube.com/watch?v=R_ty0XVhxQY.

50 Duke Ellington, 'Father Forgive' from *Sacred Concerts*, performed by combined choirs conducted by Randall Keith Horton, http://www.youtube.com/watch?v=weI3UKMn2Sg.

51 Tucker, *The Duke Ellington Reader*, 375.

52 Cecelia Tichi, *High Lonesome: The American Culture of Country Music* (Chapel Hill, NC: University of North Carolina Press, 1994), 170.

53 Jay Howard and John Streck, *Apostles of Rock: The Splintered World of Contemporary Christian Music* (Lexington, KY: University Press of Kentucky, 1999), 5.

54 Noel Erskine, "Rap, Reggae, and Religion: Sounds of Cultural Dissonance," in *Noise and Spirit: The Religious and Spiritual Sensibilities of Rap Music*, ed. Anthony Pinn (New York: New York University Press, 2003), 78.

55 Johannes Brahms, *Requiem* performed by Herbert Blomstedt conducting the Denmark Radio Symphony Orchestra, http://www.youtube.com/watch?v=dJelOS-fjrY.

56 Ernest Bloch, *Schelomo*, performed by Mstislav Rostropovich, cellist, Leonard Bernstein, conductor, and the Orchestre Nacional de France, http://www.youtube.com/watch?v=vlUQyEh_q4k.

57 John Coltrane, 'Dear Lord,' performed by John Coltrane, http://www.youtube.com/watch?v=Fp oyOwKJ1A0.

58 David Stowe, *How Sweet the Sound: Music in the Spiritual Lives of Americans* (Cambridge, MA: Harvard University Press, 2004).

59 Eric Bentley, ed., *Shaw on Music: A Selection from the Music Criticism of Bernard Shaw* (Garden City, NY: Doubleday, 1955), 243.

60 George Frideric Handel, *Messiah*, performed by the Academy of Ancient Music and Choir of King's College, Cambridge, conducted by Stephen Cleobury, https://www.youtube.com/watch?v=AZTZRtRFkvk.

61 Bentley, *Shaw on Music*, 247.

3 Knowledge and Education

Similar to science and religion, knowledge and education are two critically important themes in philosophy. Knowledge is a salient characteristic of being human and you will want to ponder whether music represents a special kind of knowledge, distinct from other ways of knowing, whether music shares an affinity with other forms of knowledge, or is even to be considered knowledge at all. Education is a major concern in nearly all societies and, although it can be shaped by many different influences such as politics and economics, often reflects a particular philosophical stance. Whether you are involved in the education of people musically in the specific sense of music education (e.g., music in preK–12 school settings) or more broadly conceived (e.g., private piano lessons, university studio teaching, etc.), you will want to consider how your approach is grounded philosophically.

Knowledge

Knowledge has been a major concern of philosophers throughout the ages. In the first chapter, we identified *epistemology* as the branch of philosophy that seeks answers to questions such as: What is knowledge? Are there limits to knowledge? How do we acquire knowledge? Can there be *a priori* knowledge, that is, knowledge independent of experience? How can we know truth? Although we will begin with some general forays into these questions, the main purpose of this discussion is to help you to think through issues related to musical knowledge. Here, of course, we are not concerned with knowledge *about* music; rather, we are interested in whether music might be a way of knowing, and, if so, what kind of knowledge it provides. What does music *mean*? What does it mean to *understand* music? What can we learn from music?

Key Ideas in Epistemology

Consider four individuals. One, we might refer to as a 'know-it-all,' a person who spouts numerous 'facts' on almost everything, whether true or not. Another is a past champion on the television quiz show *Jeopardy*, who won because of her rapid recall of an immense amount of correct information. The third person is a university professor acknowledged as an expert in his field, but who is somewhat inept in ordinary matters of life. The final person is a favorite grandparent who never went to school beyond the 8th grade, but who seems to be wise and to know so much about so many things. How would we characterize the *knowledge* that each of these four persons possesses? In fact, what is knowledge?

Evidentialism and Traditionalism are two forms of knowledge. In Evidentialism, what a person believes is considered knowledge if sufficient evidence makes it unreasonable to doubt; this is the kind of evidence needed in a court of law. How-

> "Man by nature desires to know."
> (Aristotle)

ever, as Edmund Gettier showed in a brief paper in 1963, justified belief is not necessarily truthful knowledge.[1] In Traditionalism, there is reliable communal information in which the group knows more than any given individual. However, societies can easily base long-standing customs on bias, prejudice, or faulty understanding. Thus, according to Adam Morton, "most philosophers take knowledge to be described by criteria that lie somewhere between the stringency of evidentialism and the permissiveness of traditionalism."[2] Even so, the process of defining knowledge continues. Philosophers have tried numerous strategies to deal with the 'knowledge problem,' including perception and experience, reasoning, skepticism, common sense, pragmatism, and wisdom:

- Perception and Experience. Empiricists believe that we gain knowledge through our perceptions of sights, sounds, and so on, and through our experience of living in the world. They deny the possibility of *a priori* (inborn) knowledge. One problem with this approach is that we can be deceived by our senses, as in optical or auditory illusions.
- Reasoning. The list of rationalists is a long one, running from Plato to Bertrand Russell. Because we can doubt the information that comes to us through our senses, it is the power of the mind to reason that brings us true knowledge. Critics, however, contend that a mind without sensory input would be impotent and that things exist beyond the powers of human reasoning.
- Skepticism. Skeptics use thought experiments to doubt the basis for even commonly held beliefs. According to Peter Klein, a great deal of epistemology (the study of knowledge) is concerned with defending or contradicting the arguments raised by skeptics.

  For example, rationalists could be viewed as skeptical about the possibility of empirical knowledge while not being skeptical with regard to *a priori* knowledge and empiricists could be seen as skeptical about the possibility of *a priori* knowledge but not so with regard to empirical knowledge"[3]

- Common Sense. Many cultures around the world have thrived for centuries relying on their collective experiences. Over time, people have learned that it is common sense to expect rain when you hear thunder and lightning or to expect that the sun will rise in the morning as it has every other morning since time began. Complicated logic, contrived experiments, or extended 'navel-gazing' are not required to negotiate much of daily life. Of course, there are many things, such as dealing with disease, that require far more than common sense. Folk remedies may be useful to some degree, but most of us would not want to forego the marvels of modern medicine when faced with a serious illness.
- Pragmatism. According to pragmatism, a thing is true if it works or is useful. In other words, a pragmatist is concerned with practical consequences. One can construct a hypothesis (a hunch or an idea) and then test it to see if it holds up. However, paraphrasing the influential

> "Knowledge speaks, but wisdom listens."
> (Jimi Hendrix, paraphrasing Oliver Wendell Holmes)

pragmatist William James, Bertrand Russell objected by saying, "I have always found that the hypothesis of Santa Claus 'works satisfactorily in the widest sense of the word'; therefore, 'Santa Claus exists' although Santa Claus does not exist."[4]

- Wisdom. As depicted in the opening illustration of the grandparent, being wise appears to be different from being knowledgeable. Wisdom appears to go beyond mere facts and places them into a deeper level of understanding. However, I use the term 'appears to' intentionally, because there is no clear way of separating wisdom from knowledge. Many philosophers have tried to elucidate the term, but wisdom remains a rather vague and indefinite notion.

Musical Knowledge

There are many facts *about* music such as the number of flats there are in the key of E Flat Major or the year of Bach's birth. A conductor, for example, has to have an immense amount of knowledge to lead an ensemble in an authentic performance. This is not the kind of knowledge we are concerned with at the moment, however. Rather, a different consideration is whether music itself represents a special kind of knowledge and, if so, what kind of information it provides.

James Young cites seven philosophers to substantiate the following statement: "The suggestion that music can contribute to our knowledge is, however, widely regarded as completely untenable."[5] Thus, it seems clear that many philosophers, beginning with Immanuel Kant, do not believe that music is a source of knowledge. Nevertheless, there are those who do believe that it is.

> "The art of music is a basic way of 'knowing' about reality."
> (Bennett Reimer)

Arthur Schopenhauer, for example, felt that music contributes to knowledge because it provides a direct experience of the will.[6] Here, will is construed to mean "the inner essence of everything that is" and it "consists of an undifferentiated, unitary, universal, and indestructible force."[7]

Therefore, unlike the other arts, music is in no way a copy of the Ideas; instead, it is a *copy of the will itself* . . . this is precisely why the effect of music is so much more powerful and urgent than that of the other arts; the other arts speak only of shadows while music speaks of the essence.[8]

Likewise, Susanne Langer felt that music represented a special kind of knowledge.[9] According to her, music is an unconsummated symbol that tells us about feelings. Carroll Pratt followed up on these ideas:

The design or purpose of music is thus to give alleviating expression to the inner life of emotion and will, an expression which is not an escape but rather a fulfillment and completion. The emotions and strivings of will and desire are embodied in music not directly, but indirectly by way of tonal designs which closely resemble in formal outline the inner movements of the spirit, the *Gemütsbewegungen* [emotions, strong feelings]. But here at last it may indeed be true that music becomes symbolic, for it seems to stand for and express the joy and sorrow of all mankind. Tonal ecstasy or grief takes on the meaning of reality, and the listener is profoundly moved, not by his own ecstasy or grief, but by the delight and satisfaction, sometimes almost overpowering, which come from hearing expressed in measured design what he himself could not possibly utter.[10]

Finally, consider this statement from Nelson Goodman: "a major thesis of this book is that the arts must be taken no less seriously than the sciences as modes of discovery, creation, and enlargement of knowledge in the broad sense of advancement of the understanding."[11] Without attempting to provide an exhaustive list, let us assume that there are a sufficient number of philosophers who believe that there is such a thing as musical knowledge, and that we should, thus, consider the idea seriously.

Young believed that "Music is valuable as a source of knowledge, as well as a source of pleasure."[12] Because most everyone agrees that music brings pleasure, there is little argument against the notion of hedonic value. Young, therefore, spent most of his time explaining or defending the idea that music provides its listeners with knowledge and understanding, or what he called cognitive value. He was quick to recognize that not all music has cognitive value, as some music provides only hedonic value. Nevertheless, he was convinced that some music, even absolute music that is the most controversial,[13] has cognitive value. The arts contribute to our knowledge differently than science does. Science leads us to knowledge by *systematic demonstration*, that is, providing factual information in a logical manner. The arts lead us to knowledge by *immediate demonstration* or showing. According to Young, interpretive representation symbolizes bodily movements (as in dance) and movement of voices (as in song). Body movements and patterns of vocal expression are associated with different feelings and emotions. Affective representation is more important and more common than interpretive representation and can make listeners feel a particular affect and show them something about it. "Musical compositions can, consequently, provide audiences with immediate demonstrations of facts about human experience and affective states."[14] Music, thus, not only gives pleasure, but also gives people insights into profound and important matters.

To this point, all the explanations given have derived from analytic philosophy based on consideration of aesthetic properties. There are those, however, who find these meanings of music in contrast to one in which the aim is "to locate, and to understand, music and its meanings in the social contexts in which arises."[15] Anthropologists, eth-

> "There is no truer truth obtainable by Man than comes of music."
>
> (Robert Browning)

nomusicologists, and sociologists, in particular, emphasize the importance of musical interactions within a social context. In other words, it is in the participatory acts of making music, not in the disinterested contemplation of a musical work, that the true meaning of music is found. Nicholas Cook, however, sought to "outline a way in which we can understand at least some of the meanings ascribed to music as at the same time irreducibly cultural *and* intimately related to its structural properties."[16] Thus, socially constructed meanings and critical interpretations need not be mutually exclusive.

Eleanor Stubley wrote about musical knowledge from a phenomenological perspective on constructivism. "Phenomenologists hold that knowledge is the product of a personal intentional act having social and historical dimensions."[17] We create our own 'music knowing' through listening to, performing, and creating music. Music, then, is one among many ways that we construct our own reality.

The educational psychologist Howard Gardner popularized a theory of multiple intelligences, music being one of them.[18] Through a set of eight criteria, he identified different ways that human beings can know or problem-solve. Initially, he posited seven intelligences—linguistic intelligence, musical intelligence, logical-mathematical intelligence, spatial intelligence, bodily-kinesthetic intelligence, interpersonal intelligence (awareness of others), and intrapersonal intelligence (awareness of oneself); later, he considered three additional candidates—naturalistic intelligence, spiritual intelligence, and existential intelligence. According to this theory, musical thinking is the way that composers and performers make musical decisions. A solution to a musical problem represents a way of knowing. One could take the sketchbooks of Beethoven, filled with examples of how he worked out and resolved musical problems, as a prime example.[19]

Gardner admits that the term 'musical intelligence' is far too gross and that there are a number of subintelligences or constituent units that make up musical intelligence.[20] Reimer expanded upon this idea by describing seven roles that represent particular types of musical intelligence: composer, performer, improviser, listener, music theorist, musicologist, and music teacher.[21] To this list, he could have added the role of music therapist.

Jerome Bruner, one of the pioneers in cognitive psychology, wrote a chapter entitled "Art as a Mode of Knowing." Two quotes, taken from elsewhere in the book, give a brief glimpse into his understanding of how we can know through the arts:

> Surely, knowledge of the natural world, knowledge of the human condition, knowledge of the nature and dynamics of society, knowledge of the past so that it may be used in experiencing the present and aspiring to the future—all of these, it would seem reasonable to suppose, are essential to an educated man. To these must be added another: knowledge of the products of our artistic heritage that mark the history of our aesthetic wonder and delight.[22]

> The Nobel poet or the ambassador to the United Nations, the brilliant cellist or the perceptive playwright, the historian making use of the past or the sociologist seeking a pattern in the present—these men . . . are seeking understanding and mastery over new problems.[23]

Stanford professor Elliot Eisner wrote a similarly entitled chapter called "Aesthetic Modes of Knowing," in which he said, "Both artist and scientist create forms through which the world is viewed."[24] Aesthetic knowledge takes two forms. The first kind of aesthetic knowledge is of the world and human experiences in which we can participate vicariously. We can know the rage, passion, joy, and sorrow of another. Second, the aesthetic experience has value in itself as a personal experience, not as something it refers to outside itself.

Psychologist Abraham Maslow characterized two types of knowledge as extrinsic and intrinsic.[25] Through extrinsic learning experiences, we learn information that we can communicate to others via a symbol system (e.g., language, mathematical symbols, etc.). Thus, we can talk about the music or even refer to the music itself as notation or in sounds. Intrinsic learning experiences are those that are private and personal; they cannot be shared with another in the sense that the other person will have the same experience. If two singers are standing side-by-side in a choral performance, they share a great deal of extrinsic knowledge. They both know the name of the composer, the name of the composition, the words they are singing, how many beats there are in a measure, whether to sing loudly or softly, the correct pitches and rhythms to sing, and so on. However, the intrinsic learning experiences they have are individualized. Even if they tried to share how they felt about the performance

> "[Music is the] artistic embodiment of the essence of life's great happenings."
> (Shostakovich)

afterward, neither could live the experience of the other. Maslow also writes about *peak experiences*, special intrinsic learning experiences that are connected to his concept of self-actualization.

Self-actualization is the full realization of one becoming who he or she is meant to be. The self-actualized person is one who is mature, healthy, and fulfilled, and one who is "more truly himself, more perfectly actualizing his potentialities, closer to the core of his Being, more fully human."[26] Peak experiences are mountaintop moments that help to shape the person toward self-fulfillment. Through statistical analyses of empirical reports, Maslow declared that music was one of the two most common ways to have a peak experience.[27] The upshot is that music, then, can play a significant role in self-actualization. Alf Gabrielsson provided data that confirms the powerful import of music in a project called Strong Experiences with Music (SEM).[28] He asked more than 1,300 participants to describe "the strongest, most intense experience of music that you have ever had."[29] He likened some of the responses to Maslow's concept of peak experiences.

> SEM may include reflections of the meaning of life and existence. The music may be felt as a mirror of life, its greatness as well as its transiency, its different phases, and its mixture of feelings: 'pain, sorrow, passion, joy—yes, everything, life, death, to exist as a human being'. It may lead to changed views of oneself, of other people, and of existence in general, and may give rise to action. Some respondents reported that just a few minutes of music radically changed their whole life.[30]

The notion of humanness appears frequently. A panel of experts commented that the emphasis on music education "should be to help the individual to be able to explore, identify, and develop new values throughout life—ones that help him to be more fully human."[31] Sister Wendy Beckett is an art historian who, when asked in an interview what we get from art, responded succinctly with very similar words, "You become more fully human."[32] That is, these authors, among others as we have seen, contended that art, or in our case music, provides insights into the human condition. What is the 'human condition' to which these authors refer? Bruner put it clearly when he said:

> There are features of the human condition that change only within narrow limits whether one be a cave dweller, a don in medieval Oxford, or a Left Bank expatriate of the 1920s: love, birth, hate, death, passion, and decorum persist as problems without unique solution.[33]

What do you think? Does music provide special insights into the human condition? Is it a special kind of knowledge? How can we determine whether music is a form of knowledge? If it is, what can we know through music? As you work to clarify your thoughts and mold them into a coherent philosophy of music, what we 'get from' music, whether it is a form of knowledge or not, is a central question that you will want to consider.

Education

While all animals can learn, a particular hallmark of humanity is the extent to which learning shapes us each to be a unique human being. Much of our learning is informal, as we observe another doing an action or attempt to learn something on our own. Formal learning, often in the guise of schooling, is also a salient characteristic of human societies. Thinking about learning has inevitably led to innumerable questions: What should every 'educated' member of our society know? What does it mean to be literate? What should be the primary outcomes of a formal education? Should school curricula focus on a liberal education (i.e., acquiring general knowledge for its own sake), on training and preparation for a successful career, or something else? Should schooling prepare students to address social problems or in developing each person's individual capacities? Do reading, writing, and arithmetic take precedence or are the arts equally central to what it means to be educated? Such questions as these inevitably lead to philosophical discussions.

As with nearly every other aspect of philosophy, educational philosophy can be traced back to the ancient Greeks. In Chapter 8 we will examine music philosophy of the ancient Greeks in some detail, including the role of music in education. Here, it is important to note that "To be a truly cultured person in Greek society one had to be trained *in* music and as a result *by* it."[34] In ancient China at approximately the same time, beginning around the 5th century BC, "music occupied the most prominent place in the education of a gentleman."[35] "However, the Chinese counterpart [of ancient Greeks' attitudes] is unique in that it exists with a whole system of implementing music's ethical potential . . . and is closely associated with the notion of mind-body linkage."[36] Likewise, music played an important educational role in the societies of the Aztecs and pre-Hispanic Latin America,[37] India, Native Americans,[38] Egypt,[39] Africa,[40] Japan,[41] Israel,[42] and, indeed, all over the world.[43]

Educational Philosophy

As Wayne Bowman explained, "The English word 'education' actually has two different Latin roots: *educare*, to train or to mold; *educere*, to lead out or draw out."[44] It is in formal education where the practical linkages between educational philosophy and educational practice are best seen. Ironically, many of the most prominent names in educational philosophy (e.g., Pestalozzi, Montessori, etc.) are not represented in standard textbooks on philosophy and correspondingly, many of the great philosophers did not write much about education, at least not in the sense of an educational philosophy.[45] In a contemporary sense, many educational philosophers have come to think of their discipline as "a form of applied philosophy, whose task is to clarify the aims, content, methods, and distribution of education appropriate to contemporary society."[46]

William O'Neill wrote about educational ideologies, which are related to but not the same as educational philosophies. Nevertheless, they give a good overview of the field. He said that the overall goals of education consisted of:

- Educational Fundamentalism: to revive and reaffirm older and better ways.
- Educational Intellectualism: to identify, preserve, and transmit Truth.
- Educational Conservatism: to preserve and transmit established patterns of social behavior.
- Educational Liberalism: to promote effective personal behavior.
- Educational Liberationism: to encourage necessary social reform by maximizing personal liberty.
- Educational Anarchism: to bring about immediate large-scale reform within society by eliminating compulsory schooling.[47]

A thorough accounting of educational philosophies is not practical within the scope of this chapter. However, a few examples, albeit selected somewhat arbitrarily, may suffice to provide a glimpse of how philosophical ideas about education have translated into practice in the past few centuries of Western education.

Johann Heinrich Pestalozzi (1746–1827)

Pestalozzi was a Swiss educational reformer who was born four years before Bach's death and died the same year as Beethoven. Influenced by Rousseau's *Émile*, which emphasized a person's natural growth from infancy to adulthood, he was interested in developing each student's natural abilities. "Pestalozzi's pedagogical doctrines stressed that instructions should proceed from the familiar to the new, incorporate the performance of concrete arts and the experience of actual emotional responses, and be paced to follow the gradual unfolding of the child's development."[48] In a letter to a colleague, Pestalozzi wrote, "I need not remind you of the importance of music in engendering and assisting the highest feelings of which man is capable."[49] The core of Pestalozzi's rationale for music in the curriculum was its effect on moral development.[50] Lowell Mason (1792–1872), the first to succeed in placing music in the school curriculum in the United States, based his instructional methods on Pestalozzi's ideas. Singing was a primary activity. He promoted sound before sight (i.e., listening before reading), active learning and imitation, focusing and mastering one thing at a time, and practice before theory.[51]

Friedrich Frobel (1782–1852)

Frobel was a German educator who gained recognition as the first to establish kindergartens. He was a strong proponent of allowing children at an early age to explore and discover, particularly in the form of creative play. He wrote, "A universal and comprehensive plan of human education must, therefore, necessarily consider at an early period singing, drawing, painting, and modeling."[52]

Herbert Spencer (1820–1903)

The writings of Spencer, an English philosopher in the Victorian era, were highly influential in the United States after the turn of the century. Next to Darwin, Spencer was one of the strongest proponents of evolution[53] and it was he who coined the phrase "survival of the fittest."[54] He felt that education was preparation for life and that the types of knowledge that should be taught in schools included intellectual, moral, and physical knowledge that aids self-preservation, facilitates gainful employment, prepares one for carrying out parental duties, promotes proper social and political conduct, and enhances enjoyment of nature, literature, and the fine arts.[55] Concerned that the last named should be an indication of lesser importance, he stated, "We yield to none in the value we attach to aesthetic culture and its pleasures. Without painting, sculpture, music, poetry, and the emotions produced by natural beauty of every kind, life would lose half its charm."[56]

G. Stanley Hall (1844–1924)

Hall was most widely known as a psychologist, however, he also held a professorship in philosophy at Johns Hopkins. As a psychologist, Hall was a student of William James, earned the first doctorate in psychology granted in America, and counted John Dewey among his pupils.[57] Highly influential on the development of psychology in the United States, Hall is credited as the father of child psychology and educational psychology. A strong proponent of the Child-Study Movement, Hall strove to base educational practices on scientific findings.[58] "The two main influences [of the

Child-Study Movement on music education] were the movement's effects upon some vocal series and music appreciation textbooks of the day, and the effects of music research upon later generations of music educators."[59] In 1908, Hall encouraged music teachers to become more aware of scientific research in an article entitled "The Psychology of Music and the Light It Throws upon Musical Education."[60]

Maria Montessori (1857–1952)

Montessori, an Italian educator, influenced educational practice throughout the world. Perhaps her strongest impact derived from her passion for allowing children, as well as teachers and parents, to explore and discover in a 'hands-on' approach. "Montessori had a personal mission—liberation of the developing mind through observation and support for humanity."[61] Music played a significant role in Montessori's approach as evidenced by the fact that her ideas were realized by her music consultant, Anna Maria Maccheroni, in a set of 35 unpublished booklets on Montessori music education. These books represent "a comprehensive program that is distinctive by reason of unique aspects that include (1) collaboration, (2) structure, (3) prepared environments, (4) auto-education, (5) control of error, (6) isolation of the aural sense, and (7) scope."[62]

John Dewey (1859–1952)

Dewey was a leading American philosopher among pragmatists. We will examine his philosophical ideas at some length in Chapter 15. At this point, we can begin with the notion that a pragmatic approach in education is based on learning by doing.[63]

> The thing that makes pragmatist music teachers different from rationalists and empiricists is their interest in helping the students to learn how to learn. . . . According to pragmatists, the role of the teacher is not one of collaborator in the search for truth (as it is with rationalists) or dispenser of knowledge (as it is with most empiricists), but rather one of being a combination organizer-cheerleader in helping students to learn.[64]

Lauri Väkevä characterized Dewey's idea this way: "We are not in the world merely to know, but to live fully, which entails considerably more than knowing."[65] Foster McMurray provided a pragmatic definition of education and then translated it into a statement about music education:

> The aim of general education is to use our accumulated knowledge, values, and skills to acquaint everyone with those more subtle forces in his world which influence his life, with the hope that, if he learns of their existence and their force, he can control his relations with environments to gain more of good and less of preventable bad outcomes.
>
> [The aim of music education is] to help everyone to further awareness of patterns of sound as an aesthetic component in the world of experience; to increase each person's capacity to control the availability of aesthetic richness through music; and to transform the public musical culture into a recognized part of each person's environment.[66]

As a concluding statement, McMurray wrote, "final advice from a pragmatist: Let music become known for its sounds and its felt qualities."[67]

Social Justice and Culturally Responsive Teaching

A thorough discussion of music education philosophy is beyond the scope of this chapter and there are numerous opportunities throughout the rest of the book to make connections between general educational philosophies and music education. At this juncture, we will single out a contemporary philosophical stance as an example of how practical applications can influence music education.

In Chapter 17, we will learn more about Paulo Freire's thoughts on critical pedagogy. Here, however, we look at his influence on a philosophical position in education that can be termed social justice. Freire said, "If education cannot do everything, it can achieve some things. . . . One of our challenges as educators is to discover what historically is possible in the sense of contributing toward the transformation of the world, giving rise to a world that is rounder, less angular, [and] more humane . . ."[68] Noam Chomsky echoed this sentiment when he urged educators "to take seriously the challenge of becoming agents of history so as to make this world less discriminatory, more democratic, less dehumanizing, and more just."[69]

Social justice issues in education cover a wide array of topics, including race, social class, gender, culture, and disability.[70] Estelle Jorgensen included an even more extensive list that included:

> matters of language, age, gender and sexual orientation, social class, ethnicity, race, color, physical characteristics such as size, weight, height, and dexterity, personality characteristics such as introversion, independence, sensitivity, and anxiety, intelligence, wealth, geographic location, culture and country of origin, and family background including religious and political affiliation and orientation to education.[71]

Although music can be a "vehicle for struggle for justice and against injustice,"[72] it can also be "restrictive, patronizing, paternalistic, repressive, marginalizing, and even oppressive."[73]

Among these topics, one of the ways that social justice issues can be implemented in schools is through culturally responsive teaching (CRT). "*Culturally responsive teaching* is defined as using the cultural characteristics, experiences, and perspectives of ethnically diverse students as conduits for teaching them more effectively."[74] Carlos Abril emphasized the point that CRT requires sensitivity and awareness not only of the school and community but also the students themselves and their social interactions.[75]

Here are a few examples of CRT in music education:

- Alice-Ann Darrow said, "Culturally responsive teachers understand that students with disabilities may represent a subculture within the classroom—and consequently follow certain guidelines that facilitate their inclusion."[76]
- Elizabeth McAnally found that general music classes are 'uniquely positioned' to meet the needs of children living in poverty.[77]
- Mary Junda related how composing and singing ballads are effective in enabling students to "gain a new appreciation for how earlier generations of Americans responded to immigration, war, slavery, changes in technology, unemployment, and natural disasters."[78]
- Louis Bergonzi addressed issues of sexual orientation and music education. He stated that "too often . . . high schools are developmental wastelands for youth in sexual orientation minorities, that is, those who self-identify as lesbian, gay, bisexual, or transgender (LGBT)."[79] He issued a challenge to the music education profession to include LGBT students as full members of the music education experience.

"Only the year before I lost my sight, the one and only Bessie Smith whose blues singing is still a legend, died, reportedly because, after an automobile accident, she couldn't be admitted to a white hospital. By the time a hospital that would admit Negroes was found, she had bled to death."

(Ray Charles)

- Abby Butler, Vicki Lind, and Constance McKoy wrote, "Given that music has socially constructed meanings, and represents one of several expressive forms through which diverse cultures may be known, and given that music is a source of cultural identity for many racial and ethnic groups, expanding research in multicultural music education to encompass the same areas of inquiry as multiculturalism in general education would seem entirely appropriate and necessary."[80]

Lind and McKoy covered these issues more fully in *Culturally Responsive Teaching in Music Education: From Understanding to Application*.[81]

Summary and Thought Questions

In the branch of philosophy known as epistemology, philosophers have long considered problems concerning knowledge—What is it? How do we acquire it? Do human beings have a finite or infinite capacity for knowledge? Is there ultimate knowledge beyond what we can perceive and understand? Evidentialism and Traditionalism represent two ways of organizing knowledge. Other ways of thinking about knowledge include perception and experience, reasoning, skepticism, common sense, pragmatism, and wisdom. Of more relevance for our purposes is the extent to which music represents a special kind of knowledge. Philosophers have disagreed with each other about whether music can or cannot contribute to knowledge, that is, whether it is itself a form of knowledge.

Although some major philosophers, such as Plato and John Dewey, have written major statements regarding education, other educational philosophers are not routinely included in philosophy texts. Regardless, educational philosophy can be critically influential not only in how curricula are developed, but also in how individual schools, administrators, and teachers understand their mission. Whether education is aimed at preserving the past or designed to prepare students to change the future, important decisions rest on how one views the purpose of education.

Culturally Responsive Teaching is only one example, among many that could be given, of the ways a philosophical viewpoint can impact music education. Music in the schools can either be exclusive, dismissing, and disenfranchising certain students, or inclusive, allowing all students to participate in meaningful musical experiences.

Here are some questions to ponder as you consider issues related to knowledge and education.

1. How would you characterize the difference between knowledge and wisdom? What would be the difference between someone who is musically knowledgeable and someone who is musically wise?
2. How do the following inform your own musical understanding: perception and experience, reasoning, skepticism, common sense, pragmatism, and wisdom?
3. How would you describe the difference between knowledge *about* music and knowledge *of* music?
4. Philosophers are divided on whether or not music is a form of knowledge. With which camp do you side?

5. If you decide that music is a form of knowledge, what do you *know* through music? Is this knowledge similar to other types, only in a different form, or is it a completely different kind of knowledge?

6. There are many different approaches to educational philosophy. Which one or ones seem to be most in line with your thinking? What is the basic purpose of education in your opinion? Can you connect a basic philosophy of education with a philosophy of music education?

7. There are many musicians, such as Wynton Marsalis, who move easily back and forth between different styles and genres. However, sometimes there is a cultural divide between formally and informally trained musicians. As only one example, formally trained musicians may look down upon musicians who cannot read music, while those who play without notation may be amazed that there are musicians who can only make music if it is notated. Taking these, and other aspects, into consideration, think about your own background. Are you polarized at one end or the other or do you have skills that allow you to move comfortably between the two camps (i.e., formal and informal musical skills). Is there any reason to argue that one set of skills is more important than the other, or are they simply two different, but equally important, approaches?

8. Can you think of times when you or others were disenfranchised in a music education setting because of lack of inclusiveness?

9. What examples can you provide from your own experiences where Culturally Responsive Teaching practices allowed you or others to be included in musical experiences?

10. For the moment, let us consider that a music education philosophy is an application of a philosophy of music. Especially if you are a music education major, as you progress through the book, constantly make connections between your developing philosophy of music and a philosophy of music education. Those of you who are not music education majors may still be involved in teaching (e.g., teaching private lessons, university classes, etc.). Either way, how can you connect one or two major ideas you have about the value of music to the value of a music education?

Notes

1 Edmund Gettier, "Is Justified Belief True Knowledge?" *Analysis* 23, no. 6 (1963): 121–23.

2 Adam Morton, "Knowledge," in *Western Philosophy*, ed. David Papineau (New York: Metro Books, 2009), 75.

3 Peter Klein, "Skepticism," in *The Stanford Encyclopedia of Philosophy* (2011 edition), ed. Edward Zalta. http://plato.stanford.edu/archives/sum2011/entries/skepticism/.

4 Bertrand Russell, *The History of Western Philosophy* (New York: Simon and Schuster, 1945), 818.

5 James Young, "The Cognitive Value of Music," *The Journal of Aesthetics and Art Criticism* 57, no. 1 (1999): 41.

6 Sandra Shapshay, "Schopenhauer's Aesthetics," in *The Stanford Encyclopedia of Philosophy* (2012 edition), ed. Edward Zalta. http://plato.stanford.edu/archives/sum2012/entries/schopenhauer-aesthetics/.

7 Wayne Bowman, *Philosophical Perspectives on Music* (New York: Oxford University Press, 1998), 114.

8 Arthur Schopenhauer, *The World as Will and Representation, Vol. 1*, in *The Cambridge Edition of the Works of Schopenhauer*, ed. Christopher Janaway, trans. Judith Norman and Alistair Welchman (Cambridge, UK: Cambridge University Press, 1819/2010), 285.

9 Susanne Langer, *Philosophy in a New Key, 3rd ed.* (Cambridge, MA: Harvard University Press, 1942/1963). Susanne Langer, *Feeling and Form* (New York: Charles Scribner's Sons, 1953). Susanne Langer, *Problems of Art* (New York: Charles Scribner's Sons, 1957).

10 Carroll Pratt, "The Design of Music," *The Journal of Aesthetics and Art Criticism* 12, no. 3 (1954): 299–300.

11 Nelson Goodman, *Ways of Worldmaking* (Indianapolis: Hackett, 1978), 102.

12 Young, "The Cognitive Value of Music," 43.

13 Absolute music, particularly instrumental music, poses particular problems for philosophers. Program music, that is, music that 'tells a story' or by title indicates something particular (e.g., Debussy's *La Mer*, The Sea*) or any music with lyrics, understandably represents something external to the music. It is not immediately apparent, however, how 'pure' instrumental music is able to reference anything outside itself. [*Claude Debussy: *La Mer*, performed by Valery Gergiev and the London Symphony Orchestra, http://www.youtube.com/watch?v=hlR9rDJMEiQ.]

14 Young, "The Cognitive Value of Music," 52.

15 Ian Cross and Elizabeth Tolbert, "Music and Meaning," in *The Oxford Handbook of Music Psychology*, ed. Susan Hallam, Ian Cross, and Michael Thaut (Oxford: Oxford University Press, 2009), 28.

16 Nicholas Cook, "Theorizing Musical Meaning," *Music Theory Spectrum* 23, no. 2 (2001): 173–74.

17 Eleanor Stubley, "Philosophical Foundations," in *Handbook of Research on Music Teaching and Learning*, ed. Richard Colwell (New York: Schirmer, 1992), 8.

18 Howard Gardner, *Intelligence Reframed: Multiple Intelligences for the 21st Century* (New York: Basic Books, 1999).

19 Joseph Kerman and Alan Tyson, *The New Grove Beethoven* (New York: W.W. Norton, 1983).

20 Gardner, *Intelligence Reframed*, 103.

21 Bennett Reimer, *A Philosophy of Music Education: Advancing the Vision, 3rd ed.* (Upper Saddle River, NJ: Prentice-Hall, 2003).

22 Jerome Bruner, *On Knowing: Essays for the Left Hand* (New York: Atheneum, 1969), 122.

23 Ibid., 126.

24 Elliot Eisner, "Aesthetic Modes of Knowing," in *Learning and Teaching: The Ways of Knowing. Eighty-Fourth Yearbook of the National Society for the Study of Education*, ed. Elliot Eisner (Chicago: University of Chicago Press, 1985), 26.

25 Abraham Maslow, *Motivation and Personality, 2nd ed.* (New York: Harper and Row, 1970).

26 Abraham Maslow, "Music, Education, and Peak Experiences," in *Documentary Report of the Tanglewood Symposium*, ed. Robert Choate (Washington, DC: Music Educators National Conference, 1968), 97.

27 Abraham Maslow, *The Farther Reaches of Human Nature* (New York: Penguin Books, 1971), 179.

28 Alf Gabrielsson, *Strong Experiences with Music* (Oxford, UK: Oxford University Press, 2011).

29 Alf Gabrielsson, "Strong Experiences with Music," in *Handbook of Music and Emotion*, ed. Patrik Juslin and John Sloboda (Oxford: Oxford University Press, 2010), 551.

30 Ibid., 562.

31 Max Kaplan, Page Bailey, William Cornog, Alvin Eurich, Freda Goldman, William Hartshorn, Werner Lawson, Father Norman O'Connor, and Ralph Tyler, "A Philosophy of the Arts for an Emerging Society," in *Documentary Report of the Tanglewood Symposium*, ed. Robert Choate (Washington, DC: Music Educators National Conference, 1968), 112.

32 Sister Wendy Beckett, *Sister Wendy: The Complete Collection* (BBC Video E1690, 1992).

33 Bruner, *On Knowing*, 73.

34 Mary Guerrant, "Three Aspects of Music in Ancient China and Greece," *College Music Symposium* 20 (1980). http://symposium.music.org/index.php?option=com_k2&view=item&id=1870:three-aspects-of-music-in-ancient-china-and-greece&Itemid=124.

35 Ibid.

36 Yuhwen Wang, "Cultivating Virtuous Character: The Chinese Traditional Perspective of Music Education," in *The Oxford Handbook of Philosophy in Music Education*, ed. Wayne Bowman and Ana Lucía Frega (New York: Oxford University Press, 2012), 267.

37 Luis Rodríguez, "Education in Latin American Music Schools: A Philosophical Perspective," in *The Oxford Handbook of Philosophy in Music Education*, ed. Wayne Bowman and Ana Lucía Frega (New York: Oxford University Press, 2012), 231–48.

38 Timothy Reagan, *Non-Western Educational Traditions: Indigenous Approaches to Educational Thought and Practice, 3rd ed.* (Mahwah, NJ: Lawrence Erlbaum Associates, 2005).

39 Moustafa Gadalla, *The Ancient Egyptian Culture Revealed* (Greensboro, NC: Tehuti Research Foundation, 2007).

40 John Blacking, *How Musical Is Man?* (Seattle: University of Washington Press, 1973).

41 Johannes Riedel, "The Function of Sociability in the Sociology of Music and Music Education," *Journal of Research in Music Education* 12, no. 2 (1964): 149–58.

42 Alfred Sendrey, *Music in Ancient Israel* (New York: Philosophical Library, 1968).

43 Bonnie Wade, *Thinking Musically, 2nd ed.* (New York: Oxford University Press, 2009).

44 Wayne Bowman, "Music's Place in Education," in *The Oxford Handbook of Music Education*, ed. Gary McPherson and Graham Welch (Oxford, UK: Oxford University Press, 2012), 24.

45 Anthony O'Hear, "Education, the History of the Philosophy of," in *The Oxford Guide to Philosophy*, ed. Ted Honderich (Oxford, UK: Oxford University Press, 2005), 228–31.

46 John White, "Education, Problems of the Philosophy of," in *The Oxford Guide to Philosophy*, ed. Ted Honderich (Oxford, UK: Oxford University Press, 2005), 231.

47 William O'Neill, *Educational Ideologies: Contemporary Expressions of Educational Philosophy* (Santa Monica, CA: Goodyear Publishing, 1981), 297.

48 Kate Silber, "Johann Heinrich Pestalozzi," *Encyclopædia Britannica Online* (May 23, 2014). http://www.britannica.com/biography/Johann-Heinrich-Pestalozzi.

49 Michael Mark, ed., *Music Education: Source Readings from Ancient Greece to Today, 4th ed.* (New York: Routledge, 2013), 24.

50 A. Theodore Tellstrom, *Music in American Education: Past and Present* (New York: Holt, Rinehart, and Winston, 1971).

51 Edward Birge, *History of Public School Music in the United States* (Washington, DC: Music Educators National Conference, 1928).

52 Friedrich Froebel, *The Education of Man*, trans. W.N. Hailmann (Mineola, NY: Dover, 1826/ 2005), 228.

53 William Sweet, "Herbert Spencer," *Internet Encyclopedia of Philosophy*, accessed November 10, 2015, http://www.iep.utm.edu/spencer/.

54 David Weinstein, "Herbert Spencer," in *The Stanford Encyclopedia of Philosophy* (2012 edition), http://plato.stanford.edu/archives/fall2012/entries/spencer/.

55 Tellstrom, *Music in American Education*.

56 Herbert Spencer, *Education: Intellectual, Moral, and Physical* (London: Williams and Norgate, 1861), 37.

57 "G. Stanley Hall." *Encyclopædia Britannica Online*, accessed November 10, 2015, http://www.britannica.com/biography/G-Stanley-Hall.

58 Jere Humphreys, "The Child-Study Movement and Public School Music Education," *Journal of Research in Music Education* 33, no. 2 (1985): 79–86.

59 Ibid., 82.

60 G. Stanley Hall, "The Psychology of Music and the Light It Throws upon Musical Education," *The Pedagogical Seminary* 15, no. 3 (1908): 358–64.

61 Jaan Valsiner, "Introduction to the Transaction Edition," in *The Montessori Method*, ed. Maria Montessori (New Brunswick, NJ: Transaction Publishers, 2014), xii.

62 Jeanne Rubin, "Montessorian Music Method: Unpublished Works," *Journal of Research in Music Education* 31, no. 3 (1983): 215.

63 Lauri Väkevä, "Philosophy of Music Education as Art of Life: A Deweyan View," in *The Oxford Handbook of Philosophy in Music Education*, ed. Wayne Bowman and Ana Lucía Frega (New York: Oxford University Press, 2012), 86–110.

64 Harold Abeles, Charles Hoffer, and Robert Klotman, *Foundations of Music Education, 2nd ed.* (New York: Schirmer Books, 1994), 58.

65 Väkevä, "Philosophy of Music Education as Art of Life: A Deweyan View," 99.

66 Foster McMurray, "Pragmatism in Music Education," in *Basic Concepts in Music Education: The Fifty-Seventh Yearbook of the National Society for the Study of Education*, ed. Nelson Henry (Chicago: University of Chicago Press, 1958), 41.

67 Ibid., 61.

68 Paulo Freire and Donaldo Macedo, "A Dialogue: Culture, Language and Race," *Harvard Educational Review* 65, no. 3 (1995): 397.

69 Noam Chomsky, *Chomsky on Miseducation*, ed. Donaldo Macedo (Lanham, MD: Rowman & Littlefield, 2000), 12.

70 Sharon Robinson and Jane West, "Preparing Inclusive Educators: A Call to Action," *Journal of Teacher Education* 63, no. 4 (2012): 291–93.

71 Estelle Jorgensen, "Concerning Justice and Music Education," *Music Education Research* 9, no. 2 (2007): 169.

72 Ibid., 172.

73 Ibid., 172.

74 Geneva Gay, "Preparing for Culturally Responsive Teaching," *Journal of Teacher Education* 53, no. 2 (2002): 106.

75 Carlos Abril, "Toward a More Culturally Responsive General Music Education," *General Music Today* 27, no. 1 (2013): 6–11.

76 Alice-Ann Darrow, "Culturally Responsive Teaching: Understanding Disability Culture," *General Music Today* 26, no. 3 (2013): 32.

77 Elizabeth McAnally, "General Music and Children Living in Poverty," *General Music Today* 26, no. 3 (2013): 25–31.

78 Mary Junda, "Broadside Ballads: Social Consciousness in Song," *General Music Today* 26, no. 3 (2013): 18.

79 Louis Bergonzi, "Sexual Orientation and Music Education: Continuing a Tradition," *Music Educators Journal* 96, no. 2 (2009): 21–22.

80 Abigail Butler, Vicki Lind, and Constance McKoy, "Equity and Access in Music Education: Conceptualizing Culture as Barriers to and Supports for Music Learning," *Music Education Research* 9, no. 2 (2007): 241.

81 Vicki Lind and Constance McKoy, *Culturally Responsive Teaching in Music Education: From Understanding to Application* (New York: Routledge, 2016).

4 Beauty

Many philosophers have written about beauty. For example, in the *Republic* Plato asks "for what should be the end of music if not the love of beauty?"[1] The purpose of this brief chapter is not to survey philosophical thinking on beauty through the ages, nor is there any intent to define beauty or to provide answers to pertinent questions. Rather, the purpose here is twofold: (1) to identify some of the important questions philosophers have raised about beauty over the centuries, particularly in reference to music, and (2) to stimulate your thinking so that as you read the various philosophical viewpoints presented in subsequent chapters and begin to develop your own philosophy, the topic of beauty will be uppermost in your mind. It is certainly possible to develop a philosophy of music that does not explicitly concern itself with beauty, as a number of philosophers have not made this a central focus of their thinking. However, an intentional, carefully considered omission is different from failure to take up the issue at all.

Questions about Beauty in Art

What follows are some pertinent questions, along with brief discussions, to prime the pump of your thinking. At this point in the process, you should not be overly concerned about arriving at definitive answers. However, do spend some time thinking about how you might answer such questions if called upon to do so. As you read subsequent chapters, compare your thoughts with those of some of the greatest thinkers in history. Perhaps you will be swayed to change your mind, to modify your stance slightly, or even to become attached more firmly to your own viewpoint. Any of these responses, or even uncertainty, is acceptable. The real value comes in the struggle, in the journey, not in the pat answer or in avoidance of that which is thorny and frustrating.

> "Beauty is not caused. It is."
> (Emily Dickinson)

Question 1: What Is Beauty?

Often, we recognize beauty when we see or hear it, or we are aware when it is absent. However, defining beauty is elusive. Leo Tolstoy said, "There is no objective definition of beauty" and "art is that which makes beauty manifest."[2] Before we reflect on beauty in music, let us ponder the issue in visual art. Consider Michelangelo's statue *David* (Fig. 4.1). Do you consider this beautiful? Why or why not?

Figure 4.1 Michelangelo's *David*
Photo credit: Jörg Bittner Unna / CC-BY-SA-3.0

Question 2: **Is Beauty in the Eye (Ear) of the Beholder, or Is It Inherent in an Art Object (e.g., a Statue, a Musical Composition, etc.) Independent of Human Perception?**

This issue has appeared and reappeared throughout the centuries. Some philosophers hold that beautiful art or music possess characteristics that are present whether anyone perceives them or not. Others say a work of art is neither beautiful nor ugly in and of itself. Only humans through direct perception and comprehension can make such a judgment.

Let us assume for a moment that you consider *David* to be beautiful and that it is beautiful simply because you say it is. You declare it is beautiful and there is no obligation that you specify why. Notice that this argument works equally well if you do not think it is beautiful. Now consider what the impli-

> "Beauty is whatever gives joy."
> (Edna St. Vincent Millay)

cations of this viewpoint are. If you say beauty is in the eye of the beholder, this is another way of saying that each person gets to decide whether something is beautiful or not. If that is the case, then regardless of the fact that millions of people consider *David* beautiful, it is not beautiful for the person who declares it is not. While this may be desirable from an individual rights perspective, it makes it difficult, if not impossible, to have artistic standards. For many, however, "our intuitions strongly support the feeling that there is *something* more to an object being beautiful than the mere fact of our finding it to be so."[3]

Question 3: **Does Every Opinion about What Is Beautiful Art Carry Equal Weight?**

Should the opinion of someone with no formal training whatsoever have the same validity as a carefully reasoned philosophical position of an expert? The Scottish philosopher David Hume said, "A man, who has had no opportunity of comparing the different kinds of beauty, is indeed foully unqualified to pronounce an opinion with regard to any object presented to him"[4] and thus, ". . . few are qualified to give judgment on any work of art, or establish their own sentiment as the standard of beauty."[5] Who, then, is an expert?

First, let us contend that an expert is someone who has training, expertise, and experience in the relevant field. Second, let us reiterate something stated in the first chapter: a philosophical view is much more than mere opinion. Of course, everyone is allowed to have his or her own opinion. However, this is not the same thing as a carefully reasoned philosophical position. Thus, you may wish to consider the argument that more weight should be given to the philosophical view of someone who has expertise in art and who has spent a great deal of time and thought in determining artistic beauty.

But what if experts disagree, as is commonly the case? Do we take a consensus? Can experts' judgments of beauty be tainted by personal or cultural bias? Almost in despair, although he does endeavor to answer his own questions, Hume asks of ideal judges, "But where are such critics to be found? By

> "Everything has beauty, but not everyone sees it."
> (Confucius)

what marks are they to be known? How distinguish them from pretenders?"[6] Do we even need experts to decide what is beautiful? In other words, who decides who decides?

Question 4: Can You Identify Objective Properties in Beautiful Art?

For many philosophers, "a judgment of beauty does not merely express a personal preference."[7] For example, consider two of Aristotle's comments: In *Metaphysics* he said, "The chief forms of beauty are order and symmetry and definiteness."[8] In *Poetics*, "Beauty is a matter of size and order."[9] Again, assuming for a moment you find the *David* statue beautiful, can you identify any objective properties that make it so? What might those be?

Question 5: Do Subjective Judgments Play a Role in Determining Beauty in Art?

Hume states categorically, "Beauty is no quality in things themselves. It exists merely in the mind which contemplates them."[10] Can even the most highly trained critic be free from personal preferences, from cultural, religious, or political prejudice? Is your sense of the beauty or lack of it in *David* based in any way on past associations or learned attitudes? Consider, for example, various attitudes about nudity. If one person finds great beauty in the perfection of the human body while another believes nudity is shameful, might they not arrive at different conclusions as to the beauty of *David*? What if one judge is a devout Jew, who has a deep affinity for the Old Testament hero David, while another is an atheist? Would their contrasting orientations have any bearing on their perception of beauty in this statue?

Consider a different kind of learning. Suppose one critic understands a great deal about *David*. He knows Michelangelo sculpted the statue out of the single block of marble that another sculptor, Antonio Rosselino, had already started working on and then abandoned in 1475.[11] He has learned that Michelangelo intended for *David* not only to represent the Biblical hero who defeated the giant Goliath, but also for it to represent the city of Florence. He knows *David* stood outside the Piazza Signoria until 1873 when it was replaced by a copy and the original placed in the Accademia. Is such information necessary to make a valid judgment of the statue's beauty? Is it relevant? How much knowledge should one have before being qualified to render a judgment?

Question 6: Are There Connections between Beauty in Art and Truth, Goodness, Morals, or Similar Terms?

> "Goodness is beauty in the best estate."
>
> (Christopher Marlowe)

> "Information is not knowledge.
> Knowledge is not wisdom.
> Wisdom is not truth.
> Truth is not beauty.
> Beauty is not love.
> Love is not music.
> Music is THE BEST."
>
> (Frank Zappa)

In *What Is Art?*, Tolstoy provided a historical overview of relationships among such terms.[12] For example, the Delphic Oracle stated, "The most beautiful is the most just."[13] Xenophon, in *Memorabilia III*, has Socrates say, "If, therefore, a thing is well-suited to its purpose, with respect to this it is beautiful and good . . ."[14] In *Ode on a Grecian Urn*, Keats wrote the immortal lines: " 'Beauty is truth, truth beauty,'—that is all ye know on earth, and all ye need to know."[15] Contrarily, in the *Aesthetic of Ugliness* written in 1853, Karl Rosenkranz "draws an analogy between ugliness and moral evil."[16]

Question 7: **Can Art Considered Ugly by One Standard Be Considered Beautiful in Another Context?**

According to Umberto Eco, art has the power to portray ugliness in a beautiful way, and "there is no lack of evidence regarding this concept, from Aristotle to Kant."[17] For a non-art analogy, consider Figures 4.2 and 4.3. Figure 4.2 might be considered beautiful if you were hiring a hand model to advertise hand lotion or nail polish, whereas Figure 4.3 might not be considered beautiful for the same purpose. However, suppose the hands in 4.3 are the hands of your grandfather. They represent years of toil, sacrifice, and commitment on behalf of the family. To you they may be beautiful.

How might this translate to art? Can you think of a painting or sculpture that is not pretty on the surface in a conventional sense but which represents true beauty in a deeper sense? As an example, look at Figure 4.4. Perhaps few would call this visage handsome or beautiful.

Now look at Figure 4.5, Michelangelo's *Bandini Pietà*. Notice that the face depicted in Figure 4.4 belongs to the person at the back of the group. First a few words of background and then we return to the issue at hand. Michelangelo intended this sculpture to be for his own tomb.[18] Astonishingly, at the age of 80, after nearly five years of work, he attempted to destroy the work and after being restrained, left it unfinished. Reasons why he tried to demolish his handiwork include the possibility of difficulties with the stone, lack of strength to sculpt as he once could, or unhappiness with the compositional layout.

More to the point of our discussion, however, is the realization that the face of the man in the back, Nicodemus, may be a self-portrait of Michelangelo.[19] In other words, as he prepared a memorial for his own gravesite, the artist inserted himself into the story of taking Christ down from the cross. We know from various records that Michelangelo considered himself to be ugly. Is this, then, an example of ugliness made beautiful in an artistic context, or at least ugliness serving an aesthetic purpose?

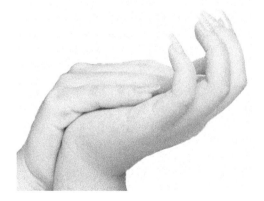

Figure 4.2 "Beautiful" hands
Photo credit: Phil Date | Dreamstime Stock Photos

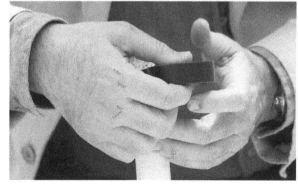

Figure 4.3 "Ugly" hands
Photo credit: Clarita | Dreamstime Stock Photos

Figure 4.4 Sculpted face

Figure 4.5 Michelangelo's *Bandini Pietà*. The face of the figure at the top is thought to be of Michelangelo himself.

Beauty in Music

Let us now consider some musical examples. In so doing, we run the risk of saying these examples are beautiful, when what we really are saying is many have considered these to be examples of beautiful music. You may feel differently, and are encouraged to supply your own examples. Examples are provided here from vocal, keyboard, instrumental, and eclectic musical styles. I encourage you to choose your own musical exemplars of beauty.

> "Whatever else the music is supposed to do, it must always be beautiful."
> (Ernst von Dohnanyi)

Each of the following examples (and those throughout the book) has a link to an online recording marked with this symbol: ♫. You are encouraged to listen to all of these, particularly ones with which you may not be familiar. Because Internet resources change from time-to-time, you may find one or more of these links does not work. It should be relatively easy, however, to find another recording. You may also go to this URL to find active links to recordings: https://sites.google.com/a/uncg.edu/https-sites-google-com-site-concisesurveyofmusphil/home.

Here are a few possibilities from the vocal-choral literature:

- Mozart: 'Sull'aria' from *The Marriage of Figaro*[20] ♫
- Delibes: 'Flower Song' from *Lakme*[21] ♫
- Bizet: 'Au fond du temple saint' from *The Pearl Fishers*[22] ♫
- Korngold: 'Marietta's Lied' from *Die tote Stadt*[23] ♫
- Strauss: 'Beim schlafengehn' from *Four Last Songs*[24] ♫
- Reynaldo Hahn: *L'Enamourée*[25] ♫
- Villa-Lobos: 'Aria' (Cantilena) from *Bachianas brasileiras* No. 5[26] ♫
- María Grever: *Júrame*[27] ♫
- Mendelssohn: 'Lift Thine Eyes' from *Elijah*[28] ♫
- Morton Lauridsen: *O Magnum Mysterium*[29] ♫

Here are representative piano pieces:

- Couperin: *Les Barricades Mystérieuses*[30] ♫
- Bach: 'Aria' from *Goldberg Variations*[31] ♫
- Mozart: Piano Concerto No. 23, 2nd movement, K. 488[32] ♫
- Beethoven: Piano Sonata No. 31, in A flat, Op. 110, 1st movement[33] ♫
- Chopin: Nocturne, Op. 9, No. 1[34] ♫
- Brahms: Intermezzo, Op. 118, No. 2 in A Major[35] ♫
- Clara Schumann: Romance, Op. 11, No. 1 in e flat minor[36] ♫
- Edvard Grieg: 'Melodie' from *Lyric Pieces*, Book II, Op. 38, No. 3[37] ♫
- Howard Hanson: *Fantasy Variations on a Theme of Youth*, Op. 40[38] ♫
- John Adams: *China Gates*[39] ♫

Here are representative instrumental selections:

- Bach: Double Violin Concerto in d minor, BWV 1043, 2nd movement[40] ♫
- Mozart: Clarinet Concerto in A Major, K. 622, 2nd movement[41] ♫
- Beethoven: Symphony No. 2 in D Major, Op. 21, 2nd movement[42] ♫
- Brahms: Piano Quartet in c minor, Op. 60, 3rd movement[43] ♫
- Elgar: 'Nimrod' from *Enigma Variations*[44] ♫
- Mahler: Symphony No. 5, 4th movement (Adagietto)[45] ♫
- Rachmaninoff: Piano Concerto No. 2 in c minor, Op. 18[46] ♫
- Percy Grainger: 'Horkstow Grange' from *Lincolnshire Posy*[47] ♫
- Eric Whitacre: *October*[48] ♫
- Michael Kamen: Brass Quintet[49] ♫

Finally, here are examples of what some may consider beautiful music from a variety of musical styles:

- Vernon Duke: 'Autumn in New York'[50] ♫
- Walter Gross: 'Tenderly'[51] ♫
- Ennio Morricone: 'Gabriel's Oboe' from *The Mission*[52] ♫
- John Barry: *Dances with Wolves* (theme)[53] ♫
- Anne Murray: 'Could I Have This Dance'[54] ♫
- Beautiful World (Phil Sawyer): 'In Existence'[55] ♫
- Goldfrapp: 'Dreaming'[56] ♫
- Dead Can Dance: 'Yolunga'[57] ♫
- Daniel Licht: 'Blood Theme' from *Dexter*[58] ♫
- David Arkenstone & Kostia: 'The Cello's Song'[59] ♫

Undoubtedly, you may say about any one of these particular selections, "Why did he pick that one?" or "Why didn't he include . . . ?" You are encouraged, of course, to nominate your own choices, not only of particular pieces but also of particular performances. This leads to an interesting aspect of music that does not occur in visual art, that is, the close connection between the work itself and representative performances of it. A weak performance of a beautiful piece of music does not mean the music is not beautiful but only that particular performance of it. Likewise, a stellar performance of a banal piece of music does not necessarily make the music itself beautiful.

As a final comment, later we will see that some philosophers do not agree with the notion of beautiful 'works' *per se*. That is, they argue for musical engagement over specific musical compositions. Beauty—value, meaning, and so on—comes from active musical experiences, not from the contemplation of a musical work. Thus, rather than prescribed lists such as the foregoing, they would offer examples such as teenagers playing in a garage band, folk or jazz musicians jamming, rehearsing in a practice room, listening to a favorite recording, or any other instance of musical engagement. We will have much more to say about this in subsequent sections, but for now, you might identify moments of beauty that occur in your musical activities. There is no reason at this juncture to choose between musical works and musical experiences.

Research on Beauty in Music

Let us begin by considering four statements concerning contemporary philosophical attitudes about the role of beauty in aesthetics:

- "We have to catch ourselves up in order to recognize that 'beauty' has receded or even disappeared from contemporary aesthetic theory. For, like other once influential ideas, it has simply faded away."[60]
- "Beauty is the most discredited philosophical notion."[61]
- "The study of beauty, however, has fallen from grace in contemporary aesthetics."[62]
- "It is remarkable that in real life, when aesthetic judgments are made, aesthetic adjectives such as 'beautiful', 'fine', etc. play hardly any role at all."[63]

Of course, there are other philosophers who would not agree, but can research help us answer the question of whether beauty is still a significant aspect of music appreciation?

> "Were it not for music, we might in these days say, the Beautiful is dead."
> (Benjamin Disraeli)

In 1942, Carl Seashore published an article entitled "In Search of Beauty in Music," in which he discussed how science can add to our understanding.[64] In particular, he discussed the singers' vibrato, saying that as one of hundreds of specific factors of a beautiful musical performance it had a biological basis as an expression of feeling. Five years later, he published a book by the same name in which he presented specific details (also on other aspects as described in Chapter 6: Aesthetics).[65] More than 60 years after that, a group of researchers published a series of studies on the use of vibrato in string playing.[66] For example, Rebecca MacLeod found differences in vibrato rate and width among four internationally recognized concert violinists—Midori, Joshua Bell, Anne Sophie Mutter, and Itzhak Perlman. Her results compared favorably with a study done in 1931 of Mischa Elman, Jascha Heifetz, and Fritz Kreisler.[67] Vibrato rates of these seven artists ranged from 6.2–7.1 Hz. When compared to the slower rates typical of high school (5.49 Hz) and college violinists (5.71 Hz),[68] one can begin to see that research can add to our understanding of how artists create musical beauty.

Attacking a different problem, researchers asked more than 300 university students to write as many adjectives as they could to describe the aesthetic value of music.[69] *Beautiful* was by far the most frequently chosen word, appearing in two-thirds of the respondents' answers. Beauty was also strongly correlated with ratings of happiness. Thus, at least according to this group of students, beauty was still very much a core aspect of why they value music.

Apparently, the notion of beauty as an important concept of music preference begins in childhood. Two groups of children, 6–7 and 8–9 years old, rated short piano pieces that were in a major key, minor key, and freely tonal.[70] Among the older children, the composition in major was rated more beautiful than the one in minor, demonstrating they were capable of making aesthetic decisions already. In another study, young adults rated emotions, preference, pleasantness, and beauty in self-selected pieces of music.[71] Once again, beauty was found to be a central aspect of finding aesthetic pleasure. This was confirmed in another study, when participants included beauty as an important criterion for both musical choice and aesthetic judgment.[72]

Because beauty is so frequently conflated with aesthetics, we will revisit research on the topic in Chapter 6: Aesthetics. In the meantime, at least two important concepts are: (1) regardless of philosophical views, beauty is a core ingredient of aesthetic value among many music listeners; and (2) research has the potential to offer something useful as you continue to develop your philosophy of music.

> "It is cruel, you know, that music should be so beautiful. It has the beauty of loneliness and of pain: of strength and freedom. The beauty of disappointment and never-satisfied love. The cruel beauty of nature, and everlasting beauty of monotony."
>
> (Benjamin Britten)

Summary and Thought Questions

Let us return to the original question: What is beauty? Instead of reviewing generic descriptions, let us focus on music. Identify in your own mind several pieces of music and/or several musical experiences you consider beautiful. Try for variety. One piece could be from your own performance medium (e.g., an oboe sonata or concerto if you are an oboist, etc.). Others could be examples from jazz, country, rock, or any genre. With these musical compositions and activities in mind, review the seven questions we have been discussing, now paraphrased to be music specific:

1. What is beautiful music?
2. Is beautiful music in the ear of the listener or is beauty inherent in the music independent of a listener's perception?
3. Does every opinion about what is beautiful music carry equal weight?
4. Can you identify objective properties in beautiful music?
5. Do subjective judgments play a role in determining beauty in music?
6. Are there connections between beauty in music and truth, goodness, or other similar terms?
7. Can music considered ugly by one standard be considered beautiful from another perspective?

These are only a few of the questions philosophers have asked regarding artistic beauty. However, by now you may be feeling overwhelmed and confused. Do not despair. As stated at the outset, the purpose of asking all these questions is not to force you into uncomfortable or arbitrary choices. Rather, if you have started thinking about these issues and continue to do so as you read the ensuing chapters, you will have a head start on clarifying your own philosophy of music.

Notes

1 Plato, *Republic*, trans. Benjamin Jowett. The Project Gutenberg Ebook #1497, 2008, 81. http://www.gutenberg.org/ebooks/1497.
2 Leo Tolstoy, *What Is Art?* trans. by Almyer Maude (Indianapolis: Liberal Arts Press, 1896/1960), 43–44.
3 Ben Dupré, *50 Philosophy Ideas You Really Need to Know* (London: Quercus, 2007), 145.
4 David Hume, "Of the Standard of Taste," in *Aesthetics: The Big Questions*, ed. Carolyn Korsmeyer (Malden, MA: Blackwell, 1757/1998), 144.
5 Ibid., 145.

6 Ibid., 146.
7 Jennifer McMahon, "Beauty," in *The Routledge Companion to Aesthetics*, ed. Berys Gaut and Dominic Lopes (London: Routledge, 2002), 228.
8 Albert Hofstadter and Richard Kuhns, *Philosophies of Art & Beauty: Selected Readings in Aesthetics from Plato to Heidegger* (Chicago: University of Chicago Press, 1976), 96.
9 Ibid., 105.
10 Hume, "Of the Standard of Taste," 139.
11 Enrica Crispino, *Michelangelo*, trans. Silvia Silvestri (Florence: Giunti, 2001).
12 Tolstoy, *What Is Art?*
13 Umberto Eco, ed. *History of Beauty*, trans. Alastair McEwen (New York: Rizzoli, 2002), 37.
14 Ibid., 48.
15 John Keats, "Ode on a Grecian Urn," in *One Hundred and One Famous Poems*, ed. Roy Cook (Chicago: The Cable Co., 1820/1929), 141.
16 Umberto Eco, ed., *On Ugliness* (New York: Rizzoli, 2007), 16.
17 Eco, *History of Beauty*, 133.
18 Robert Liebert, "Michelangelo's Mutilation of the Florence *Pietà*: A Psychoanalytic Inquiry," *Art Bulletin* 59, no. 1 (1977): 47–54.
19 Rolf Wirtz, *Art and Architecture of Florence* (Florence: Könemann, 2005).
20 Wolfgang Mozart, 'Sull'aria' from *The Marriage of Figaro*, sung by Kiri te Kanawa and Mirella Freni, http://www.youtube.com/watch?v=goYSEpSsX3o.
21 Leo Delibes, 'Flower Duet' from *Lakme*, duet sung by Anna Nerebko and Elina Garanca, http://www.youtube.com/watch?v=M9NK-EbUAao.
22 Georges Bizet, 'Au fond du temple saint' from *The Pearl Fishers*, sung by Dmitri Hvorostovsky and Jonas Kaufmann, http://www.youtube.com/watch?v=p2MwnHpLV48.
23 Erich Korngold, 'Marietta's Lied' from *Die tote Stadt*, performed by Leontyne Price, http://www.youtube.com/watch?v=vh_8Sos4szY.
24 Richard Strauss, 'Beim schlafengehn' from *Four Last Songs*, sung by Kiri te Kanawa, http://www.youtube.com/watch?v=3XP2chJ6Ujc.
25 Reynaldo Hahn, *L'Enamourée*, sung by Anna Netrebko, http://www.youtube.com/watch?v=kUZPljVpWak.
26 Heitor Villa-Lobos, 'Aria' (Cantilena) from *Bachianas brasileiras* No. 5, sung by Anna Moffo, http://www.youtube.com/watch?v=anxdAcilnsM.
27 María Grever, *Júrame*, performed by Ramón Vargas, tenor, and Alun Francis conducting the Orquesta Filharmónca de la UNAM (National Autonomous University of Mexico), https://www.youtube.com/watch?v=8JbbWpknygM.
28 Felix Mendelssohn, 'Lift Thine Eyes' from *Elijah*, sung by Choristers of Canterbury Cathedral, http://www.youtube.com/watch?v=BT7rFMrrkYU.
29 Morton Lauridsen, *O Magnum Mysterium*, sung by King's College Choir, http://www.youtube.com/watch?v=Q7ch7uottHU.
30 François Couperin, *Les Barricades Mystérieuses*, performed by Scott Ross on harpsichord, http://www.youtube.com/watch?v=sf-LMHrslHw.
31 J.S. Bach, 'Aria' from *Goldberg Variations*, performed by András Schiff, piano, https://www.youtube.com/watch?v=o_lQ36vxYAI.
32 Wolfgang Mozart, Piano Concerto No. 23, 2nd movement, K. 488, played by Vladimir Horowitz, http://www.youtube.com/watch?v=9LqdfjZYEVE.
33 Ludwig van Beethoven, Piano Sonata No. 31, in A Flat, Op. 110, 1st movement, played by Hélène Grimaud, http://www.youtube.com/watch?v=lPpy5YrhMp4.
34 Frédéric Chopin, Nocturne, Op. 9, No. 1, performed by Arthur Rubinstein, https://www.youtube.com/watch?v=WnFs85pLmj4.
35 Johannes Brahms, Intermezzo, Op. 118, No. 2 in A Major, performed by Arthur Rubinstein, http://www.youtube.com/watch?v=cqBzK5tKFVc.
36 Clara Schumann, Romance, Op. 11, No. 1 in e flat minor, performed by Tomer Lev, https://www.youtube.com/watch?v=1L3WPzNr-og.
37 Edvard Grieg, 'Melodie' from *Lyric Pieces*, Book II, Op. 38-3, performed by Walter Gieseking, http://www.youtube.com/watch?v=yK8EjfG_dH4.

38 Howard Hanson, *Fantasy Variations on a Theme of Youth*, Op. 40, performed by Carol Rosenberger, piano, and the New York Chamber Symphony, Gerard Schwarz, conductor, https://www.youtube.com/watch?v=M4J6B6fUzis.

39 John Adams, *China Gates*, performed by Fraser Graham, http://www.youtube.com/watch?v=sV0JFg0xlF0.

40 J. S. Bach, Double Violin Concerto in d minor, BWV 1043, 2nd movement, performed by Isaac Stern and Itzhak Perlman, with the New York Philharmonic, conducted by Zubin Mehta, http://www.youtube.com/watch?v=axFUvA_he-o.

41 Wolfgang Mozart, Clarinet Concerto in A Major, K. 622, 2nd movement, performed by Karl Leister and the Berlin Philharmonic, conducted by Herbert von Karajan, http://www.youtube.com/watch?v=zsvgIW2YMWA.

42 Ludwig van Beethoven, Symphony No. 2 in D Major, Op. 21, 2nd movement, performed by Bernard Haitink conducting the Royal Concertgebouw Orchestra, http://www.youtube.com/watch?v=YmNxqMxZoRk.

43 Johannes Brahms, Piano Quartet in c minor, Op. 60, 3rd movement, performed by Sara Okamoto, piano; Stefano Succi, violin; Wolfgang Tluck, Viola; Ulrich Horn, cello, http://www.youtube.com/watch?v=UCIo1LP4G_8.

44 Edward Elgar, 'Nimrod' from *Enigma Variations*, performed by Daniel Barenboim conducting the Chicago Symphony, http://www.youtube.com/watch?v=sUgoBb8m1eE.

45 Gustav Mahler, Symphony No. 5, 4th movement (Adagietto), performed by Leonard Bernstein conducting the Vienna Philharmonic, http://www.youtube.com/watch?v=yjz2TvC2TT4.

46 Sergei Rachmaninoff, Piano Concerto No. 2 in c minor, Op. 18, performed by Evgeny Kissin, pianist, and Andrew Davis conducting the BBC Symphony Orchestra, http://www.youtube.com/watch?v=DgYhcM5TB_c.

47 Percy Grainger, 'Horkstow Grange' from *Lincolnshire Posy*, performed by the United States Marine Band, conducted by Col. Michael J. Colburn, https://www.youtube.com/watch?v=G2q8oxHUaMI.

48 Eric Whitacre, *October*, performed by the United States Navy Band, conducted by Russell Gross, http://www.youtube.com/watch?v=WZaYOGYdI4w.

49 Michael Kamen, Brass Quintet, performed by The Canadian Brass, http://www.youtube.com/watch?v=HjBT8ElQ7Pw.

50 Vernon Duke, 'Autumn in New York,' performed by Ella Fitzgerald and Louie Armstrong, http://www.youtube.com/watch?v=50zL8TnMBN8.

51 Walter Gross, 'Tenderly,' performed by Miles Davis, https://www.youtube.com/watch?v=ISnrLn4LnZs.

52 Ennio Morricone, 'Gabriel's Oboe' from *The Mission*, performed by the London Philharmonic Orchestra, conducted by Ennio Morricone, https://www.youtube.com/watch?v=Ixby9BzJfEo. Listen also to Yo-Yo Ma's version of 'Gabriel's Oboe,' with the Roma Sinfoneitta Orchestra, conducted by Ennio Morricone, https://www.youtube.com/watch?v=XISBJ-MJ0HI.

53 John Barry, *Dances with Wolves* (theme) performed by the London Symphony, conducted by John Williams, https://www.youtube.com/watch?v=EuaDf0L11E4.

54 Anne Murray, 'Could I Have This Dance,' https://www.youtube.com/watch?v=iE3z-6XO2Ds.

55 Beautiful World (Phil Sawyer), 'In Existence,' https://www.youtube.com/watch?v=gIt-B5dujCI.

56 Goldfrapp, 'Dreaming,' http://www.youtube.com/watch?v=OxdC-FhTPfQ.

57 Dead Can Dance, 'Yulunga,' https://www.youtube.com/watch?v=sJqUbb-WuPQ.

58 Daniel Licht, 'Blood Theme' from *Dexter*, https://www.youtube.com/watch?v=e2xxizpHuoo.

59 David Arkenstone & Kostia, 'The Cello's Song,' http://www.youtube.com/watch?v=GUv9AH6JkpQ.

60 Jerome Stolnitz, "Beauty: Some Stages in the History of an Idea," *Journal of the History of Ideas* 22, no. 2 (1961): 185–204, p. 185.

61 Alexander Nehamas, "An Essay on Beauty and Judgment," *The Threepenny Review* 80 (Winter, 2000). http://www.threepennyreview.com.

62 Ruth Lorand, "In Defense of Beauty," *American Society of Aesthetics* (2007),. http://aesthetics-online.org/default.asp?page=lorandbeauty&terms=%22ruth+and+lorand%22#.V2sAaIiJPwY.gmail.

63 Ludwig Wittgenstein, *Lectures and Conversations on Aesthetics, Psychology and Religious Beliefs* (Berkeley, CA: University of California Press, 1967), 3.

64 Carl Seashore, "In Search of Beauty in Music," *The Musical Quarterly* 28, no. 3 (1942): 302–8.

65 Carl Seashore, *In Search of Beauty in Music: A Scientific Approach to Musical Aesthetics* (New York: The Ronald Press, 1947).

66 Michael Allen, John Geringer, and Rebecca MacLeod, "Performance Practice of Violin Vibrato: An Artist-Level Case Study," *Journal of String Research* 4 (2009): 27–38. John Geringer, Michael Allen, Rebecca MacLeod, "Initial Movement and Continuity of Vibrato among High School and University String Players," *Journal of Research in Music Education* 53, no. 3 (2005): 248–59. John Geringer, Michael Allen, and Rebecca MacLeod, "String Vibrato: Research Related to Performance and Perception," *String Research Journal* 1 (2010): 7–23. John Geringer, Rebecca MacLeod, and Michael Allen, "Perceived Pitch of Violin and Cello Vibrato Tones among Music Majors," *Journal of Research in Music Education* 57, no. 4 (2010): 351–63. Rebecca MacLeod, "Influences of Dynamic Level and Pitch Register on the Vibrato Rates and Widths of Violin and Viola Players," *Journal of Research in Music Education* 56, no. 1 (2008): 43–54. Rebecca MacLeod, "A Pilot Study of Relationships between Pitch Register and Dynamic Level and Vibrato Rate and Width in Professional Violinists," *String Research Journal* 1 (2010): 75–83.

67 Data from L. Cheslock, "An Introductory Study of the Violin Vibrato," *Research Studies in Music* 1 (Baltimore: Peabody Conservatory, 1931), as cited in Geringer, Allen, and MacLeod, "String Vibrato," 7–23.

68 MacLeod, "Influences of Dynamic Level."

69 Eva Istók, Elvira Brattico, Thomas Jacobsen, Kaisu Krohn, Mira Müller, and Mari Tervaniemi, "Aesthetic Responses to Music: A Questionnaire Study," *Musicae Scientiae* 13, no. 2 (2009): 183–206.

70 Sirke Nieminen, Eva Istók, Elvira Brattico, and Mari Tervaniemi, "The Development of the Aesthetic Experience of Music: Preference, Emotions, and Beauty," *Musicae Scientiae* 16, no. 3 (2012): 372–91.

71 Suvi Saarikallio, Sirke Nieminen, Elvira Brattico, "Affective Reactions to Musical Stimuli Reflect Emotional Use of Music in Everyday Life," *Musicae Scientiae* 17, no. 1 (2012): 27–39.

72 Patrik Juslin and Sara Isaksson, "Subjective Criteria for Choice and Aesthetic Value of Music: A Comparison of Psychology and Music Students," *Research Studies in Music Education* 36, no. 2 (2014): 179–98.

5 Emotion

What are we to make of the following opposing comments of two musical giants? Igor Stravinsky said, "Do we not, in truth, ask the impossible of music when we expect it to express feelings?"[1] In contrast, Leonard Bernstein wrote, "Therefore, what it is that the composer is telling is never factual, can never be literal, but *must* be emotional."[2] Clearly, we have a difference of opinion here. Philosophers represent this disagreement as well. Eduard Hanslick stated Stravinsky's position a century earlier when he said, ". . . is it not a psychologically unavoidable conclusion, that it [music] is likewise incapable of expressing emotion?"[3] A few years before Hanslick's statement, Georg Hegel said that music "finds utterance in its tones for the heart with its whole gamut of feelings and passions."[4] Regardless of their take on the matter, musicians and philosophers alike have had to deal with what has always been a controversial issue. In fact, as we will see in a moment, music psychologists, too, are divided in their conclusions about the role emotions play in music.

As odd as it may seem, one of the critical issues you will need to face in developing your own philosophy of music is the role of emotions. Do you agree with Stravinsky, Hanslick, and Paul Hindemith, who declared that "music does not express feelings"?[5] Or, do you find yourself aligned with

> "Music is the shorthand of emotion."
> (Leo Tolstoy)

Bernstein, Hegel, and legendary jazz trumpeter Louis Armstrong, who said about jazz, "You use it to say all kinds of things and explain all kinds of moods."[6] Because you will read many of the differing views about musical emotions—that is, emotional responses to creating, performing, or listening to music—in Section II, the purpose of this chapter is to help you think through some of the important aspects of this issue in preparation both for understanding various positions and for clarifying your own thinking. A secondary purpose is to share some of the recent positions held by music psychologists based on their research.

One issue we can dispense with rather quickly is whether emotions reside in the music itself. When we say things like 'that is a happy song' or 'that was sad music,' what do we mean? Surely, the notes on the page or the sounds in the air are neither happy nor sad. Perhaps the composer or performer was happy or sad, though there is not necessarily a direct connection between how the artist felt at the moment of composition or performance and the music itself (e.g., a sad composer could write happy music and a happy person could sing a sad song). As Bernstein saw it, there "is a lot of nineteenth-century romantic nonsense that always pictures the creator creating in the mood of the piece he is writing."[7] Writing about Beethoven's third cello sonata, Op. 69,[8] ♫ cellist Carlos Prieto wrote, "The easy, lighthearted flow of the piece might suggest that Beethoven composed it during one of his rare moments of happiness. However, the following words appear on the manuscript: *Inter lacrimas et luctum* (Between tears and sadness)."[9] Hindemith agreed when he argued that it might take several months to write a piece of music and that a single emotional focus could not last that long.[10] Suppose, for example, that a composer worked for six months on a funeral mass. Are we to imagine that the emotions attendant on such a work were the only ones he experienced during that time?

If the emotions are not in the music itself and not necessarily in the composer, at least at the moment of composition, how is it that music and emotions are so often aligned? To stimulate your thinking on this critical topic, we will first examine what an emotion is, and then present brief overviews of the thoughts of philosophers and music psychologists. As always, however, it is crucial that you begin formulating your own thoughts.

What Is an Emotion?

One of the difficulties in understanding emotions is the variety of definitions used by various writers. Understanding that not all scholars would agree with the following, here are brief definitions of terms as we will use them in this book. These are paraphrased and abridged definitions from the *APA Dictionary of Psychology*:[11]

- *Moods* are short-term, low intensity emotional states (e.g., jovial or moping) or longer lasting, sometimes ill-defined dispositions. They differ from emotions in that they lack an object (i.e., one may be generally unhappy rather than sad about something specific).
- *Emotions* are complex reactions with experiential, behavioral, and physiological components (e.g., anger, grief). Emotions usually involve feelings, but are different from them in that emotions involve direct engagement with the world.
- *Feelings* are subjective appraisals of the sensations, thoughts, or images that evoke them. Feelings typically have a pleasant–unpleasant valence and are purely internal, as opposed to emotions that involve direct interactions with something external.
- *Affect* is an umbrella term that includes any experience of feeling or emotion.

Neuroscientist Antonio Damasio wrote three books about emotion that provide a good overview. In *Descartes' Error: Emotion, Reason and the Human Brain* (1994), he argued that the schism between mind and body, thoughts and feelings, reason and emotion, that began with the Greeks and received its strongest affirmation from René Descartes in the 17th century, is false. That is, "The brain and the body are indissociably integrated by mutually targeted biochemical and neural circuits."[12] Under most circumstances, we do not feel without thinking and do not think without feeling. In *The Feeling of What Happens: Body and Emotion in the Making of Consciousness*, Damasio clarified definitions of feelings and emotions when he said, "It is through feelings, which are inwardly directed and private, that emotions, which are outwardly directed and public, begin their impact on the mind."[13] Another point that Damasio made is that while we are most often consciously aware of our feelings, we are not always cognizant of them. Both emotions and feelings can happen nonconsciously; thus, we can experience an emotion without necessarily feeling it. Awareness of our feelings is related directly to consciousness. Let us tie this idea to another one and then apply it to music. Emotions are induced when we process sensory information, such as when we hear sounds or when the mind recalls certain images from memory, and these images can be auditory as well as visual, tactile, and so on. It is very likely, then, that listening to music, either processing the sounds themselves or recalling certain memories attached to the sounds, induces emotions and that this can happen without our being consciously aware of it.

In *Looking for Spinoza: Joy, Sorrow and the Feeling Brain*, Damasio continued his examination of emotions. Here he distinguished among three types:[14]

- *Background emotions* are essentially the same as the first definition given above for moods; that is, they are relatively short-term, low intensity emotional states that result from regulatory processes involved in homeostasis, pain and pleasure, and appetites.
- *Primary (or basic) emotions* include such familiar ones as fear, anger, disgust, surprise, sadness, and happiness. These are sometimes called universal emotions because they are inborn and commonly found among different cultures.
- *Social emotions* are learned, and include sympathy, embarrassment, shame, guilt, pride, jealousy, envy, gratitude, admiration, indignation, and contempt.

Emotions arise from complicated patterns of interacting chemical and neural responses and are colored by a positive–negative valence. Nonconscious emotions occur very rapidly, while feelings based on appraisal appear more slowly. Interestingly, "the appraisal can modulate the ensuing emotional state and, in turn, be modulated by it."[15] Collectively, these ideas, based as they are on modern neuroscientific findings, should be kept in mind as you ponder those philosophical views that polarize musical responses as primarily rational or primarily emotional.

What Have Philosophers Thought about Musical Emotions?

Specific details about the role of emotions in music philosophy are presented in Section II, especially in Chapter 12: Expressionism. In the meantime, however, what follows is a general overview of the issue. Philosophers have taken positions at either extreme and at nearly every point in between. In a book concerned with the connection of emotions to music, Malcolm Budd presented a variety of philosophical positions that he divided into three categories:[16]

1. Theories that deny a connection between music and emotions:

    a. Eduard Hanslick claimed that music could not represent definite feelings or emotions. After discussing preludes and fugues from Bach's *Well-Tempered Clavier*,[17] ♪ he wrote, "this alone is enough to prove that music need not necessarily awaken feelings, or that it must necessarily be the object of music to represent them."[18]

    > ". . . philosophical blood, sweat, and tears had been spilled through the centuries in various contentions as to the relation, if any, of musical feeling to feeling outside musical experience."
    > (Bennett Reimer)

    b. Carroll Pratt contended that music cannot embody emotions when he said, "If taken literally, however, the notion that music can embody or contain an emotion is psychological nonsense."[19]

    > A few people do undoubtedly soak in some sort of emotional bath while listening to the heart-rending measures of Tschaikowsky or to the sickening despair of Ravel; but for

every one whose visceral processes are thus aroused there are ninety and nine who in proper psychical distance gladly lend an attentive ear to the sadness of Tschaikowsky and the sorrow of Ravel without themselves descending into any slough of despond.[20]

c.　Edmund Gurney stated that "the great point, which is often strangely ignored . . . is that expressiveness of the literal and tangible sort is either absent or only slightly present in an immense amount of impressive music; that to suggest describable images, qualities, or feelings . . . makes up no inseparable or essential part of its [music's] function . . ."[21]

2.　Theories that propose a connection between music and emotions.

a.　In writing about melody, Arthur Schopenhauer said, "it tells the will's most secret story, it paints every emotion, every striving. . . . Thus music has always been described as the language of feeling and of passion."[22]
b.　Susanne Langer wrote, "Music is a tonal analogue of the emotive life."[23]
c.　Deryck Cooke felt that emotionally expressive music has persisted from plainsong throughout the history of Western music.[24]

3.　A theory that attempts to bridge both views.

a.　Leonard Meyer described two opposing positions, Absolutism and Referentialism. In the first position, the "musical meaning lies exclusively within the context of the work itself."[25] In the second, "music also communicates meanings which in some way refer to the extra-musical world of concepts, actions, emotional states, and character."[26] He further stated, "In spite of the persistent wrangling of these two groups, it seems obvious that absolute meanings and referential meanings are not mutually exclusive: that they can and do coexist in one and the same piece of music."[27] This position is called Absolute Expressionism.

Even taken out of context, these quotes, some of which come from books not discussed by Budd, give a fair representation of the disparity of views expressed by various philosophers over time. It is not our concern at this juncture that Budd argues that none of these views is correct, for we will be revisiting each of these philosophers in Section II. Let us turn instead to music psychologists to see if they can clarify this core aspect of musical experiences.

Does Psychological Research Support or Contradict Various Philosophical Views?

Music psychologists characterize the theoretical positions described in the previously mentioned book by Budd with the terms cognitivism and emotivism. Cognitivists believe that listeners can perceive emotional expressiveness in the music without necessarily feeling those emotions (perception). Emotivists believe that listeners sometimes do feel the emotions being expressed by the music (induction). Through experiments, researchers have collected data that uphold both positions. In support of the cognitivists' position, Geoffrey Collier conducted five experiments demonstrating that listeners could reliably identify emotions being expressed in the music.[28] Supporting the emotivists' position, researchers contacted college students randomly seven times a day and they reported experiencing emotions 64% of the time when they were listening to music.[29] Of course, theoretically, nothing would preclude a listener from perceiving emotions in the music and experiencing induced emotions in rapidly shifting patterns or even parallel streams during a single listening occurrence. A third position, discussed later, provides an alternative to these two viewpoints.

As a means of providing an overview of the interactions of philosophers and music psychologists on the matter of musical emotions, we will take an extended look at an article by Vladimir Konečni. In this article he reviews a debate between philosophers Noël Carroll and Peter Kivy in order "to clarify matters that seem to be of interest to most camps in both philosophy and psychology of music."[30] The focus of discussion, both in the debate and in Konečni's article, is on absolute music, that is, on instrumental music from the Western art music tradition that has no program or any overt extramusical references. This is a common approach among philosophers because vocal music and instrumental program music represent a separate issue, as we can more obviously understand how they convey emotions. Thus, a core question is whether absolute music can induce emotional responses in listeners.

Konečni's first criticism of music psychology experiments was that researchers are sometimes careless and use excerpts from program music as stimuli, even when the focus is purportedly on perception versus induction. A second criticism was that music psychologists tend to conflate perception and induction. For example, researchers may ask listeners to rate musical stimuli in terms of perceived emotions but later discuss the listeners' emotional experience, without the latter having been monitored in any way.

Konečni leveled a third criticism at the position taken by Patrik Juslin and Daniel Västfjäll that absolute music can induce basic emotions.[31] Although these authors posit six mechanisms for how absolute music may cause emotions, Konečni contended that three of them concern nonmusical mediating events. In other words, it is not the music *per se* that causes the emotions, but extramusical referents, including remembering real-world emotional situations (episodic memory), mental representations of nonmusical events (visual imagery), and a pairing of a nonmusical emotion with the music (evaluative conditioning). The fourth mechanism, brain stem reflexes, and the fifth mechanism, musical expectancy, are not sufficient to raise responses beyond brief startle or surprise reactions to more complex emotions. Finally he stated that even Juslin and Västfjäll admit the speculative nature of the sixth mechanism, emotional contagion, an internal mimicking of music's expressiveness.

Konečni closed this section of his article by stating,

> In short, I am contending that absolute music may induce a *basic emotion* only by profiting—like some other art works do—from various types of associations of music with nonmusical events and also from the visual imagery to which music may give rise, and it is these *nonmusical events that are the true proximal causes of the fundamental emotions.*[32]

He declared that although "it is conceptually and logically impossible for absolute music to induce basic emotions directly, it can do so by means of various nonmusical mediators."[33] In this, he supported Kivy's philosophical position.

Next, however, Konečni criticized an important aspect of Kivy's philosophy, the fact that his viewpoint is based on 'formalist canonical listening.' This is a very restricted, particular type of listening experience that involves absolute music heard in a concert hall or on a recording in an undisturbed setting by a listener who subscribes to enhanced formalism (i.e., that absolute music has expressive qualities that one perceives in the music), and a listener concentrating on structural, phenomenological, and expressive properties of the music, ignoring as much as possible any extraneous, nonmusical elements. Under these circumstances, "Absolute music, the enhanced formalist claims, is frequently *deeply moving*—arouses *deep emotion*—in listeners who listen in the enhanced formalist manner, when the music is of the high artistic quality exemplified by the masterpieces of the Western canon."[34] The problem is that as philosophically attractive as this position might be to Kivy and others of like mind, it is not only impractical that many listeners could achieve this exalted level on a regular, consistent basis, but also that it eliminates so many possibilities of meaningful listening.

Responses to the beauty of absolute music can include non-basic emotions, such as excitement, enthusiasm, and ecstasy (Kivy) and aesthetic awe (Konečni). Here, we come to Konečni's Aesthetic Trinity Theory (ATT). "In ATT, a tripartite hierarchy of responses is proposed: *Aesthetic awe*, as the peak experience; the state of *being moved* (or *being-touched*), as a less pronounced experience; and *thrills* (or *chills*), as the most common experience."[35] In addition to Konečni's own philosophical and psychological work,[36] support also comes from the work of Alf Gabrielsson, although he used different language.[37] As mentioned in Chapter 3, in a project involving Strong Experiences in Music (SEM), Gabrielsson performed a content analysis of more than 1,300 responses to a prompt to describe "the strongest, most intense experience of music that you have ever had."[38]

> ". . . the seeming emotionality of music is an absolute, unfathomable mystery."
> (Kingsley Price)

Vivid descriptions of transcendent, overwhelming, life-changing peak experiences sound very much like Kivy's ecstasy and Konečni's ATT. However, the matter is still complicated and unresolved in that a variety of other responses, including experiencing deep emotions of the kind supported by emotivists, are also included.

What Role Will Musical Emotions Play in Your Philosophy?

As frustrating as it may be to have the previous discussion end in limbo, that is the state of both philosophy and psychology on the matter. In Chapter 11: Formalism, we will discuss the position in which value is found in an intellectual appreciation of relationships within the music, and in Chapter 12: Expressionism, we will be concerned with the viewpoint that value is found in the expression of feelings and emotions.

Bennett Reimer, while framing the discussion with different language, provided an alternative to polarized, extremist views.[39] First, he used the labels *inherence* and *delineation*. By inherence, he was referring to how the music is arranged so that "feeling is contained and expressed in sounds configured within some musical system and that the way the sounds are disposed in relation to each other within that system is the way they will be felt."[40] Delineation refers to what the music is 'about' and is "the capturing in sounds of an emotion, mood, situation, or message delineated by those sounds and made apparent to others by the clarity of the delineation."[41] Recognizing that many have taken positions at opposite ends of the spectrum, Reimer was concerned with "preserving the validity of both inherence and delineation while also unifying them in musical practice."[42] He does this, acknowledging that this only moves us closer to a useful answer rather than arriving at absolute truth, by saying that,

> The affective experiences music offers, I submit, are necessarily functions of what sounds are made to do that add inherent meanings to any and all delineations, or to put it differently, that transmute delineations into musical inherence while also including the delineations as a

dimension of that inherence. That transmutation is what is called "musical," and people who accomplish it are called "musicians."[43]

In other words, extramusical references are made in and through the music; this is a restatement of the position called absolute expressionism.

Perhaps one of the most important things you can do to resolve these issues in your own mind is to spend time in introspection. Konečni makes an almost impassioned plea for both philosophers and psychologists to think deeply and thoughtfully about musical experiences.[44] Take time to reflect on your music listening experiences in a variety of settings and with a variety of musical styles. Is listening to masterpieces of Western absolute music in a concert hall different from listening to music with friends at a party? Of course, they are different in many, many ways. But, what about your affective responses? Do you perceive emotions expressed in the music without actually feeling those emotions—sometimes, always, never? Can you identify times and circumstances when you actually feel the same emotions that you identify as being expressed in the music? What about terms such as ecstasy or awe; do you ever experience them? Are there times when the musical experience transcends or seems to go beyond *mere* emotions?

Finally, while this entire discussion has been focused on listening, what about performing, improvising, or composing? As indicated previously, Bernstein and Hindemith did not believe that a composer had to feel the emotion concurrently with writing it into the music. Or, take the case of an opera singer. If you were singing an emotionally expressive aria, could you do it effectively while being unemotional or would being truly emotional restrict the vocal apparatus such that your singing would be compromised?[45] When you perform or conduct, do you focus on technique and musical elements or are you more apt to concentrate on extramusical aspects such as what the music is *about* or on expressiveness? One clue to this issue may be found in a report that the famous conductor Herbert von Karajan had higher heart rates when conducting very expressive passages than when conducting more physical or energetic passages.[46] We can suppose that he experienced heightened emotions at these times, but that he maintained control nonetheless. At any rate, these are all questions that may be highly individualized and your philosophy will only be useful to you if it truly represents what you experience as a musician.

Summary and Thought Questions

As you can see, the issue of musical emotions is not a simple or easy one. In considering all the different philosophies, opinions, and research findings presented in this chapter, I encourage you to spend some time thinking about your own experiences and perhaps querying your friends about theirs. Think about the different kinds of music you listen to and the different situations in which you hear music. The next time you listen to music, engage in some metacognition, or more simply, think about your own thoughts. You might even surreptitiously jot down some notes on the margins of a program or in a small notebook. You could also ruminate on your performing experiences, though this would of necessity be after the fact. Here are the kinds of questions you might ask yourself:

1. Do I agree with Stravinsky, Hindemith, Hanslick, Pratt, Gurney, and others who contend that music is incapable of expressing emotions? If so, how would I account for the fact that so many people say that music expresses feelings?
2. Do I fall into the camp of those like Bernstein, Armstrong, Hegel, Schopenhauer, Langer, and Cooke who say that the whole point of music is to express emotions? If so, how can music—especially pure instrumental music—do that?

3. Do I experience different emotions when I listen to classical music than when I listen to jazz or country or any other genre?
4. Do I experience music differently in various formal—concert and recital halls, opera houses— and informal settings—nightclubs, coffee houses, in the car, alone with headphones?
5. Do I agree with Meyer and Reimer that intellectual and emotional approaches can co-exist? Does absolute expressionism sound like a viable alternative?
6. Using the language of music psychologists, am I a cognitivist or an emotivist?
7. Do I find merit in Konečni's Aesthetic Trinity Theory of aesthetic awe, being moved, and thrills?
8. Do the reactions I have to music when I listen to music, whether emotional or not, extend to my experiences as a performer? How about when I compose, teach, or work with clients as a music therapist?

There are two aspects of this chapter that are very similar to the previous one on beauty. First, to develop your philosophy of music you will need to consider the role of emotions very carefully. Second, the subject of emotions is also conflated somewhat with the notion of aesthetic experiences and it is to that topic that we turn in the next chapter.

Notes

1 Igor Stravinsky, *Poetics of Music in the Form of Six Lessons*, trans. Arthur Knodel and Ingolf Dahl (New York: Vintage Books, 1960), 79.
2 Leonard Bernstein, *The Infinite Variety of Music* (New York: Simon and Schuster, 1966), 274.
3 Eduard Hanslick, *The Beautiful in Music*, ed. Morris Weitz, trans. Gustav Cohen (New York: Bobbs-Merrill, 1854/1957), 35.
4 Bernard Bosanquet (trans.), *The Introduction to Hegel's Philosophy of Fine Art* (London: Kegan Paul, Trench, Trübner, 1905), 20.
5 Paul Hindemith, *A Composer's World: Horizons and Limitations* (Cambridge, MA: Harvard University Press, 1950), 42.
6 Louis Armstrong, "Jazz Is a Language," in *They Talk about Music, Vol. 2*, ed. Robert Cumming (Rockville Centre, NY: Belwin/Mills, 1971), 129.
7 Bernstein, *The Infinite Variety*, 275.
8 Ludwig van Beethoven: Cello Sonata No. 3 in A Major, Op. 69, performed by Yo-Yo Ma, cello, and Emmanuel Ax, piano, https://www.youtube.com/watch?v=X9pivx91mVk.
9 Carlos Prieto, *The Adventures of a Cello*, trans. Elena Murray (Austin, TX: University of Texas Press, 2006), 233.
10 Hindemith, *A Composer's World*.
11 Gary VandenBos, ed., *APA Dictionary of Psychology* (Washington, DC: American Psychological Association, 2007).
12 Antonio Damasio, *Descartes' Error: Emotion, Reason, and the Human Brain* (New York: Avon Books, 1994), 87.
13 Antonio Damasio, *The Feeling of What Happens: Body and Emotion in the Making of Consciousness* (New York: Harcourt Brace, 1999), 36.
14 Antonio Damasio, *Looking for Spinoza: Joy, Sorrow, and the Feeling Brain* (New York: Harcourt Brace, 2003).
15 Ibid., 79.
16 Malcolm Budd, *Music and the Emotions: The Philosophical Theories* (London: Routledge and Kegan Paul, 1985).
17 J.S. Bach, *Well-Tempered Clavier*, BWV 846–893. *Book I*, performed by Léon Berben, harpsichord, https://www.youtube.com/watch?v=Qm59Vn7ak-I. *Book II*, performed by Kenneth Gilbert, harpsichord, https://www.youtube.com/watch?v=hms_PF_CKV4.
18 Hanslick, *The Beautiful in Music*, 28.

19 Carroll Pratt, *Music as the Language of Emotion: A Lecture Delivered in the Whittall Pavilion of the Library of Congress* (December 21, 1950), 6. http://www.questia.com/PM.qst?a=o&d=6090173.
20 Carroll Pratt, "The Design of Music," *The Journal of Aesthetics and Art Criticism* 12, no. 3 (1954): 291–92.
21 Edmund Gurney, *The Power of Sound* (London: Smith, Elder, & Co., 1880), 314.
22 Arthur Schopenhauer, *The World as Will and Representation, Vol. 1*, in *The Cambridge Edition of the Works of Schopenhauer*, ed. Christopher Janaway, trans. Judith Norman and Alistair Welchman (Cambridge, UK: Cambridge University Press, 1819/2010), 287.
23 Susanne Langer, *Feeling and Form* (New York: Charles Scribner's Sons, 1953), 27.
24 Deryck Cooke, *The Language of Music* (Oxford: Oxford University Press, 1963).
25 Leonard Meyer, *Emotion and Meaning in Music* (Chicago: The University of Chicago Press, 1956), 1.
26 Ibid., 1.
27 Ibid., 1.
28 Geoffrey Collier, "Beyond Valence and Activity in the Emotional Connotations of Music," *Psychology of Music* 35, no. 1 (2007): 110–31.
29 Patrik Juslin, Simon Liljeström, Daniel Västfjäll, Gonçalo Barradas, and Ana Silva, "An Experience Sampling Study of Emotional Reactions to Music: Listener, Music, and Situation," *Emotion* 8, no. 5 (2008): 668–83.
30 Vladimir Konečni, "Music, Affect, Method, Data: Reflections on the Carroll v. Kivy Debate," *American Journal of Psychology* 126, no. 2 (2013): 180.
31 Patrik Juslin and Daniel Västfjäll, "Emotional Responses to Music: The Need to Consider Underlying Mechanisms," *Behavioral and Brain Sciences* 31, no. 5 (2008): 559–621.
32 Konečni, "Music, Affect, Method, Data," 184.
33 Ibid., 185.
34 Peter Kivy, "Moodology: A Response to Laura Sizer," *Journal of Aesthetics and Art Criticism* 65, no. 3 (2007): 312.
35 Vladimir Konečni, "Aesthetic Trinity Theory and the Sublime," *Philosophy Today* 55, no. 1 (2011): 64.
36 Vladimir Konečni, "The Aesthetic Trinity: Awe, Being Moved, Thrills," *Bulletin of Psychology and the Arts* 5, no. 2 (2005): 27–44. Vladimir Konečni, "Does Music Induce Emotion? A Theoretical and Methodological Analysis," *Psychology of Aesthetics, Creativity, and the Arts* 2 (2008): 115–29. Vladimir Konečni, Amber Brown, and Rebekah Wanic, "Comparative Effects of Music and Recalled Life-events on Emotional State," *Psychology of Music* 36, no. 3 (2008): 289–308. Vladimir Konečni, Rebekah Wanic, and Amber Brown, "Emotional and Aesthetic Antecedents and Consequences of Music-Induced Thrills," *American Journal of Psychology* 120, no. 4 (2007): 619–43.
37 Alf Gabrielsson, "Emotions in Strong Experiences with Music," in *Music and Emotion: Theory and Research*, ed. Patrik Juslin and John Sloboda (New York: Oxford University Press, 2001), 431–49. Alf Gabrielsson, "Strong Experiences with Music," in *Handbook of Music and Emotion*, ed. Patrik Juslin and John Sloboda (Oxford: Oxford University Press, 2010), 547–74. Alf Gabrielsson, *Strong Experiences with Music* (Oxford, UK: Oxford University Press, 2011). Alf Gabrielsson and Siv Wik, "Strong Experiences Related to Music: A Descriptive System," *Musicae Scientiae* 7, no. 2 (2003): 157–217.
38 Gabrielsson, "Emotions in Strong Experiences with Music," 434.
39 Bennett Reimer, "Once More with Feeling: Reconciling Discrepant Accounts of Musical Affect," *Philosophy of Music Education Review* 12, no. 1 (2004): 4–16.
40 Ibid., 6.
41 Ibid., 8.
42 Ibid., 12.
43 Ibid., 12–13.
44 Konečni, "Music, Affect, Method, Data."
45 For an extended discussion of what is referred to as the 'singer's paradox' (i.e., whether singers should fake emotions on the stage or actually experience them while singing), see Klaus Scherer, "The Singer's Paradox: On Authenticity in Emotional Expression on the Opera Stage," in *The Emotional Power of Music: Multidisciplinary Perspectives on Musical Arousal, Expression, and Social Control*, ed. Tom Cochrane, Bernardino Fantini, and Klaus Scherer (Oxford, UK: Oxford University Press, 2013).
46 G. Herrer and H. Harrer, "Music, Emotion, and Autonomous Function," in *Music and the Brain*, ed. Macdonald Critchley and R. Henson (London: William Heinemann Medical Books, 1977), 202–16.

6 Aesthetics

In 1933, Harvard professor George Birkhoff developed a scientific aesthetic measure expressed in a mathematical formula.[1] In 1993, Clifford Madsen, Ruth Brittin, and Deborah Capperella-Sheldon measured aesthetic responses by means of a Continuous Response Digital Interface.[2] What exactly were they measuring? What is an aesthetic response? In fact, what does the word *aesthetics* mean?

For many, "aesthetics is an investigation of the beautiful."[3] Thus, you should keep the chapter on beauty in mind as you read and think about aesthetics. Although aesthetics is often concerned with beauty, it includes a great deal more as well. For example, some even contend that the concept of aesthetics is not restricted to art, that it could include nature, too. However, for our purposes we will consider aesthetics as dealing with art in general and music specifically. In this regard, " 'aesthetics' refers to theories about the fundamental nature and value of art."[4] Because this definition relies on further definitions of 'art' and 'music,' let us begin there.

What Is Art? What Is Music?

Defining art or music is so difficult that there is no general agreement, and many philosophers have given up the attempt altogether.[5] However, "the question 'What is art?' would hardly provoke such wide interest unless it mattered whether something is or is not art."[6] Attempts to define art range from simple statements to complex books. Abbé Batteux reduced the issue to a single principle when he said that the object of the fine arts is pleasure, as the arts "were born only in the womb of joy and of feelings that plenty and tranquility produce."[7] In contrast, Leo Tolstoy argued against pleasure as a basis for art. Instead, he stated,

> "The first step in the direction of beauty is to understand the frame and scope of the imagination, to comprehend the act itself of esthetic apprehension."
>
> (James Joyce)

Art is a human activity consisting in this, that one man consciously, by means of certain external signs, hands on to others feelings he has lived through, and that other people are infected by these feelings and also experience them.[8]

Denis Dutton provided a considerably more detailed approach when he presented 12 characteristics of art, based upon the creation/performance of art, the artworks that sometimes result, and art experiences:[9]

- *Direct pleasure.* We derive pleasure from reading a novel, viewing a sculpture, or listening to music. This 'aesthetic pleasure' is a direct, immediate experience, undertaken for the pleasure it brings, not primarily for utilitarian purposes. [Jerrold Levinson makes a further point that even when music conveys negative emotions such as sadness or anger, we find the experience worthwhile although it may not be predominantly pleasant.][10]

- *Skill and virtuosity.* Creating art often demands special skills and even when many members of a community share in the process (e.g., communal singing), there are those whose expertise rises above the norm. We admire and delight in observing an expert in action or in the result of their action, and, of course, those who are composers or performers may also find deep pleasure in the act of music making.
- *Style.* Art objects and performances adhere to a particular style as found in a particular culture in a particular time and place.
- *Novelty and creativity.* We value art for its inventiveness and originality. "Creativity and novelty are a locus of individuality or genius in art, referring to that aspect of art that is not governed by rules or routines."[11]
- *Criticism.* Wherever there is art, there is bound to be discussion, critique, judgment, and evaluation. It is hard to imagine an audience leaving a jazz concert with nary a word said about what was just heard. We enjoy talking about art experiences.
- *Representation.* Art often represents real or imaginary things. Although there is controversy about whether absolute instrumental music can refer to anything extramusical, a great deal of music—including program music, opera, and songs—refers to *something* outside the music.
- *Special focus.* Often, the way we experience art is 'bracketed off' from everyday life, as performers and listeners alike intently concentrate their energies on the music event. In these cases, and even in many private musical experiences, music is in the foreground rather than in the background.
- *Expressive individuality.* Art provides opportunities for individual expression. This can be somewhat more restricted, as in ensemble performances, or considerably more free, as in solo performances, improvisation, or composition.
- *Emotional saturation.* Although the issue is complicated, as we discovered in Chapter 5, there is no denying a connection between art and emotions. Whether music represents emotions or we actually experience them or however it is characterized, there is an emotionality to the art experience.
- *Intellectual challenge.* Art can provoke, stimulate, tease, or confuse. However, "the full exercise of mental capacities is in itself a source of aesthetic pleasure."[12] The brevity of a three-minute Schubert lied and dramatic scope of a four-hour Wagner opera pose infinite opportunities for us to stretch our cognitive muscles.
- *Art traditions and institutions.* All cultures give significance to art in various ways through their customs, rituals, and institutional practices. Frequently, we listen to or perform music in concert halls or in jazz clubs, we dress appropriately and act in a particular, socially-approved manner, such as not clapping between movements at classical concerts, but enthusiastically applauding after a solo ride in a jazz concert or actively participating in a rock concert.
- *Imaginative experience.* Those who produce and those who experience art utilize their imaginations. "Artistic experience takes place in the theater of the imagination."[13]

There are three things to note about this list. First, not everyone would agree with these characteristics of art. Second, any claim to universality must be qualified to mean that it is more likely to be found everywhere than not; there are always exceptions. Finally, we can find many, if not all, of these characteristics in experiences other than art. We can admire skill in sports, for example, or find intellectual challenges in many realms, such as solving a mathematical problem. Nevertheless, for Dutton, at least, these are the common characteristics of art. Perhaps we can conclude our definitions of art with Monroe Beardsley's simpler answer when he said, "an artwork is an arrangement of conditions intended to be capable of affording an experience with marked aesthetic character."[14] This definition firmly connects art and aesthetics.

Regarding music specifically, Andrew Kania wrote that many philosophers are disinterested in coining a definition. Nevertheless, after reviewing inherent difficulties, he offered his own version: "Music is (1) any event [including silence] intentionally produced or organized (2) to be heard, and (3) *either* (a) to have some basic musical feature, such as pitch or rhythm, *or* (b) to be listened to for such features."[15] Ian Cross added the concept of *floating intentionality* to indicate that "music's meanings appear intimately bound to the contexts in which it is experienced."[16]

As we can see from even this brief smattering of examples, although philosophers and artists have made many attempts, there is still no consensus on a definition of art or music. If so many bright minds have failed to arrive at a satisfactory solution, perhaps you may be excused if you do not craft one yourself. While you do not necessarily need to create a perfect definition of music to have a music philosophy, issues may arise in which you will need to make some declarations. For example, if you say that rap/hip-hop is not music, you would have to explain why that is so. Or, are bird songs or thunderstorms music? Before you give up in disgust, maybe we should all take a cue from Louis Armstrong, who is reported to have said, "If you have to ask what jazz is, you'll never know" (source unknown).

What Does the Word 'Aesthetic' Mean?

Alexander Baumgarten coined the term 'aesthetics' in 1735 in an attempt to develop "an aesthetic theory (chiefly of poetry, but extensible to the other arts) based upon Cartesian principles and using the rationalistic deductive method, with formal definitions and derivations."[17] Although his conception is not the way most would construe the term aesthetics today, at least it did enter the lexicon at that time. One point worth noting before continuing with an exploration of the word 'aesthetic' is John Dewey's recognition that there is ambiguity in the meanings of aesthetic (or esthetic as he spelled it) and artistic.[18] Often, artistic refers to the production of art and aesthetic refers to perception and enjoyment. While most of the following definitions and discussions more frequently use the term in the sense of perceiving art rather than producing it, there is no reason why we cannot extend our understanding to include both senses.

Philosophers often use the word 'aesthetic' as an adjective. Rafael De Clercq, for example, wrote in describing aesthetic objects, "Prototypical *aesthetic properties* [*underlining* added here and following] include beauty, elegance, gracefulness, balance, harmony, delicacy, loveliness, and unity."[19] Other properties include powerfulness, vividness, boldness, or emotion words such as mournful, sad, angry; another consideration could be the position an artwork occupied in history, such as being original or influential. Maxine Greene made the point that an aesthetic object is not an external, physical thing, but that it is created in the mind. "The *aesthetic object* here means much more than the musical notes";[20] "it depends upon a living subject for its coming into being: that each work of art, in order to become an aesthetic object must be transmuted by a person into an event in his own life world."[21]

> "Art is the imposing of a pattern on experience, and our aesthetic enjoyment is recognition of the pattern."
> (Alfred North Whitehead)

Here are a few additional uses of the term aesthetic as an adjective. Jerome Stolnitz described the *aesthetic attitude* as "disinterested and sympathetic attention to and contemplation of any object of awareness whatever, for its own sake alone."[22] By 'disinterested' he meant that there is no ulterior purpose; aesthetic disinterestedness is often indicated by the phrase 'art for art's sake.' By 'sympathetic' he meant that one should engage the object with openness and readiness to meet it on its own terms. By this description, Stolnitz was willing to expand the concept of aesthetics to things/experiences beyond art.

As with everything else in philosophy, such a definition is not universally accepted. George Dickie, for example, thought that an aesthetic attitude was a myth, writing that disinterestedness "cannot properly be used to refer to a special kind of attention."[23] Even a century earlier, George Santayana wrote against the notion of disinterestedness.[24] Thus, few, if any, of these definitions have consensual agreement. Nevertheless, they give some flavor of what issues concern philosophers about aesthetics.

For Gerard Kneiter, "*Aesthetic sensitivity* is man's capacity to respond to the emotional values and cognitive meanings of art."[25] In searching for the basis of *aesthetic emotion*, Bell found it in 'significant form,' "the essential quality in a work of art, the quality that distinguishes works of art from all other classes of objects."[26] Monroe Beardsley's Instrumentalist definition of *aesthetic value* stated that it was "the capacity to produce an *aesthetic experience* of some magnitude."[27] Because the phrase 'aesthetic experience' is so central, it deserves its own section.

What Is an Aesthetic Experience?

In the first edition of his book on aesthetics, Beardsley (1958) described five aspects of an aesthetic experience:[28]

- First, attention is focused firmly on the art experience.
- Second, the experience involves a degree of intensity; that is, a vibrancy in expressive elements.
- Third, the aesthetic experience is one of unity or coherence; the various parts fit together.
- Fourth, the experience is complete in itself; it does not blend into the rest of our experience, but rather seems to stand alone.
- Fifth, there is a sense of 'make believe' about an aesthetic experience; for example, in music we may have a sense of movement, but nothing moves.

Gerard Kneiter also identified five aspects of a musical aesthetic experience, including:[29]

- *Focus.* Unless one is focused intently on the art experience, one is not likely to have an aesthetic experience.
- *Perception.* During an aesthetic experience with music, one perceives melody, harmony, rhythm, and so on.
- *Affect.* Both physiological change and feeling reactions occur during an aesthetic experience.
- *Cognition.* Thoughtful engagement with music involves such cognitive processes as analysis, synthesis, abstraction, generalization, or evaluation.
- *Cultural matrix.* Musical experiences occur in a particular social-cultural environment.

Perhaps another way to gain an understanding of an aesthetic experience is through its opposite: anesthetic, "nothingness, no life, no feeling, no humanness."[30] When we go to the dentist, we may receive an anesthetic to deaden or dull our senses. By contrast, the aesthetic experience is one in which we are fully alert and completely absorbed. Consider two people sitting side-by-side at a concert. Suppose that one listener is not paying attention to what is happening on stage. According to both Beardsley and Kneiter, this person is not going to have an aesthetic experience. After all, if he is not focused on the music, he will hardly be able to satisfy the other criteria. The second listener, however, focuses intently on the music. Furthermore, she perceives the musical elements of melody, rhythm, and so on. She engages both cognitively and affectively. Her experience is holistic rather than fragmented; she may be having an aesthetic experience. Note, however, that this does not necessarily mean that the person having the aesthetic experience is having a *better* experience. For now, let us simply agree that it is a different experience.

What Are Aesthetic Values?

People all over the world value music. Why? Alan Goldman wrote that there are instrumental (i.e., functional) values, such as therapeutic uses in music therapy, and social uses such as for weddings and funerals. Aesthetic value, however, is intrinsic, not instrumental. "We can define the aesthetic value of music as the value of the way in which music sounds when experienced with understanding."[31] We need to have a direct experience with music before we can gain the intrinsic value. We understand music when we can follow it, relate what is happening *now* to what has happened previously in the piece, organize perceptions, anticipate what is about to happen, and so on. Understanding means grasping meanings—not external meanings, since in pure music there are none, only internal or musical meanings. "All perception and cognition seek order in complex data, and success in actively finding it is pleasurable."[32]

Echoing Beardsley's fifth point that aesthetic experiences have an element of 'make believe,' Goldman wrote about the other-worldliness of music. Where novels create a world of fiction and paintings refer to things or to forms (e.g., squares, etc.) that exist, "a musical work is therefore a self-contained world that provides a more thorough escape from the everyday world in which to exercise our human capacities than the other arts provide."[33] "Its peculiar value lies not only in its providing us models of perfect order that we seem to cooperate in creating while listening to them, but also in the purity of its revelation of the creative mind itself."[34]

Aesthetic judgments come into play when determining aesthetic values. Ever since Immanuel Kant's *Critique of Aesthetic Judgment*, philosophers have argued and discussed various positions. Kant's notion was that "aesthetic pleasure is shown to reside in forms or appearances *per se*, and not in an object's real-world status or connections."[35] Since the purpose of this chapter is not a historical review, let us move now to consider a fairly modern conception. Roger Scruton wrote that aesthetic judgments are not simply made on determinations of beautiful/ugly or good/bad, rather they are made:[36]

- in terms denoting aesthetic values, including beautiful, sublime, elegant, ugly, unsightly;
- in terms describing music's effect on us, such as moving, exciting, uplifting;
- in terms that describe the aesthetic character of something without conveying an evaluation, as a material object, an object of perception, or as an aesthetic object of interest, as in "the sharply outlined theme of a fugue by Bach, the balance, intricacy, ardour, or sadness of a melody by Brahms";[37]
- in approval terms such as good, great, a triumph;
- in terms of the virtues and vices of a work of art, as in sentimental, cruel, vapid, or noble.

What Can We Gain from Art?

What is the value of art? What do we expect to get from it? Gordon Graham wrote that two central values of music are that it brings pleasure and expresses emotions.[38] However, he found limitations in each of these values and concluded that the uniqueness of music was its greatest aesthetic value. He argued that while photography could theoretically replace painting, and cinema could replace theatre, nothing could replace the experience of music. "Music is unique in providing us with extended structures of organized sound by means of which we may explore human experience."[39] "It is by enlarging and exploring this dimension of experience that music assists us in understanding better what it is to be a human being."[40] This is reminiscent of Sister Wendy's response, as given in Chapter 3, that what we get out of art is to become more fully human.

Bennett Reimer used similar language when he argued that "the arts offer meaningful, cognitive experiences unavailable in any other way, and that such experiences are necessary for all people if their essential humanness is to be realized."[41] Scruton wrote:

> Art is the record of human ideals, and in abstract music, those ideals concern the higher order of our feelings—the order that is free from pretense, which confronts hardship in the way that we hear Beethoven confronting hardship in the first movement of the Ninth Symphony;[42] ♪ which gives itself completely as Mozart does in his instrumental works; or which wins from tragedy the consolations of tenderness that Schubert finds in the sublime C major Quintet.[43] ♪

In a discussion of greatness in art, Louis Reid acknowledged that there are no objective, scientific principles by which to determine the greatest works of art. However, we can, he said, distinguish great works of art from good ones.

> In some of Bach's Chorales and in some of his great Passion music, as well as in some of Beethoven's later work (to cite but two names), our intuition tells us that there is embodied this range and comprehensiveness of experience convergent upon, and making vivid and real, some of the profoundest values of human life.[44]

Jerrold Levinson echoed this sentiment in a statement he wrote about listening to Beethoven's Piano Sonata, No. 30, Op. 109:[45] ♪

> when we hear such music adequately, we understand something about human life and the process of living. . . . This understanding is its own reward, apart from any quantum of pleasure or satisfaction it brings with it. The sonata Op. 109 is not music to enjoy, one wants to say; it is music to commune with and be transfigured by.[46]

Levinson further identified three aspects of profound music, including:

- an exploration of emotions and the inner psychological world in a more powerful or insightful way than other music;
- references to extramusical modes of growth and development more so than other music;
- concerns with critically important aspects of the human experience, such as death, the meaning of life, and so on.[47]

He also wrote that profound music might reveal something about life of particular importance.

As examples of what many might call profound music, consider Johannes Brahms's *Four Serious Songs*[48] ♫ and Richard Strauss's *Four Last Songs*.[49] ♫ Brahms wrote his songs when his dear friend Clara Schumann was nearing death, and he was ill and in the last year of his own life.

> In July he wrote to her daughters Marie and Eugenie; 'Such texts have long preoccupied me; and although I did not expect having to receive worse news about your mother, something often speaks and works within the human being, almost unknown to us, and this may well sometimes resound as poetry or music.'[50]

Strauss also wrote his *Four Last Songs* just a year before his own death in 1949. The titles of the four songs are 'Spring,' 'September,' 'Going to Sleep,' and 'At Sunset.' The texts of the first three songs are from poems by Hermann Hesse (1877–1962). In the final song, from a poem by Joseph von Eichendorff (1788–1857), the opening words are: "Through trouble and joy we have walked hand in hand; we can rest from our wanderings now."[51] Although the words of both sets of songs are meaningful, according to some it is the musical settings that give them such profundity.

Many philosophers prefer to focus on pure, absolute instrumental music, pondering how it is that mere musical sounds, without text, program, or extramusical referents, can be profound. Some contend that instrumental music can be profound; for example, John Sullivan felt that the Beethoven string quartets, especially the late ones, were profound works.[52] However, others demurred. In his book *Music Alone*, Peter Kivy concluded that absolute music cannot be profound.[53] Years later he refined and restated his position this way; music must:

> (1) have a profound subject matter and (2) treat this profound subject matter in a way adequate to its profundity—which is to say (a) profound things about this subject matter and (b) do it at a very high level of artistic or aesthetic excellence . . .[54]

He felt that pure instrumental music is not *about* anything and thus could not be profound.

Although Kivy received several criticisms (e.g., David White),[55] it was an article by Stephen Davies that caused him to respond with a rebuttal. Davies felt that absolute music could be profound "for what it exemplifies and thereby reveals about the capacities of the human mind."[56] "More than this, the greatest masterpieces can be revealing of human capacities for representing, understanding, controlling, balancing, and reflecting on the emotions, and thereby exhibit the affective dimension of our nature, as well as our more purely cognitive side."[57]

Kivy's response to Davies in a nutshell is this:

> I argue in the present paper that Davies's attempt to rescue profundity for absolute music will not work, because it does not allow what I take to be the crucial distinction between great works of absolute music that *are* profound and great works of absolute music that are *not*. In other words, it has the unwelcome implication that all great works of absolute music are profound works.[58]

At the end of his article, Kivy says, "In my view, absolute music at its greatest can be profoundly moving and profoundly arresting; but not in spite of lacking profundity; rather, in part, *because of it*."[59] Undoubtedly the argument will continue. In the meantime, it is important for you to make up your own mind.

Who Determines Aesthetic Values?

Recall from Chapter 4 our brief discussion of David Hume's point that only qualified judges should make determinations of beauty, now expanded to include assessments of aesthetic value. Set aside, for a moment, questions of authority: Who is qualified to make judgments? What if different experts disagree?, and so on. Instead, let us consider a rather simplistic model, called the Ring Model, that may help you in determining your role in this process.

> "All aesthetic judgment is really cultural evaluation."
>
> (Susan Sontag)

Suppose for a moment that you have received a package in the mail from a recently deceased distant relative that contains an item he or she bequeathed to you. Upon opening the package, you discover a ring. More than likely you would have several, simultaneous reactions. At least three of them can be artificially lifted out of the context of the situation and examined in more detail.

One reaction you might have would be one of almost immediate like/dislike. You might think or utter such comments as: "Oh, what a pretty ring," or "Ugh, what a gaudy piece of jewelry." Another reaction might be one of trying on the ring. A third reaction might be to wonder how much the ring was worth.

Considering each of these reactions separately, the first one identified was one of personal like/dislike. For example, your feelings about the person to whom the ring originally belonged may color your judgment. If you did not care for Aunt Bessie or were particularly close to Grandpa Smith, your reactions would be different. Many external forces may shape your like/dislike reactions, such as family background, peer pressure, and socioeconomic status; however, such reactions are still primarily internal. A private decision only you can make will determine the ring's personal value for you.

The second reaction was a functional one—does it fit? Other functional reactions might include the gender identity of the ring and the particular type—school class ring, party ring, engagement ring, wedding band, and so on. A ring's functional purpose will vary according to several aspects, including how well the ring suits the intended purpose.

Regarding the third reaction, most persons are not qualified to establish how much a ring is worth. Therefore, to determine the monetary value of a ring, you must consult one who is qualified by training and experience. In determining the value of a ring, a jeweler or appraiser must base her decision not on her own personal likes and dislikes, though they may inevitably come into play, nor on the functional aspects of the ring, but on several more objective criteria. The appraiser must consider the kind, size, and quality of materials used, the craftsmanship, history, and rarity of the ring, among other things. An exquisitely fashioned or one-of-a-kind heirloom ring with a large diamond is likely to be worth more money than one of the thousands of relatively nondescript high school class rings produced yearly.

While personal, functional, and monetary values are related, they are not necessarily the same and may fluctuate independently. One might have a sentimental attachment (high personal value) to a ring that no longer fits (low functional value) and that is worth very little (low monetary value). High value in one area will not necessarily influence the value of the remaining areas.

In making value judgments in music, three similar conditions might apply—that is, there are personal, functional, and musical values to be considered. First, a value may be assigned to music on the basis of like/dislike; the music we like has higher personal value than the music we dislike. Each person makes his own choices and, again, these choices are the result of all manner of complex influences—peers, disc jockeys, family, opportunities, training, and so on. Nevertheless, there is great variety in the individuality of our preferences. We are free to like and dislike what we wish to and furthermore have the right to change our minds.

Value may be assigned to music on the basis of its functionality, that is, on the basis of how well it fits particular circumstances. Certain musical styles function best in certain situations. Thus, a Bartok string quartet does not function well in a dance club and a Chopin waltz is not useful for helping a band march down the street. Functional value may also be determined by such considerations as how well the music is suited to performers' ages and ability levels.

Finally, musical value may be assigned to a piece of music based upon the musical qualities it possesses. Based on the ring analogy, an expert, one who has training and experience, is the person qualified to assign musical values. Just as a jeweler determines the worth of a ring by predetermined criteria, so a musical expert can evaluate a musical composition based on similar criteria. For example, one might consider compositional craftsmanship, creativity, profundity of content, and so on. None of these aspects can be used single-handedly to determine a composition's musical value. However, an expert may use them collectively to make an assessment.

The musical value assigned to a composition by an expert does not necessarily indicate the personal or functional value. For example, a Mahler symphony may be determined to have high musical value, but it has limited suitability for the elementary school classroom and it is doubtful that many children would like it. Similarly, a marching band director may choose a piece of music that he feels is not a great work of art but that fits perfectly the theme of a half-time show; the students' personal reactions to the piece are likely to be independent of either of these considerations.

Transferring the ring analogy to the question of musical or aesthetic valuing seems to imply that there is a set, predetermined standard for judging the musical value of a composition. While, as we have seen, various authors have attempted to set forth criteria by which the quality of music should be determined, the result is that there is, of course, no final, fixed scale by which one can permanently quantify the musical value of a given composition. It would be naive and simplistic to think that there are any absolute answers of this sort. The lack of final and absolute truth does not make it impossible to make some relative judgments, however. In fact, what this entire discussion suggests is that *you* are the person in your situation who by training and experience is qualified to make aesthetic judgments.

You probably perform and listen to a great deal of music for the simple reason that it brings you pleasure. If you enjoy a particular style of music, no matter what it is, that is the end of it. You do not need to defend or explain your choices. Also, throughout your career, you will most likely encounter numerous situations in which the circumstances will dictate or influence the music you choose. Singing at a dear friend's wedding or conducting a middle school choir at a school Thanksgiving program will necessitate particular choices that may or may not reflect your personal preferences. Finally, as a composer, conductor, performer, teacher, or therapist, you have an obligation to spend time thinking carefully about aesthetic values. Once you have a clearly articulated philosophy, you will need to use that philosophy in an intentional, applied way. You, then, become an expert who makes aesthetic choices.

Experimental Aesthetics

Recall the question posed at the outset concerning experiments by Birkhoff and Madsen, Brittin, and Capperella-Sheldon: 'What exactly were they measuring?' Now that we have a better understanding of the phrase 'aesthetic response,' let us return to the notion of studying this phenomenon. Can science add anything useful to the discussion? At least some people think so. "The potential for the cognitive sciences to inform long-standing philosophical debates has not gone unnoticed by many philosophers working on the aesthetics of music."[60] Dustin Stokes wrote that "the explanatory goals and resources of both aesthetics and cognitive science should expand to include those of the other."[61]

Birkhoff expressed his aesthetic measure in a ratio based on order and complexity:[62]

Aesthetic Measure = Order divided by Complexity

He attempted to quantify the feeling of value that comes from attending to increasing complexity in an artwork. Harold McWhinnie reviewed a number of experiments designed to test Birkhoff's formula.[63] Most of the studies involved visual art and they met with only mixed success. As Paul Farnsworth put it, Birkhoff's formula and the follow-up experiments "have not captured the interests of any substantial number of aestheticians."[64] Although Gustav Fechner founded Experimental Aesthetics as the second oldest branch of psychology in 1876,[65] James Mainwaring felt that it had restricted value for "it can supply no single rule whereby the artist can create that which is beautiful and no single principle by which beauty can be judged."[66] Conversely, after reviewing a number of studies in experimental aesthetics, Adrian North and David Hargreaves concluded that research does offer some worthwhile insights.[67]

As mentioned previously, music psychologist Carl Seashore published a book in 1947 entitled *In Search of Beauty: A Scientific Approach to Musical Esthetics*. He stated, "Science can clarify and define essential concepts in esthetics."[68] To that end, he conducted experiments on vibrato, deviations from the musical score (e.g., phrasing, ornaments, musical license), timbre, harmony (consonance), rhythm, aspects of beauty in piano performance, violin performance, and in song. He also conducted experiments on subjective variables, such as like/dislike, musical imagery, musical intelligence, musical temperament, and artistic talent.

Following all these experiments, Seashore stated that "love of music, for those who really do love it, rests upon five fundamental grounds: the physiological, the perceptual, the esthetics, the social, and the creative."[69] We have a body/brain that responds to music. We can perceive beautiful elements in music.

> "Music is a language of emotion."
> (Carl Seashore)

We engage in aesthetic behaviors, such as admiring the harmonic structure, melodic progressions, and so on. Music conveys emotions and as such has great social value (e.g., in worship, romance, and entertainment). Music furnishes a medium of expression without ulterior motive. This is play and "through it we express our love, our fears, our sympathy, our aspirations, our feelings of fellowship, our communion with the Divine."[70]

To complete this section, let us finally return to the other experimental study of aesthetics mentioned in the opening of this chapter, the study by Madsen, Brittin, and Capperella-Sheldon.[71] They asked 30 faculty members and graduate students from a large university school of music to indicate perceived aesthetic response while listening to a 20-minute excerpt from Puccini's *La Bohème*[72] ♪ by manipulating the dial on a Continuous Response Digital Interface (CRDI). Each listener made an individual determination of what an aesthetic response was and moved the dial from negative to positive along a 256-degree arc. They also indicated whether they had an aesthetic experience during the listening. All listeners reported having an aesthetic experience, and while the dial movements were reflective of individual differences, there were 'aesthetic response' clusters at similar places in the music.

Madsen and colleagues subsequently conducted a series of experiments concerned with various elements of an aesthetic experience. In one such study, for example, he asked 50 musicians to rate the first movement of Haydn's Symphony No. 104[73] ♪ along two dimensions: arousal (i.e., relaxing–exciting) and affect (i.e., ugly–beautiful), manipulating the cursor of a two-dimensional CRDI.[74] The relationship between the two dimensions was moderately inverse, indicating a nearly mirror-image relationship between them. These results lead to many ensuing questions, calling for more research.

The Golden Mean

The Golden Mean is a mathematical ratio that many composers have used either intuitively or intentionally. The Golden Mean is a ratio of 0.618 derived from dividing any number by the one following in the Fibonacci Series. The Fibonacci Series starts with 0 and 1. Adding these two together, then continuing in the following fashion: 0+1=1, 1+1=2, 1+2=3, 2+3=5, 3+5=8, and so on—leads to this series: 0, 1, 2, 3, 5, 8, 13, 21, 34, 55, . . . Dividing any number by the following one gradually settles around 0.618 or what is called the Golden Mean.

A musical climax at approximately two-thirds through the movement or other uses of the Fibonacci Series have been found in the music of de la Halle, Machaut, Dufay, Bach, Mozart, Beethoven, Chopin, Bartok, Stockhausen, Nono, and Krenek among others.[75] Of course, composers have used many other mathematical structures in their music. The idea is not that there is only one particular way of composing, but that there is most often a rational basis for it. Alexander Voloshinov called symmetry a superprinciple of both science and art, and discussed approximate symmetry as a means of avoiding the creation of artworks perceived as static and frigid.[76]

Berlyne's Arousal Theory

Perhaps the person who contributed most to experimental aesthetics was Canadian psychologist D. E. Berlyne.[77] Berlyne's hypothesis was that aesthetic preferences are determined by physiological arousal. Arousal potential comes from three types: (1) Psychophysical variables such as pitch, tempo, or loudness; higher, faster, louder music has more arousal potential. (2) Ecological variables are related to past associations with reward or punishment and the meaningfulness of the musical experience; the possibility of a richly rewarding musical experience increases arousal. (3) Collative variables—the "most significant of all for aesthetics"[78]—include properties of the music such as complexity, energy, predictability, and tension/release. As illustrated in his adaptation of the Wundt inverted U-curve (Fig. 6.1), maximum pleasure increases, up to an optimal point, as collative variables increase. If they increase past an optimal point, maximum pleasure, or what he called hedonic value, decreases. Maximum pleasure is not static, that is, it is altered through many personal and situational variables, such as age, training, experience, and so on. For example, what we found enjoyable as children is generally less pleasing as we mature and gain more musical understanding.

Preference for Prototype Theory

Personal musical preferences are a central concept in aesthetic choices. One theoretical construct, with a foundation in cognitive psychology and some supportive evidence from experimental studies,

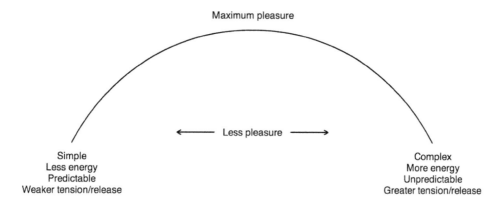

Figure 6.1 Maximum pleasure is based upon an optional level of arousal potential.

Source: Hodges, D. *Music in the Human Experience: An Introduction to Music Psychology.* New York: Routledge, 2011, p. 202. Used with permission.

is the Preference for Prototype Theory (PPT).[79] According to PPT, listeners match incoming music to previously formed models or prototypes. Preferred music is represented in the brain in well-defined schema. Over time, we form discrete categories for features of the music we hear most often and that we like. An adolescent who has listened to hundreds (and probably thousands) of hours of popular music has established well-defined categories for certain timbres, rhythms, and other features that make up the preferred style. While scanning a radio dial, she could rapidly determine which music matches and does not match the music she wants to hear. In fact, in one study, listeners could identify with surprising accuracy (76% overall) the appropriate genre from among classical, jazz, country, metal, and rap/hip-hop excerpts that were as brief as one-eighth of a second.[80] They were significantly more accurate with styles they preferred than non-preferred styles.

The more fluently listeners can process various features of music they hear, the more positive their aesthetic judgments.[81] This does not mean, of course, that you cannot enjoy or find aesthetic pleasure in unfamiliar music. It does mean, however, that you are more likely to have an aesthetic experience with music that matches your preferred prototypes. PPT is resonant with the arousal mediating theory of Berlyne, and as we shall see in a subsequent section, is also supported by brain research.

Chills as an Indicator of Aesthetic Response

Chills, sometimes referred to as thrills or frisson, refer to "the shiver that usually starts at the back of the neck, with piloerection [goose bumps], and spreads down the back and arms, sometimes reaching other parts of the body."[82] In an early study, Avram Goldstein found that approximately half of those he surveyed (*n* = 249) experienced thrills to emotionally arousing music.[83] Numbers vary from study-to-study as to how many people experience chills. John Sloboda reported that 90% of people surveyed experienced chills while listening to music over a period of years,[84] a figure that was confirmed by Paul Silvia and Emily Nusbaum, who obtained a figure of 92%.[85]

Numerous factors undoubtedly play into the likelihood of having chills or goose bumps while listening to music. Surveying people is one way of finding out, but Experience Sampling Methods (ESM) provides a more naturalistic way to approach everyday music listening. In ESM, participants are contacted randomly throughout the day and asked to respond to what they are experiencing at that moment. Modern software allows people to be contacted on their cell phones. Using this approach, researchers found that 106 college students who responded to ten daily contacts were listening to music 22% of the time they were surveyed.[86] Of these 106 participants, 79 reported at least one chill episode during a random call and the average was 3.73 chills. A reported feeling of happiness or sadness was more conducive to chills than being worried. Thus, existing emotional states were important factors. Another key finding was that people were more likely to experience chills to music that they selected rather than to music playing in the environment beyond their control.

Juslin's BRECVEMA Model

In Chapter 5: Emotion, reference was made to a model developed by Patrik Juslin and Daniel Västfjäll that contained six mechanisms to explain musical emotions. In a recent paper, Juslin presented his BRECVEMA model, a revised version that contains eight mechanisms that operate in addition to cognitive appraisal:[87]

- Brain Stem Reflex: responses to sudden sounds, such as a cymbal crash, that lead to arousal and emotional responses such as surprise.
- Rhythmic Entrainment: bodily rhythms (e.g., heart rate) entrain or synchronize with musical rhythms leading to feelings of communion and being connected.
- Evaluative Conditioning: emotional responses arise because a specific piece of music has been associated with certain events; for example, in the United States, Elgar's *Pomp and Circumstance* March No. 1[88] ♫ is often associated with graduation from high school or college and its attendant feelings.
- Emotional Contagion: the listener mimics the feelings expressed in the music.
- Visual Imagery: emotions arise when inner visual images are conjured up as a result of the music.
- Episodic Memory: emotions are induced when the music calls to mind past experiences.
- Musical Expectancy: emotions arise when predictions about musical movement are met in unusual ways or not met at all.
- Aesthetic Judgment: aesthetic emotions arise as a result of aesthetic judgments.

For each of these mechanisms, Juslin identifies relevant brain structures and evolutionary development. Most mechanisms are supported by research; others are awaiting confirmation based on research strategies that have been suggested.

Neuroaesthetics

Neuroaesthetics is a relatively new study of the aesthetics of art using neuroscience.[89] A great deal of the work in neuroaesthetics has been done in visual art. For example, V. S. Ramachandran and William Hirstein proposed eight laws of aesthetic principles based on the brain circuitry involved in processing visual images.[90] However, several of their principles, such as perceptual grouping, perceptual problem solving, and symmetry, may be applicable to music as well, as reviewed by Mari Tervaniemi.[91]

Rather than providing an extensive overview here, let us consider one study as an exemplar. Before we get to the actual experiment, two brief detours are necessary, one to describe the Default Mode Network (DMN) and another to introduce Network Science. The DMN is a network of brain regions that is more active during inwardly directed consciousness, such as during prayer, meditation, daydreaming, or mind wandering.[92] When we turn our attention outward, the DMN tends to submerge as other areas of the brain become more active. The DMN has been implicated in the processing of autobiographical memories, self-relevant emotions, and empathetic awareness of others.[93] One indication of this is that the DMN is impaired in cognitive deficits such as Alzheimer's disease, autism, and schizophrenia in which a sense of self is compromised.[94] Expressed in more poetic than scientific language, we might say that the Default Mode Network is a part of the brain that identifies a person as a human being in general and as a specific human being in particular; it is the seat of conscious awareness[95] and personal identity.

Now let us briefly consider Network Science. In the past several decades, enormous strides have been made in brain imaging methodologies. PET (positron emission tomography) and fMRI (functional magnetic resonance imaging) are two that have been applied extensively in investigations of music processing. While these approaches indicate those parts of the brain involved in playing the piano[96] or in processing simultaneous visual and auditory information as conductors do,[97] for example, they do not provide a means of showing how the various brain regions communicate with each other in real time. Network Science is a novel way of analyzing fMRI data to indicate connectivity.[98]

With information on the DMN and Network Science as background, let us now consider an experiment in which 21 listeners were recruited for their musical preferences: five each preferred classical, country, rap/hip-hop, and six preferred rock.[99] Inside a brain scanner, they indicated their preferences as they listened to five-minute selections of these four genres plus an excerpt from Chinese opera selected to be an unfamiliar example. In addition, each participant heard a personally selected 'all-time favorite,' for a total listening time of 30 minutes. Network analysis indicated that listening to their personal favorite piece of music strongly activated the Default Mode Network.

Once again, to put the findings into more poetic than scientific language, listening to personally selected favorite music engaged the network of the brain that first identifies the listener as a human being and second as someone with a personal history and core emotional memories. Whenever we listen to music that has a deep and profound impact on us, we are tapping into the neural resources involved in our personal understanding of the human condition. Thus, the 'Sister Wendy philosophy' discussed at the end of Chapter 3 has substantiation from modern neuroscience. As the neurologist Oliver Sacks wrote,

> In the last 20 years, there have been huge advances here [in neuromusical research], but we have, as yet, scarcely touched the question of why music, for better or worse, has so much power. It is a question that goes to the heart of being human.[100]

Summary and Thought Questions

This is a long chapter with much food for thought. My advice at this point would be not to worry too much initially about the smallest details of aesthetics. Rather, continue thinking about the musical experiences in performing, listening, creating, teaching, and so on that move you the most. Think of very specific instances when you have had a peak experience and reflect on what it was that made the experience so memorable. As you move through the rest of the book, you will have numerous occasions to encounter aesthetics, and each time you will have the opportunity to refine and clarify your understanding.

1. Do you agree with Kania's definition of music? Would you add, delete, or modify anything?
2. How would you describe an aesthetic experience? Rather than conducting this as a dry, academic exercise, think of some of the most profound, sublime musical experiences you have had. Would you call those *aesthetic*? Why?
3. Thinking back to the two previous chapters, what roles do beauty and emotion play in your concept of aesthetics?
4. What is the value of an aesthetic experience to you? Are aesthetic experiences a frequent and important part of your life? What would be missing from your life if you could no longer have an aesthetic experience?
5. Asked in another way, what do you gain from aesthetic experiences? Are those who live without aesthetic experiences missing anything of importance?
6. Previously, it was stated that an aesthetic experience is not necessarily better than a non-aesthetic experience. Under what circumstances, if any, might either an aesthetic or non-aesthetic experience be considered better than the other?
7. Is everyone qualified to make aesthetic judgments or does it take a certain amount of education or experience? Is there a difference between making personal aesthetic judgments and judgments that relate to others, for example, in the way a teacher might make aesthetic judgments about repertoire her students might study? Can you give some examples of aesthetic judgments that you have made recently?
8. Identify what seems to you to be great absolute music, that is, pure instrumental music without program, text, or any extramusical references. Are any of these profound works? What, in your mind, makes them profound?
9. Is the extant body of research on musical aesthetics convincing? What do you wish researchers would do differently or study next?

Considerations of aesthetics have appeared so frequently in various music philosophies that you will encounter them repeatedly throughout the remainder of this book. However, as we will see in Chapter 17, David Elliott and others argue that aesthetics are not an important part of the musical experience. Thus, while there is no absolute requirement that you incorporate aesthetics as part of your philosophy, you will want to consider very carefully whether and to what extent it will be included. In the next chapter, we will see how philosophers have tended to organize themselves in a grand overview of music philosophy. Perhaps this review will give you some ideas of where you might want to head in your pursuit of your own views.

Notes

1 George Birkhoff, *Aesthetic Measure* (Cambridge, MA: Harvard University Press, 1933).
2 Clifford Madsen, Ruth Brittin, and Deborah Capperella-Sheldon, "An Empirical Method for Measuring the Aesthetic Experience to Music," *Journal of Research in Music Education* 41, no. 1 (1993): 57–69.
3 Christopher Janaway, "Beauty," *The Oxford Companion to Philosophy*, ed. Ted Honderich (Oxford: Oxford University Press, 1995), 80.

4   Richard Anderson, "From Calliope's Sisters," in *Aesthetics: The Big Questions*, ed. Carolyn Korsmeyer (Malden, MA: Blackwell, 1998), 19.

5   Carolyn Korsmeyer, *Aesthetics: The Big Questions* (Malden, MA: Blackwell, 1998).

6   Susan Feagin and Patrick Maynard, *Aesthetics* (Oxford: Oxford University Press, 1997), 5.

7   Abbé Batteux, "The Fine Arts Reduced to a Single Principle," in *Aesthetics*, ed. Susan Feagin and Patrick Maynard, trans. Robert Walters (Oxford: Oxford University Press, 1746/1997), 104.

8   Leo Tolstoy, *What Is Art?*, trans. Almyer Maude (Indianapolis: Liberal Arts Press, 1896/1960), 51.

9   Denis Dutton, *The Art Instinct* (Oxford: Oxford University Press, 2009).

10 Jerrold Levinson, *The Pleasures of Aesthetics: Philosophical Essays* (Ithaca, NY: Cornell University Press, 1996).

11 Dutton, *The Art Instinct*, 54.

12 Ibid., 57.

13 Ibid., 58–59.

14 Monroe Beardsley, *Aesthetics: Problems in the Philosophy of Criticism, 2nd ed.* (Indianapolis, IN: Hackett, 1981), xix.

15 Andrew Kania, "Definition," in *The Routledge Companion to Philosophy and Music*, ed. Theodore Gracyk and Andrew Kania (London: Routledge, 2011), 12.

16 Ian Cross, "The Evolutionary Nature of Musical Meaning," *Musicae Scientiae*, Special Issue: Music and Evolution (2009): 180.

17 Monroe Beardsley, *Aesthetics from Classical Greece to the Present* (Tuscaloosa, AL: The University of Alabama Press, 1966), 157.

18 John Dewey, *Art as Experience* (New York: Perigree Books, 1934/1980).

19 Rafael De Clercq, "Aesthetic Properties," in *The Routledge Companion to Philosophy and Music*, ed. Theodore Gracyk and Andrew Kania (London: Routledge, 2011), 144.

20 Maxine Greene, "Teaching for Aesthetic Experience," in *Toward an Aesthetic Education* (Washington, DC: Music Educators National Conference, 1971), 23.

21 Ibid., 24.

22 Jerome Stolnitz, "The Aesthetic Attitude," in *Aesthetics: The Big Questions*, ed. Carolyn Korsmeyer (Malden, MA: Blackwell, 1998), 80.

23 George Dickie, "The Myth of the Aesthetic Attitude," *American Philosophical Quarterly* 1, no. 1 (1964): 60.

24 George Santayana, *The Sense of Beauty: Being the Outline of Aesthetic Theory* (New York: Dover, 1896).

25 Gerard Kneiter, "The Nature of Aesthetic Education," in *Toward an Aesthetic Education* (Washington, DC: Music Educators National Conference, 1971), 3.

26 Clive Bell, "Significant Form," in *Introductory Readings in Aesthetics*, ed. John Hospers (New York: The Free Press, 1913/1969), 87.

27 Monroe Beardsley, "The Instrumentalist Theory of Aesthetic Value," in *Introductory Readings in Aesthetics*, ed. John Hospers (New York: The Free Press, 1969), 318.

28 Monroe Beardsley, *Aesthetics* (New York: Harcourt, Brace & World, 1958).

29 Kneiter, "The Nature of Aesthetic Education," 3–5.

30 Harold Abeles, Charles Hoffer, and Robert Klotman, *Foundations of Music Education, 2nd ed.* (New York: Schirmer Books, 1994), 76.

31 Alan Goldman, "Value," in *The Routledge Companion to Philosophy and Music*, ed. Theodore Gracyk and Andrew Kania (London: Routledge, 2011), 157.

32 Ibid., 161.

33 Ibid., 162.

34 Ibid., 164.

35 Levinson, *The Pleasures of Aesthetics*, 4.

36 Roger Scruton, *The Aesthetics of Music* (Oxford: The Clarendon Press, 1997).

37 Ibid., 372.

38 Gordon Graham, *Philosophy of the Arts: An Introduction to Aesthetics, 3rd ed.* (London: Routledge, 2005).

39 Ibid., 101.

40 Gordon Graham, *Philosophy of the Arts: An Introduction to Aesthetics, 2nd ed.* (London: Routledge, 2000), 87.

41 Bennett Reimer, *A Philosophy of Music Education, 2nd ed.* (Englewood Cliffs, NJ: Prentice-Hall, 1989), 28–29.
42 Ludwig van Beethoven, Symphony No. 9 in d minor, Op. 125, performed by Leonard Bernstein conducting the Vienna Philharmonic Orchestra, http://www.youtube.com/watch?v=3MnGfhJCK_g.
43 Roger Scruton, *Understanding Music: Philosophy and Interpretation* (London: Continuum UK, 2009), 55. Franz Schubert, C Major Quintet, Op. 163, D. 956, performed by Isaac Stern, Alexander Schenider, Milton Katims, Pable Casals, and Paul Tortilier, http://www.youtube.com/watch?v=S3tmFhrOgNk.
44 Louis Reid, "Greatness," in *A Modern Book of Esthetics: An Anthology, 3rd ed.*, ed. Melvin Rader (New York: Holt, Rinehart, and Winston, 1960), 485.
45 Ludwig van Beethoven, Piano Sonata No. 30 in E Major, Op. 109, performed by Daniel Barenboim, https://www.youtube.com/watch?v=qqSetFrR-Xo.
46 Jerrold Levinson, *The Pleasures of Aesthetics*, 20–21.
47 Jerrold Levinson, "Musical Profundity Misplaced," *Journal of Aesthetics and Art Criticism* 50, no. 1 (1992): 58–60.
48 Johannes Brahms, *Four Serious Songs*, Op. 121, performed by Dietrich Fischer-Dieskau, baritone, and Gerald Moore, piano, https://www.youtube.com/watch?v=knHeiIjzvYU.
49 Richard Strauss, *Four Last Songs*, performed by Renée Fleming, soprano, and the Lucerne Festival Orchestra conducted by Claudio Abbado, https://www.youtube.com/watch?v=z5xFL-iFh0Q.
50 Eric Sams, *The Songs of Johannes Brahms* (Bolton, UK: Biddles, Guildford and King's Lynn, 2000), 20.
51 Jason Sundram, "Vier Letzte Lieder by Richard Strauss," *Program Notes*, 2004. http://jsundram.freeshell.org/ProgramNotes/Strauss_Leider.html.
52 J. Sullivan, *Beethoven: His Spiritual Development* (New York: Vintage Books, 1927).
53 Peter Kivy, *Music Alone: Philosophical Reflections on the Purely Musical Experience* (Ithaca, NY: Cornell University Press, 1990).
54 Peter Kivy, *Philosophies of Arts: An Essay in Differences* (Cambridge, UK: Cambridge University Press, 1997), 145.
55 David White, "Toward a Theory of Profundity in Music," *The Journal of Aesthetics and Art Criticism* 50, no. 1 (1992): 23–34.
56 Stephen Davies, "Profundity in Instrumental Music," *British Journal of Aesthetics* 42, no. 4 (2002): 343.
57 Ibid., 356.
58 Peter Kivy, "Another Go at Musical Profundity: Stephen Davies and the Game of Chess," *British Journal of Aesthetics* 43, no. 4 (2003): 401.
59 Ibid., 411.
60 Tom Cochrane, "Music, Emotions and the Influence of the Cognitive Sciences," *Philosophy Compass* 5, no. 11 (2010): 978.
61 Dustin Stokes, "Aesthetics and Cognitive Science," *Philosophy Compass* 4, no. 5 (2009): 727.
62 George Birkhoff, *Aesthetic Measure*, 12.
63 Harold McWhinnie, "A Review of Research on Aesthetic Measure," *Acta Pscyhologia* 28 (1968): 363–75.
64 Paul Farnsworth, *The Social Psychology of Music* (Ames, IA: The Iowa State University Press, 1969), 47.
65 Adrian North and David Hargreaves, *The Social and Applied Psychology of Music* (Oxford: Oxford University Press, 2008).
66 James Mainwaring, "An Examination of the Value of the Empirical Approach to Aesthetics," *British Journal of Psychology* 32, no. 2 (1941): 128.
67 North and Hargreaves, *The Social and Applied Psychology of Music*, 88.
68 Carl Seashore, *In Search of Beauty in Music: A Scientific Approach to Musical Aesthetics* (New York: The Ronald Press, 1947), 17.
69 Ibid., 378.
70 Ibid., 380.
71 Madsen, Brittin, and Capperella-Sheldon, "An Empirical Method for Measuring the Aesthetic Experience to Music."
72 Giacomo Puccini, *La Bohème*, performed by Carlos Kleiber conducting at La Scala, with Luciano Pavarotti and Ileana Cotrubas, http://www.youtube.com/watch?v=kHAS7r8Pd0k.
73 Franz Haydn, Symphony No. 104 in D Major, H 1/104, performed by Mariss Jansons conducting the Bavarian Radio Symphony Orchestra, https://www.youtube.com/watch?v=zRfGwzHCSSU.

74 Clifford Madsen, "Emotion versus Tension in Haydn's Symphony No. 104 as Measured by the Two-dimensional Continuous Response Digital Interface," *Journal of Research in Music Education* 46, no. 4 (1998): 546–54.

75 Jonathan Kramer, "The Fibonacci Series in Twentieth-Century Music," *Journal of Music Theory* 17, no. 1 (1973): 110–48. Newman Powell, "Fibonacci and the Golden Mean: Rabbits, Rumbas, and Rondeaux," *Journal of Music Theory* 23, no. 2 (1979): 227–73. Margaret Sandresky, "The Golden Section in Three Byzantine Motets of Dufay," *Journal of Music Theory* 25, no. 2 (1981): 291–306. Alexander Voloshinov, "Symmetry as a Superprinciple of Science and Art," *Leonardo* 29, no. 2 (1996): 109–13.

76 Voloshinov, "Symmetry as a Superprinciple of Science and Art."

77 Daniel Berlyne, *Aesthetics and Psychobiology* (New York: Appleton-Century-Crofts, 1971). Daniel Berlyne, ed., *Studies in the New Experimental Aesthetics: Steps Toward an Objective Psychology of Aesthetic Appreciation* (Washington, DC: Hemisphere Publishing, 1974).

78 Berlyne, *Aesthetics and Psychobiology*, 69.

79 Colin Martindale and Kathleen Moore, "Priming, Prototypicality, and Preference," *Journal of Experimental Psychology: Human Perception and Performance* 14, no. 4 (1988): 661–70.

80 Sandra Mace, Cynthia Wagoner, David Teachout, and Donald Hodges, "Genre Identification of Very Brief Musical Excerpts," *Psychology of Music* 40, no. 1 (2011): 112–28.

81 Bruno Repp, "The Aesthetic Quality of a Quantitatively Average Music Performance: Two Preliminary Experiments," *Music Perception* 14 (1997): 419–44. J. David Smith and Robert Melara, "Aesthetic Preference and Syntactic Prototypicality in Music: 'Tis the Gift to be Simple," *Cognition* 34 (1990): 279–98.

82 Vladimir Konečni, Rebekah Wanic, and Amber Brown, "Emotional and Aesthetic Antecedents and Consequences of Music-Induced Thrills," *American Journal of Psychology* 120, no. 4 (2007): 619.

83 Avram Goldstein, "Thrills in Response to Music and Other Stimuli," *Physiological Psychology* 8, no. 1 (1980): 126–29.

84 John Sloboda, "Music Structure and Emotional Response: Some Empirical Findings," *Psychology of Music* 19 (1991): 110–20.

85 Paul Silvia and Emily Nusbaum, "On Personality and Piloerection: Individual Differences in Aesthetic Chills and Other Unusual Aesthetic Experiences," *Psychology of Aesthetics, Creativity, and the Arts* 5 (2011): 208–14.

86 Emily Nusbaum, Paul Silvia, Roger Beaty, Chris Burgin, Donald Hodges, and Thomas Kwapil, "Listening between the Notes: Aesthetic Chills in Everyday Music Listening," *Psychology of Aesthetics, Creativity, and the Arts* 8, no. 1 (2014): 104–9.

87 Patrik Juslin, "From Everyday Emotions to Aesthetic Emotions: Towards a Unified Theory of Musical Emotions," *Physics of Life Reviews* 10, no. 3 (2013): 235–66.

88 Edward Elgar, *Pomp and Circumstance*, March No. 1, Op. 39, performed by Jiří Bělohlávek conducting the BBC Symphony Orchestra and Chorus, http://www.youtube.com/watch?v=Vvgl_2JRIUs.

89 Martin Skov and Oshin Vartanian, eds., *Neuroaesthetics* (Amityville, NY: Baywood, 2009).

90 V. Ramachandran and William Hirstein, "The Science of Art: A Neurological Theory of Aesthetic Experience," *Journal of Consciousness Studies* 6, nos. 6–7 (1999): 15–51.

91 Mari Tervaniemi, "Musical Sounds in the Human Brain," in *Neuroaesthetics*, ed. Martin Skov and Oshin Vartanian (Amityville, NY: Baywood, 2009), 221–31.

92 Peter Fransson and Guillaume Marrelec, "The Precuneus/Posterior Cingulate Cortex Plays a Pivotal Role in the Default Mode Network: Evidence from a Partial Correlation Network Analysis," *Neuroimage* 42 (2008): 1178–84. Marcus Raichle, Ann MacLeod, Abraham Snyder, William Powers, Debra Gusnard, and Gordon Shulman, "A Default Mode of Brain Function," *Proceedings of the National Academy of Sciences USA* 98, no. 2 (2001): 676–82.

93 Debra Gusnard, Erbil Akbudak, Gordon Shulman, and Marcus Raichle, "Medial Prefrontal Cortex and Self-referential Mental Activity: Relation to a Default Mode of Brain Function," *Proceedings of the National Academy of Sciences* 98 (2001): 4259–64.

94 Samantha Broyd, Charmaine Demanuele, Stefan Debener, Suzannah Helps, Christopher James, and Edmund Sonuga-Barke, "Default-Mode Brain Dysfunction in Mental Disorders: A Systematic Review," *Neuroscience & Biobehavioral Reviews* 33, no. 3 (2009): 279–96.

95 Silvina Horovitz, Allen Braun, Walter Carr, Dante Picchioni, Thomas Balkin, Masaki Fukunaga, and Jeff Duyn, "Decoupling of the Brain's Default Mode Network During Sleep," *Proceedings of the National Academy of Sciences* 106, no. 27 (2009): 11376–81.

96 Lawrence Parsons, Justine Sergent, Donald Hodges, and Peter Fox, "The Brain Basis of Piano Performance," *Neuropsychologia* 43, no. 2 (2005): 199–215.

97 Donald Hodges, Jonathan Burdette, and David Hairston, "Aspects of Multisensory Perception: The Integration of Visual and Auditory Information Processing in Musical Experiences," in *The Neurosciences and Music II: From Perception to Performance*, ed. Giuliano Avanzini, Luisa Lopez, Stefan Koelsch, and Maria Majno, *Annals of the New York Academy of Sciences* 1060 (2005): 175–85.

98 Ed Bullmore and Olav Sporns, "Complex Brain Networks: Graph Theoretical Analysis of Structural and Functional Systems," *Nature Reviews Neuroscience* 10 (2009): 186–98. Mikail Rubinov and Olav Sporns, "Complex Network Measures of Brain Connectivity: Uses and Interpretations," *Neuroimage* 52 (2010): 1059–69.

99 Robin Wilkins, Donald Hodges, Paul Laurienti, Matthew Steen, and Jonathan Burdette, "Network Science: A New Method for Investigating the Complexity of Musical Experiences in the Brain," *Leonardo* 45, no. 3 (2012): 282–83. Robin Wilkins, Donald Hodges, Paul Laurienti, Matthew Steen, and Jonathan Burdette, "Network Science and the Effects of Music Preference on Functional Brain Connectivity: From Beethoven to Eminem," *Nature Scientific Reports* 4 (2014): 6130. DOI: 10.1038/srep06130.

100 Oliver Sacks, "The Power of Music," *Brain* 129 (2006): 2532.

7   A Philosophical Framework

In this chapter, we will consider two broad questions in preparation for the closer inspection of specific philosophical views that are presented in Section II. What is the basis for determining musical meaning and value? What kind of music has aesthetic value? Because both of these issues will be dealt with in considerable detail in ensuing chapters, the intent here is to present an introduction to the different kinds of meanings and values that philosophers have found in music and the ways in which different genres of music might influence those values. As has been the case with other topics in this first section—science, religion, knowledge, education, beauty, emotion, and aesthetics—you are encouraged to keep an open mind and to allow yourself to consider a variety of viewpoints. Later, as you read the detailed discussions of various philosophers in Section II, you will have some context and some preparatory thinking as a basis for considering disparate views.

What Is the Basis for Determining Musical Meaning and Value?

Philosophers have proposed so many different ways of finding meaning and value in music that it can be somewhat confusing and difficult to form a mental organizational scheme. As an aid, we will begin with a simplified organization involving two dichotomies and eventually move to a more nuanced understanding. The first dichotomy involves a question of whether the meaning and value of music is found in the music itself or in what music points to outside itself. One view is called Absolutism and the other is called Referentialism (see Table 7.1).

The first main difference of opinion exists between those who insist that musical meaning lies exclusively within the context of the work itself, in the perception of the relationships set forth within the musical work of art, and those who contend that, in addition to the abstract, intellectual meanings, music also communicates meanings which in some way refer to the extramusical world of concepts, actions, emotional states, and character. Let us call the former group the 'absolutists' and the latter group the 'referentialists.'[1]

Table 7.1 Dichotomy 1

Absolutism	*Referentialism*
Meaning and value are found in the music itself.	Meaning and value are found in what the music points to outside itself.

Figure 7.1 Fugue No. 11 in F Major from *The Well-Tempered Clavier*, BWV 846² ♫

Image created by author

You might naturally wonder why one has to choose. Can you not find meaning and value both inside and outside the music? We will come to positions later that will give you this option, but for many philosophers this dichotomy is an either-or proposition. Consider two musical examples, admittedly chosen for their oppositional natures. On the one hand, we might imagine a Bach fugue, as depicted in Figure 7.1. Here, it is easy to imagine that the focus of a listener might be on the music alone, since the notes do not refer to anything external.

In contrast, the famous clip-clop of 'On the Trail' from the *Grand Canyon Suite* by Ferde Grofé is meant to depict a donkey as it makes its way down the trail (Fig. 7.2). Here, it is not difficult to suppose that a listener might be imagining that very donkey on an internal visual screen.

A skeptic might say that I have unfairly opposed two very different kinds of music. Very well, I would reply, what if you listen to the Bach fugue and your mind wanders to visual imagery, such as the scene in Walt Disney's *Fantasia* when the Bach Toccata and Fugue in d minor was animated with moving colored lines and shapes?[4] ♫ It is likely that many listeners create internal visual imagery regardless of whether the composer intended it or not. In his analysis of over 1,300 descriptions

Figure 7.2 Excerpt from 'On the Trail,' from *Grand Canyon Suite* by Ferde Grofé[3] ♫

Image created by author

of strong experiences with music, Alf Gabriels-son found wide variation in the inclusion of visual imagery as a response to music, with some reporting it frequently, some occasionally, and others very infrequently.[5] Or, take the Grofé example. Could we not focus on the musical elements themselves, ignoring or minimizing the fact that it is supposed to mimic a donkey, and noticing instead the very creative juxtaposition of duplets against triplets? It is certainly possible that a listener can recognize that

> "Songwriting is my way of channeling my feelings and my thoughts. Not just mine, but the things I see, the people I care about. My head would explode if I didn't get some of that stuff out."
>
> (Dolly Parton)

the music is referring to something extramusical, but deem that irrelevant and focus on the formal aspects instead. In other words, it is not the music that dictates how one views the meaning and value, it is the person who chooses to find meaning and value in the music in a particular way.

At this point, it is important to reiterate distinctions between what is called absolute or pure instrumental music—music containing no text, no story, no extramusical referents—and program music—music with a title, a story (e.g., Richard Strauss's *Don Quixote*[6] ♪ or Dolly Parton's 'Coat of Many Colors'),[7] ♪ lyrics, or some intentional extramusical reference. As we will see throughout Section II, many philosophers restrict their discussion to pure instrumental music. They ask, for example, how can mere music, consisting only of pitches, rhythms, and so on, refer to anything outside itself? We will come to that conundrum in time, but for the moment it is important to recognize that an immense amount of music is programmatic to some degree. For example, when the chorus explodes with 'Dies Irae' (Day of Wrath) in the Mozart *Requiem*[8] ♪ (Fig. 7.3), they are clearly referring to the day of final judgment when the faithful are rewarded with eternal life and the wicked are punished with everlasting fire. Thus, while one can reasonably argue absolutism versus referentialism in pure instrumental music, it goes without saying that an enormous amount of music does, or at least can, refer to things outside itself.

Figure 7.3 Opening measures of 'Dies Irae' (Day of Wrath) from Mozart's *Requiem in d minor*, K. 626
Image created by author

Table 7.2 Dichotomy 2

Formalism	Expressionism
Meaning and value are found in musical relationships and are primarily intellectual.	Meaning and value are found in expression of human feelings and emotions.

Figure 7.4 Schubert's Octet in F Major, Op. 166 (D. 803), opening of second movement

Image created by author

In, addition to the absolutism–referentialism schism, a second dichotomy concerns the extent to which one's response to music is primarily intellectual or emotional. Formalists contend that meaning and value arise from the mental apprehension of musical elements and their relationships; expressionists find meaning and value in the musical expression of feelings and emotions (see Table 7.2).

Let us consider the opening of the second movement of Schubert's Octet in F Major, Op. 166, D. 803 (Fig. 7.4).[9] ♪ A formalist might note the expansive clarinet solo over the moving lines of the strings. She would marvel at Schubert's creativity in spinning out such a beautiful melody. An expressionist would notice the same things. However, for him, the meaning of the music comes from how the clarinet solo seems to express a sense of longing, perhaps even wistfulness.

The next step in refining our understanding of various philosophical positions is to delineate three positions out of these two dichotomies (see Table 7.3):

Table 7.3 Simplified chart of music philosophies

	Absolutism (meaning is found within the music itself)	*Referentialism (meaning is found in extramusical referents)*
Formalism (meaning is in musical relationships and is primarily intellectual)	**Absolute Formalism** (meaning is found in the music and is primarily intellectual)	*
Expressionism (meaning is found in the expression of human feelings)	**Absolute Expressionism** (meaning is found in the music and is primarily emotional)	**Referential Expressionism** (meaning derives from the expressiveness of external referents)

*There is no position labeled Referential Formalism because the two are antithetical; formalists find meaning in the music itself and referentialists find it outside the music.

Figure 7.5 Music and musical experiences of any kind
Image created by author

Absolute formalism is more frequently referred to simply as formalism. Meaning and value come from an understanding of relationships among musical elements; the experience is primarily intellectual. In absolute expressionism, the focus remains on the music itself, and the meaning and value come from the expression of emotions in and through the music. Referential expressionists believe that the meaning and value of music comes from what music refers to outside itself, such as emotions, thoughts, actions, and so on.

Let us depict these positions in a series of images. First, in Figure 7.5, imagine that this 'musical circle' represents any kind of musical experience, including a musical work, or improvising, composing, performing, listening, and so on.

Figure 7.6 is a depiction of formalism, where the focus is on the music itself whether that is a notated score, a performance, or a listening experience. Furthermore, the primary meaning and value of the musical experience is the mental apprehension of the interplay of musical elements. "The experience of art, for the Formalist, is primarily an intellectual one; it is the recognition and appreciation of form for its own sake."[10]

A formalist might listen to 'Take Five'[11] ♪ by Paul Desmond, made famous by Dave Brubeck, and consider that this piece has enormous musical value (Fig. 7.7). She would notice the unusual key and meter signatures, along with the tricky off-beat rhythmic feel. She would take into account the elongated fourth beat that contrasts with the staccato notes surrounding it. Intellectually, she would appreciate the exquisite formal properties of 'Take Five.'

Figure 7.6 Formalism: The focus is on the music or musical experience and the meaning and value come from intellectual appreciation.

Image created by author

Figure 7.7 'Take Five' by Paul Desmond

Image created by author

In Figure 7.8, we have a depiction of referentialism where a musical experience of whatever kind refers one to 'things' outside the music. These things can be visual images, feelings, memories, and so on. To a referentialist,

> the meaning and value of a work of art exist outside of the work itself. To find that art work's meaning, you must go to the ideas, emotions, attitudes, events, which the work *refers* you to in the world outside the art work.[12]

Figure 7.8 Referentialism: The focus is on what the music refers to outside itself.
Image created by author

Imagine, for example, that a referentialist is listening to a recording of Alan Jackson singing his song 'Where Were You When the World Stopped Spinning?'[13] ♫ This song was written following the tragedy of the terrorist bombing on September 11th, 2001. Of course, the listener follows the melody, attends to the sound of Jackson's voice, and so on, but the real meaning and value come from where the listener's mind and heart are drawn in thinking about the events of that awful day. "Did you rejoice for the people who walked from the rubble and sob for the ones left below?"

Figure 7.9 is a depiction of absolute expressionism. "Absolute Expressionism insists that the meaning and value are internal; they are functions of the artistic qualities themselves and how they are organized. . . . Nonartistic references in a work of art, say, the words in a song, the story in program music, the crucifixion scene in a painting, the political conflicts in a play, and so on, . . . are always transformed and transcended by the internal artistic form."[14]

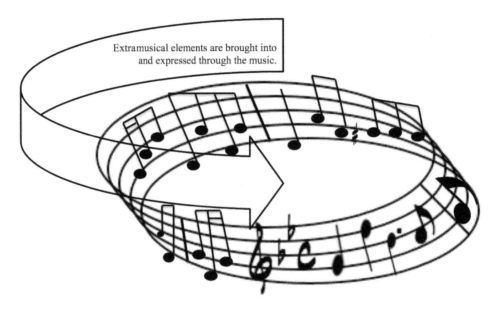

Figure 7.9 Absolute expressionism: Anything external to the music, such as lyrics, programmatic titles, and so on, are expressed in musical elements

Image created by author

Consider Tchaikovsky's *Romeo and Juliet Fantasy Overture*.[15] ♫ Based on Shakespeare's play, there are numerous obvious external references, including the characters, dramatic scenes such as fighting between the Montagues and Capulets, visual images, and so on. An absolute expressionist is certainly aware of these extramusical elements, but she keeps her attention focused on the music and everything external to the music is realized in and through the music. For example, in hearing the love theme (Fig. 7.10), she is aware of the fact that it is expressing love between the two main characters and perhaps even symbolizing eternal love in a broader sense, but she does not leave the music and go (in her mind) to these extramusical aspects; rather, she hears love being expressed in the music.

Figure 7.10 The love theme from Tchaikovsky's *Romeo and Juliet Fantasy Overture*

Image created by author

Figure 7.11 The beginning of the main theme of Fantaisie and Variations on *The Carnival of Venice* as arranged by Arban and revised by Goldman; only the solo trumpet part is shown.

Image created by author

An absolute expressionist position is easier to understand with something as overtly programmatic as *Romeo and Juliet*, but what about something that has fewer obvious external referents? Can you still view it from the same stance? The answer is yes, and to illustrate, let us imagine how a trumpeter, who is an absolute expressionist, might view the Fantaisie and Variations on *The Carnival of Venice*[16] ♪ as arranged by Jean-Baptiste Arban and revised by Edwin Franko Goldman. Formally, this piece contains an introduction, the main theme (shown in Fig. 7.11), and four variations, each exceeding the other in demanding technical virtuosity. Our absolute expressionist could spend hours analyzing the different variations and noting how the technical virtuosity was achieved. But, he could also note how each variation expresses a different mood. In particular, the third variation, which is slower, more lyrical, and legato, stands in contrast to the other variations. In his preparation for a performance of this work, his focus would be on how he can convey different feelings through a musically expressive performance.

As stated previously, it may appear that the music determines how one finds meaning and value. That is, pure instrumental music is valued for its formal properties and program music is valued for the extramusical things it references. However, this is not the case. It is the individual who determines the value. To illustrate, let us consider George Gershwin's *An American in Paris*[17] ♪ from all three perspectives (Fig. 7.12). A formalist finds meaning and value in the interrelationships among music elements. A notable feature, for example, is Gershwin's use of a jazz-like rhythmic feel within a classical music context; the focus is on the music itself and not on how it makes the listener feel or what it attempts to represent. An absolute expressionist marvels at how well Gershwin seems to

Figure 7.12 Opening measures of George Gershwin's *An American in Paris*; reduced piano score

Image created by author

capture the feel of an American walking along the streets of a major city like Paris by his control of musical elements. Although he concentrates on the music, he finds the real meaning and value in how he responds emotionally. Finally, the referentialist shifts his focus away from the music onto the things it represents. These 'things' can be internal images of walking along, of a taxi's honking, and so on, or it can be the 'feel' of Paris or the 'feel' of being an American, and so on. To the extent that these extramusical referents have meaning and value, so does the music.

From this perspective, any piece of music can be valued from whatever philosophical viewpoint the listener has adopted. A referentialist may, for example, place less value on a Haydn string quartet because it does not represent anything extramusical in an effective way. Another referentialist might value the same quartet because it reminds him of the first date he had with his future wife when he took her to a concert where this was performed.

It might be natural at this point for you to be thinking that you can see yourself adopting each of these viewpoints in different circumstances or with different pieces of music. As indicated, such flexibility is not disallowed and you will find some support in Section II for an eclectic or pluralistic philosophy. However, more often than not, philosophers have tended to be more restrictive in their views, arguing for a particular orientation in finding primary musical meaning and value. Finally, one might object that all the examples, except for the trumpeter, have involved music listening. What about the experiences of performing, improvising, or composing? These, too, we will come to in time. However, the bulk of philosophical discussion has focused on the experience of listening.

As a preliminary overview of many different philosophical views, let us preview the chapters in Section II, Chapters 8–19. These thumbnail sketches should be considered only teasers; considerably more detail is presented in each chapter.

Chapter 8. Contributions to Music Philosophy from the Ancient Greeks (Pythagoras, Plato, Aristotle). There are at least three central issues raised by the ancient Greeks that have resonated down through the centuries and are still relevant today. In greatly simplified form, the Greeks believed that: (1) Music is based on mathematical ratios and thus is best understood with the rational mind. Even today, some use theoretical analyses to 'explain' music. (2) Music has value as it imitates absolute ideals, such as Truth, Beauty, and Harmony. The simpler and purer mathematical ratios (e.g., the 2:1 ratio of the octave or 3:2 perfect fifth) are more desirable as they represent the balance sought for in the human soul. (3) Music has the power to influence human character, morals, and ethical behavior. Music has an important role to play in education because understanding the rational basis for music leads one to choose the music best suited for positive moral development.

Chapter 9. From Classical Antiquity to the Renaissance (Plotinus, St. Augustine, Boethius, Thomas Aquinas, Martin Luther). Centuries later, Plotinus continued to espouse the ideas of Plato with some new twists of his own. Essentially, he was more flexible than Plato, allowing for a continuum between music and absolute ideals rather than a sharp division. Also, he did not distrust musicians as much as Plato did, believing that their ability to create beauty was a positive contribution.

St. Augustine attempted to blend Plato's views with Christian ideals; the proper use of music was as an aid to the development of Christian character. Influenced by Pythagoras and Plato, Boethius wrote several important works in the 6th century, including one that was still used as a textbook as late as the 18th century. Centuries after Augustine, Thomas Aquinas continued to incorporate the ideas of Plato, as well as those of Aristotle, in his views of Christian theology. The rational mind was paramount over bodily feelings in reverencing God. Martin Luther gave music a central role in both worship and education. An enthusiastic amateur musician, he was instrumental in tilling the artistic soil that eventually led to Bach and many other German composers.

Chapter 10. Rationalism, Empiricism, and Idealism (Rationalists: Descartes, Spinoza, Leibniz; Empiricists: Hobbes, Locke, Berkeley, Hume, Rousseau; Idealists: Kant, Schiller, Hegel, Schopenhauer). Rationalists found meaning, in music and elsewhere, through reasoning. They put a modern spin on Plato's notions that the intellect is superior to the senses. To the contrary, empiricists believed that we can only understand music as we experience it through our senses. Rational thought about music, in the absence of actually hearing it, was limited and misguided. Any basis for understanding and valuing music must be founded on direct interactions with it. Idealists attempted to bridge these polarized positions, bringing thought and feeling, mind and body together. In this approach, however, Immanuel Kant, Friedrich Schiller, Georg Hegel, and Arthur Schopenhauer varied widely. Although all tried to find a balance, Kant tipped more toward thought and Schopenhauer leaned more toward emotion.

Chapter 11. Formalism (Hanslick, Gurney, Bell, Meyer). Formalists find the meaning of music in itself and its inner relationships and not in anything external to the music. Furthermore, they believe that musical meaning is intellectual and not emotional. Eduard Hanslick was a music critic who found profound meaning and beauty in the music of Beethoven and Brahms because of the formal clarity of their writing and was dismissive of the music of Liszt and Wagner because of their over-reliance on extramusical elements to the detriment of the structure. Edmund Gurney wrote about the preeminence of form in beauty and Clive Bell coined the phrase 'significant form,' a core property in aesthetic emotions. For both men, aesthetic emotions were completely different from ordinary emotions. One of Leonard Meyer's strong contributions was the application of Expectancy Theory to music listening. Formal properties in the music (e.g., rhythm and meter, melodic line, harmonic movement, etc.) lead an experienced listener to expect certain resolutions. Uncertainty in the listener's mind can heighten affective responses. Absolute expressionism retains formalism's focus on the music, but incorporates extramusical elements into the music as a means of expressing human feelings.

Chapter 12. Expressionism (Tolstoy, Croce, Collingwood, Cooke, Kivy, Davies, Robinson). Expressionism is the notion that music expresses feelings and emotions and that the value of music is in those expressions. We value music because of the way it makes us feel. Leo Tolstoy felt that music could *infect* listeners with definite feelings such as joy. Benedetto Croce felt that art exists in the mind, not as a physical fact; art is not useful, nor is it moral, nor does it supply conceptual knowledge. Rather, art leads to intense feeling through intuition. R. G. Collingwood's ideas were similar to Croce, although he used the term *imagination* instead of Croce's *intuition*. Deryck Cooke felt that the elements of music provide a vocabulary that can express emotions. Peter Kivy and Stephen Davies promoted the idea that music expresses emotions by resembling or mimicking how human beings express themselves. Music can express more basic emotions that are represented by characteristic behavioral expressions, but not complex, nuanced emotions. Jenefer Robinson disagreed, feeling that music can also mirror more complex emotions.

Chapter 13. Symbolism (Langer, Nelson, Goodman, Beardsley, Nattiez). Referentialists find meaning and value in whatever the music refers to outside itself. Beethoven's 9th Symphony, for example, might be valued highly because of its overt references to brotherhood. Extending ideas first stated by the Greeks and idealists, symbolists understand music as a symbolic representation of ideas, feelings, things, and so on. Susanne Langer said that language denotes literal meanings but is limited in dealing with emotions. Music's very ambivalence allows it to symbolize the inner, feelingful life. Nelson Goodman felt that music not only symbolized, but also exemplified qualities of what it referenced. Monroe Beardsley, though not a symbolist, went even further in saying that music actually exhibited or possessed particular qualities. Jean-Jacques Nattiez recognized both internal referring (e.g., how musical elements interacted with each other) and external referring (i.e., extramusical elements).

Chapter 14. Phenomenology (Husserl, Merleau-Ponty, Dufrenne, Clifton, Burrows, Stubley, Johnson). Instead of a focus on the mind or the senses, phenomenologists find that the meaning and value of music is in the lived, bodily experience. Rather than on an after-the-fact contemplative reflection, they focus on the musical experience in the moment-by-moment here and now. Edmund Husserl did not write about music or aesthetics, but his work on bringing conscious awareness of space and time to the forefront was instrumental. Maurice Merleau-Ponty put an emphasis on the bodily experience of space and time. Mikel Dufrenne wrote about how we share the same time–space as music and become one with it. Clifton and Burrows continued to discuss bodily experiences, and Stubley emphasized the social-cultural context of musical performances. Johnson reversed the notion that the mind is in the body, to say that the body is in the mind.

Chapter 15. Pragmatism (Peirce, James, Dewey). Pragmatists take a practical approach. John Dewey connected an aesthetic experience, described as *an* experience, to the natural ebb and flow of living. He felt that it was a consummatory experience, characterized by completeness, distinctness, identifiableness, seamlessness, and cumulativeness. Those who hold a utilitarian view consider that the value of music lies primarily in its usefulness, for example, in the important roles music plays in religious and civil ceremonies, in sporting events, or in celebrations ranging from birthdays to holidays, or merely in accompanying daily events such as exercising or doing the dishes.

Chapter 16. Social Philosophy (Adorno, Attali). Social philosophers understand music in its social context. To them, extracting a musical experience from its surroundings robs it of its most potent feature. Theodor Adorno felt that certain music, especially the music of Schoenberg, Berg, and Webern, has the power to influence and effect social progress. According to Jacques Attali, music is a means of understanding the social and political world. Where noise is violent, music can bring order out of chaos. In a broader sense, music can be seen as a means of effecting positive social change, as happened during the Civil Rights Movement or the Vietnam War. Music programs such as El Sistema can be outlets for at-risk children to find success and gain self-esteem.

Chapter 17. Praxialism (Elliott, Alperson, Regelski). Praxialism is a multifaceted view of the meaning and value of music as found in direct engagement through performing, composing, improvising, and listening. David Elliott wrote that critical thinking, knowing, and reflection are important components of a meaningful musical experience that have significance in terms of human values such as self-growth. Philip Alperson's robust praxialism is similarly multifaceted, but broadened to include tenets of aesthetic education (e.g., appreciating, understanding, and responding to expressive elements in a musical experience). Regelski promoted the notion of music as social praxis, that is, that the primary values of music come from the social interactions people have when musicing.

Chapter 18. Feminism (Göttner-Abendroth, Cusick, McClary, Citron). Historically, women have been under-represented in classical music; however, there are important figures such as

Hildegard von Bingen, Fanny Mendelssohn, Clara Schumann, and Alma Mahler, along with numerous contemporary composers. Heide Göttner-Abendroth wrote that a matriarchal view of art is different from a patriarchal view. She emphasized processual, participatory, and collective processes; for her there are no clear divisions between thought and emotion or reflection and action. Suzanne Cusick explored ways in which hurtful or demeaning messages can be embedded in beautiful music. Susan McClary felt that traditional elements of Western art music (e.g., tonality, sonata-allegro form) were examples of male hegemony.

Chapter 19. Postmodernism abandons many of the traditional or conventional views of art and music. Rather than focusing on a single approach (e.g., rationalism or idealism), postmodernists adopt a pluralistic view. There are many ways to value music and no one way is privileged. Furthermore, no particular musical style or genre is privileged. Bennett Reimer proposed a synergistic view between modernism and postmodernism. Rather than take each modernistic philosophical view at its extreme, disparate views can work together. For example, music's value need not be found solely in a musical work or in the performance of music; process and product can work together in a balanced approach.

After reading these brief descriptions of the chapters in Section II, you may be excited and eagerly anticipating your journey. However, if you are feeling bewildered, overwhelmed, or even frightened, there is good news. The good news is that with so many competing theories, it is clear that no answer is the single, correct one. If all the brilliant minds in the history of the world have not arrived at THE answer, you should not expect that you will either. Each philosophical position has strengths and weaknesses. One way to think about this is that rather than one correct answer, great thinkers have come up with many good answers. Your answer—whether adopted wholesale from others, modified, or unique—can be a good one, too. The primary purpose of this book is to help you find yours.

What Kind of Music Has Aesthetic Value?

Historically, most philosophers have not written about musical genres other than so-called serious, classical, or art music.[18] Remember that until quite recently, philosophers were restricted to the types of music they could hear. Unless it was music they heard in church, at court, in someone's home, or at a concert, or unless an artist was touring from another country, they had no access to different kinds of music. They could only experience the music of their environment, the music of their time and place. Public concerts only began to be fashionable in the 18th century and public orchestral concerts in the early 19th century.[19] However, with increasing access to an ever-expanding repertoire, philosophers have begun to consider many different genres. Examining all the different genres and styles of music is far beyond the scope of this chapter. Therefore, we will look more closely at just three—popular music, school music, and world music.

Does Popular Music Have Aesthetic Value?

Noël Carroll provided a brief overview of the main reasons why philosophers have historically dismissed popular music, or what he calls mass art:

There are a number of recurring themes that run through the preceding six arguments against mass art, including: that the mass artwork is formulaic, not unique; that it is a commodity, and, therefore, neither is it disconnected from society and practical concerns, nor is it disinterested; that mass art encourages neither an imaginative nor an active response from spectators; and that the responses it does elicit are 'canned' (i.e., generic) and not unique.[20]

As another example of the dismissive attitude of many philosophers, here is one eminent philosopher's take on whether popular music has aesthetic value: "Much modern pop is cheerless, and meant to be cheerless. But much of it is also a kind of *negation* of music, a dehumanizing of the spirit of song."[21] Before you respond in indignation, remember that "there is an important distinction between liking something very much—or even in thinking that a great many people will take pleasure in it—and thinking that it is of great value."[22] In other words, if we are to evaluate the aesthetic value of rock music or any other popular genre, we must do it on a basis other than personal preference, as discussed in the Ring Model presented in Chapter 6. The purpose of this section is not to arrive at definitive answers concerning the aesthetics of popular music, a term used here as a catchall for non-classical art music (e.g., pop, rock, country, jazz, etc.). In fact, the section is somewhat truncated intentionally, allowing a few, brief examples to prime your thinking and then stopping to allow you to arrive at your own conclusions.

Perhaps a review of four connected articles will help to frame the discussion. Bruce Baugh wrote an article in which he set out some introductory considerations on the aesthetics of rock music.[23] James Young wrote a critique of the article[24] and Baugh responded to him.[25] Finally, Stephen Davies responded to both of them.[26] Let us take each article in turn.

According to Baugh, the aesthetic value of rock music cannot be based on traditional ways of valuing art music because rock music has different concerns and aims.

> If I were to indicate this difference in a preliminary way, I would say that traditional musical aesthetics is concerned with form and composition, whereas rock is concerned with the *matter* of music . . . by "matter" I mean the way music feels to the listener, or the way that it affects the listener's body.[27]

The performance of tones, loudness, and rhythm are important aspects that are felt more by the body than judged by the mind. By the standards of traditional aesthetics as applied to classical music, rock music fares poorly because it is deemed too simple. A 'good' rock song is one that has a strong beat that engages the body. Also important is the use of the voice and instruments to convey a feeling. Some rock vocalists may not be considered good singers from a trained voice perspective, but they do express raw emotions in such a way as to engender a visceral response. Another means of expressiveness is in the loudness of the music, which again has a direct connection to the body. "Rhythm, the expressivity of the notes themselves, loudness: These are three material, bodily elements that would, I submit, constitute its essence, and might form the basis for a genuine aesthetics of rock."[28] In other words, the focus is more on the performance and less on the 'work.'

Young did not criticize Baugh in the sense that the standards for classical and rock are different, nor that rock music is not an aesthetic endeavor. Rather, Young contended that the standards that Baugh used to judge rock music could be applied to other types of music as well. "In criticizing Baugh, I argue that the criteria of good rock music can also apply to classical music."[29] Classical music also involves emotional expression, classical musicians are concerned with tonal expressivity, and classical music also involves loud dynamics that can be visceral (e.g., Tchaikovsky's *1812 Overture*[30] ♪ with its use of cannons, etc.). "A good classical performance can be expressive, stress the beauty of individual notes, bear a loose relation to a score, inspire the body to movement, be very loud, and employ unsophisticated means of expression."[31] Baugh responded to Young's criticism by saying, "In short, although both rock music and classical music may be judged by formalist or non-formalist criteria, it does not follow that formalist criteria are as inappropriate when applied to classical music as to rock music."[32]

Finally, Davies gave Young and Baugh their due, but disagreed with both of them. He provided a point-by-point refutation of most of Baugh's and some of Young's ideas. In the end, he decided that the question of whether or not rock music should be judged by a different aesthetic depends on the level.

> If you take it as low level, as asking if we attend to different features in appreciating and evaluating rock and classical music, the answer might be 'yes.' If you take it as high level, as asking if the principals of evaluation and appreciation are radically different for these two kinds of music, the answer might be 'no.'[33]

In other words, on the one hand, we do listen for or respond to different things in different genres. By making this distinction, Davies allowed for the possibility that each genre—country, rap/ hip-hop, heavy metal, punk rock, blues, gospel, and so on—can be appreciated in different ways and for different reasons. On the other hand, many aesthetic features, such as expressive ones, are common to a variety of different genres, hence, they can be judged by the same criteria.

Richard Shusterman provided an example of both uniqueness and commonality when he described the philosophical value of country music. He believed that it comes from a combination of affect (feelings and emotions shared by all) credence (country music's authenticity and believability), and verbal narrative (stories that are often personal and autobiographical).

> This reinforcing dialectic of affect, credence, and verbal narrative constitutes, I shall argue, the philosophical core of country music's aura of authenticity and its ability to sustain this appealing image of down-home purity that, paradoxically, clearly flouts and distorts the hard empirical facts of its real history.[34]

Obviously, this does not end the discussion, as there are others who have contributed their thoughts.[35] However, a more important thing is to ask: What do you think? If you set aside your personal proclivities (e.g., I hate rap; I love alternative rock), what is the aesthetic value of non-classical art music? If you wish to defend or slight any particular genre, you must do so in a thoughtful, reflective manner that represents something other than personal bias.

A Special Case of 'School' Music

Issues surrounding school music are related, but somewhat different. First, it bears saying that although music educators are more directly involved in school music, all musicians have a vested interest because school music programs are the training grounds for a large percentage of both performers and audiences. The primary issue is that a great deal of music listened to, performed, and studied in K–12 music programs is not 'authentic.' That is, at least according to critics, it is not music composed for artistic purposes but rather for student use. In 1963, a group of 31 musicologists, composers, music educators, performing artists, administrators, ethnomusicologists, conductors, and music critics met at the Yale Seminar on Music Education to discuss the state of music instruction in the schools. Panel members criticized the music literature being used as "of appalling quality, representing little of the heritage of significant music,"[36] calling it "pseudo-music."[37]

In an attempt to rectify the situation, the U.S. Office of Education provided a grant to the Juilliard School of Music for the Juilliard Repertory Project "to research and collect music suitable for use in grades kindergarten through six."[38] The result was a compendium of authentic literature transcribed and edited for young students. Included in the collection were compositions by such illustrious names as Josquin des Prez, Telemann, Haydn, Mozart, Beethoven, Schubert, Brahms, Schumann, Tchaikovsky, and contemporary composers such as Otto Leuning. The set also included folk music from Japan, Scotland, Croatia, Ghana, and elsewhere around the world.

Fifteen years after the Yale Seminar, several highly respected music educators offered their perspectives. Here are excerpts from three of them. Two of the quotations are quite lengthy, because they set up a subsequent discussion of school music that took place many years later.

- Charles Hoffer

    The Final Report also indirectly draws attention to the curious 'third stream' musical tradition of American music education. That tradition was neither art music nor popular music, but rather 'school music.' The composers whose music school bands played and choral groups sang often wrote only for school groups and were not recognized in the larger world of music. The basal series books contained a sizable number of songs by the series authors, who were not composers of any distinction. With the exception of orchestras and a number of resourceful school music teachers in other areas of the field, it must be admitted that the Report is correct in implying that much of the music performed in schools had little to do with the music known by the rest of the society.[39]

    Although the materials [the Juilliard Repertory Library] are useful and of good quality, they hardly shook the foundations of music education, something the supporters of the project had hoped for and its opponents had feared.[40]

- Charles Leonhard

    The effort to expand the repertory of school music programs, has not, however, met with unqualified success; the staple of the musical diet remains music familiar in style.[41]

- Bennett Reimer

    The gap between 'school music' and music in our culture was clearly recognized in a list of indictments: music used in schools was of appalling quality; constricted in scope; condescending to children; corrupted by tasteless arrangements, artificial and demeaning to both music and children; chosen more according to the limitations of classroom teachers than the needs of children; reflecting banality in texts, accompaniments, taste; leaving whole segments of music literature untouched; including no authentic music by children themselves. . . . As mentioned earlier school music has indeed moved significantly in many of the directions [proposed], for which we can be grateful and reasonably proud. Yet in rereading it one is tempted to publish the chapter again as a kind of prod to continuing self-assessment.[42]

As can be seen, the Yale Seminar and subsequent Juilliard Repertory Project had limited success in raising the quality of music used in the schools. The Tanglewood Symposium had, perhaps, a stronger impact, particularly in fostering the inclusion of world music, jazz, and other musical styles into the music curriculum.[43]

The use of so-called 'school music' has persisted, however. In a brief but highly polemic article in the *Washington Post*, Stephen Budiansky took the music education profession to task over repertoire that he called "rather slick but soulless numbers cranked out by the music ed [*sic*] publishing industry."[44] Although his criticisms were of school music generically, he reserved his harshest comments for band music, calling it 'pseudo-music,' in a term reminiscent of the Yale Seminar report.

> Many critics have noted that much of the music composed specifically for school band is formulaic, emotionally superficial, monotonously alike, dull, and didactic; that it fails to inspire students; and that by being removed from any genuine living musical tradition, classical or popular, it fails to provide students with a true musical education or the basis for further independent exploration of music, either as a performer or a listener.[45]

Many responses to the original article concurred, describing school band repertoire as schlock music, band fodder, junk music, crap, and even less flattering terms. In about 140 responses received, respondents were 7–1 in support of his comments.[46]

In an attempt to document his opinion, Budiansky, along with Timothy Foley, reviewed a number of published studies. They found that overwhelmingly compositions ranked by band directors as 'high quality' were performed only about one-third of the time, with the more frequently performed pieces rated as inferior. Budiansky and Foley referenced an article by Guy Forbes,[47] who surveyed high school choral directors concerning the basis for their repertoire selections. Recall our previously stated distinctions from Chapter 6 between personal likes and judgments of aesthetic quality as you read the following:

> Personal appeal was also identified as a factor in determining the quality of a composition. Most directors citing personal appeal as a factor stated that their perception of the quality of a composition was related to how appealing they found the work. High appeal was almost always equated to high quality. . . . Those who emphasized personal appeal in determining quality generally found decisions regarding quality relatively easy to make, stating that it was simply a matter of knowing what one likes.[48]

Some of the directors interviewed stated that they never considered quality in selecting repertoire, believing that it was not important. Interestingly, in a nod to the previous discussion of aesthetic values in popular music, 85% of the directors surveyed felt that much of the popular music that was programmed by choirs was of poor quality.

Rather than continue with a diatribe against school music, let us get to the main point of this section, and that is the need for serious discussions of aesthetic merits among music educators. According to Budiansky, "Many defenders of the status quo [in school music literature] argue that it is impossible to define artistic 'quality.' "[49] "In part, a reluctance to say what is good music—and perhaps more important, what is bad music—reflects insecurity and ignorance."[50]

> One of the things that I strongly sense is missing from the training of music educators is the tools, apparatus, vocabulary, and skills to make critical aesthetic judgments. . . . The whole project of intelligent artistic criticism is to dig beyond individual taste and explore what makes good art and bad art; what is original and what is derivative; what has integrity and what is overblown and clichéd; what is deep and what is superficial.[51]

Finally, among his suggestions for improving the situation is this one: "Make aesthetic criticism part of the essential teaching of music educators. Give them the tools and confidence to make aesthetic judgments so they won't be suckers for schlock."[52]

As stated at the outset, all musicians have a vested interest in this issue. It is likely that the vast majority of music majors in American universities received at least some of their preparatory training in public school music education programs. So, let us conclude this lengthy section by reiterating the need for all musicians to have a clearly articulated philosophy that is put into action. Whatever aspects of this discussion apply to you—popular music (including jazz, rock, country, etc.), world music, or school music—it is not too early to begin thinking about aesthetic judgments concerning these genres.

World Music

World music has gained considerable attention among Western listeners in recent decades. Because our discussions are focused primarily on Western music philosophy, as stated in Chapter 1, this brief section is meant only to convey the idea that there is a considerable literature on the aesthetics of non-Western music, not to survey it in any detail. Here are a few, admittedly selective and out of context, comments on the aesthetics of world music:

- India. Sanskrit texts from roughly 1,000 BC to the 16th century relate music to Hindu cosmology. Taken collectively,

    > the series of texts represents, whether explicitly or implicitly, a relatively coherent and consistent body of cosmological discourse relating directly or indirectly to music—especially ritual music and what may be retrospectively understood as art music, that is, that sustained by elite patronage and grounded in theory explicitly articulated in the *shâstras* [Sanskrit texts].[53]

Rasa theory refers to both what the music expresses and what emotion the listener experiences. There are links between the eight *rasas* (e.g., erotic, humorous, sorrowful, etc.) and basic, real-life emotions. When Muslim rulers prevailed after the 13th century, especially in the North, music aesthetics became increasingly secular. Today,

> Performed in concert halls, reviewed in newspapers, and increasingly learned in conservatories, Indian art musics are enjoyed in much the same way as Western concert music, evaluated with many of the same criteria, and amenable to being discussed in the terms of Western academic writing on music aesthetics.[54] ♪

- Java. *Rasa* is also central to Javanese gamelan music.[55] ♪ The inner, hidden meaning of gamelan music, its *rasa*, is never stated directly, but rather hinted at obliquely. In this way, gamelan music has a strong spiritual dimension. In gamelan, the 'inner melody' is a composite of many instruments playing together and is only revealed in the minds of the musicians and listeners. The search for the inner melody is similar to a search for absolute spiritual truths, which are revealed as one progresses from outer surfaces through meditation to deeper, inner meanings.
- China. *Record of Music*, a treatise on music written around the last few centuries BC, has been highly influential in Chinese musical aesthetics. Musical development is seen as a journey that ends in a person becoming a creative being.

  > Throughout this process, music itself is seen in a continual process of constant growth: from mere sound, on to ordered sound, and finally on to the supreme type of Music which exemplifies nothing less than all the order of the natural world and man's place within it.[56] ♪

- Korea. Central to the concept of Korean musical aesthetics are *mŏt* and *mat*. These terms are difficult to define in terms understandable to Westerners. The more common of the terms, *mŏt*, refers to a spiritual linkage between a person and an object. When the listener perceives *songmŏt* (lit., deep or inner *mŏt*), she is responding to the essence of the music, rather than its sensuous surface. *Mat* refers to the emotional content that arises when we reflect upon our inner nature.[57] ♪
- Zimbabwe. Among the Shona people, the verb *kunzwa*, 'to hear,' involves perception by touch, sight, or hearing; to understand.[58] In other words, it is closely related to the role of sensory perception in aesthetic experiences. Restricting our brief discussion here to the sense of touch, Shona music involves tactile senses through dancing, handclapping, drumming, and physical aspects of playing instruments such as mouth bows. Playing the *mbira*, or thumb piano, involves feeling/touch as much or more so than hearing. Even this snippet "is sufficient to show that we must approach African music on the aesthetic level if we are going to properly understand it and if we are going to avoid the Western tendency to isolate sound from context."[59] ♪

Perhaps to continue would be more of a disservice to the integrity and sophistication of non-Western musical aesthetics than to ignore it altogether. To reiterate, the sole point of this brief section is to make you aware that non-Western musical styles have a vast, intricate, and nuanced literature in musical aesthetics of their own. In so doing, we must also acknowledge that not all cultures concern themselves with what we understand as aesthetics, focusing instead on social interactions.[60]

Although many postmodernist philosophies include non-Western musics along with Western music, this is not a position to be taken blithely. Rather, it should come from a deeper understanding of the role and meaning of music around the world. Considering the many differences to be found, Peter Manuel makes the point that many non-Western musical styles can be appreciated in ways similar to appreciating Western musics.

> Accordingly, many Western analytical approaches—whether Leonard Meyer's theories of the dynamics of tension and resolution (Meyer 1956)[61] [discussed in Chapter 11], or the ongoing academic debates on the nature of the psycho-acoustic process—might be fruitfully applied to a variety of global genres, from Indian classical music to a pop song played in an African nightclub. However, in many traditional cultures worldwide, one can find a rich and dramatic

variety not only of musical styles but also of conceptions of musical meaning, much of which could be understood as constituting distinctive forms of music aesthetics.[62]

Summary and Thought Questions

In this chapter, we have considered two topics that will be central in the development of your philosophy—the basis for determining musical meaning and value and the kind of music that has aesthetic value. In the questions that follow, do not worry about making hard and fast decisions. Rather, ponder the questions to see which way you might be leaning at this point, not locking yourself into a particular viewpoint but keeping yourself open as you read further. Also, do not worry about labeling yourself as a formalist, a pragmatist, or any other label. Labels can sometimes be useful as they provide structure to a coherent set of beliefs, but they can also be restrictive and inaccurate. As before, test yourself to see which ideas you resonate more strongly with or have more adverse reactions to, but give yourself permission to change your mind later. Finally, do not worry if you cannot choose between competing alternatives. What if you do not want to choose between being an absolutist or a referentialist? That is perfectly fine for now; simply acknowledging that you do not want to make that choice right now is a step in the right direction toward finding your own voice.

1. Do you find the value of music more in the music itself (absolutism) or in what the music refers to (referentialism)? Is your feeling about this fairly consistent or does it change in different circumstances or with different musical genres?
2. Do you find music more meaningful from an intellectual (formalism) or an emotional (expressionism) perspective?
3. If you were asked to choose, which of the following positions seems to match most closely with your own experiences?

    a. absolute formalism
    b. absolute expressionism
    c. referentialism
       One way to help with this decision is to identify a familiar piece of music, one that you do find pleasure and value in, and consider it from each of these three perspectives. For example, you might write three paragraphs, one for each view as applied to the piece you identified. Which paragraph is most representative of how you feel?
          There are three caveats to Question 3. One, you do not have to make a choice if you later adopt a pluralistic view. Two, there are many more choices than just these three. Three, your illustration does not have to be a musical 'work.' It can be an activity or experience, such as composing or performing. In other words, if you were performing the piece that you identified, either alone or with others, would you find the experience to be more meaningful from one of these three viewpoints than the others? Or, perhaps you want to consider which of these viewpoints is most compatible with your teaching style.

4. Do you think aesthetic values are restricted to Western classical art music?
5. What is your feeling about other Western musical genres such as jazz, popular music, rock, heavy metal, country western, rap/hip-hop, gospel, and so on? Would you include/exclude some or all of these genres in ascribing aesthetic values? On what basis?

6. You may have an intimate experience with so-called 'school' music or a more limited one. Regardless, how do you feel about 'school' music in terms of its aesthetic value? Can you give examples from your own personal experiences as teacher or student that support either a positive or a negative view? What role, if any, does music composed specifically for school groups have? Should it be eliminated entirely or does it serve a useful purpose as preparation for 'greater' aesthetic artworks (whatever that phrase might mean)?

7. Is it reasonable for anyone constructing a philosophy of music to consider the role of world music or should some level of expertise and understanding be expected? How do you view world music from an aesthetic values standpoint?

Notes

1 Leonard Meyer, *Emotion and Meaning in Music* (Chicago: The University of Chicago Press, 1956), 1.
2 J.S. Bach, Fugue No. 11 from *The Well-Tempered Clavier, Book 1*, performed by Wanda Landowska, https://www.youtube.com/watch?v=-ay0ihqjT4o.
3 Ferde Grofé, 'On the Trail' from *The Grand Canyon Suite*, performed by Leonard Bernstein conducting the New York Philharmonic Orchestra, John Corigliano, Sr., violin, http://www.youtube.com/watch?v=bVKVB0MImOg.
4 J.S. Bach—Leopold Stokowski, Toccata and Fugue in d minor, BWV 565, arranged by Leopold Stokowski as it appeared in Walt Disney's *Fantasia*, http://www.youtube.com/watch?v=z4MQ7GzE6HY.
5 Alf Gabrielsson, *Strong Experiences with Music* (Oxford, UK: Oxford University Press, 2011).
6 Richard Strauss, *Don Quixote*, Op. 35, performed by the NHK Philharmonic, Wolfgang Sawallisch, conductor; Mischa Maisky, cellist, http://www.youtube.com/watch?v=dJNEuvfeshg.
7 Dolly Parton, 'Coat of Many Colors,' performed by Dolly Parton, https://www.youtube.com/watch?v=9zLsAf6SCwY.
8 Wolfgang Mozart, 'Dies Irae' from *Requiem in d minor*, K. 626, performed by John Eliot Gardner conducting the English Baroque Soloists and Monteverdi Choir, http://www.youtube.com/watch?v=DFq-HHA0k2E.
9 Franz Schubert, Octet in F Major, Op. 166, D. 803, 2nd movement, performed by Janine Jansen, violin; Julia-Maria Kretz, violin; Maxim Rysanov, viola; Jens Peter Maintz, cello; Stacey Watton, contrabass; Chen Halevi, clarinet; Sergio Azzolini, bassoon; Radovan Vlatkovic, horn, http://www.youtube.com/watch?v=g5flFNalapk.
10 Bennett Reimer, *A Philosophy of Music Education, 2nd ed.* (Englewood Cliffs, NJ: Prentice-Hall, 1989), 23.
11 Paul Desmond, 'Take Five,' performed by The Dave Brubeck Quartet, http://www.youtube.com/watch?v=PQLMFNC2Awo.
12 Reimer, *A Philosophy of Music Education, 2nd ed.*, 17.
13 Alan Jackson, 'Where Were You When the World Stopped Turning?', performed by Alan Jackson, http://www.youtube.com/watch?v=fvj6zdWLUuk.
14 Reimer, *A Philosophy of Music Education, 2nd ed.*, 27.
15 Pytor Tchaikovsky, *Romeo and Juliet Fantasy Overture*, performed by Valery Gergiev conducting the London Symphony Orchestra, https://www.youtube.com/watch?v=ZxOtYNf-eWE.
16 Jean Arban—Edwin Goldman, Fantaisie and Variations on *The Carnival of Venice*, performed by Ronald Romm, https://www.youtube.com/watch?v=F0rTi3i1zOw.
17 George Gershwin, *An American in Paris*, performed by Lorin Maazel conducting the New York Philharmonic, http://www.youtube.com/watch?v=BUfI6v6SwL4.
18 John Fisher, "Popular Music," in *Routledge Companion to Philosophy and Music*, ed. Theodore Gracyk and Andrew Kania (London and New York: Routledge, 2011), 405–15.
19 William Weber, "Mass Culture and the Reshaping of European Musical Taste, 1770–1870," *International Review of the Aesthetics and Sociology of Music* 25, nos. 1/2 (1994): 175–90.
20 Noël Carroll, *A Philosophy of Mass Art* (Oxford, UK: Clarendon Press, 1998), 89.
21 Roger Scruton, *The Aesthetics of Music* (Oxford, UK: The Clarendon Press, 1997), 504.

22　Theodore Gracyk, "Valuing and Evaluating Popular Music," *The Journal of Aesthetics and Art Criticism* 57, no. 2 (1999): 206.

23　Bruce Baugh, "Prolegomena to Any Aesthetics of Rock Music," *The Journal of Aesthetics and Art Criticism* 51, no. 1 (1993): 23–29.

24　James Young, "Between Rock and a Harp Place," *The Journal of Aesthetics and Art Criticism* 53, no. 1 (1995): 78–81.

25　Bruce Baugh, "Music for the Young at Heart," *The Journal of Aesthetics and Art Criticism* 53, no. 1 (1995): 81–83.

26　Stephen Davies, "Rock versus Classical Music," *The Journal of Aesthetics and Art Criticism* 57, no. 2 (1999): 193–204.

27　Baugh, "Prolegomena to Any Aesthetics of Rock Music," 23.

28　Ibid., 28.

29　Young, "Between Rock and a Harp Place," 78.

30　Pyotr Tchaikovsky, *1812 Overture*, performed by Eugene Ormandy conducting the Philadelphia Orchestra with the Mormon Tabernacle Choir, http://www.youtube.com/watch?v=r3ZMpv9CnZk.

31　Young, "Between Rock and a Harp Place," 81.

32　Baugh, "Music for the Young at Heart," 83.

33　Davies, "Rock versus Classical Music," 202.

34　Richard Shusterman, "Moving Truth: Affect and Authenticity in Country Musicals," *The Journal of Aesthetics and Art Criticism* 57, no. 2 (1999): 223.

35　For a recent review of the literature on the aesthetics of rock music, see Allan Moore, "Rock," in *Routledge Companion to Philosophy and Music*, ed. Theodore Gracyk and Andrew Kania (London and New York: Routledge, 2011), 416–25.

36　Claude Palisca, *Music in Our Schools: A Search for Improvement*. Report of the Yale Seminar on Music Education (Washington, DC: U.S. Department of Health, Education and Welfare, Office of Education, OE-33033, bulletin 1964, No. 28), 11.

37　Claude Palisca, *Seminar in Music Education*. ERIC document ED003429 (New Haven, CT: Yale University, 1963), 86.

38　Juilliard Repertory Library, *Juilliard Repertory Library: Reference/Library Edition* (Cincinnati, OH: Canyon Press, 1970), Preface, n.p.

39　Charles Hoffer, "Some Thoughts on the Final Report of the Yale Seminar," *Bulletin of the Council for Research in Music Education* 60 (1979): 28.

40　Ibid., 29.

41　Charles Leonhard, "Was the Yale Seminar Worthwhile?" *Bulletin of the Council for Research in Music Education* 60 (1979): 62.

42　Bennett Reimer, "The Yale Conference: A Critical Review," *Bulletin of the Council for Research in Music Education* 60 (1979): 10.

43　Robert Choate, ed., *Documentary Report of the Tanglewood Symposium: Music in American Society* (Washington, DC: Music Educators National Conference, 1968).

44　Stephen Budiansky, "The Kids Play Great, but That Music . . ." *Washington Post* (Saturday, January 30, 2005): Page B03. Retrieved from http://www.washingtonpost.com/wp-dyn/articles/A46383-2005Jan29.html.

45　Stephen Budiansky and Timothy Foley, "The Quality of Repertoire in School Music Programs: Literature Review, Analysis, and Discussion," *Journal of the World Association for Symphonic Bands and Ensembles* 12 (2005): 17.

46　Stephen Budiansky, "The Repertoire *Is* the Curriculum: Getting Back to the Basics in Music Education," Paper based on a talk presented to the World Association of Symphonic Bands and Ensembles, Cincinnati, OH (July 10, 2009). Retrieved from http://www.budiansky.com/MUSIC.html.

47　Guy Forbes, "The Repertoire Selection Practices of High School Choral Directors," *Journal of Research in Music Education* 49, no. 2 (2001): 102–21.

48　Ibid, 115.

49　Stephen Budiansky and Timothy Foley, "The Quality of Repertoire in School Music Programs," 20.

50　Ibid, 21.

51 Stephen Budiansky, Talk to the College Band Directors National Association, Eastern Division. West Chester, PA, March 13, 2010, 19. http://www.budiansky.com/MUSIC.html.

52 Ibid., 22.

53 Peter Manuel and Stephen Blum, "Classical Aesthetic Traditions of India, China, and the Middle East," in *Routledge Companion to Philosophy and Music*, ed. Theodore Gracyk and Andrew Kania (London and New York: Routledge, 2011), 246.

54 Ibid., 250. Music from ancient India, https://www.youtube.com/watch?v=BoAoqT55Wos.

55 Susan Walton, "Aesthetic and Spiritual Correlations in Javanese Gamelan Music," *Journal of Aesthetics and Art Criticism* 65, no. 1 (2007): 31–41. You can hear an example of Javanese gamelan music at: https://www.youtube.com/watch?v=wwjXwEO8_NU.

56 Scott Cook, "'Yue Ji' 樂記—*Record of Music*: Introduction, Translation, Notes, and Commentary," *Asian Music* 26, no. 2 (1995): 13. Traditional Chinese music, https://www.youtube.com/watch?v=6SMgRkhwHg0.

57 Hwang Byong-ki, "Aesthetic Characteristics of Korean Music in Theory and in Practice," *Asian Music* 9, no. 2 (1978): 29–40. Music from Korea, https://www.youtube.com/watch?v=XwrnoWaJb2g.

58 Robert Kauffman, "Some Aspects of Aesthetics in the Shona Music of Rhodesia," *Ethnomusicology* 13, no. 3 (1969): 507–11.

59 Ibid., 511. From Zimbabwe, *Sarangarike*, performed by Frank Mgomba, https://www.youtube.com/watch?v=Tdw5IoqUOhs.

60 Fremont Besmer, *Horses, Musicians, & Gods: The Hausa Cult of Possession-Trance* (Zaria, Nigeria: Ahmadu Bello University Press, 1983).

61 Leonard Meyer, *Emotion and Meaning in Music*.

62 Peter Manuel, "Ethnomusicology," in *Routledge Companion to Philosophy and Music*, ed. Theodore Gracyk and Andrew Kania (London and New York: Routledge, 2011), 535.

Section II

A Review of Major Music Philosophies

8 Contributions to Music Philosophy from the Ancient Greeks

Because of the tremendous importance of music in ancient Greece, philosophers wrote extensively about music. Many of their thoughts are still influential today and anyone seeking to develop a philosophy of music should have a basic familiarity with the main ideas they espoused. In the brief account that follows, it is important to remember that the time span is so extensive and the writing so voluminous that what follows is only a synopsis. Synthesizing nearly 1,300 years of historical writings from approximately 800 BC to AD 500 means that many details and interesting points have been omitted. Nevertheless, it is possible to identify some major ideas that you may wish to consider. Before we delve into these philosophical ideas, a brief look at music in ancient Greece will provide some context.

Music in Ancient Greece

What we know about ancient Greek music comes from physical remains of musical instruments and depictions of musicians, music making, and dance on vase paintings and sculptures, and even a few fragments of musical scores.[1] There are also a few archeological finds, such as monuments and the Odeion,[2] a roofed concert hall that was built in the Athenian acropolis in the second half of the 6th century BC. Numerous written sources provide descriptions of the role of music in society and its perceived aesthetic functions. These literary references include hymns, wedding songs, threnodies (songs of mourning or lamentation), drinking songs, love songs, and work songs, among others.[3]

   Music played a vital role in both private and public life in ancient Greece. It was heard in religious worship and festivals, in public ceremonies, in performances of both tragedies and comedies in the theatre, in athletic contests, in warfare, and, of course, at home for dinner parties and other intimate family gatherings.[4] In addition to vocal music, three instruments (among many others) were the most commonly used—the kithara, the lyre, and the aulos.

- The *kithara*[5] ♫ was a large, wooden lyre associated with Apollo.[6] Most often, the kithara had seven strings and was plucked. It had a hollow sound box that became narrower near the flat base, and a cross-bar at the top to which the strings were attached. A highly trained male musician stood while playing the kithara and sang while he played.
- Lyre refers to many different types of plucked string instruments, including the kithara. Unlike the larger kithara, the smaller and lighter lyre or *chelys-lyre*[7] ♫ (tortoise lyre) was played sitting, reclining, or walking.[8] The right hand plucked the strings with a plectrum, similar to playing

the kithara. The sound box was made by covering a tortoise shell with leather. Women are depicted playing the chelys-lyre in wedding processions and domestic scenes.[9]

- Although the term *aulos*[10] ♫ may refer to other hollow tube instruments such as a single-tube pipe or even a trumpet, most often it refers to a double-pipe wind instrument with double reeds.[11] Amateur musicians, such as shepherds, likely made their auloi from reeds. However, specialist instrument makers made professional instruments of wood, ivory, bone, or metal, and fashioned reeds from specially grown reed plants that came from specific islands.

In addition to these three, other instruments included the *krotala* (hand clappers), *kroupezai* (foot clappers), *kumbala* (finger cymbals), *seistron* (similar to krotala with a higher, more metallic sound), *rhombos* (bullroarer), *rhoptron* (similar to a snare drum), drums, *syrinx* (reed pipe), *hydraulis* (a system of flue pipes blown by wind pressure), *salpinx*, and *keras* (horns).[12]

Shepherds played the pipe to their flocks, women and children played the lyre at home, and music likely occurred as a matter of daily living, although much less was written about these informal ways of music making. Commonly, educated males were taught to play and sing competently. However, professional musicianship was somewhat polarized. At one end, musicians were considered at the lower end of the social scale and they often led a meager existence.[13] At the other end, the best virtuoso performers competed for prizes and occupied a very high social status. As we will see subsequently, philosophical beliefs also reflected this dichotomy.

Greek melodies were shaped by three aspects—rhythm, genus, and mode. Rhythm patterns, such as dactylic (long-short-short) or iambo-trochaic (long-short) followed the poetic stress-release patterns of the text.[14] The basic interval in a genus was the tetrachord, or a perfect fourth. The upper and lower notes were fixed and the inner notes varied according to three principal types: diatonic, chromatic, and enharmonic.[15] Finally, the modes consisted of scale structures called *harmoniai* (literally 'tunings'): "The ones most often mentioned are the Dorian, Phrygian, and Lydian, but we also hear of Ionian, Aeolian, Locrian, Mixolydian, and others."[16] In spite of the information we have about Greek theory, we know remarkably little about the actual melodies that were played or sung. Altogether, we have only 45 intact melodies or fragments that span over 900 years,[17] hardly enough to give us a very thorough picture of how the music actually sounded.

Philosophical Ideas

To the ancient Greeks, *mousike* was a broad term encompassing not only music, as we understand the word, but also poetry, drama, and dance.[18] As indicated previously, music saturated nearly every aspect of life and philosophers were bound to comment on anything that assumed such importance. For our purposes, we will discuss these ideas under three major headings: music as mathematics, music as an imitation of harmonious balance, and music as an influence on human behavior.

Music as Mathematics

Pythagoras was a philosopher and mathematician who lived in the 6th century BC (perhaps 570–490 BC). Many students are likely to be familiar with the Pythagorean theorem from geometry class. More pertinent for our purposes, Pythagoras conducted experiments with a monochord.[19] ♫ Dividing a fixed string length by adjusting a movable bridge, Pythagoras established mathematical ratios for various musical intervals: an octave is 2:1, a fifth 3:2, and so on. Thus, when he moved the bridge so that the longer portion of the string was twice as long as the shorter portion (i.e., 2:1), the result was that plucking the shorter section produced a tone one octave above the tone produced with the longer section. These ratios became the foundation for tuning systems in Western music, as Pythagorean tuning led to just intonation, meantone tuning, and eventually to equal temperament, among many different variants.

The discovery of simple mathematical proportions of musical intervals led to a much broader concept called the 'harmony of the spheres.' Pythagoras proposed that the sun, moon, and planets all co-existed in harmonious relationships, much like music. Thus, life on earth is part of a harmonious balance. These ideas were hugely influential and even centuries later Johannes Kepler wrote a book

> "There is geometry in the humming of the strings, there is music in the spacing of the spheres."
> (Pythagoras)

entitled *Harmonices Mundi* (Harmony of the World, 1619). Largely because of Pythagoras's work, music was grouped with mathematics, geometry, and astronomy in the educational system adopted by Plato. Later, the seven liberal arts as codified in the Middle Ages included the *Quadrivium* (mathematics, geometry, music, and astronomy) and the *Trivium* (grammar, rhetoric, and logic).

A major philosophical idea from antiquity that is worth considering in terms of music is the notion that music has a strong relationship with mathematics and science. Because of this, rational thinking became the primary way to understand music. This 'theoretical' approach to music, as opposed to performing, continues to be visible today, for example, as music theory classes continue to be taught separately from music performance classes in university academic structures and curricula. Pythagoras's ideas had a profound effect on subsequent philosophers, as we will see in the next two sections.

Music as an Imitation of Harmonious Balance

Socrates (469–399 BC) was the teacher of **Plato** (429–347 BC), who was the teacher of **Aristotle** (384–322 BC). No writings of Socrates have come down to us, so everything we know of his philosophical ideas comes from the writings of Plato and others. Although Plato often quotes Socrates, it is impossible to know which ideas come from Socrates and which from Plato. Aristotle generally agreed with Plato's ideas on music, although there were some differences.

Over time, writers expanded the notion of the harmony of the spheres. Plato wrote about harmony as it related to the world, society, and even to attributes of human character.[20] However, this harmoniousness was not apprehended through actual sense perceptions, but only through the mind in rational thought. In other words, based on Pythagorean thought, all things were composed of numbers and the simpler, purer relationships (e.g., 2:1, 3:2) were most desirable. For example, in *Timaeus*, Plato discussed the composition of the cosmos and the human soul, both in terms of intervals and ratios.[21] Although he never mentioned it in this context, it is clear that music is built on the same Pythagorean ratios that form the basis of everything. Thus, mathematical relationships provide connections among music, the cosmos, and the human soul.

Plato's *Theory of Forms* and his notion of *mimesis* are worth considering. The Theory of Forms is that there is an ideal truth, an ideal beauty, an ideal harmonious balance, and so on. These are universal archetypes that are only apprehended by the mind. As a mundane example, consider a time when I went in search of the perfect 'leaf.' It was fall and the trees in some nearby woods were aflame with yellow, red, and orange leaves. At a distance, they all looked amazing. However, when I searched for the perfect leaf that would represent all the others, I could not find one that did not have some blemish. Sometimes the color was uneven, or there was a small tear in the edge, or there was some other minor imperfection. All of the individual leaves pointed toward the perfect image that apparently only existed in my mind. So it is with concepts the Greeks were contemplating.

The idea of mimesis is that all particular things are imitations of their ideal forms. Just as any of the individual leaves I found only approximated an ideal leaf, particular examples that we appre-hend with our senses are only imitations that point to ultimate truth or beauty.[22] Music's primary value to Plato was that it could imitate the harmonious balance found in the cosmos. Note again, music's importance stems from the rational contemplation of the proportions found in music as they represent ideal Forms, not from listening to music and responding emotionally.

> "Philosophy is the highest music."
>
> (Plato)

Ideal harmoniousness could never be understood fully, but was most closely approached through rational thought by those who understood Pythagorean ratios. Those who listened to actual music were vulnerable to being swayed by their emotional responses. Thus, while music might provide glimpses into the nature of divine harmony, there was also a danger that it could appeal to the appetitive or lower part of the soul. Plato did not trust musicians because they were concerned with performing and not with thinking about abstract musical concepts.

The second important idea the Greeks gave us that informs a philosophy of music is that music can provide important insights by imitating ultimate truth, beauty, and harmonious balance. These insights come from the rational contemplation of mathematical ratios. Alternatively, music can be degrading and misleading if one merely responds emotionally. In other words, Plato held conflict-ing opinions regarding music; he praised it as a means of understanding important concepts, but denigrated both the potential emotional effects of music, as well as performing musicians who did not understand the rational basis for music. These ideas lead to the notion that music can have both positive and negative effects on human behavior, an idea explored in the next section.

Music as an Influence on Human Behavior

Plato felt that music had the power to create ideal citizens by balancing the soul through the study of music's harmonious relationships. Contrarily, those who listened to 'inappropriate' music with-out rational contemplation were liable to be led astray and to develop inferior moral character. In this doctrine of *ethos*, each harmoniai had a specific character, as Plato outlined in *Republic III:*

- Lydian[23] ♪ and Mixolydian (tenor Lydian): expressive of lamentation and sorrow; "These then, I said, must be banished; even to women who have a character to maintain they are of no use, and much less to men."[24]
- Ionian and Lydian: "In the next place, drunkenness and softness and indolence are utterly unbecoming the character of our guardians. Utterly unbecoming. And which are the soft or drinking harmonies? The Ionian, he replied, and the Lydian; they are termed 'relaxed.' "[25]
- Dorian[26] ♪ and Phrygian: "These two harmonies I ask you to leave [i.e., to keep or to use]; the strain of necessity and the strain of freedom, the strain of the unfortunate and the strain of the

fortunate, the strain of courage, and the strain of temperance; these, I say, leave. And these, he replied, are the Dorian and Phrygian harmonies of which I was just now speaking."[27]

As a result, some forms of music had a positive effect on moral character, while other types had a deleterious effect.

Listening to music could bring pleasure, but what was important was the way harmonious relationships in the music appealed to the mind. One could only derive the true meaning through rational thought processes. Because reasoning was paramount, it was necessary to be well educated, and because of music's influential nature, it was a necessary part of education. *Paideia* was the term given to a total education that involved intellectual, artistic, social, and moral development. Music was central to education according to Plato, who wrote,

> musical training is a more potent instrument than any other, because rhythm and harmony find their way into the inward places of the soul, on which they mightily fasten, imparting grace, and making the soul of him who is rightly educated graceful, or of him who is ill-educated ungraceful.[28]

Thus, we see that the third major contribution of the ancient Greeks is that music can influence human character for good or for ill.

Aristotle's Contributions

As stated previously, Aristotle mostly agreed with his teacher Plato. However, Aristotle had a more open, relaxed view of music. He recognized that music should be included in education because it provides "an amusement and refreshment," as something that produces virtue, and as a "service in the conduct of life, and an assistant to prudence."[29] He also wrote that

> we all agree that music is one of the most pleasing things, whether alone or accompanied with a voice . . . for which reason it is justly admitted into every company and every happy life, as having the power of inspiring joy.[30]

Thus, every boy should be instructed in music and the pleasure that comes from it is valuable. "All music which has the power of purifying the soul affords a harmless pleasure to man."[31]

Another point of departure concerned the relationship of music and what it imitated. To Plato, the value of imitating the ideal Form was more important than the excellence of the imitation. As we have seen, Plato did not trust musicians since they did not spend time contemplating harmonious relationships, nor did they have the education necessary to do so. Aristotle, however, recognized and appreciated the skill and artistry necessary to create an excellent imitation.

On the main point of music's power to alter human character, teacher and pupil agreed. Aristotle ascribed to the harmoniai nearly the same powers as Plato. The 'mixed Lydian' occasions grief and contracts the soul, "others soften the mind, and as

> "Music directly represents the passions of the soul. If one listens to the wrong kind of music, he will become the wrong kind of person."
>
> (Aristotle)

it were dissolve the heart," Dorian strengthens the heart, and "the Phrygian fills the soul with enthusiasm."[32] When we hear music "our very soul is altered"[33] and "it is evident what an influence music has over the disposition of the mind."[34] Thus, music is central to a total education.

Summary and Thought Questions

Our greatly truncated view of ancient Greek philosophical views on music has identified three major themes. We will consider each of these independently, and in combination, by means of some thought questions. Although gaining an understanding of these ideas is important and useful, for the purposes of developing your own philosophy of music it is more critical to examine how you feel about these ideas. It may be helpful to set aside the ideas you agree with for further consideration as you begin to articulate your own philosophy. It is perfectly acceptable to reject one or more of these ideas, as long as you do so on the basis of a carefully reasoned argument. One final caveat before we continue: two thousand years of history has brought about so many changes and our knowledge of music from the period of the ancient Greeks is so limited that their ideas should not be applied literally to present-day circumstances. Rather, we will interpret these ideas somewhat broadly in an effort to determine whether they have something useful to add to your own philosophical understanding of the nature, value, and meaning of music.

Music Is Based Upon Rational, Mathematical, and Scientific Principles

1. This idea has led to a dichotomy between the theory of music and the practice of music (i.e., performance) throughout the Middle Ages and even to our own times. What implications does this have for contemporary music learning?
2. Separating theoretical and practical aspects has sometimes led to feelings of superiority of one side over the other. Have you ever had a sense that the academic side of the house holds 'mere performers' in some disdain or that performers look upon music academicians as inferior or failed artists?
3. One example of the theoretical (i.e., scientific and mathematical) and practical sides of music coming together might be in the development of the next generation of electronic instruments (e.g., synthesizers or computer software). What other examples can you give?

A Primary Value of Music Is Its Ability to Imitate Things Outside Itself, Such as Truth, Beauty, Harmonious Balance, and Attributes of Human Character

4. 'Music as imitation' is a referentialist view; things outside the music are more important than the music itself. Are you a referentialist? Do you believe that what music points to is more important than the music itself?
5. According to Plato, music imitated ideal Forms. Do you believe that there are Absolute Truths that lie beyond human comprehension? If so, what might those be? In what ways does music provide insights into these Absolute Truths?
6. Does the relative value of what is being pointed to make a difference? In other words, is music that imitates something that is considered trivial, mundane, immoral, or socially inappropriate less valuable than music that imitates things that are considered profound, uplifting, morally upright, or excellent?

Music Can Influence Human Character in a Positive or Negative Way

7. Do you believe that music has this power?
8. In Plato's time, the term 'music' included poetry, drama, and dance as well as music. Certain popular styles intermix music, dance, lyrics, and visual effects such as costumes and stage effects. If music has the power to influence human character, is it the music itself in terms of melodies, rhythms, and so on, or music in the broader context of a 'show'?
9. How would you reconcile these two polarized issues? (a) Some music involves lyrics that promote illicit sex, violence, hatred, or are degrading to women and are inappropriate for children and youth. (b) Censorship is a slippery slope and once an external agency, other than parents (i.e., the government, school boards, etc.), makes decisions about what is and what is not appropriate, artistic freedom is lost.
10. If you adopted one or more of these ideas into your own philosophy, what effect would this have on you in your musical career? How would we hear any of these ideas reflected in your performances? What would we observe in your teaching that would lead us to conclude that you share a philosophical mindset with the ancient Greeks?

As a final statement, our concern of the moment is not so much whether the ancient Greeks were right or not in their estimation of music's value. More to the point, what do you think? Do you reject all these ideas or would you like to put some of these into your 'I want to think about it some more' folder? Thinking about these ideas from so long ago may be useful in that they sharpen your thinking in opposition or in giving you some ideas upon which to build your own philosophy.

Notes

1 Colette Hemingway and Seán Hemingway, "Music in Ancient Greece," in *Heilbrunn Timeline of Art History* (New York: The Metropolitan Museum of Art, 2000). http://www.metmuseum.org/toah/hd/grmu/hd_grmu.htm (October 2001).
2 "The Odeion of Ephesus," *Ephesus*, 2010–2015. http://www.ephesus.ws/the-odeion-of-ephesus.html.
3 Thomas Mathiesen, Dimitri Conomos, George Leotsakos, Sotirios Chianis, and Rudolph Brandi, "Greece," in *Grove Music Online. Oxford Music Online*, 2012. http://www.oxfordmusiconline.com/subscriber/article/grove/music/11694pg1.
4 John Landels, *Music in Ancient Greece and Rome* (New York: Routledge, 1999).
5 Kithara played by Sean Folsom, http://www.youtube.com/watch?v=tOqCwIV9ztU.
6 Martha Maas, "Kithara," in *Grove Music Online. Oxford Music Online*, 2012. http://www.oxfordmusiconline.com/subscriber/article/grove/music/15077.
7 Chelys-lyre played by Paul Butler, http://www.youtube.com/watch?v=7KcETZ7OImA&list=PLZM9yT8vav_IqixwPTzjbW2bKh19au7hb.
8 Martha Maas and Jane Synder, *Stringed Instruments of Ancient Greece* (New Haven, CT: Yale University Press, 1989).
9 Maas, "Kithara."
10 Aulos played by Sean Folsom, http://www.youtube.com/watch?v=KCZBPtjwZMo.
11 Annie Bélis, "Aulos," in *Grove Music Online. Oxford Music Online*, 2012. http://www.oxfordmusiconline.com/subscriber/article/grove/music/01532.
12 Mathiesen et al., "Greece."
13 Bélis, "Aulos."
14 Martin West, *Ancient Greek Music* (New York: Oxford University Press, 1992).
15 J. Peter Burkholder, Donald Grout, and Claude Palisca, *A History of Western Music, 7th ed.* (New York: W.W. Norton, 2006).

16 West, *Ancient Greek Music*, 177.

17 Peter Burkholder et al., *A History of Western Music, 7th ed.*

18 Gerald Abraham, *The Concise Oxford History of Music* (Oxford: Oxford University Press, 1985).

19 Monochord played by Sean Folsom, http://www.youtube.com/watch?v=KCZBPtjwZMo.

20 Edward Lippman, *A History of Western Musical Aesthetics* (Lincoln, NE: University of Nebraska Press, 1992).

21 Plato, *Timaeus*, trans. Benjamin Jowett, The Project Gutenberg Ebook #1572, 2013, 28–29. http://www.gutenberg.org/ebooks/1572.

22 Christopher Janaway, "Plato," in *The Routledge Companion to Aesthetics*, ed. Berys Gaut and Dominic Lopes (London: Routledge, 2002), 3–13.

23 Music in the Lydian mode composed and performed by Michael Levy, http://www.youtube.com/watch?v=xBZ7Ogb8EJ4.

24 Plato, *Republic*, trans. Benjamin Jowett, The Project Gutenberg Ebook #1497, 2012, 193. http://www.gutenberg.org/ebooks/1497.

25 Ibid., 193–94.

26 Music in the Dorian mode composed and performed by Michael Levy, http://www.youtube.com/watch?v=JNBfy1tjJXk.

27 Plato, *Republic*, 194.

28 Ibid., 200–201.

29 Aristotle, *Politics: A Treatise on Government*, trans. William Ellis (New York: E. P. Dutton, 350 BC/1928), 611–12.

30 Ibid., 614.

31 Ibid., 628.

32 Ibid., 618.

33 Ibid., 617.

34 Ibid., 619.

9　From Classical Antiquity to the Renaissance

In the centuries following his life, Plato's ideas influenced numerous philosophers, such as Philo of Alexandria and Numenius of Apamea (Syria).[1] Collectively, they have been called Neoplatonists (literally, 'new Platonists'). We will briefly examine the views of Plotinus, St. Augustine, and Boethius, who are among the most important Neoplatonists. Thomas Aquinas was more influenced by Aristotle than Plato, but he was also significantly influenced by St. Augustine's Neoplatonic views. We end with a discussion of Martin Luther, not frequently thought of as a philosopher, but one who is included for defensible reasons.

There is rarely a consensus in dating historical periods, but for our purposes we will consider the end of the Greco-Roman period of Classical Antiquity to be in the 5th century with the fall of Rome. The Middle Ages we will take as that period from 500–1400, and the Renaissance from 1400–1600. The individuals we will consider in this chapter include two who lived at the end of the Classical Antiquity period, one at the beginning and one near the end of the Middle Ages, and one who lived at the beginning of the Renaissance.

Classical Antiquity (8th c. BC–5th c. AD)	Plotinus	204/5–270
	St. Augustine	354–430
Middle Ages (500–1400)	Boethius	475/7–526?
	Thomas Aquinas	1225–1274
Renaissance (1400–1600)	Martin Luther	1483–1546

Neoplatonism

Music in Ancient Rome

The ancient Romans did not develop a very distinctive musical identity. In the earliest years, they employed Etruscan musicians, from a region north of Rome in what is now known as Tuscany, and later they imported Greek musicians. Generally, they "were content to listen to foreign professionals."[2] Music formed a part of civic and religious rituals and ceremonies, and was included in theatrical performances, especially comedies. The Romans continued to use Greek instruments, such as the kithara and lyre, with some modifications. They also developed military trumpets and horns, such as the cornu, lituus, and tuba.[3] Probably the most famous Roman musician was Nero, who sang and played on a number of instruments. Music schools formed a part of Roman education,

> for, although music did not play so fundamental a part in Roman education as in Greek, and the Romans were not so impressed with its influence in the formation of character as were the Greeks, it was far from being neglected as an accomplishment.[4]

Plotinus

Plotinus (204/5–270) was one of the most influential Roman philosophers who based many of his ideas on Plato.[5] Writing some 600 years after Plato, he was instrumental in continuing to spread the master's philosophical views. For Plotinus, as for Plato, the rational, harmonious aspects of music were paramount.

> Now in the case of music, tones high and low are the product of Reason-Principles which, by the fact that they are Principles of harmony, meet in the unit of Harmony, the absolute Harmony, a more comprehensive Principle, greater than they and including them as its parts.[6]

> "for the measures of our sensible music are not arbitrary but are determined by the Principle whose labor is to dominate Matter and bring pattern into being."
> (Plotinus)

Furthermore, music has the power to affect human character.

> There is a class—rhetoric, music and every other method of swaying mind or soul, with their power of modifying for better or for worse—and we have to ascertain what these arts come to and what kind of power lies in them.[7]

He also wrote about

> the concordance of the Souls with the ordered scheme of the kosmos . . . and out of this concordance rises as it were one musical utterance: the music, the harmony, by which all is described is the best witness to this truth.[8]

Although Plotinus continued to promote many of Plato's ideas, there were some differences. For one thing, Plotinus did not adhere to Plato's rigid distinction between the ideal Form and perceived form, rather he saw it as a continuum from the thing perceived (e.g., music heard) and the Absolute Truth (e.g., beauty). Earthly experiences, including music, had value in their own right and not just as a representation of the ideal. In the following passage, Plotinus recognizes the beauty in music, but also goes on quickly to reiterate the Platonic ideal of rational thought beyond the perception of the music itself.

> Beauty addresses itself chiefly to sight; but there is a beauty for the hearing too, as in certain combinations of words and in all kinds of music, for melodies and cadences are beautiful; and minds that lift themselves above the realm of sense to a higher order are aware of beauty in the conduct of life, in actions, in character, in the pursuits of the intellect; and there is the beauty of the virtues.[9]

Similarly, Plotinus did not distrust musicians to the degree that Plato did. He described some of their attributes in a positive manner (e.g., the musician is "exceedingly quick to beauty");[10] however, he emphasized the need to go beyond performance.

> This natural tendency [to deal with tones, etc.] must be made the starting-point to such a man; . . . he must learn to distinguish the material forms from the Authentic-Existent [the Ideal Realm] . . . he must be shown that what ravished him was no other than the Harmony of the Intellectual world and the Beauty in that sphere, not some one shape of beauty but the All-Beauty, the Absolute Beauty.[11]

Thus, according to Plotinus, music "must be the earthly representation of the music there is in the rhythm of the Ideal Realm."[12]

Music in the Early Church

Just as it was with other ancient music, we obviously have no recordings of music in the early Christian church. What we know comes primarily from scattered writings of early church fathers. Commentary on music in worship in the first three centuries of the Christian era is exceedingly sparse; however, Calvin Stapert quotes this passage from Pliny the Younger (who lived from 61–112): Christians "were accustomed to assemble on a set day before dawn and to sing a hymn among themselves."[13] Congregational singing arose in the 2nd and 3rd centuries as the church began to establish a formal program of worship, and "antiphonal singing by the whole congregation began in Antioch about the year 350."[14] Gradually, a new more ornate style of singing arose and, as we shall see in the subsequent discussion of St. Augustine, this caused some problems as singing in the new style stirred feelings more strongly than was deemed appropriate.

Niceta was a 4th century Bishop in modern-day Serbia who promoted sacred music during worship. He is said to have composed several liturgical hymns, including a *Te Deum*.[15] While some were objecting that poor congregational singing was detracting from the worship services, Niceta encouraged members of his flock to sing, though preferably in tune and in time.[16] He based his promotion of congregational singing on such scriptural stories as David singing and dancing and Paul and Silas singing hymns while in prison.

St. Augustine

Aurelius Augustinus (354–430) or St. Augustine of Hippo (modern-day Annaba, Algeria)[17] is considered a Christian Neoplatonist.[18] He was a principal proponent of merging Plato's ideas with Christian perspectives. We know that at least some of his concerns were with what we would call aesthetics when he asked, "What then is the beautiful? And what is beauty?"[19] Because beauty is an attribute of God, it was seen consequently as Good.[20]

Music played an important role in Augustine's conversion experience in 386 and his decision was reinforced by his response to David's psalms and the sound of the brothers singing hymns. "How freely did I weep in the hymns and canticles; how deeply was I moved by the voices of thy sweet-speaking church!"[21] He also describes how the Ambrosian hymn *Deus, creator omnium* assuaged his grief over the death of his mother, Monica.[22] ♪ Because David used music to praise God, Augustine saw it as good and valuable.[23]

> "For he who sings praise, does not only praise, but also praises joyfully; he who sings praise, not only sings, but also loves Him whom he is singing to."
>
> (St. Augustine)

Although St. Augustine set out to write a series of books on the liberal arts, *De Musica* is the only one that survives. "The treatise on music, as planned, was to comprise twelve books: six would treat rhythm, including metrics, and a further six would deal with melody."[24] He completed the rhythm books by 389, but not the ones on melody. *De Musica* is not a practical music book, but rather one that deals with mathematical and philosophical issues. Basing his ideas on those of Pythagoras, Plato, and Plotinus, St. Augustine held that the most important aspects of beauty are "unity, number, equality, proportion, and order."[25] Also, "Music, it was maintained, was capable of affecting the soul and able to induce or qualify an ethical state."[26]

One of the most notable aspects of St. Augustine's writings about music is his ambivalence. On the one hand, he rejoices in "the delights of the ear" and in "those melodies which thy words inspire when sung with a sweet and trained voice";[27] yet on the other hand he recognizes that "the pleasures of the flesh . . . often beguile me" and "thus, in these things I sin unknowingly."[28] Then, he realizes that if he works to "avoid very earnestly this kind of deception, I err out of too great austerity"[29] and he remembers the comfort he has received in singing and listening to hymns.

> Thus I vacillate between dangerous pleasure and healthful exercise. I am inclined—though I pronounce no irrevocable opinion on the subject—to approve of the use of singing in the church, so that by the delights of the ear the weaker minds may be stimulated to a devotional mood. Yet when it happens that I am more moved by the singing than by what is sung, I confess myself to have sinned wickedly, and then I would rather not have heard the singing.[30]

Music Philosophy in the Middle Ages and Renaissance

Boethius

Neoplatonic ideas continued to persist during the Middle Ages and throughout the Renaissance. In the 6th century, the Roman scholar Boethius (475/7–526?) wrote a series of books that were used later throughout the Middle Ages as textbooks for the Quadrivium (i.e., arithmetic, geometry, astronomy, and music). These included *De institutione musica* (500), in which he elaborated on relationships between music and mathematics. Music was considered in three categories, with a fourth category added in *De consolatione Philosophiae*:[31]

- *Musica mundane*—music of the spheres/world
- *Musica humana*—harmony of the human body and spiritual harmony
- *Musica instrumentalis*—instrumental music, which included the human voice
- *Musica divina*—music of the gods

De institutione musica was so highly regarded as a standard textbook on music theory that it was still being required at Oxford in the 18th century.[32] In it, "number and proportion are said to be the principles of reality, through which music expresses the divine."[33]

Boethius explained Pythagorean principles in considerable detail and even recounted the probably apocryphal story of Pythagoras discovering the musical-mathematical ratios when he passed by a blacksmith shop and heard the beating of hammers of different weights. That Boethius perpetuated Platonian ideas can be seen in the very first heading of Book I: "Introduction: Music Forms a Part of Us through Nature, and Can Ennoble or Debase Character."[34] He felt that due to the strong ethical value of music, it was the most important discipline in the Quadrivium for improving the mind and body.[35] Boethius also followed Plato's lead in promoting rationalism, for although he grants a certain role to hearing, "reason ought to be more trusted."[36]

Later, following Boethius, Christians perpetuated his views that music was mathematically structured and that it influenced moral character.[37] Since music was scientifically determined, only certain forms were acceptable. Church leaders then reasoned that music that did not follow the proper form, did not exert the proper moral influence, and was thus forbidden. Even though Boethius was a pagan, his ideas were an important influence on church music.

> "That person is a musician who applies the faculty of reason and thought to what is fitting and appropriate for music."
>
> (Boethius)

Thomas Aquinas

Although Thomas Aquinas (1225–1274) grew up in Italy, he was the son of a German nobleman. He was educated in Naples and Cologne, entered the Dominican Order as a monk, and spent time at the University of Paris.[38] Aquinas shaped Christian philosophy more toward Aristotelian ideas,[39] incorporating both "Augustine's use of Neoplatonism and Aristotelian philosophical resources in his well-known union of faith and reason, *Summa Theologiae*."[40] His notions of pleasure, which conformed to the Church's position, were that the pleasures of reason and intellect are preferable to those of the senses.[41] Reason must control emotion.

Aquinas did not write much about aesthetics, which is somewhat odd given the explosion of scholastic work during his time, as well as his prolific output in scholastic philosophy.[42] His total output is conservatively estimated at eight million words;[43] one modern translation of *Summa Theologiae* (Summation of Theology) runs to 4,032 pages[44] and in it, he wrote little on aesthetics and even less about music. In several passages he did write, however, about beauty.

> Beauty and goodness in a thing are identical fundamentally; for they are based upon the same thing, namely, the form. . . . Beauty consists in due proportion; for the senses delight in things duly proportioned . . .[45]
>
> For beauty includes three conditions, *integrity* or *perfection*, since those things which are impaired are by the very fact ugly; due *proportion* or *harmony*; and lastly, *brightness* or *clarity*, whence things are called beautiful which have a bright color.[46]

He connected music to perfection and proportion when he said that music proceeds "from principles established by arithmetic"[47] or that it depends on arithmetic.[48]

In another section of *Summa Theologiae*, Aquinas questioned whether God should be praised by song. First he raised five objections resulting in the conclusion that God should not be praised by song—because we should employ spiritual rather than bodily canticles, because God should be

> "One will observe that all things are arranged according to their degrees of beauty and excellence, and that the nearer they are to God, the more beautiful and better they are."
>
> (Thomas Aquinas)

praised with the heart not the voice, because ministers at the altar should not sing, because singing might seem to be imitating [others], and because praise of the lips interferes with praise of the heart.[49] Then, he answered his objections with contrary evidence, quoting St. Augustine and Boethius in the process, eventually concluding that God can be praised with song.[50] Whitwell wrote a concise statement of Aquinas's views on music:

> Thomas Aquinas, as a philosopher, was a 13th century regression to the schools of Greek philosophy which trusted only Reason. As a teacher he was no doubt outstanding in his ability to explain this older material, but nowhere in Aquinas is there the slightest evidence that he was aware of the tremendous cultural explosion going on all around him in music and literature, of the rebirth of philosophy or the blossoming of commerce, trade, travel and politics. His vision was firmly fixed on the past, while the Renaissance was beginning all around him! He must have seen it all, but, for a man who loved Aristotle almost as much as he loved the Church, to acknowledge it was probably a price too high.[51]

Still, Thomas Aquinas may not have been as disinterested as it seems. Around 1262 Pope Urban IV asked him to compose an Office for a celebration with appropriate hymns and prayers. The result was the *Feast of Corpus Christi*, first celebrated in 1311, some 37 years after his death.[52]

Martin Luther

As indicated in the opening paragraph, the inclusion of Martin Luther (1483–1546) stretches the boundaries of this chapter. He was not a philosopher, at least not in the usual sense of the word; however, he is placed in this chapter for four reasons:

1. Many standard 'introduction to' or 'history of' philosophy books do not mention Martin Luther, or do so only in passing. However, he is included in such works as *The Oxford Guide to Philosophy*. There is a rather lengthy entry on Luther in the *Internet Guide to Philosophy*, with a section entitled "Relationship to Philosophy" to which we will turn subsequently, as his ideas influenced many philosophers.
2. His appointment at the University of Wittenberg was first as professor of Philosophy and then of Theology.[53]

> "Next to the Word of God, the noble art of music is the greatest treasure in the world."
>
> (Martin Luther)

3. Although Luther was born at the very end of what we now call the Middle Ages, his adult life was spent in the early Renaissance. Thus, if we begin with Plotinus and end with Luther, we have spanned a period of over 1,300 years.
4. Music played a prominent role in his life and thinking and, in many respects, prepared the soil for the later flowering of Germanic contributions to music (e.g., Handel, Bach, Beethoven, etc.).

Luther was an avid amateur musician, even composing some music on his own. He is widely credited with composing the hymn *Ein Feste Burg* (A Mighty Fortress),[54] ♫ which Bach later famously set in his cantata *Ein feste Burg is unser Gott*, BWV 80,[55] ♫ although there are those who contend Luther did not compose the melody.[56] He expressed his feelings about music and its role in worship in a letter to a court composer, Ludwig Senfl:

> There is no doubt that there are many seeds of good qualities in the minds of those who are moved by music. Those, however, who are not moved by music I believe are definitely like stumps and blocks of stone. For we know that music, too, is odious and unbearable to the demons. Indeed I plainly judge, and do not hesitate to affirm, that except for theology there is no art that could be put on the same level with music, since except for theology, music alone produces what otherwise only theology can do, namely, a calm and joyful disposition. . . . This is the reason why the prophets did not make use of any art except music; when setting forth their theology they did it not as geometry, not as arithmetic, not as astronomy, but as music, so that they held theology and music most tightly connected, and proclaimed truth through Psalms and songs. But why do I now praise music and attempt to portray . . . such an important subject on such a little piece of paper? Yet my love for music, which often has quickened me and liberated me from great vexations, is abundant and overflowing.[57]

Luther felt, in a similar way to the ancient Greeks, that music had the power to bring about positive changes in people. The great body of German Protestant church music is largely attributable to Luther's enthusiasm.

> Because of his intense interest in music and because of his philosophy concerning its nature, uses, import, and purposes, men like Schütz, Buxtehude, Pachelbel, Bach, and a host of others have been encouraged and impelled to write some of the world's greatest music. Luther's whole approach to music ultimately helped substantially to produce not only great hymns, notably the chorales of the Lutheran Church, but also great choral as well as great instrumental music.[58]

Summary and Thought Questions

In this chapter we ranged from Plotinus in the 3rd century to Luther in the 16th, a period that stretches from Classical Antiquity to the Renaissance. Simplistically, two major themes arose: Neoplatonism and music in the early church. In Neoplatonsim, the basic ideas are still based primarily on those of Plato; however, there is some relaxation and softening of hard positions, as well as an infusion of ideas foreign to Plato. Music grew in importance and sophistication over the first one thousand years of the Catholic church and played a strong role in the fledgling Protestant church. Throughout, church leaders wrestled with concerns over the extent to which music appealed to the senses more than the intellect. Music could be very useful if it strengthened a worshiper's faith, but also it could be seductive in drawing them away from faith. Spend some time thinking about the following questions as you determine whether any of these ideas will influence your own philosophy of music.

1. In Chapter 8, you had the opportunity to consider the philosophical ideas of the ancient Greeks, particularly Plato. Does the brief discussion of Neoplatonism encourage you to retain

your previous stance? That is, whether you agreed or disagreed with some or all of Plato's ideas, have your views softened with the refinements of Neoplatonism or are you inclined to accept/reject as you did before?

2. Plotinus recognizes beauty in music and the musician's role in it; however, he finds that beauty in the intellectual realm is superior. Do you agree? If so, what examples can you give to support your position? If you disagree, what arguments would give to support beauty in music as equivalent to beauty in the intellect, virtues, and conduct of life?

3. Do you see musical beauty as good because it is an attribute of God? Or, is beauty related to goodness for other reasons? Or, is beauty not related to goodness at all?

4. St. Augustine adopts the tenets of Pythagoras, Plato, and Plotinus in saying that the most important aspects of beauty are unity, number, equality, proportion, and order. Do you believe that these are the most important aspects of musical beauty? If not, what would you say are the most important aspects?

5. If you have a strong faith tradition, do you understand St. Augustine's ambivalent attitude toward music? That is, can you see how beautiful music might distract one from worship? Have you dealt with this issue and, if so, how?

6. Boethius felt that music was a strong moral force in education. Do you agree? If you do agree, do you think it is appropriate for music to play a moral role within a public school setting? If you do not agree with Boethius, how would you support the contention that music is not a moral force in education?

7. Describe some pleasures of the intellect and pleasures of the senses. Do you agree with Thomas Aquinas when he says that the pleasures of reason and intellect are preferable to those of the senses?

8. As have many who preceded him, Aquinas links music to perfection and proportion or, in other words, to mathematics. How do you assess the connections between music and mathematics?

9. Luther felt that those who were not moved by music were "like stumps and blocks of stone." Do you know anyone who is not moved by at least some kind of music? Does this have any implications for their moral character? How would you account for the fact that they are unmoved by music?

10. In the final quote, Walter Buszin credits Luther with an enormous influence on the flowering of German music in the Baroque era and beyond. Do you think this is an exaggeration or would you agree?

Notes

1 Monroe Beardsley, *Aesthetics from Classical Greece to the Present* (Tuscaloosa, AL: The University of Alabama Press, 1966).
2 John Landels, *Music in Ancient Greece and Rome* (New York: Routledge, 1999), 172.
3 Curt Sachs, *Our Musical Heritage*, 2d ed. (Englewood Cliffs, NJ: Prentice-Hall, 1955).
4 Stanley Bonner, *Education in Ancient Rome* (New York: Routledge, 2012), 44.
5 A. Lacey, *A Dictionary of Philosophy* (London: Routledge, 1986).
6 Plotinus, *The Six Enneads*, trans. Stephen MacKenna and B. Page, 250/1994–2009. http://classics.mit.edu//Plotinus/enneads.html, p. 108.
7 Ibid., 209.
8 Ibid., 178.
9 Ibid., 58.
10 Ibid., 51.

11 Ibid., 12.

12 Plotinus, *The Six Enneads*, Fifth Ennead, Ninth Tractate, Section 11, trans. Stephen MacKenna and B. Page, 250/1917–1930. http://www.sacred-texts.com/cla/plotenn/enn502.htm.

13 Calvin Stapert, *A New Song for an Old World. Musical Thought in the Early Church* (Grand Rapids, MI: Wm. B. Eerdmans, 2007), 38.

14 Andrew Burn, *Niceta of Remesiana: His Life and Works* (Cambridge, UK: Cambridge University Press, 1905), xci.

15 "Niceta of Remesiana," *Encyclopedia Britannica*, 2015 http://www.britannica.com/biography/Nicetas of-Remesiana.

16 Burn, *Niceta of Remesiana*.

17 Christopher Kirwan, "Augustine: City of God," in *Central Works in Philosophy, 1: Ancient and Medieval*, ed. John Shand (Montreal: McGill-Queen's University Press, 2005), 140–68.

18 Michael Mendelson, "Saint Augustine," in *The Stanford Encyclopedia of Philosophy* (2012 edition), ed. Edward Zalta. http://plato.stanford.edu/archives/win2010/entries/augustine/. Samuel Stumpf and James Fieser, *Philosophy: History and Problems, 6th ed.* (New York: McGraw-Hill, 2003).

19 St. Augustine, *Confessions*, trans. Albert Outler, 398/1994. http://www.fordham.edu/halsall/basis/confessions-bod.asp, p. 49.

20 Joseph Margolis, "Medieval Aesthetics," in *The Routledge Companion to Aesthetics*, ed. Berys Gaut and Dominic Lopes (London: Routledge, 2002), 27–36.

21 Ibid., 116.

22 Ambrose, *Deus, creator omnium*, performed by Schola Gregoriana Mediolanensis, http://www.youtube.com/watch?v=7B2AY3avN8Q.

23 St. Augustine, *The City of God*, trans. Marcus Dods (New York: C. Scribner, 413/1871), 199.

24 Brian Brennan, "Augustine's *De Musica*," *Vigiliae Christianae* 42, no. 3 (1988): 270.

25 Beardsley, *Aesthetics from Classical Greece to the Present*, 93.

26 Brennan, "Augustine's *De Musica*," 271.

27 St. Augustine, *Confessions*, 145.

28 Ibid., 146.

29 Ibid., 146.

30 Ibid., 146.

31 David Chamberlain, "Philosophy of music in the *Consolatio* of Boethius," *Speculum* 45, no. 1 (1970): 80–97.

32 Calvin Bower, *Boethius' The Principles of Music: An Introduction, Translation, and Commentary* (Nashville, TN: George Peabody College for Teachers, 1966).

33 Beardsley, *Aesthetics from Classical Greece to the Present*, 91.

34 Anicius Boethius, *Fundamentals of Music*, ed. Claude Palisca and trans. Calvin Bower (New Haven, CT: Yale University Press, 1989), 1.

35 Julius Portnoy, *The Philosopher and Music: A Historical Outline* (New York: Da Capo Press, 1954).

36 Boethius, *Fundamentals of Music*, 16.

37 Portnoy, *The Philosopher and Music*.

38 Will Durant, *The Story of Philosophy* (New York: Simon and Schuster, 1953).

39 Bertrand Russell, *Wisdom of the West* (London: Rathbone Books, 1959).

40 Margolis, "Medieval Aesthetics," 31.

41 David Whitwell, *Ancient Views on Music and Religion* (Austin, TX: Whitwell Publishing, 2013).

42 Beardsley, *Aesthetics from Classical Greece to the Present*.

43 Alexander Broadie, "Aquinas, St. Thomas," in *The Oxford Guide to Philosophy*, ed. Ted Honderich (Oxford, UK: Oxford University Press, 2005), 45.

44 Thomas Aquinas, *Summa Theological*, trans. Fathers of the English Dominican Province, 1265–75/1947. http://www.basilica.org/pages/ebooks/St.%20Thomas%20Aquinas-Summa%20Theologica.pdf.

45 Ibid., 33.

46 Ibid., 270.

47 Ibid., 3.

48 Ibid., 5.

49 Ibid., 2124.

50 Ibid., 2125.
51 Whitwell, *Ancient Views on Music and Religion*, 138.
52 Barbara Walters, "The Feast and Its Founders," in *The Feast of Corpus Christi*, ed. Barbara Walters, Vincent Corrigan, and Peter Ricketts (University Park, PA: The Pennsylvania State University Press, 2006), 3–56.
53 Anthony O'Hear, "Luther, Martin," in *The Oxford Guide to Philosophy*, ed. Ted Honderich (Oxford, UK: Oxford University Press, 2005), 547–48.
54 Martin Luther, *A Mighty Fortress Is Our God*, performed by the Roger Wagner Chorale, http://www.youtube.com/watch?v=ADamVJaXZMg.
55 J.S. Bach, *Ein Feste Burg is Unser Gott*, BWV 80, performed by Phillipe Hereweghe conducting La Chapelle Royale and Collegium Vocale, https://www.youtube.com/watch?v=x0zBmcckFoM.
56 Walter Buszin, "Luther on Music," *The Musical Quarterly* 32, no. 1 (1946): 80–97.
57 Martin Luther, "Letter to Louis Senfl (1530)," in *Instructions for the Visitors of Parish Pastors in Electoral Saxony*, quoted in David Whitwell, *Ancient Views on Music and Religion*, 187.
58 Buszin, "Luther on Music," 96–7.

10 Rationalism, Empiricism, and Idealism

Idealism arose out of Immanuel Kant's responses to both rationalism and empiricism. Other philosophers, such as Georg Hegel, Friedrich Schiller, and Arthur Schopenhauer, were highly influenced by his writings and further developed this viewpoint. The result is a set of ideas that are dissimilar in their individuality and yet unified by their adherence to a core principle. Although they arrive at this core idea by different routes, the main point of agreement is that while music is comprised of sounds that must be perceived, these sounds actually become music in the mind. Stated more succinctly, music is a product of the mind. In this chapter, we will review rationalism and empiricism, and then move to a review of the contributions of the idealists, Kant, Schiller, Hegel, and Schopenhauer. We finish with some musical examples.

Before we proceed, a quick note about labels is in order. Sometimes it is not so easy to place a given philosopher into a particular philosophical viewpoint. Consider George Berkeley, for example. Some classify him as an empiricist or as one among the British Empiricists.[1] Brian Duignan classified him as both an empiricist and an idealist,[2] while still others included Berkeley in discussions of empiricism, but wrote of his idealism.[3] In a book on British Empiricists, the author stated, "The Anglican Irish bishop George Berkeley (1685–1753) is an empiricist and an idealist."[4] In another book, the authors began a section entitled "The Idealism of George Berkeley" with this sentence: "Berkeley (1685–1753), was a great British Empiricist who carried Locke's premises to their ultimate conclusion . . ."[5] and later, "Since Berkeley portrays all substances as identical with ideas, restricting the metaphysically real universe to the realm of the spiritual or ideal, he is known as a philosophical Idealist."[6] In other words, Berkeley pushed empiricism to its logical conclusions, leading to idealism.

Bertrand Russell also classified Berkeley as an empiricist, but proceeded to discuss what he called 'Berkeley's idealism.' He then went on to say, in a comment that applies to all the philosophers in this chapter and to the book as a whole:

> It is important not to apply these labels too rigidly. One of the great obstacles to understanding in philosophy, as indeed in any other field, is a blind and over-rigid classification of thinkers by labels. Still, the conventional division is not arbitrary, but points to some leading features of the two traditions [i.e., rationalism and empiricism]. This is true even though in political theory the British empiricists show a marked streak of rationalist thinking.[7]

Rationalism

Rationalists take the position that reasoning is the source of truth. Major figures associated with rationalism include René Descartes, Baruch Spinoza, and Gottfried Leibniz. Socrates and Plato laid the groundwork, but new perspectives and an increased emphasis on rationality came with Descartes and the subsequent Age of Enlightenment, which was also known as the Age of Reason. Musicians can place these philosophers into chronological context with the following comparisons:

René Descartes (1596–1650)	Heinrich Schütz (1585–1672)
Baruch Spinoza (1632–1677)	Dieterich Buxtehude (1637–1707)
Gottfried Leibniz (1646–1716)	Arcangelo Corelli (1653–1713)

Nearly everyone, even those with only a smattering of knowledge about philosophy, has heard the famous statement of **René Descartes** (1596–1650): "I think, therefore I am" (*Cogito, ergo sum*).[8] While he could doubt his body's existence, he could not doubt that he was using his mind to think. This separation of mind and body, a strengthening of Plato's position, has resonated throughout Western thought for centuries. Since the body has always been associated with emotions, this dichotomy also places a schism between thinking and feeling. Even as recently as 1994, as we read in Chapter 5, neuroscientist Antonio Damasio published a book called *Descartes' Error*,[9] in which he put the mind and body back together in a more integrated view. Descartes held the view that music was essentially mathematical. Because rhythms had moral values that influenced the human soul, he preferred simpler rhythms that would not excite the passions.[10]

Baruch (Benedictus) Spinoza (1632–1677) was highly influenced by Descartes, although he moved beyond the elder's ideas. In *Ethics* (1677), he wrote that there were three kinds of knowledge: imagination, reason, and intuition.[11] The first kind of knowledge, imagination, comes from random experience and involves sensory perceptions that are superficial and haphazard in nature. This kind of knowledge is inadequate to convey a true sense of the world, primarily because it lacks a systematic order and can lead us into false impressions. Reason, the second kind of knowledge, provides adequate ideas in a systematic, logical order. To understand something involves apprehension in the mind, not just a sensory experience. Sensory experience provides knowledge of something as it is in the moment; reason provides knowledge of its abstract aspects.

> "The object of music is a Sound. The end: to delight, and move various Affections in us."
>
> (René Descartes)

The third type of knowledge was intuition, "a perception of things . . . in their eternal aspects and relations."[12] Unlike Descartes, Spinoza did not see the mind and body as separate, but rather as aspects of the same entity. Thus, perceptions and reason were fused into a higher level of understanding. In this, Spinoza prepared the way for the later idealists. He also pointed toward idealism in his

> "One and the same thing can at the same time be good, bad, and indifferent, for example, music is good to the melancholy, bad to those who mourn, and neither good nor bad to the deaf."
>
> (Baruch Spinoza)

recognition of the importance of affects (drives, motivations, emotions, and feelings) to human nature.[13] We shall see both of these ideas elaborated upon by the idealists.

Gottfried Leibniz (1646–1716) was a student of Spinoza. The following statement of his shows a remarkable continuation of the ideas of Pythagoras, Plato, and Descartes:

> The pleasures of the senses themselves come down in the end to intellectual pleasures—they strike us as sensory rather than intellectual only because they are known in a confused way. Music that we hear can charm us, even though its beauty consists only in relations among numbers, and in the way the beats or vibrations of the sounding body return to the same frequency at certain intervals. (We are not aware of the numbers of these beats, but the soul counts them all the same!)[14]

As we read in Chapter 6, Alexander Baumgarten, who first used the term aesthetics, developed his theory on rational principles. Thus, rationalists have had a profound effect on the philosophy of music.

Empiricism

In contrast to rationalists, empiricists claim that knowledge comes through the senses. Major figures include Thomas Hobbes, John Locke, George Berkeley, David Hume, and Jean-Jacques Rousseau. As we did previously, it may help to place these scholars with some musical contemporaries:

Thomas Hobbes (1588–1679)	Samuel Scheidt (1587–1654)
John Locke (1632–1704)	Jean-Baptiste Lully (1632–1687)
George Berkeley (1685–1753)	J. S. Bach (1685–1750)
David Hume (1711–1776)	W. F. Bach (1710–1784)
Jean-Jacques Rousseau (1712–778)	C.P.E. Bach (1714–1788)

Thomas Hobbes (1588–1679) felt that empirical experience is the only source of knowledge. That is, we construct knowledge from actual interactions with the physical, material world.[15] **John Locke** (1632–1704) believed that we are born with the mind a blank slate (*tabula rasa*).[16] Lived experiences imprint themselves on the mind. The genesis for this idea can be traced back at least to Aristotle. Locke's emphasis upon it, however, gave it new impetus. He further insisted that no knowledge is *a priori*; in other words, no knowledge is innate. We gain information and rules for processing this information through experience.

A famous quote from **Bishop Berkeley** (1685–1753) is "esse est principi"—"to be is to be perceived."[17] Any 'thing' is merely a group of perceptions. Think of all the ingredients that went into making your lunch. While it is the mind that puts the label 'lunch' onto these ingredients as they are organized, it is the sensory experience of tasting your lunch (and smelling, seeing, and touching) that gives rise to the naming of it as 'lunch.' Without the sensory experience, the mind would have no conception of lunch. However, since perceptions do gain their meaning in the mind, Berkeley, as noted in the introduction, was leading toward idealism. **David Hume** (1711–1776) wrote that the sensory perception of music was more important than rational contemplation.[18] He believed that music was emotional and sensory rather than rational. Finally, **Jean-Jacques Rousseau** (1712–1778) stated that "instinct and feeling are more trustworthy than reason."[19]

Idealism

Idealism is often referred to as German Idealism because the leading figures were Germans. They are also grouped together because no matter how varied their ideas were, they all made an attempt to bridge the gap between rationalism and empiricism. Whatever their differences, they agreed that art is ultimately a product of the mind, an idea. Finally, they are also unified from the unfortunate fact that on the whole, their writing is dense, difficult, and obtuse. Will Durant said, "Kant is the last person in the world whom we should read on Kant."[20] Hegel's notions of aesthetics are tied to his larger philosophical views and, at least according to Monroe Beardsley, "that system does not yield readily to intelligible paraphrase."[21] Peter Singer added that Hegel's style is impenetrable and "anything but 'user-friendly'; at first glance most readers will find his sentences simply incomprehensible."[22] Bertrand Russell found that "Hegel's writings are amongst the most difficult works in the entire literature of philosophy."[23]

Schopenhauer is an exception, for according to Durant, "here is no Chinese puzzle of Kantian terminology, no Hegelian obfuscation, no Spinozist geometry; everything is clarity and order."[24] In spite of these difficulties, however, their work, individually and collectively, has had an enormous influence on subsequent philosophical views on musical aesthetics. It is well worth the time and effort to understand at least the basic ideas they put forth. Here are their musical contemporaries:

Immanuel Kant (1724–1804)	Franz Joseph Haydn (1732–1809)
Friedrich Schiller (1759–1805)	Wolfgang Amadeus Mozart (1756–1791)
Georg Wilhelm Friedrich Hegel (1770–1831)	Ludwig van Beethoven (1770–1827)
Arthur Schopenhauer (1788–1860)	Gioachino Rossini (1792–1868)

Immanuel Kant

By the time Immanuel Kant (1724–1804) arrived on the scene, the philosophical world was in a state of contentiousness, caught between the mindfulness of rationalism and the sensuousness of empiricism. His goal was to bring the two opposing views together into one balanced, coherent view. In the *Critique of Pure Reason*,[25] he set out to provide a critical analysis of reasoning. For example, he refuted Locke's notion that all knowledge comes to us through our senses. He asserted that mathematics is an example of *a priori* knowledge. Two plus two will always equal four and that truth does not depend on our experiences to make it so. Similarly, he dismissed the notion of the mind as *tabula rasa*. He said that the mind contains inherent structures that organize sensory perceptions into ideas. Durant encapsulated Kant's position this way: "Sensation is unorganized stimulus, perception is organized sensation, conception is organized perception, science is organized knowledge, wisdom is organized life: each is a greater degree of order, and sequence, and unity."[26]

Regarding the arts, Kant is the first philosopher to integrate aesthetics into a broader philosophy.[27] He pondered how judgments of beauty, which are mindful, differ from rational and moral judgments and everyday sensual experiences. He determined that aesthetic experiences involve contemplative delight in perception of imaginative form. Finding beauty in art is not a matter of individual preference. Rather anyone who uses cognitive faculties of imagination and free play will discover underlying unity, a universal property of beauty. Kant believed that "successful works of fine art normally have intellectual content and please us in virtue of the harmony among their content, form, and material."[28] On this basis, Kant gave music a lower rating than the other arts, because it was more sensual than intellectual. He used more subtle arguments than references to Pythagorean mathematical relationships, but orderly and rational principles were important.

> "We would declare music either ... to be the *beautiful* play of sensations (of hearing), or [to be the play] of *agreeable* sensations."
>
> (Immanuel Kant)

Kant also posited four distinguishing features of aesthetic judgments:

1. They are disinterested. Aesthetic judgments are free from external interests. "The judgment results in pleasure, rather than pleasure resulting in judgment."[29]
2. We make aesthetic judgments as if they were universal. When we make aesthetic judgments, we do so on the basis that everyone will agree. "Although I may be perfectly aware that all kinds of other factors might enter in to make particular people in fact disagree with me, never-the-less I at least implicitly demand universality in the name of *taste*."[30]
3. Aesthetic judgments identify beautiful objects that are purposive but without a definite purpose. Artworks may have been created for a particular purpose (e.g., ceremonial music to crown a new king), but such facts must be abstracted from making an aesthetic judgment of the work.
4. Aesthetic judgments are necessary in the sense that they are made according to principle.

In general, judgments of beauty rest on design, pattern, coherence, unity, and finality. Aesthetic pleasure is derived from contemplation and reflection. Music appeals too much to the senses and not enough to the mind. Because of that, it reigns supreme as an agreeable art, but does not qualify as a fine art (where poetry is ranked first).

Friedrich Schiller

Although Friedrich Schiller (1759–1805) was a contemporary of Mozart, many musicians know of him because his *Ode to Joy* appears as the text for the last movement of Beethoven's 9th Symphony.[31] ♪ In addition to being a poet, Schiller was a philosopher who was highly influenced by the writings of Kant.[32] One of his important contributions was *On the Aesthetic Education of Man in a Series of Letters.*[33] He wrote these letters to Friedrich Christian of Schleswig-Holstein-Augustenburg, a Danish Prince who had befriended him and supported him financially. Although a fire at the Danish court destroyed the originals,[34] Schiller later revised and extended them in a series of journal articles.

> "Art is the daughter of freedom."
>
> (Friedrich Schiller)

While it is always good to place scholarly writings in context, it is particularly important when studying Schiller's views. He wrote during the Reign of Terror in France, when all of Europe was considering newly articulated humanitarian ideals.

> [Schiller] made it clear that in his view mankind must first learn to serve Beauty before it could faithfully serve freedom—the world, he felt, was not ready for political liberty, and it was necessary to prepare for a true conception of it by developing first a sense of the beautiful. That is,

in fact, the whole theme of the letters.[35] . . . The whole burden of the argument in these letters is, in a single sentence, that Man must pass through the aesthetic condition, from the merely physical, in order to reach the rational or moral.[36]

Schiller believed that humans are driven by two opposing forces. Sensuous drive (*stofftrieb*) derives from our physical existence and explains how we are changed by feelings, instincts, and pleasure. Formal drive (*formtrieb*) deals with the capacity for reason to impose conceptual and moral order on the world. These two are roughly akin to Cartesian duality. However, Schiller resolves this polarization through Play drive (*spieltrieb*), uniting body and mind to achieve artistic beauty. Schiller stressed the humanizing and cultural value of music. Aesthetic education and artistic beauty impart balance and harmony to the human spirit. In his *Fifteenth Letter*, Schiller said,

> The object of the play impulse, conceived in a general notion, can therefore be called *living shape*, a concept which serves to denote all aesthetic qualities of phenomena and—in a word— what we call beauty in the widest sense of the term.[37]

Schiller wrote of the importance of beauty in inculcating good citizenship: "Though need may drive Man into society, and Reason implant social principles in him, Beauty alone can confer on him a *social character*."[38] Beauty symbolizes morality and enables us to become good citizens.[39] Art, then, plays a central role in educating people to act morally[40] and aesthetic education "makes man whole, and . . . man is only whole when he engages in such activity."[41]

Georg Wilhelm Friedrich Hegel

A contemporary of Beethoven, Hegel (1770–1831) was born in the same year but outlasted the composer by four years. Interestingly, Hegel never mentioned Beethoven, but expressed fondness for Bach, Handel, Mozart, Rossini, and von Weber.[42] Remembering previously expressed concerns—Hegel's theory of art "is obscure to the point of being unintelligible"[43]—this brief section can only present a general notion of his ideas about art. For Hegel, art is fundamentally human and thus differs from natural beauty. Art plays an important role in the development of the mind, for we learn about ourselves and the world through art and religion, as well as through cognition.[44] Art reveals rationality and spirituality.

> "Music is a higher revelation than all wisdom and philosophy."
>
> (Beethoven)

Hegel calls the highest evolution of mind and spirit 'Absolute Idea.' As he put it,

> The Idea is the truth. . . . The Absolute Idea, or the Idea in its absolute form, is what we have spoken of above as Mind or Spirit, and Mind or Spirit in its absolute form begins at the stage of art.[45]

Art reveals Absolute Idea and makes it manifest. Man is capable of understanding the universe because the universe is rational, and according to Hegel, "Reason is the Sovereign of the World."[46] Art plays an important role in the development of the human mind from infancy to adulthood. Hegel said, "The artist, the poet, the musician, reveal the meaning, the truth, the reality of the world: they teach us, they help us . . . to see, to hear, to feel what our rude senses had failed to detect."[47]

Music is uniquely capable of revealing to mind and soul their innermost nature; it offers insight into an otherwise unfathomable inner life. Although art is a vehicle for Absolute Idea's expression, when humankind's spiritual awareness has been elevated to new heights through art, art has outlived its usefulness. Hegel saw this evolutionary progress resulting from stating a thesis, providing an antithesis that moves the idea forward, and then combining the two in a synthesis.[48] These steps lead ever upward toward Absolute Idea. As art evolves into higher spiritual realms, it is superseded by religion and philosophy.[49] One reason for this is that art occupies a middle ground between purely objective reality and purely inner ideas.[50] Stephen Houlgate provides a succinct synopsis of Hegel's view of art.

> The principal aim of art is not, therefore, to imitate nature, to decorate our surroundings, to prompt us to engage in moral or political action, or to shock us out of our complacency. It is to allow us to contemplate and enjoy created images of our own spiritual freedom—images that are beautiful precisely *because* they give expression to our freedom. Art's purpose, in other words, is to enable us to bring to mind the truth about ourselves, and so to become aware of who we truly are. Art is there not just for art's sake, but for beauty's sake, that is, for the sake of a distinctively sensuous form of human self-expression and self-understanding.[51]

"If we are in a general way permitted to regard human activity in the realm of the beautiful as a liberation of the soul, as a release from constraint and restriction, in short to consider that art does actually alleviate the most overpowering and tragic catastrophes by means of the creations it offers to our contemplation and enjoyment, it is the art of music which conducts us to the final summit of that ascent to freedom."

(Georg Wilhelm Friedrich Hegel)

In Hegel's view, music is an important way of expressing our humanity. According to him, music provides unique insights into human nature.

Arthur Schopenhauer

Schopenhauer (1788–1860) was not only a contemporary of Rossini; his lifespan overlapped many other composers, including Nicoló Paganini (1782–1840), Carl Maria von Weber (1786–1826), Mendelssohn (1809–1847), Chopin (1810–1849), and Schuman (1810–1856). In contrast to the rationalists, Schopenhauer felt that the world was irrational, a ceaselessly striving place, devoid of meaning. The name he gave to this is 'Will,' a blind, impotent force that cannot be grasped by the rational mind. The arts are important because they can give us insights into the phenomenal world. The phenomenal world is that world we experience through the senses; the noumenal world is the world of thought, independent of sensory apprehension. In addition, the arts can provide a release from the incessant, driving force. Music gives us

"Accordingly, we could just as well call the world embodied music as embodied will."

(Schopenhauer)

insights more profound than reason can give. "If the form of the world is best reflected in the form of music, then the most philosophical sensibility will be a musical sensibility."[52] This may partially explain why Wagner and Nietzsche were both drawn to Schopenhauer in combining musical and philosophical interests.

Music stands quite alone, as Schopenhauer wrote:

> Therefore it [music] does not express this or that individual and particular joy, this or that sorrow or pain or horror or exaltation or cheerfulness or peace of mind, but rather joy, sorrow, pain, horror, exaltation, cheerfulness and peace of mind as such *in themselves*, abstractly, as it were, the essential in all these without anything superfluous, and thus also in the absence of any motives for them.[53]

In other words, to him, music expresses the essence of joy or sorrow, not the joy or sorrow of a particular situation. Furthermore, pure, undiluted joy or sorrow is being presented through the music.

Schopenhauer also said that music "is a *copy of the will itself* . . . this is precisely why the effect of music is so much more powerful and urgent than that of the other arts: the other arts speak only of shadows while music speaks of the essence."[54] John Dewey provided a succinct statement of Schopenhauer's philosophy in one sentence: "Music is the highest of the arts, because it gives us not merely the external objectifications of Will but also sets before us for contemplation the very *processes* of Will."[55]

Musical Examples

As a rationalist, Descartes thought that music was essentially mathematical. Leibniz concurred when he contended that the beauty in music was only relationships among numbers. An outstanding example, although not necessarily known to the rationalists, is found in parallel constructions of an isorhythmic motet by Guillaume Dufay and the dome of the cathedral at Florence built by Filippo Brunelleschi. The motet was written for the dedication ceremony of the new dome, and mathematical aspects of Dufay's *Nuper rosarum flores*[56] ♫ "are not purely musical after all, but the results of a deliberate attempt on the part of Dufay to create a sounding model of Brunelleschi's architecture."[57] For example, the 6:4:2:3 proportions found in the motet are precisely those that Brunelleschi used in the construction of the vault. "In its overall dimension, then, *Nuper rosarum flores* has exactly the same proportions as the interior of the cross and dome of Santa Maria del Fiore."[58] There are many additional points of correspondence between the motet and the dome, sufficient to serve as support for a rationalist view of music.

Empiricists believed that music was more emotional and sensory, rather than rational. Here, let us consider another connection between music and architecture, but this time with attention to the acoustical aspects. Perhaps no finer example, and again one not necessarily known to the empiricists, can be given than the music of Giovanni Gabrieli in connection with the cathedral of St. Mark's in Venice. He served as organist and composer at St. Mark's from 1585 until his death in 1612. Although polychoral music with separated choirs (*cori spezzati*) was not restricted to Gabrieli or to St. Mark's,[59] his music provides particularly good illustrations. The size and layout of the cathedral provided wonderful opportunities to create dazzling effects by placing performing forces in different places around and across the large open space. For example, the motet *In Ecclesiis*[60] ♫ calls for two choruses and organ, with three cornetti, a tenor violin, and two trombones functioning as a third choir.[61] Venetian music was characteristically expressive with an emphasis on beautiful sonorities.[62] David Bryant quotes documents of the time saying that various instruments were added because "it would make the sound more excellent."[63]

As with the prior Dufay example, this Gabrieli example is used merely as an illustration and not necessarily as a composition known to any of the empiricists. Furthermore, it must be remembered from the discussion in Chapter 7 that the music does not determine how one perceives it philosophically. That is, one could view the Dufay and Gabrieli motets from either an empiricist or a rationalist position.

Somewhat parallel with these developments is the rise of the Doctrine of Affections, whose roots are found during the Renaissance with the Florentine Camerata, as they tried to mimic music of the ancient Greeks. Their understanding was that text and music were highly integrated, so they sought a word-to-music correspondence. The Doctrine of Affections, as further developed during the 17th–18th centuries, was the idea that musical motives could embody the affects (i.e., specific feelings).

In his *Passions of the Soul*,[64] Descartes attempted to provide systematic definitions of feelings and emotions. This rational way of dealing with emotions highly influenced music theory treatises. These included Jean-Philippe Rameau's *Treatise on Harmony: Reduced to Its Natural Principles Divided into Four Books* (*Traité de l'harmonie réduite à ses principes naturels*),[65] Johann Joseph Fux's *Ascent to Mount Parnassus* (*Gradus ad Parnassum*),[66] and Johann Mattheson's *The Perfect Chapelmaster* (*Der vollkommene Capellmeister*).[67] The Doctrine of Affections was primarily a word-to-music relationship. Different musical formulas or figures (e.g., falling bass line, a sequence of rising thirds, etc.) led to a depiction of specific affections. This passage from Mattheson makes the connection between words and music explicit:

> However, one must know here that even without words, in purely instrumental music, always and with every melody, the purpose must be to present the governing affection so that the instruments, by means of sound, present it almost verbally and perceptibly.[68]

Another important aspect was the maintenance of a single affection throughout one movement.[69]

Contemporary definitions demonstrate the role of the mind in emotions, a position somewhat resonant with idealism. According to Claude Palisca, Lorenzo Giamcomini, a 16th-century poetic critic, defined an affection as "a spiritual movement or operation of the mind in which it is attracted or repelled by an object it has come to know."[70] In opera, "an affection was understood to be a state of mind that could occupy a character's thoughts and sentiments over a period of time until he was moved by dialogue or action to another state."[71] The role of the mind is reinforced when Rameau said, "reason alone enabled them [the ancients] to discover the greater part of music properties."[72] However, in a more extended passage, he sounded much more like an idealist when he said,

> We may judge of music only through the intervention of hearing, and reason has authority in it only so far as it agrees with the ear; at the same time, nothing can be more convincing to us than their union in our judgments. Our nature is satisfied by the ear, our mind by reason; let us then judge of nothing excepting through their cooperation.[73]

Summary and Thought Questions

The German Idealists are notoriously difficult to understand. Nevertheless, they have made tremendous contributions to the world of philosophy in general and to aesthetics specifically. Their views are so widely divergent that it may seem arbitrary to place them all under one umbrella. However, what ultimately unifies them is the centrality of the mind. Music provides sensory delights and Schiller, Hegel, and Schopenhauer all found value in its beauty. That value was, nevertheless, superseded by the superior role of the mind. The actual sounds (and additional empirical experiences) and the mind's rational understanding of those sounds combine to create the music, which exists only in the mind. By analogy, consider constellations. The stars themselves have no notion of a big dipper or Orion or whatever. Likewise, they are hundreds of thousands of light-years apart and are not connected in any logical way. However, when we look at the night sky and in our minds 'connect the dots,' we create the idea of constellations. They exist in our minds, but not out in space.

In our own times, contemporary music psychologists have generally recognized views that are resonant with idealism. Recall the discussion in Chapter 5: Emotion. According to considerable experimental research, listeners are able to recognize emotions being expressed in the music without necessarily experiencing those emotions. This is called a cognitivist or perceived emotions position. An alternative view, the emotivist or induced emotions position, makes the claim that listeners can actually feel the emotions being expressed, at least some of the time. Of course, there is the possibility that one can listen to music from both perspectives and there are competing theories as well (e.g., Konecki's Aesthetic Trinity Theory). To bring the discussion back to the idealists, the point is that even today there is acknowledgement of the fact that the mind plays a central role in musical experiences.

Idealists get their name essentially because on the whole they believe that ideas are the ultimate reality. We understand the universe, ourselves, and our place in the world through the power of our minds to reason and understand. Unlike the rationalists, idealists recognize sensory experiences as important contributors to mindfulness. Unlike the empiricists, they do not give primacy to the senses. A more even-handed balance is sought between mind and body, and music, specifically, can contribute to an understanding of Absolute Idea (Hegel) or Will (Schopenhauer). However, it is also considered an inferior art (Kant), fades in importance as one approaches ultimate reality (Hegel), or reigns supreme as an expression of the Will (Schopenhauer).

1. *Rationalists separate the mind and the body, elevating the mind and denigrating bodily experiences.* Do you think a mindful (i.e., contemplative) musical experience is more important than a bodily one? If so, how does that influence your teaching, performing, and other musical experiences?
2. *By contrast, empiricists claim that bodily, sensory experiences are more trustworthy than reasoning.* Can you give examples of bodily experiences that provide better insights into reality than rational thought? Is music primarily emotional or mindful?
3. *Kant, Schiller, Hegel, and Schopenhauer expressed considerably divergent views about the nature of music.* Do your ideas resonate with one of these philosophers more than another? Or, do you reject all four of them?
4. *Idealists attempted to synthesize rationalist and empiricist positions.*

   • Do you think they succeeded?
   • To an idealist, music allows for a kind of 'knowing' that is different from our usual conception of knowledge. Do you feel that music can impart a special kind of knowledge? If so, how would you characterize this knowledge?
   • If you claimed to be an idealist, how would that be reflected in your teaching or performing?

Notes

1 For example: Will Durant, *The Story of Philosophy* (New York: Simon and Schuster, 1953). Daniel Flage, "George Berkeley (1685-1753)," *The Internet Encyclopedia of Philosophy*, accessed on June 22, 2016, http://www.iep.utm.edu. Ted Honderich, ed., *The Oxford Guide to Philosophy* (Oxford, UK: Oxford University Press, 2005). Samuel Stumpf and James Fieser, *Philosophy: History and Problems, 6th ed.* (New York: McGraw-Hill, 2003).

2 For example, Brian Duignan, "George Berkeley," *The Encyclopedia Britannica* (July 31, 2014). http://www.britannica.com/biography/George-Berkeley.

3 Stephen Law, *Philosophy* (New York: Metro Books, 2007). Robert Solomon, *Introduction to Philosophy, 8th ed.* (New York: Oxford University Press, 2005).

4 Stephen Priest, *The British Empiricists, 2nd ed.* (New York: Routledge, 2007), 5.

5 William Sahakian and Mabel Sahakian, *Ideas of the Great Philosophers* (New York: Fall River Press, 2005), 135.

6 Ibid., 137.

7 Bertrand Russell, *Wisdom of the West* (London: Rathbone Books, 1959), 214.

8 The complete context of this famous statement is quite lengthy. However, this brief excerpt perhaps puts it into a broader perspective:

But immediately upon this I observed that, whilst I thus wished to think that all was false, it was absolutely necessary that I, who thus thought, should be somewhat; and as I observed that this truth, I think, therefore I am (COGITO ERGO SUM), was so certain and of such evidence that no ground of doubt, however extravagant, could be alleged by the skeptics capable of shaking it, I concluded that I might, without scruple, accept it as the first principle of the philosophy of which I was in search.

In the next place, I attentively examined what I was and as I observed that I could suppose that I had no body, and that there was no world nor any place in which I might be; but that I could not therefore suppose that I was not; and that, on the contrary, from the very circumstance that I thought to doubt of the truth of other things, it most clearly and certainly followed that I was; while, on the other hand, if I had only ceased to think, although all the other objects which I had ever imagined had been in reality existent, I would have had no reason to believe that I existed; I thence concluded that I was a substance whose whole essence or nature consists only in thinking, and which, that it may exist, has need of no place, nor is dependent on any material thing; so that 'I,' that is to say, the mind by which I am what I am, is wholly distinct from the body, and is even more easily known than the latter, and is such, that although the latter were not, it would still continue to be all that it is.

(René Descartes, Chapter 4, *Discourse on the Method of Rightly Conducting the Reason, and Seeking Truth in the Sciences.* The Project Gutenberg Ebook #19796, 1637/2006, n.p. http://www.literature.org/authors/descartes-rene/reason-discourse/chapter-04.html)

9 Antonio Damasio, *Descartes' Error: Emotion, Reason, and the Human Brain* (New York: Avon Books, 1994).

10 Julius Portnoy, *The Philosopher and Music: A Historical Outline* (New York: Da Capo Press, 1954).

11 Stumpf and Fieser, *Philosophy: History and Problems, 6th ed*, 238.

12 Durant, *The Story of Philosophy*, 129.

13 Antonio Damasio, *Looking for Spinoza: Joy, Sorrow, and the Feeling Brain* (New York: Harcourt Brace, 2003).

14 Gottfried Leibniz, *Principles of Nature and Grace Based on Reason*, trans. Jonathan Bennett (1714/2006). http://www.earlymoderntexts.com/assets/pdfs/leibniz1714a.pdf, 7.

15 Russell, *Wisdom of the West.*

16 Solomon, *Introduction to Philosophy, 8th ed.*

17 George Berkeley quoted in Stumpf and Fieser, *Philosophy: History and Problems, 6th ed.*, 262.

18 David Hume, "Of the Standard of Taste," in *Aesthetics: The Big Questions*, ed. Carolyn Korsmeyer (Malden, MA: Blackwell, 1757/1998), 137–50.

19 Durant, *The Story of Philosophy*, 197.

20 Ibid., 192.

21 Monroe Beardsley, *Aesthetics from Classical Greece to the Present* (Tuscaloosa, AL: The University of Alabama Press, 1966), 234.

22 Peter Singer, "Hegel, Georg Wilhelm Friedrich," in *The Oxford Guide to Philosophy*, ed. Ted Honderich (Oxford, UK: Oxford University Press, 2005), 365–367.

23 Russell, *Wisdom of the West*, 246.

24 Durant, *The Story of Philosophy*, 233.

25 Immanuel Kant, *Critique of Pure Reason*, trans. J. Meiklejohn, 1781, accessed on June 22, 2016, http://philosophy.eserver.org/kant/critique-of-pure-reason.txt.

26 Durant, *The Story of Philosophy*, 205.

27 Beardsley, *Aesthetics from Classical Greece to the Present.*

28 Paul Guyer, "18th Century German Aesthetics," in *The Stanford Encyclopedia of Philosophy* (2008 edition), ed. Edward Zalta. http://plato.stanford.edu/archives/fall2008/entries/aesthetics-18th-german/.

29 Douglas Burnham, "Immanuel Kant: Aesthetics," *Internet Encyclopedia of Philosophy* (2005). http://www.iep.utm.edu/kantaest/.

30 Ibid.

31 Ludwig van Beethoven: Symphony No. 9 in d minor, Op. 125, 4th movement, performed by Leonard Bernstein and the Vienna Philharmonic Orchestra, https://www.youtube.com/watch?v=QDViACDYxnQ.

32 Beardsley, *Aesthetics from Classical Greece to the Present.*

33 Friedrich Schiller, *On the Aesthetic Education of Man in a Series of Letters*, trans. Reginald Snell (New York: Continuum, 1795/1990).

34 Reginald Snell, Introduction to *On the Aesthetic Education of Man in a Series of Letters*, by Friedrich Schiller, trans. Reginald Snell (New York: Continuum, 1795/1990).

35 Ibid., 4.

36 Ibid., 12.

37 Schiller, *On the Aesthetic Education of Man in a Series of Letters*, 76.

38 Ibid., 138.

39 Solomon, *Introducing Philosophy, 8th ed.*

40 Michael Inwood, "Schiller, Johann Christoph Freidrich von," in *The Oxford Guide to Philosophy*, ed. Ted Honderich (Oxford, UK: Oxford University Press, 2005).

41 Melvin Rader, *A Modern Book of Esthetics* (New York: Holt, Rinehart and Winston, 1960), xxxii.

42 Stephen Houlgate, "Hegel's Aesthetics," in *The Stanford Encyclopedia of Philosophy* (2014 edition), ed. Edward Zalta. http://plato.stanford.edu/archives/spr2014/entries/hegel-aesthetics/.

43 Gordon Graham, *Philosophy of the Arts: An Introduction to Aesthetics, 2nd ed.* (London: Routledge, 2000), 201.

44 Michael Inwood, "Hegel," in *The Routledge Companion to Aesthetics*, ed. Berys Gaut and Dominic Lopes (London: Routledge, 2002), 65–74.

45 Albert Hofstadter and Richard Kuhns, eds., *Philosophies of Art & Beauty: Selected Readings in Aesthetics from Plato to Heidegger* (Chicago: University of Chicago Press, 1976), 379.

46 Georg Hegel, *The Philosophy of History*, trans. J. Sibree (Kitchener, Ontario, CA: Batoche Books, 1837/2001), 22.

47 Georg Hegel, "Philosophy of Mind," in *The Encyclopaedia of the Philosophical Sciences with Five Introductory Essays*, trans. William Wallace. Project Gutenberg EBook #39064, 1830/1894/2012. http://www.gutenberg.org/files/39064/39064-h/39064-h.html#toc37, p. xlii.

48 Tim Crane, "Hegel," in *Western Philosophy*, ed. David Papineau (New York: Metro Books, 2009), 30.

49 Paul Guyer, "History of Modern Aesthetics," in *The Oxford Handbook of Aesthetics*, ed. Jerrold Levinson (Oxford, UK: Oxford University Press, 2005), 25–60.

50 Georg Hegel, *Aesthetics: Lectures on Fine Art, 2 Vols.* trans. T. Malcolm Knox (Oxford, UK: Clarendon Press, 1835/1975).
51 Houlgate, "Hegel's Aesthetics."
52 Robert Wicks, "Arthur Schopenhauer," in *The Stanford Encyclopedia of Philosophy* (2012 edition), ed. Edward Zalta. http://plato.stanford.edu/archives/win2011/entries/schopenhauer/.
53 Arthur Schopenhauer, *The World as Will and Representation, Vol. 1*, in *The Cambridge Edition of the Works of Schopenhauer*, ed. Christopher Janaway, trans. Judith Norman and Alistair Welchman (Cambridge, UK: Cambridge University Press, 1819/2010), 289.
54 Ibid., 285.
55 John Dewey, *Art as Experience* (New York: Perigree Books, 1934/1980), 296.
56 Guillaume Dufay, *Nuper rosarum flores*, performed by the Hilliard Ensemble. https://www.youtube.com/watch?v=EOWHvIZzXPI.
57 Charles Warren, "Brunelleschi's Dome and Dufay's Motet," *The Musical Quarterly* 59, no. 1 (1973): 92.
58 Ibid., 97.
59 Valerio Morucci, "Reconsidering *cori spezzati*: A New Source from Central Italy" *Acta Musicologica* 84, no. 1 (2013): 21–41.
60 Giovanni Gabrielli, *In Ecclesiis*, performed by the Choir of King's College, Cambridge, and the Philip Jones Brass Ensemble: www.youtube.com/watch?v=q2BOBnAD1Es.
61 Claude Palisca, *Baroque Music* (Englewood Cliffs, NJ: Prentice-Hall, 1968).
62 J. Burkholder, Donald Grout, and Claude Palisca, *A History of Western Music, 7th ed.* (New York: W.W. Norton, 2006).
63 David Bryant, "The 'cori spezzati' of St. Mark's: Myth and Reality," *Early Music History* 1 (1981): 180.
64 René Descartes, *Passions of the Soul*, trans. Jonathan Bennett (1649/2015). http://www.earlymoderntexts.com/assets/pdfs/descartes1649part2.pdf.
65 Jean-Phillippe Rameau, *Treatise on Harmony: Reduced to Its Natural Principles Divided into Four Books*, trans. with an introduction and notes by Philip Gossett (Mineola, NY: Dover Books, 1722/1971).
66 Johann Fux, *The Study of Counterpoint from Johann Joseph Fux's Gradus ad Parnassum*, ed. and trans. by Alfred Mann (New York: W.W. Norton, 1965).
67 Johann Mattheson, *Der vollkommene Capellmeister*. A revised translation with critical commentary by Ernest Harriss (Ann Arbor, MI: UMI Press, 1739/1981).
68 Ibid., 291.
69 Manfred Bukofzer, *Music in the Baroque Era* (New York: W.W. Norton, 1947).
70 Claude Palisca, *Baroque Music*, 3–4.
71 Ibid., 174.
72 Jean-Phillippe Rameau, *Traité de l'harmonie* as quoted in Oliver Strunk, *Source Readings in Music History: The Baroque Era* (New York: W.W. Norton, 1722/1965), 204.
73 Ibid., 207.

11 Formalism

Formalism is a philosophical stance that the value of music lies in the music itself and that the meaning is primarily intellectual. Sometimes this is referred to as Absolute Formalism. While this position can be applied to all art, it may have particular explanatory value for music. After all, "could it even be music, the formalist might ask rhetorically, if it did not have form? Formless sound, so it might be said, just is not music."[1] Although there are ancient precursors to these views in the writings of Aristoxenus, Philodemus, and Sextus Empiricus,[2] we will focus our attention on more contemporary accounts. Eduard Hanslick and Edmund Gurney promoted formalism strenuously in the 19th century, and Clive Bell and Leonard Meyer expounded upon these ideas in the 20th. We will review these major contributors in turn.

Eduard Hanslick

For many years, Eduard Hanslick (1825–1904) was a music critic in Vienna for the *Weiner Zeitung*, the *Presse*, and the *Neue Freie Presse*. He was also a professor at the University of Vienna where he taught musicology and originated music appreciation courses. He is most famous for his book, *The Beautiful in Music*.[3] We will also look at excerpts from some of his concert reviews, because they give particular examples of his philosophical ideas.

The core of Hanslick's philosophy was that beauty is found in the music itself and not in references to things outside the music. He said, "the beauty of a composition is *specifically music*, i.e., it inheres in the combinations of musical sounds and is independent of all alien, extramusical notions."[4] Hanslick did not deny that people experienced emotions or feelings when they listened to music. However, in his view, that is not the point of the music and furthermore, "definite feelings and emotions are unsusceptible of being embodied in music."[5] Apprehending exquisite beauty by focusing on the music itself is not the same thing as being swept away by emotions that lie outside the music. Beauty in music comes from melody, rhythm, harmony, form, and what he called 'euphony,' an agreeableness of sound.

It is easier, perhaps, to understand Hanslick's viewpoint when considering 'absolute' or 'pure' music, that is, instrumental music without a text or program. However, he deals often and at length with programmatic music and opera. In a rather lengthy excerpt, taken from a review of Liszt tone poems, he makes it clear that, for him, it is still the musical elements that are paramount.

> It is hardly necessary here to raise the issue of whether programme music can be justified or not. Nobody now is so narrow-minded as to deny the composer the poetical stimulation

offered by reference to an external theme. Music certainly will never be able to express a definite object, or to represent its essential characteristics in a manner recognizable without the title; but it may take the basic mood from it and, with the title given, present an allusion, if not a graphic representation. The main prerequisite is that music be based on its own laws and remain specifically musical, thus making, even without programme, a clear, independent impression.[6]

One of the implications of Hanslick's philosophy is that the educated mind is better able to apprehend the beauties of music. "The habit of reveling in sensation and emotion is generally limited to those who have not the preparatory knowledge for the aesthetic appreciation of musical beauty."[7] This position is clarified in the following review: "The full enjoyment of such a work [Bach's *St. Matthew Passion*][8] ♫ is vouchsafed, of course, only to those who come to it well prepared and who are able to appreciate the fathomless depths of the technical accomplishment."[9]

At first glance, Hanslick may appear to be an unfeeling, purely rational person. This is not a fair understanding, however. He does find a great deal of meaning and beauty, but these are found in the music itself. What follows are excerpts from his concert reviews. As can be seen, he finds great pleasure in those composers whose artistry is focused on musical ideas (e.g., Beethoven and Brahms), but he is highly critical of those who attempt to portray extramusical ideas (e.g., Berlioz, Bruckner, Liszt, Strauss, and Wagner).

- Beethoven: "In artistic richness, in intrepid greatness, in the free unleashing of an immeasurable fantasy, the Mass in D [*Missa Solemnis*][10] ♫ and the 9th Symphony[11] ♫ stand unique and alone, like colossal Pillars of Hercules, at the gates of modern music, saying, 'No farther!'—the one to sacred music, the other to the symphony."[12]
- In speaking of Brahms's progress in writing piano pieces, Hanslick lauds his gain in "formal clarity."[13] Comparing Brahms to Schumann, Hanslick writes, "Brahms often matches him [Schumann] in wealth of purely formal structure."[14] This emphasis on form is elaborated upon in the following comment: "The term 'form' in musical language is peculiarly significant. The forms created by sound are not empty; not the envelope enclosing a vacuum, but a well, replete with the living creation of inventive genius."[15]
- Brahms 2nd Symphony:[16] ♫ "Its essential characteristics can best be defined as serene cheerfulness, at once manly and gentle, animated alternately by pleased good humour and reflective seriousness."[17]
- About Berlioz, Liszt, Wagner, and Strauss, he wrote, "Colour is everything, musical thought nothing."[18] Specifically about Richard Strauss, he said, "The composer of *Don Juan*[19] ♫ has again proved himself a brilliant virtuoso of the orchestra, lacking only musical ideas."[20]
- Liszt: "His piano compositions were consistently of such mediocre invention and execution that barely one of them could have claimed lasting existence in musical literature."[21]
- Bruckner's 8th Symphony:[22] ♫ "Thus, tossed about between intoxication and desolation, we arrive at no definite impression and enjoy no artistic pleasure. Everything flows, without clarity and without order, willy-nilly into dismal long-windedness."[23]

Hanslick wrote a great deal about Wagner. Upon their initial acquaintance, the critic was favorably impressed with the composer. However, as Wagner continued on his path to merging music with text, dramatic action, and scenery in his conception of *Gesamtkunstwerk* (total artwork), Hanslick became increasingly critical:

- *Tristan and Isolde:*[24] ♪ "Musical form, already considerably relaxed in *Tannhäuser*[25] ♪ and *Lohengrin,*[26] ♪ is totally destroyed, making way for a type of dramatic representation reminiscent of a boundless flood, and governed not by the musical idea but by the word."[27] "It would be hard to find music more unvocal, more unsingable, than is to be found in *Tristan and Isolde.*"[28]
- Overture to *Die Meistersinger von Nürnberg:*[29] ♪ "All the leitmotivs of the opera are dumped consecutively into a chromatic flood and finally tossed about in a kind of tonal typhoon."[30] Of the opera as a whole, he said, "It consists of the intentional dissolution of every fixed form into a shapeless, sensually intoxicating resonance; the replacement of independent, articulate melody by vague melodization."[31] In a different review of a Munich performance, "This system is erroneous in principle and, in its consistent implementation, unbeautiful and unmusical."[32] At the risk of overkill, it is amusing to read Hanslick's review of a different performance of the overture. "The only thing which prevents me from declaring it to be the world's most unpleasant overture is the even more horrible Prelude to *Tristan* and *Isolde*. The latter reminds me of the old Italian painting of that martyr whose intestines were slowly unwound from his body onto a reel. The Prelude to *Die Meistersinger*, at best, goes about it quickly, with spirit and a club."[33] Ironically, it is in this very opera that Wagner "pilloried Hanslick as the foolish pedant Beckmesser."[34]
- In a review of *Parsifal,*[35] ♪ Hanslick comments on the compositional approach: "This method, which purports to elevate opera to true drama, involves the exclusion of the old organic forms, assigning the leading role to the ceaselessly moving orchestra and leaving the voices to declaim rather than sing."[36]
- In a review of the Italian singer Adelina Patti, Hanslick made these comments about singers preparing to sing Wagner's *Ring* cycle operas: "They may learn a lot doing it—but one thing they will certainly unlearn: what singing actually means. Under such conditions it would be regrettable if there were not in at least one German capital (Vienna) an excellent Italian company to remind us from time to time of the vanishing art of beautiful singing."[37]

Whether one agrees with Hanslick or not, one at least has to admire his consistency. He evaluated music from a perspective of formalism; how the musical elements were arranged and related to each other was paramount. Extramusical references were considered irrelevant. He considered a piece of programmatic music beautiful if it had good form. However, he considered music inferior that did not follow good form, whether programmatic or absolute. Finally, Hanslick did find a great deal of beauty and feeling in music; however, these came from musical expressiveness, not from extramusical referents. As we shall see, many critics have attacked the lack of a clear definition of what constitutes 'good form.'

Edmund Gurney

According to Malcolm Budd, Edmund Gurney (1847–1888) was "the most impressive representative of the opposed formalist theory that the abstract art of music is devoid of any human meaning."[38] In *Power of Sound*,[39] Gurney presented a lengthy and detailed account of music's meanings. A similarly detailed review will not be given in these pages; rather, only a few points will be presented to underscore some fundamental aspects of the formalist position.

At the outset, Gurney made the following blunt statement: "The world of Beauty is preeminently the world of form."[40] He believed that music does express emotion, but it is emotion of a very unique kind; we struggle to analyze and explain musical emotions, "while really the beauty has the unity and individuality pertaining to clear and definite form."[41] Gurney also took the position that aesthetic emotions are "totally different from the emotions of life and occasioned only by the perception of works of art."[42] Finally, regarding emotion, Gurney stated that "musical works may be throughout independent of any emotion now conceivable outside the musical sphere."[43]

Another aspect of formalism is that music occupies a separate realm in the mind. Gurney said that the musical faculty and pleasure, "which have to do with music and nothing else, are the representatives and linear descendants of a faculty and pleasure which were music and nothing else."[44] In spite of what may seem like extreme positions, especially when taken so far out of context, Gurney's work "remains one of the most impressive in the field of musical aesthetics."[45]

> "I see music as fluid architecture."
> (Joni Mitchell)

Clive Bell

Clive Bell's (1881–1964) work primarily concerned visual art. Nevertheless, a very brief accounting of his principal idea, encapsulated in the phrase 'significant form,' will be helpful in understanding the formalist position. To Bell, "the starting point for all systems of aesthetics must be the personal experience of a personal emotion."[46] Emotions provoked by artworks are called aesthetic emotions. If all artworks express aesthetic emotions, there must be some common denominator. To Bell, this ubiquitous feature is significant form, by which he meant "arrangements and combinations that move us in a particular way."[47]

Bell also provided a clear accounting of a typically formalist position that "regarded representation in art as an incidental rather than as an essential property of artworks."[48]

> But if a representative form has value, it is as form, not as representation. The representative elements in a work of art may or may not be harmful; always it is irrelevant. For, to appreciate a work of art we need bring with us nothing from life, no knowledge of its ideas and affairs, no familiarity with its emotions. Art transports us from the world of man's activity to a world of aesthetic exaltation. For a moment we are shut off from human interests; our anticipations and memories are arrested; we are lifted above the stream of life.[49]

Bell confessed to being "not really musical" and that "my opinion about music is not worth having."[50] He was unable to grasp the significant form of most music.

> But at moments I do appreciate music as pure musical form, as sounds combined according to the laws of a mysterious necessity, as pure art with a tremendous significance of its own and no relation whatever to the significance of life.[51]

He then described how sometimes when he was tired or distracted and let his mind wander, his grasp of form slipped, his aesthetic emotion collapsed, and he "tumbled from the superb peaks of aesthetic exaltation to the snug foothills of warm humanity."[52]

A position that Bell hinted at previously—that art is removed from life—is made explicit in this passage:

> Great art remains stable and unobscure because the feelings that it awakens are independent of time and place, because its kingdom is not of this world. To those who have and hold a sense of the significance of form what does it matter whether the forms that move them were created in Paris the day before yesterday or in Babylon fifty centuries ago? The forms of art are inexhaustible; but all lead by the same road of aesthetic emotion to the same world of aesthetic ecstasy.[53]

> "I call architecture frozen music."
> (Johann Wolfgang von Goethe)

In sum, then, Bell articulated an extremely formalistic position. Significant form is the common denominator of all art, extra-artistic representations are irrelevant, and aesthetic emotions are removed from daily life and everyday emotions.

Leonard Meyer

Leonard Meyer (1918–2007) approached formalism from the perspective of 20th-century psychology. His exposition of Expectancy Theory was based on Gestalt psychology.[54] Gestalt principles, here applied to music, include such aspects as:

- The whole is different from the sum of its parts. A piece of music heard as a coherent whole is different from one that is analyzed into its constituent parts.
- *Figure–ground relationships* are at play in listening to music when we pay attention to certain elements that we pull into the foreground (e.g., the melody) and relegate other elements to the background (e.g., the accompaniment). Modern cognitive psychology extends this idea by pointing out that we can selectively choose which elements to pay attention to; for example, we could decide to focus on the left-hand accompaniment pattern in a piano sonata rather than on the melody in the right hand.
- The *Law of Prägnanz* states that we tend to make sense of unfamiliar music by these strategies:
  - *Proximity*: pitches that are closer together, generally an interval of a third or less, are easier to group, say, as notes of a melody, than pitches farther apart. Thus, we expect melodies to move more by step than by leap; when there is a leap, the tendency is to expect the notes following a leap to move in a stepwise motion in the opposite direction of the leap.
  - *Simplicity*: we tend to reduce complex musical patterns into a simpler form, such as feeling a 6/8 meter in two beats per measure. As we encounter musical elements in the flow of the music, we expect they will fit into the established harmonic and rhythmic structure.
  - *Good continuation*: we expect a musical line to continue in an established way more than we expect it to move in a different direction. Think of the descending scale line in the opening of *Joy to the World*;[55] ♪ each consecutive pitch leads us to expect the next one in the scale until it reaches a resting point.
  - *Closure*: the feeling of rest we expect when the music has brought us to that point.

Unlike language, where single words can be meaningful (e.g., eat!, why?, stop!), music's meaning arises from one musical event leading to another. The first note of a melody is followed by another and another, the first phrase (the antecedent) implies a second phrase (the consequent), a series of chords may lead us to expect a cadence or a continuation. Beyond this simplicity is a mechanism for explaining how the complexity of music leads to a meaningful musical experience. Once expectations are under way, composers may lead audiences astray by inserting a deceptive cadence, changing the expected cadential point of relaxation into one that suggests incompletion. Major may shift to minor, dynamic levels may instantly become louder or softer, and so on. Composers employ a variety of strategies to create surprise, delay, suspense, ambiguity, and a host of other techniques to create and maintain interest.

According to Meyer, Expectancy Theory plays an important role in emotional responses to music. One of his most well-known statements is that "emotion or affect arises when a tendency to respond is delayed or inhibited."[56] As a simple example, consider the second movement of Haydn's Symphony No. 94 in G Major, the *Surprise Symphony*.[57] ♫ Notice how the opening is very clear and simple—a simple tune, simple duple meter, simple harmonies (not shown)—and how the repetition, slightly softer so that the listener is drawn in, leads to an expectation of a full cadence at the end of the second phrase (see Fig. 11.1). The emotional response is elicited by a disruption in the expectation of a quiet closure.

In Chapter 7 we made a distinction between absolute formalism and absolute expressionism. Absolute formalists are characterized by two things: (1) Their focus is on the music itself and not on extramusical elements. (2) The meaning of music is primarily intellectual, not emotional. Absolute expressionists agree primarily with the first premise, but not the second. At the same time that they agree the focus should be on the music, they also believe that extramusical elements can be brought into the music rather than disregarded and that meaning and value comes from musical expressiveness. Consider Smetana's *Die Moldau*,[58] ♫ for example. While absolute formalists would not find it necessary to consider the fact that the Moldau is a river that runs through Bohemia in determining aesthetic value, absolute expressionists would say that depiction of the river is a result of the way the composer arranged the melody, rhythm, and so on. Furthermore, it is our feelingful response to the music depicting the Moldau River growing from a small stream into a mighty torrent as it flows on its way to Prague. This is the point Bennett Reimer was making when he said that extramusical references are made in and through the music (see Chapter 5).

Figure 11.1 Opening melody in the second movement of Haydn's Symphony No. 94

Image created by author

Early on, in a discussion of absolute expressionism, Meyer's position was that there need not be such a strong division between formalism and expressionism.

> Once it is recognized that affective experience is just as dependent upon intelligent cognition as conscious intellection, that both involve perception, taking into account of, envisaging, and so forth, then thinking and feeling need not be viewed as polar opposites but as different manifestations of a single psychological process.
>
> There is no diametric opposition, no inseparable gulf between the affective and the intellectual responses made to music. . . . Seen in this light, the formalist's conception of musical experience and the expressionist's conception of it appear as complementary rather than contradictory positions. They are considering not different processes but different ways of experiencing the same process.[59]

However, in a later work, Meyer contradicted his earlier position by saying that:

> The sensuous-associative is of minor importance in the consideration of value. Music must be evaluated syntactically.[60]

Here, 'sensuous-associative' refers to emotional responses and referential meanings. Syntactic evaluation refers to consideration of music's formal properties and arrangements.

Finally, in a much later essay, Meyer emphasized the role of uncertainty in emotional processes (changes involving functionally differentiated relationships) and emotional states (e.g., happy, sad, etc.).[61] Normally we desire an optimal level of uncertainty in the music we most prefer. With too little uncertainty, music is completely predictable and that may lead to boredom or disinterest. Music that is completely baffling in its unpredictability may have too much uncertainty and, in turn, may cause us to be frustrated or even angry. As always, however, he connects uncertainty to a formalist position:

> Finally, the aesthetic importance of uncertainty lies not only in the shaping of emotional *processes*, as distinguished from the evocation of emotional *states*, but in the articulation of musical structure. When the tensions of instability are resolved to the cognitive security of stable patterning, functional relationships have at once articulated and unified musical structure.[62]

On balance, then, while Meyer strives to include absolute expressionism as a viable possibility, inevitably and ultimately he ends up with a formalist position. "In short, structure, syntax, and the 'mindful' relationships they implicate are more valuable than the particular, the immediate, and the sensuous."[63]

An Evaluation of Formalism

Noël Carroll provided a succinct, but clear critique of formalism as a viable philosophical viewpoint.[64] He reviewed and then dismissed several arguments put forth by formalists to support their views. In the *common denominator argument*, formalists say that the presence of form is a necessary criterion for something to have the status of art. To support this contention, they discount two alternative views—all art is representational and all art is expressive. Formalists claim that not all art is representational—for example, Bach fugues—and not all art is expressive, such as aleatoric compositions. All artworks do contain form, however. Because things other than art contain form, formalists must qualify the phrase. Thus, a work of art is something that possesses *significant* form. Carroll contends, however, that many works of art were created to explore the lack of significant form. John Cage's *4'33"*[65] ♪ is a famous (or infamous, depending on your viewpoint) example. This is a piece where a pianist sits at the keyboard without playing a single note. The sounds of the 'music' come from the audience and ambient noises in the recital hall. (See Chapter 19: Postmodernism for an extended discussion of John Cage's music.)

Carroll points out that there are many examples of art that were originally intended for purposes other than to present significant form. Thus, the presentation of form is not a *necessary* condition for art. In response, formalists put forward a *function argument*. While other things, such as a sermon or a computer, may possess significant form, they say, only art exists for the purpose of presenting form. While a sermon may possess form, it does not exist primarily to present that form. Likewise, other things besides music are expressive. However, again, only art exists for the purpose of expression. Cheers at a football game are expressive. However, their main purpose is not to be expressive but to be supportive of the team. The primary purpose of art, then, is to exhibit significant form. However, Carroll is quick to show that significant form can be found in many other disciplines besides art. Mathematicians often search for a more elegant solution and athletes may display beauty while fielding a ball or hitting a serve, yet none of these are considered art.

A final criticism is that formalists have no way of distinguishing between significant and insignificant form. There are no guiding principles by which one can decide which artwork exhibits significant form and which does not. Because of the impossibility of defining significant form, "obscurity lies at the heart of formalism; the theory turns out to be useless, because its central term is undefined."[66] Thus, in sum, to Carroll's way of thinking, formalism is a greatly flawed philosophical perspective.

Nigel Warburton adds two additional criticisms of formalism.[67] First, he says that the argument is circular; that is, we only know that 'significant form' gives rise to 'aesthetic emotion' and that 'aesthetic emotion' occurs in the presence of 'significant form.' Without knowing more precisely what either term is or without recognizing one or the other independently, the notion is too vague to be useful. His second objection is irrefutability. If those who experience the aesthetic emotion are deemed sensitive critics and those who do not are considered inexperienced or insensitive critics, then the theory cannot be refuted. "And many philosophers believe that if a theory is logically impossible to refute because every possible observation would confirm it, then it is a meaningless theory."[68]

Musical Examples

Because several musical examples have already been mentioned in this chapter, this section will be somewhat shorter than it could be. First, it bears mentioning that any piece of music or musical experience can be viewed from a formalist perspective. Thus, even the most overtly expressive piece of music or musical experience (e.g., a jam session in which participants give free rein to individual expressions) can be valued on the basis of the internal musical relationships. We might, for example, attend a performance of Richard Strauss's opera *Salome* and be mesmerized by the 'Dance of the Seven Veils,'[69] ♪ surely an expressive piece if there ever was one! However, we could also hear a purely orchestral performance or study the score and focus on the music alone, without the costumes, staging, and dancing.[70] ♩ Either way, the piece could be valued for Strauss's compositional techniques, never mind the story and acting. In Hanslick's view, such a focus reveals a weakness of form, and thus it would have less value.

More often, formalists are apt to talk about pure, instrumental music, using pieces such as a Bach fugue, a Haydn string quartet, or a Mozart symphony as examples. Here, the focus can be on contrapuntal techniques, the use of sonata or rondo form, and so on without the distraction of programmatic elements. Consider theme and variations—or variants such as chaconne, ground bass, or passacaglia; formalists would contend that the primary value of the following compositions rests in the inventiveness, cleverness, and creativity in presenting a major theme in different guises:

- Corelli: *La Folia*[71] ♩
- Bach: *Goldberg Variations*[72] ♩
- Beethoven: *Diabelli Variations*[73] ♩
- Brahms: *Variations on a Theme of Haydn*[74] ♩
- Rachmaninoff: *Rhapsody on a Theme of Paganini*[75] ♩
- Ives: *Variations on America*[76] ♩
- Schoenberg: *Theme and Variations for Wind Band*, Op. 43a[77] ♩

And, of course, so much of jazz is characterized by embellishments and creative explorations of a given tune, such as ''Round Midnight' by Thelonius Monk.[78] ♩ As you think about or listen to each of these examples, consider them first from a formalist point of view. Can you see how one would find meaning and value in the internal musical relationships? If you do not wish to be a formalist, how else could you find value in these pieces? What arguments could you give that a formalist view is not the only way to find meaning and value in these sets of variations?

Music Psychology Research

We can view a great deal of music psychology research from a formalist perspective. That is, researchers have been concerned with how the interplay of musical elements leads to musical understanding. Researchers have generally based their work on the Gestalt principles outlined in the section on Leonard Meyer. Experiments on the role of tonality in Western tonal music are but one example. Carol Krumhansl used a probe tone technique to investigate tonal hierarchies, that is, the relationships and relative importance of notes and chords within a given key.[79] In one study, listeners rated how well each note of a chromatic scale completed an ascending or descending C major scale that was missing the final note. Similarly, in another experiment, listeners rated how well each note of the chromatic scale exhibited 'goodness-of-fit' with scales, triads, and chord sequences in a musical context. On the basis of these and many other experiments, music psychologists have confirmed the tonal hierarchies that composers and listeners expect in 'common-practice' music.

These tonal hierarchies help us understand musical performance behaviors. For example, string players routinely adjust individual notes up or down depending on where they fall in the musical context, as when they raise leading tones. Researchers have demonstrated that tonal hierarchies influence music perception, tracking melodic contour, memorization of melodies, sense of musical stability, perceptual expectancy, and even emotional responses.[80] At a higher level, tonal hierarchies feed into event hierarchies. Tonal hierarchies combine with rhythm to create a series of events that are understood across time as periods, phrases, sections, movements, and so on.[81]

As we have seen, Meyer developed his Expectancy Theory to account for how we derive meaning by following from one musical event to another. Meyer's student Eugene Narmour developed a highly detailed set of implicative rules that help explain how we navigate our way through a music listening experience.[82] The term *functional harmony* implies that chords in a musical context have movement or direction.

David Huron has done extensive work to demonstrate how harmonic movement can lead to emotional responses, even in the absence of text or program.[83] A brief outline of his work, which can be used to support an absolute expressionist position, demonstrates that:

- Listeners describe tonic as stable and satisfying and the leading tone as unstable and restless. Huron gave descriptors such as these the name *qualia*, indicating that these tones, even in isolation, conveyed a certain feeling.
- Next, following the work of Krumhansl described previously, his student[84] and others analyzed the frequency of occurrence of individual pitches in thousands of pieces of music. As would be expected, certain tones (i.e., tonic, fifth, third, etc.) occurred much more frequently than other tones, especially non-diatonic ones. Thus, listeners come to expect certain tones more than others.
- Then researchers examined the regularity of tonal patterns; that is, which tone is more likely to follow any given tone in a melodic sequence? Huron analyzed more than a quarter million pairs of tones in order to construct probability tables.
- Finally, he paired the qualia of scale degrees with the likelihood that one note would move to another. From this, he was able to determine just how it is that pitches moving in a tonal context, without text or program, can convey different feelings. An obvious, simple example would be that an unresolved leading tone elicits a feeling of instability and tension, while resolution to the tonic brings relief and a feeling of comfort and closure.

Composers do many things to delay, disguise, or thwart movement toward a simple cadence, thus heightening the feelings aroused. Musical meaning can come from the music itself, without resorting to extramusical associations. As noted, research of this type can be used to support an absolute expressionist position.

Summary and Thought Questions

Although there are divergent offshoots, formalists are grouped under this label because at the core, it is the arrangement and relationships of musical elements within the music itself from which meaning arises. Hanslick did not deny that there were extramusical elements that accompany many musical experiences, but these were secondary or even irrelevant compared to the music. For him, meaning and value are to be found in melody, harmony, rhythm, form, and all the other musical elements that come into play in a powerful musical experience. There are two additional implications that arise from Hanslick's position. One is that the 'prepared' listener is apt to derive more of the meanings of music than one who is unprepared. Although he does not specifically say that the prepared listener is formally trained necessarily, it is clear that knowledge (e.g., of the composer, the specific piece, of musical styles, etc.) is important. The second implication is that absolute music has greater value than program music. If we recognize that Hanslick was writing during the height of the Romantic era, we can imagine that he was disturbed by the movement away from the structural clarity of Haydn, Mozart, and Beethoven.

Meyer's Expectancy Theory, the notion that each musical idea leads us to expect the next, also favors the knowledgeable listener. Again, knowledgeable listening does not need to come from formal musical training; many knowledgeable listeners gain their skills by repeated listening and increasing familiarity with particular musical styles. The general notion of *uncertainty* is one that captures Meyer's approach in a single word. Generally, we desire an optimal level of uncertainty. Too much predictability or unpredictability most often leads to negative responses.

Absolute expressionism shares with formalism a focus on the music itself. However, where formalists declare extramusical elements irrelevant and eschew emotional responses, absolute expressionists seek to discover how extramusical elements are drawn into and expressed by the music. Furthermore, according to them, these musical expressions are evocative of human feeling.

As is true of any philosophical position, there are critics. Carroll provided a detailed refutation of a formalist position, focusing primarily on the realization that many works of art were not created to present highly structured form and that form is not a necessary or a sufficient condition for meaningful music. What do you think?

1. Do you believe that the central value and meaning of art comes from the formal properties that reside in the music itself?
2. Are all extramusical references irrelevant?
3. Are aesthetic emotions completely separate from emotions experienced in daily life?
4. Either by listening to familiar or unfamiliar music or by imagining the same, can you describe how the Expectancy Theory applies to your experiences? Can you see how focusing on the way musical elements move from point to point leads to a meaningful musical experience?
5. Do the brief explanations of music psychology research convince you that pure instrumental music can convey feelings?
6. Do you feel yourself more aligned with absolute formalism or absolute expressionism? Or perhaps neither? Explain your choice.
7. Suppose you agree with the absolute formalism position. How would this impact your professional musical activities, choices, and attitudes? In other words, what difference would it make if you were an absolute formalist?
8. Ask yourself the same questions if you were to take the absolute expressionist position.
9. Perhaps you agree more with Carroll and do not agree with either absolute formalists or absolute expressionists. Why do you disagree with an absolutist position?

Notes

1 Noël Carroll, *Philosophy of Art* (New York: Routledge, 1999), 111.
2 Wayne Bowman, *Philosophical Perspectives on Music* (New York: Oxford University Press, 1998).
3 Eduard Hanslick, *The Beautiful in Music*, ed. Morris Weitz, trans. Gustav Cohen (New York: Bobbs-Merrill, 1854/1957).
4 Ibid., 5.
5 Ibid., 21.

6 Eduard Hanslick, *Music Criticisms (1846–99)*, ed. and trans. Henry Pleasants (Baltimore: Penguin Books, 1950), 54–55.

7 Ibid., 99.

8 J.S. Bach, *St. Matthew Passion*, BWV 244, performed by Ton Koopman conducting the Amsterdam Baroque Orchestra, https://www.youtube.com/watch?v=ZgA6twxoLRM.

9 Hanslick, *Music Criticisms (1846–99)*, 99.

10 Ludwig van Beethoven, *Missa Solemnis*, Mass in D Major, Op. 123, performed by Kurt Masur conducting the Leipzig Gewandhaus Orchestra, http://www.youtube.com/watch?v=njCCxCQa9sI.

11 Ludwig van Beethoven, Symphony No. 9 in d minor, Op. 125, performed by Leonard Bernstein conducting the Vienna Philharmonic, http://www.youtube.com/watch?v=3MnGfhJCK_g.

12 Hanslick, *Music Criticisms (1846–99)*, 73.

13 Ibid., 83.

14 Ibid., 83.

15 Hanslick, *The Beautiful in Music*, 50.

16 Johannes Brahms, Symphony No. 2 in D Major, Op. 73, performed by Carlos Kleiber conducting the Vienna Philharmonic, https://www.youtube.com/watch?v=XHmkl7GM_es.

17 Hanslick, *Music Criticisms (1846–99)*, 158.

18 Ibid., 291.

19 Richard Strauss, *Don Juan*, Op. 20, performed by Fritz Reiner conducting the Chicago Symphony Orchestra, http://www.youtube.com/watch?v=obEYUa_U8sc.

20 Hanslick, *Music Criticisms (1846–99)*, 293

21 Ibid., 53.

22 Anton Bruckner, Symphony No. 8 in c minor, performed by Herbert van Karajan conducting the Vienna Philharmonic, https://www.youtube.com/watch?v=iU-lNkqbUbI.

23 Hanslick, *Music Criticisms (1846–99)*, 289.

24 Richard Wagner, *Tristan and Isolde* (end of Act 3, *Liebestod*), performed by Daniel Barenboim, conductor, with Siegfried Jerusalem and Waltraud Meier at Bayreuth, http://www.youtube.com/watch?v=OAEkTK6aKUM.

25 Richard Wagner, *Tannhäuser*, performed by Sir Colin Davis, conductor, at Bayreuth, http://www.youtube.com/watch?v=8du71AE0h6o.

26 Richard Wagner, *Lohengrin*, performed by Andris Nelsons, conductor, at Bayreuth, http://www.youtube.com/watch?v=VXwSV0sjYzg.

27 Hanslick, *Music Criticisms (1846–99)*, 222.

28 Ibid., 224.

29 Richard Wagner, Overture to *Die Meistersinger von Nürnberg*, performed by Christian Thielemann conducting the Vienna Philharmonic, http://www.youtube.com/watch?v=uyypHlrZsgg.

30 Hanslick, *Music Criticisms (1846–99)*, 112.

31 Ibid., 119.

32 Ibid., 122.

33 Ibid., 112.

34 Jenefer Robinson ed., *Music and Meaning* (Ithaca, NY: Cornell University Press, 1997), 3.

35 Richard Wagner: *Parsifal*, performed by Herbert von Karajan conducting the Berlin Philharmonic, https://www.youtube.com/watch?v=p1BFR5UfXe0.

36 Hanslick, *Music Criticisms (1846–99)*, 197.

37 Ibid., 183.

38 Malcolm Budd, *Music and the Emotions: The Philosophical Theories* (London: Routledge and Kegan Paul, 1985), 52.

39 Edmund Gurney, *The Power of Sound* (London: Smith, Elder, & Co., 1880).

40 Ibid., 8.

41 Ibid., 120.

42 Jerrold Levinson, "Music and Negative Emotion," in *Music and Meaning*, ed. Jenefer Robinson (Ithaca, NY: Cornell University Press, 1997), 218.

43 Edmund Gurney, "On Some Disputed Points in Music," *Fortnightly Review* 20, no. 115 (1876): 119.

44 Gurney, *The Power of Sound*, 492.

45 Edward Lippman, *A History of Western Musical Aesthetics* (Lincoln, NE: University of Nebraska Press, 1992), 319.

46 Clive Bell, "Significant Form," in *Introductory Readings in Aesthetics*, ed. John Hospers (New York: The Free Press, 1913/1969), 87.

47 Ibid., 90–91.

48 Carroll, *Philosophy of Art*, 110.

49 Bell, "Significant Form," 91.

50 Ibid., 93

51 Ibid., 94

52 Ibid., 94

53 Ibid., 96.

54 Leonard Meyer, *Emotion and Meaning in Music* (Chicago: The University of Chicago Press, 1956).

55 Isaac Watts (text) and Lowell Mason (music, arr. of Handel), *Joy to the World*, performed by Faith Hill, http://www.youtube.com/watch?v=x-8i_N-thek.

56 Meyer, *Emotion and Meaning in Music*, 31.

57 Franz Haydn, Second movement of Symphony No. 94 in G Major, *Surprise*, Hob.1.94, performed by Leslie Jones conducting the Little Orchestra of London, http://www.youtube.com/watch?v=mNwMXj0Y1_Y.

58 Bedrich Smetana, *Die Moldau* (or *Vltava*), performed by Nikolaus Harnencourt conducting the Chamber Orchestra of Europe, http://www.youtube.com/watch?v=h3_EsIKarl8.

59 Meyer, *Emotion and Meaning in Music*, 39–40.

60 Leonard Meyer, *Music, the Arts, and Ideas* (Chicago: The University of Chicago Press, 1967), 36.

61 Leonard Meyer, "Music and Emotion: Distinction and Uncertainties," in *Music and Emotion*, ed. Patrik Juslin and John Sloboda (New York: Oxford University Press, 2001), 341–60.

62 Ibid., 359.

63 Bowman, *Philosophical Perspectives on Music*, 192.

64 Noël Carroll, "Formalism," in *The Routledge Companion to Aesthetics*, ed. Berys Gaut and Dominic Lopes (London: Routledge, 2002), 87–96.

65 John Cage, *4'33"*, performed by William Marx, http://www.youtube.com/watch?v=JTEFKFiXSx4.

66 Carroll, "Formalism," 94.

67 Nigel Warburton, *Philosophy: The Basics, 3rd ed.* (London: Routledge, 1999).

68 Ibid., 155.

69 Richard Strauss, 'Dance of the Seven Veils' from *Salome*, performed by Karita Mattila, with James Conlon conducting the l'Orchestra de l'Opéra National Paris, https://www.youtube.com/watch?v=owdJmtuMSIw.

70 Richard Strauss, 'Dance of the Seven Veils' from *Salome*, performed by Erich Leinsdorf conducting the London Symphony Orchestra, http://www.youtube.com/watch?v=C14LfoE8G14.

71 Arcangelo Corelli, Violin Sonata No. 12 in d minor, *La Folia*, performed by Henryk Szeryng, violin, and Huguette Dreyfus, harpsichord, http://www.youtube.com/watch?v=XS-Nqzprais.

72 J.S. Bach, *Goldberg Variations*, BWV 988, performed by Murray Perahia, http://www.youtube.com/watch?v=4ppcbLdtghE.

73 Ludwig van Beethoven, *Diabelli Variations*, Op. 120, performed by Rudolf Serkin, piano, http://www.youtube.com/watch?v=PebmYKm-BE4.

74 Johannes Brahms, *Variations on a Theme by Haydn*, Op. 56, performed by Ricardo Muti conducting the Philadelphia Orchestra, http://www.youtube.com/watch?v=SJO4aXoKptM.

75 Sergei Rachmaninoff, *Rhapsody on a Theme by Paganini*, performed by Daniil Trifonov, piano, and Zubin Mehta conducting the Israel Philharmonic Orchestra, http://www.youtube.com/watch?v=AAu6BRWL8p8.

76 Charles Ives, *Variations on America*, performed by Timothy Foley conducting the United States Marine Band, http://www.youtube.com/watch?v=hs0VjhNWqn8.

77 Arnold Schoenberg, *Theme and Variations for Wind Band*, Op. 43a, performed by Gunther Schuller conducting the United States Marine Band, http://www.youtube.com/watch?v=JEVZwr8GP1s.

78 Thelonious Monk, ''Round Midnight,' performed by Thelonious Monk, Dizzy Gillespie, and the Giants of Jazz, http://www.youtube.com/watch?v=VUVuX3lLrdg.

79 Carol Krumhansl, *Cognitive Foundations of Musical Pitch* (New York: Oxford University Press, 1990).

80 Emmanuel Bigand and Bénédicte Poulin-Charronat, "Tonal Cognition," in *The Oxford Handbook of Music Psychology*, ed. Susan Hallam, Ian Cross, and Michael Thaut (Oxford, UK: Oxford University Press, 2009), 59–71.

81 Fred Lerdahl and Ray Jackendoff, *A Generative Theory of Tonal Music* (Cambridge, MA: The MIT Press, 1983).

82 Eugene Narmour, *The Analysis and Cognition of Melodic Complexity: The Implication-Realization Model* (Chicago: The University of Chicago Press, 1992).

83 David Huron, *Sweet Anticipation: Music and the Psychology of Expectation* (Cambridge, MA: The MIT Press, 2006).

84 Bret Aarden, "Dynamic Melodic Expectancy" (Ph.D. dissertation, Ohio State University, 2003). http://rave.ohiolink.edu/etdc/view?acc_num=osu1060969388.

12 Expressionism

Previously, we discussed referentialism, the notion that the primary value of music comes from what the music points to rather than the music itself. Here, we have divided referentialist positions into two camps, expressionism in this chapter, and symbolism in the next. Recall, also from a previous discussion, the fact that labels can be confusing and sometimes even arbitrary. Although not everyone would make this division, many others have. Thus, in this chapter we take a look at philosophers who find the primary value of music in the expression of human emotions.

"That the expression of emotion is among the principal purposes of art is a thought with a pedigree stretching back at least as far as the Ancient Greeks."[1] This notion, which on the surface seems simple and straightforward, rapidly turns into a complex and confusing discussion in the hands of philosophers. 'Expression' can refer to the feelings of the composer, the performer, the audience, the "intrinsic expressiveness of music itself,"[2] or to any or all of these in combination. Do listeners actually feel the emotions expressed through music or are they only cognitively aware of those emotions? Are the emotions expressed in music the same as other emotions or are there separate aesthetic emotions? Further, there are issues of whether the music merely presents sounds, which listeners interpret as expressive of certain feelings, or whether the music sonically exemplifies characteristics of emotions, as in the slowly descending, chromatic lines of 'Dido's Lament' from Purcell's opera *Dido and Aeneas*.[3] ♪ The Purcell example introduces additional confounds, that of language, costumes, scenery, and acting. Is it the words "when I am laid in earth" that provide the emotional expressiveness, along with the behavioral expressions of grief, the music, or both? What, then, about pure instrumental music; can a Bach fugue, a Haydn string quartet, or a Mozart symphony express emotions? Terminology is important, too, as philosophers make a distinction between music *expressing* an emotion and music being *expressive of* an emotion.[4] In fact, some prefer the term *expressivism* rather than expressionism.[5]

Our purpose in this chapter will be to review some of the major ideas of philosophers who have dealt with emotional expression in music. We will begin with Leo Tolstoy and proceed through Benedetto Croce, R. G. Collingwood, Deryck Cooke, Peter Kivy, Stephen Davies, and Jenefer Robinson. Many musical examples will accompany the discussion and, as always, the important thing is for you to think carefully through the issues as they are presented and eventually to come to your own understanding of the matter. The final major section presents an overview of research on musical emotions.

Leo Tolstoy

The great novelist Leo Tolstoy (1828–1910) wrote a highly influential book entitled *What Is Art?* In it, as presented previously in Chapter 6, he articulated a very clear stance of expressionism.

> Art is a human activity consisting in this, that one man consciously, by means of certain external signs, hands on to others feelings he has lived through, and that other people are infected by these feelings and also experience them.[6]

George Bernard Shaw agreed with Tolstoy's notion of art as an expression of feelings when he said, "The moment it [this notion] is uttered, whoever is really conversant with art recognizes in it the voice of the master."[7]

> "Music is the shorthand of emotion."
> (Leo Tolstoy)

Notice the use of the verb 'infected.' In another passage, Tolstoy described how he, himself, was *infected* with the feelings expressed in music. He was returning home feeling depressed when he heard a group of peasant women greeting the return home of his daughter from her marriage.

> In this singing, with its cries and clanging of scythes, such a definite feeling of joy, cheerfulness, and energy was expressed that, without noticing how it infected me, I continued my way toward the house in a better mood and reached home smiling and quite in good spirits.[8]

The process of being infected by the expressions of music extends to performers, as it "is a thing we receive only when the performer finds those infinitely minute degrees which are necessary to perfection in music."[9]

Infectiousness is the hallmark of great art. If there is no 'infection' there is no art; "the stronger the infection, the better is the art as art."[10] Infectiousness depends on the individuality of the feeling being expressed, the clarity with which the feeling is transmitted, and the sincerity of the artist. Sincerity, that is the extent to which the artist feels the emotion he is expressing, is the most important criterion. Subsequently, Tolstoy adds two qualifiers to distinguish great art. It must be Christian art that (a) expresses a union of man to God and to one another, or (b) expresses universal feelings of common life accessible to all. In making these criteria of great art, Tolstoy decided that there are very few works from the classical repertoire that qualify—"Bach's famous violin aria, Chopin's nocturne in E-flat major,[11] ♫ and perhaps a dozen bits (not whole pieces, but parts) selected from the works of Haydn, Schubert, Beethoven, and Chopin."[12] Conversely, nearly all the "chamber and opera music of our times, beginning especially from Beethoven (Schumann, Berlioz, Liszt, Wagner), by its subject matter devoted to the expression of feelings accessible only to people who have developed in themselves an unhealthy, nervous irritation evoked by this exclusive, artificial, and complex music"[13] is to be considered bad art, even including Beethoven's 9th Symphony.[14] ♫

Charles Daniels is among those who have criticized Tolstoy's view. He said that if you were to adopt Tolstoy's view you have to believe that art is a means of communication and that it must communicate with everyone.[15]

Benedetto Croce

The Italian philosopher Benedetto Croce (1860–1952) was "unquestionably the most influential aesthetician of our time," according to Monroe Beardsley;[16] however, thereafter his influence has waned.[17] Gary Kemp succinctly stated the essence of Croce's aesthetic position this way: "art is expression that we engage with via the intuitive capacity."[18] Croce explained what he meant by the phrase "art is intuition"[19] in terms of four negations:

- "It denies, above all, that art is a *physical fact*."[20] Croce believed that artworks exist in the mind. Thus, when a person listens to music, the symphony or pop tune or jazz ballad becomes reality in the listener's mind.
- "Art cannot be a utilitarian act; . . . [it] has nothing to do with the *useful* and with *pleasure* and *pain*."[21] This is because intuition involves contemplation, not action.
- "A third negation, effected by means of the theory of art as intuition, is that art is a *moral act*." This, again, is because intuition is "opposed to the practical of any sort."[22]
- "With the definition of art as intuition, we deny that it has the character of *conceptual knowledge*." Conceptual knowledge establishes reality in contrast with unreality, "but, intuition means, precisely, indistinction of reality and unreality."[23]

> "Art is a true aesthetic synthesis, 'a priori' of feeling and image in the intuition, as to which it may be repeated that feeling without image is blind, and image without feeling is void."
>
> (Benedetto Croce)

In summary, he said that "art is distinguished from the physical world and from the practical, moral, and conceptual activity as *intuition*."[24] Furthermore, "what lends coherence and unity to intuition is intense feeling. Intuition is truly such because it expresses an intense feeling."[25] Croce is thus an expressionist: "Not the idea, but the feeling, is what confers upon art the airy lightness of the symbol."[26] It is impossible to be "a great composer who cannot express himself."[27] "Expression and beauty are not two concepts, but a single concept."[28]

R. G. Collingwood

R. G. Collingwood (1889–1943) wrote an aesthetic theory of expressionism that was very similar to Croce's. He used the term 'imagination' in place of Croce's 'intuition,' but they mean basically the same thing. For Collingwood, "art is expression at the level of imagination."[29] His primary work was *The Principles of Art*,[30] in which he attempted "to offer an account of just what it is to express an emotion and how that differs from simply feeling an emotion."[31] A primary aspect of his position is that there is no distinction between artistic expressions and everyday expressions of art. "Every utterance and every gesture that each one of us makes is a work of art."[32] An artist, or in our case, composer, discovers what he feels through the act of expressing it in his music. The emotion and the artwork are bound together because "the identity of an emotion expressed in a work of art is inextricably linked to the identity of the work of art."[33] In revealing his own emotions to himself through his music, the composer also reveals those same emotions to the audience. Thus, "The artist's business is to express emotions; and the only emotions he can express are those which he feels, namely, his own."[34]

Gordon Graham listed six objections to Croce's ideas and concluded that "expressivism is seriously flawed."[35] Likewise, Anne Sheppard stated, "In the end Croce and Collingwood fail because they concentrate too much on what they take to be going on in the mind of the creative artist and because they exaggerate the importance of their notion of expression."[36] We shall see whether contemporary philosophers were able to overcome these limitations.

> "If 'work of art' means work of art proper, a piece of music is not something audible, but something which may exist solely in the musician's head."
>
> (R. G. Collingwood)

Deryck Cooke

Deryck Cooke (1919–1976) wrote a book "to show that the conception of music as a language capable of expressing certain very definite things is not a romantic aberration, but has been the common unconscious assumption of composers for the past five-and-a-half centuries at least."[37] To him, the elements of music create a vocabulary capable of expressing emotions. For example, pitches can create tonal or intervallic tensions, whether placed successively in a melody or simultaneously in harmony. Time-based tensions include rhythmic accents, syncopation, and duration (including tempo, movement, and phrasing). Three additional means of musical expression are volume (i.e., loudness), tone-color, and texture.

Limiting himself to tonal music, he provided numerous musical examples. For example, he endeavored to show "the strong contrast between the 'natural' pleasurable major third and the 'unnatural' painful minor third"[38] with examples ranging from Dufay to Haydn, Schubert, Tchaikovsky, and Irving Berlin.

> "Instead of responding to music as what it is—the expression of man's deepest self—we tend to regard it more and more as a purely decorative art; and by analyzing the great works of musical expression purely as pieces of decoration, we misapprehend their true nature, purpose, and value."
>
> (Deryck Cooke)

> Hence the major third, when emphasized strongly in the triadic context, is the supremely satisfied, straightforwardly and contentedly joyful note, firmly 'looking on the bright side of things'; the minor third, emphasized strongly in the triadic context, is the supremely stern, straightforwardly and dignifiedly tragic note, firmly 'looking on the dark side of things'.[39]

Cooke did recognize that isolated notes or intervals taken out of context have no genuine musical meaning and he subsequently discussed phrases and large-scale structures. From there, he attempted to show how an entire work functions as an expressive whole. He showed how composers work from an original conception to inspiration and creative imagination. Cooke also discussed the communication pathway from composer through the performer to the listener. Especially assuming both musical performers and listeners, the emotion experienced by listeners is as close to the composer's original intention as "the emotions of one human being can ever resemble those of another."[40] That is, "we can never know exactly how another person feels."[41] If Beethoven, for example, wrote music to express joy, he asked players to play certain notes at certain times in certain ways.

> Thus Beethoven still shouts for joy, and we still listen to him; but since the shout is a musical one, we do not merely have a vague impression that he felt joyful (as those who only heard his vocal shoutings did)—we feel, to the best of our capacity, just how vitally and intensely joyful he felt, and we are renewed and inspirited by our direct emotional contact with his indomitable being.[42]

As Beethoven himself wrote in the manuscript of the *Missa Solemnis*:[43] ♪ "From the heart—may it go back—to the heart!"[44]

In the final paragraph of his book, Cooke sums up his thesis in this way:

> The composer, expressing unconscious emotions in the inexplicit language of music, and often not fully realizing himself exactly what he is saying, does indeed 'give himself away': being certain that whatever he has said can only be felt by the musically sensitive, and not clearly identified, explained and discussed, he can let out all that he obscurely feels in the depths of his being, while still remaining 'silent' (i.e., inexplicit).[45]

Peter Kivy

Peter Kivy (1934–) presented a 'doggy' theory of musical expressiveness, more formally called the 'contour theory.' Just as the face of a St. Bernard can express sadness without our imagining that the dog itself is sad, so music can express emotions by resembling how humans express themselves.[46] Music can express human utterances, or the way we move or gesture. Consider, for example, differences in how we express grief and joy. We might slump with grief or leap with joy. Music mimics these bodily expressions in slow versus fast tempo, or falling versus rising melodic lines, and so on. In addition, some musical elements are associated with emotional expressions by convention, as in music in a minor key often being understood to express sadness. "Cheerful people express themselves in bright, loud, sometimes even raucous—certainly not subdued—tones; and cheerful music tends to be bright, loud, and in the high register."[47]

In *Music Alone*, Kivy explained that pure instrumental music can express what he calls 'garden-variety emotions,' such as grief and joy, but not cognitively complex emotions such as pride or envy.[48] This is because garden-variety emotions have standardized behavioral responses, such as described previously, and are not necessarily about something in particular. In other words, we can be generally sad without being sad about some particular thing, and our bodily and behavioral expressions of sadness have universal features that can be mimicked by music. In contrast, expressions of more complex or subtle emotions such as jealousy require that it be about someone or something and there are no standard expressions; thus, pure instrumental music cannot mimic or express jealousy or other complex emotions.

> "Music, alone of the fine arts, makes us free of the world of our everyday lives. . . . Only music, music alone, is the true art of liberation."
>
> (Peter Kivy)

Stephen Davies

Stephen Davies (1950–) presented a theory of musical expressiveness similar to Kivy's.[49]

> The sadness of music is a property of the sounds of the musical work. The sadness is presented in the musical work. There need be no describing, or representing, or symbolizing, or other kinds of denoting that connect the musical expressiveness to occurrent emotions, for the expressive character of the music resides within its own nature.[50]

Davies adds basset hounds to Kivy's St. Bernards in agreement with the contour theory.

Again, similar to Kivy, he believed that "the expressiveness of music depends mainly on a resemblance we perceive between the dynamic character of music and human movement, gait, bearing, or carriage."[51] Davies also placed a limitation on the kinds of emotions that could be expressed in music, feeling that they must be restricted to emotions that have "characteristic behavioral expressions."[52]

> "No doubt composers sometimes express their feelings in what they write, but they do so not by conveying what they feel to, or betraying it in, the music but, instead, by creating music with an expressive character that independently matches what they are inclined to feel."
>
> (Stephen Davies)

Jenefer Robinson

Jenefer Robinson identified several criticisms of the type of contour theory espoused by Kivy and Davies.[53] She felt that it does not adequately represent the richness and complexity of human emotions.

> Before leaving the doggy theory, I would like to point out that in addition to denying or ignoring (1) the expression (in the sense of articulation) of particular emotions by a piece of music, the doggy theory does not adequately distinguish between (2) the possession of emotional qualities such as sadness and cheerfulness by music, and (3) emotional *expressiveness* in music.[54]

She felt that music can mimic or mirror more complex emotions such as aspiration or nostalgia. For example, a musical theme that repeatedly struggles for completion and finally achieves closure might mimic desire.

Robinson also addressed the limitations placed on pure instrumental music by the contour theory. She based some of her ideas on the work of Edward Cone,[55] albeit with some differences. Although not all instrumental music is necessarily experienced as emotionally expressive, "once the notion of Romantic expression in music has been introduced, then we can, if we wish, listen to different kinds of music *as if* it were an expression by some character in the music . . ."[56] Allowing pure instrumental music to express emotions has the following consequences:

- In contrast to the contour theory that deals with individual emotions, one can experience an entire piece as expressive of a range of emotions. "It is not just isolated gestures that are expressive, but the way one theme or harmony transforms into another, the way that the end of the piece sheds new light on the beginning, and so on and so forth."[57]

- Purely instrumental music can express cognitively complex emotions as they represent agents, characters, or personae. Again, from Cone: "The violin of a Bach partita, the piano of a Beethoven sonata—the agents these bring to life are coterminous with the musical personas of their respective compositions."[58] "The persona of a violin partita is a violinistic persona; the persona of a piano sonata is a pianistic persona. And the persona implied by a combination of instruments is realized in the sound of the combination."[59]
- Assuming these personae, then, "pure instrumental music can be *about* the emotions it expresses."[60] The composer, having created the character or characters in a work, is then free to comment on their emotions.
- "Finally, if there is a persona or set of characters in a piece of instrumental music, then a piece of 'music alone' can be a genuine Romantic expression of emotion in a protagonist, just like a song, and not just a sequence of expressive contours."[61] Even if there is no hint from the composer, such as a descriptive title (e.g., Schubert's *Wanderer Fantasy*),[62] ♪ "it is reasonable to interpret certain kinds of Romantic instrumental music as expressions of emotion in a persona, because that was how composers of the time thought of (some of) their compositions."[63]

Robinson finds that the formal and expressive elements of music are interdependent. That is, it is not that the formal elements are 'decorated' by expression but form and expression are co-dependent. In an extended analysis of the Brahms Intermezzo in b flat minor, Opus 117, No. 2,[64] ♪ including both structural and expressive details, Robinson pointed out that the "overall bittersweet character of the piece *emerges* from this dramatic interplay between melodies and harmonies."[65] She noted that "Brahms referred to the three Intermezzi of his Opus 117 as 'three cradle-songs of my sorrows'. Never a man to pour out his feelings in words, Brahms communicates what he has to say in his music."[66] Brahms communicates what he wants to through the combination of structural and expressive elements.

> "Once we hear the structure of a piece of music as a psychological as well as a musical structure, then we are able to hear in it not just specific emotions but patterns of emotion."
>
> (Jenefer Robinson)

As can well be expected, there are critics of expressionism as a philosophy of music. After systematically reviewing various expressionist theories, Malcolm Budd presented his criticisms.[67] "And the result of the examinations is that each of the theories . . . is found wanting; no theory does justice to the phenomenon of music."[68] Likewise, Noël Carroll was critical of expressionist theories. "Though superior to representational theories of art, they fail to track all art satisfactorily in both its richness and its specificity."[69] That is, although some art may be expressive of human emotions, not all art is. In particular, expressionist philosophers have failed to show, according to these and other critics, how pure instrumental music might express emotions and other things outside itself.

Musical Examples

The notion that art is expressive can be traced back to ancient philosophers, but it was Romantic artists of the 18th–19th centuries who heightened that perspective.[70] "It is important to remember that the concept of art as a personal expression of emotion originated in Romanticism."[71] Recognizing this, most of the examples in this section come from the Romantic period or later. As was the case with musical examples in the previous chapter, the point of including these examples is more to stimulate your thinking than to state categorically that these pieces of music are expressing specific emotions.

Let us begin with opera. From so many choices, consider two arias from Puccini's *Madama Butterfly*. In the second act, Cio-Cio San, known as Butterfly, is waiting for her American soldier husband, Lt. Pinkerton, to return after a three-year absence. In the famous aria 'Un bel di,' she is nearly giddy with excitement as she imagines that she will stand on top of a hill overlooking the ocean and see the puff of smoke off on the far horizon announcing the arrival of the ship carrying her husband.[72] ♫ By the end of the opera, Cio-Cio San knows that Pinkerton has married an American wife and that they have come to take the child Butterfly had with him to raise as their own. In the opera's tragic and dramatic finale, Cio-Cio San sings 'Con onor muore' (To die with honor) as she blindfolds her son, then kills herself.[73] ♫

Probably few, if any, who have heard *Madama Butterfly* would deny that these two arias, and indeed the entire opera, express powerful emotions. But, a critic might contend, these emotions arise as much or more from the costumes, staging, storyline, lyrics, and so on. Much as we could argue about music's role in this expressiveness, let us move to oratorio, removing the costumes and staging, but retaining a storyline and lyrics. In *Elijah*, Mendelssohn tells the story of the Biblical prophet who is fighting against the pagan priests of Baal. He sings "It is enough; O Lord now take away my life," surely a piece expressing despair and resignation.[74] ♫ Here again, both sides of the argument can be made—the lyrics and setting create the emotional response against the position that the music enhances the emotional impact far beyond the words alone.

There are similar examples from other musical genres. Consider the iconic performance of 'Candle in the Wind' by Elton John at Princess Diana's funeral.[75] ♫ Moving to an entirely different style, consider Pussy Riot, a feminist, punk protest band based in Moscow. Two of their members were jailed for hooliganism after performing a song critical of then-Prime Minister Vladimir Putin.[76] The song 'Punk Prayer,' performed in an Orthodox cathedral, included the words "Drive away Putin," along with other highly critical lyrics.[77] ♫ "The 'punk prayer' was inspired by the women's anger about the relationship between the Russian government and the Orthodox Church, according to the band's manager, who is married to one of the women."[78] Listening to the music, even with an inability to understand the Russian lyrics, one gets an unmistakable sense of the expression of anger.

Let us conclude these vocal-choral examples with two thoughts: (1) an enormous amount of Western music is vocal and (2) this music is expressive. One might argue about how or what elements make it expressive, but it is unlikely that many would argue that music with text, and often with costumes, staging, or stage effects (e.g., smoke machines at rock concerts) is inexpressive. Assuming at least temporary agreement with these points, let us turn, then, to instrumental music, beginning with Romantic program music. A significant amount of this music gains at least some impetus for expressivity through titles or programs. For example, Mussorgsky's *Pictures at an Exhibition*, originally written for the piano,[79] ♫ but more famously known, perhaps, in the orchestrated version by Ravel,[80] ♫ is intended to represent a tour of an art gallery featuring paintings by Viktor Hartmann. Titles of the various movements give clues to what is being expressed; for example, the 'Promenade' depicts a patron walking amongst the paintings, 'Ballet of the Unhatched Chicks' comes from costume and set designs Hartmann made for a ballet performed at the Bolshoi, and 'The Great Gate of Kiev' was a design for a city gate (never built) to honor Tsar Alexander II's survival from an assassination attempt.

One could easily create a long list of instrumental pieces that have titles. Never mind that some of these titles were added after the fact by someone other than the composer, or that the title is not necessarily reflective of the musical expressiveness. For example, the descriptive title of Beethoven's piano rondo *Rage Over a Lost Penny*[81] ♫ seems not to have come from him[82] and the music hardly expresses rage. Rather, the major question facing most philosophers is whether, and if so how, pure instrumental music can express feelings and emotions. Recall the musical examples given in the previous chapter on formalism. Can any of these be said to express anything extramusical? Let us revisit just one of those examples, the Schoenberg *Theme and Variations for Wind Band*.[83] ♫

Whether you have performed or conducted this piece many times or never heard it before, I encourage you to listen to it in its entirety twice, once with your 'formalist' hat on and once with your 'expressionist' hat on. Of course, there are many more positions from which to consider this piece, but the question of the moment is whether, and if so how, pure instrumental music can be said to be expressive of anything outside the music, particularly emotions. While listening as a formalist—whether you are one, uncertain, or decidedly not—listen with a specific focus on the musical interrelationships. Try to follow the theme through its various iterations. Concentrate on Schoenberg's creativity in manipulating melody, harmony, form, and so on. Schoenberg's *Theme and Variations* is one of the few pieces originally written for wind band (Op. 43a) and later transcribed for orchestra (Op. 43b). According to the composer, "It is one of those works that one writes in order to enjoy one's own virtuosity."[84]

In listening a second time, this time as an expressionist, try to separate out your own feelings from what is being expressed in the music. You might feel confusion, boredom, elation, or any number of feelings. However, on what basis would you say that this music expresses these or other feelings? If your answer is yes, it does do that, can you explain how this is done? This is the challenge that the formalists put before expressionists.

Research on Musical Emotions

Kate Hevner is one of the pioneers of music psychology research on musical emotions. She started by assuming that music is expressive, recognizing that

> in the history of musical culture, there has been a lengthy controversy over the problem of expressiveness in music, and much difference of opinion as to whether music can be made to express definite emotions and concepts and sentiments, or whether it is merely suggestive and moving in a very general way and to be interpreted quite variously by the different listeners who are attending to it.[85]

She developed what has become known as the Hevner Adjective Cycle, a series of emotion adjectives arranged in groups. There are eight categories, with as many as 11 adjectives in each group: (1) spiritual, (2) sad, (3) dreamy, (4) tranquil, (5) playful, (6) happy, (7) exhilarated, and (8) vigorous.

In one experiment, Hevner had participants listen to the following selections and indicate as many adjectives that "seemed appropriate for describing the music:"[86]

- Debussy: 'Reflections in the Water' from *Images, Book I*[87] ♫
- Mendelssohn: Scherzo from *Midsummer Night's Dream*, Op. 21[88] ♫
- Liszt–Busoni arrangement of Paganini: *Étude* No. 2 in E Flat Major[89] ♫

- Tchaikovsky: Symphony No. 6 in b minor, *Pathetique*[90] ♫
- Wagner: Prelude to Act III from *Lohengrin*[91] ♫

In analyzing the results, Hevner was struck by the "striking uniformity and consistency in the interpretations."[92] Listeners tended to check or avoid similar adjectives for each piece. Collapsing all the adjectives in a given category into one label, here are the highest rated adjectives for each selection:

- Debussy: dreamy and exhilarated
- Mendelssohn: exhilarated and playful
- Paganini: playful and exhilarated
- Tchaikovsky: spiritual and dreamy
- Wagner: exhilarated and vigorous

Picking just one example, "Mendelssohn's Scherzo, to be played after the first act of Shakespeare's *Midsummer Night's Dream*, is outstandingly exciting-impetuous and playful-graceful, and there is a total lack of such affective states as serenity, sadness, dignity, and solemnity."[93] The point for our purposes is not whether these are the 'correct' responses, rather that listeners are able to assign emotion words to music and can do so with some degree of consistency. Note especially that the Paganini *Étude*, an example of pure instrumental music, "(a composition characterized by its emphatic rhythms and rapid tripping arpeggios, and presented by Horowitz with great brilliance and precision) lacks entirely the feeling-tone of sadness, dignity, or serenity, and suggests playfulness, gayety, excitement, and vigor."[94]

In 2004, Patrik Juslin and Petri Laukka confirmed Hevner's findings and many researchers who followed her when they said, "the results from over 100 studies have indicated that listeners are generally consistent in their judgments of emotional expression in music."[95] In their own study, Juslin and Laukka obtained responses to a questionnaire from 141 music listeners between the ages of 14 and 74. Participants, half of whom were musically trained and half who were not, indicated how frequently particular emotions occurred during music listening in a variety of situations. In responding to the prompt, "What can music express?," 100% of the respondents indicated 'emotions,' followed by psychological tension/relaxation (89%), physical aspects (88%), beauty (82%), and sound patterns (80%). In contrast to the philosophers discussed previously, listeners did not restrict music's expressive abilities to garden-variety emotions. In addition to such familiar terms as joy and sadness, they included emotion words such as longing, solemnity, loneliness, pride, desire, nostalgia, contempt, regret, curiosity, disappointment, guilt, admiration, jealousy, shame, trust, and humiliation. These results, which are relatively similar to an updated version of Hevner's adjective cycle, were confirmed by a parallel study of 135 musicians using the same questionnaire. In another confirmatory study, the two most common responses to a survey about why people listened to specific types of music were "moves me emotionally" and "is expressive."[96] Over a third identified "music is a way of expressing and communicating emotions."[97]

Research has not been limited to music listening. Juslin created the GERMS model to identify five sources of expression in musical performance:[98]

- Generative Rules. Performers can mark or emphasize various structural features, such as accents or pulse.

- **Emotional Expression.** Performers can alter tempo and dynamics, or change tone colors to express different emotions.
- **Random Fluctuations.** Performers are not machines and random changes in timing and other performance variables lead to expressive nuances.
- **Motion Principles.** Performers often make tempo adjustments to reflect or mimic human movement patterns expressive of emotion.
- **Stylistic Unexpectedness.** Performers add variety and surprise by deliberately deviating from expectations.

Each of these five sources is supported by considerable experimental evidence. For example, 28 musicians evaluated ten different performances of the Chopin *Prelude*, Op. 28, No. 4[99] ♪ by rating expressivity both in moment-to-moment and post-performance ratings.[100] The authors summarized their conclusions by saying, "this study showed that musical structure had a very important impact on the emotionality ratings made by listeners during performance."[101] In other words, what the different pianists did in the way of emphasizing different structural features was not only perceived by listeners but was related to emotional expression. The notion of performers expressing emotions is eloquently captured in these quotes by the famous blues guitarist B. B. King:

> I wanted to connect my guitar to human emotions. By fooling with the feedback between my amplifier and instrument, I started experimenting with sounds that expressed my feelings, whether happy or sad, bouncy or bluesy.[102]

> If I was feeling lonely, I'd pick up the guitar; feel like talking, pick up the guitar; if something's bugging me, just grab the guitar and play out the anger; happy, horny, mad, or sad, the guitar was right there, a righteous pacifier and comforting companion.[103]

Recent findings from neuroscience provide clues for how music, even pure instrumental music such as B. B. King describes, can convey emotion. A beginning place is with a brief introduction to mirror neurons. Mirror neurons fire when one person observes or hears another's actions.[104] These areas of the brain provide the ability for us to understand and represent actions and intentions of others. When we observe someone playing or singing, the same regions involved in making these actions are activated in our brains. Thus, the physical actions involved in aggressive drumming or softly strumming are mirrored in our brains. When we watch or listen to B. B. King perform, mirror neurons in our brains fire in similar regions as in his brain.

This is true of the sounds themselves, absent a visual component, as when we listen to recordings. Language, music, and action share perceptual resources in the mirror neuron system. Thus, the supposition is that interpretation of auditory signals involves understanding of the motor actions necessary to create those sounds. Both actions and sounds can convey emotions. Music consists of "intentional, hierarchically organized sequences of expressive motor acts behind the signal."[105]

Several neuroimaging experiments have corroborated the role of mirror neurons in music listening. For example, observation of piano playing, both with and without sound, activated mirror neurons in professional pianists and in non-pianists (more strongly in the former).[106] Mirror neuron activations also occurred in professional pianists when they only heard piano playing, without accompanying visual observations.[107] One explanation is that when we perceive something, we experience what it would take to achieve a similar condition. Listeners have reported perceived anger in jazz improvisations by various saxophonists, even when the performers contended that anger is not the emotion they were trying to convey.[108] When listeners heard high, fast playing, they imagined the actions necessary to create those sounds and interpreted this feeling as anger.

Because the shared signals arise from both performer and listener, there is a *shared affective motion experience* (SAME).[109] As described in the previous paragraph, neuroimaging work supports this model.[110] Another component of the SAME model is that music can convey a sense of agency, that is, a perception of the person behind the sounds and his or her affective state. "With its ability to link perceptual and behavioral representations of a stimulus during the perception of emotionally arousing music, the mirror neuron system may simulate an emotional state in the listener."[111]

Summary and Thought Questions

As a means of summarizing this discussion, let us return briefly to a model previously presented in Chapter 6. In the BRECVEMA model, Juslin provided a framework to explain both *everyday* and *aesthetic* emotions.[112]

- Brain Stem Reflex. We are wired to respond immediately, and often emotionally, to sudden sounds that potentially signal an urgent event. Sudden loud or dissonant sounds in music may trigger this response.
- Rhythmic Entrainment. Emotional responses can be evoked when a strong musical rhythm influences internal bodily rhythms. Rock music often has this visceral effect, harnessing heart and breathing rates to the beat.
- Evaluative Conditioning. Often, past associations between a piece of music and an emotional experience lead to a pairing. Thus, couples may have a favorite that they call 'our song.'
- Emotional Contagion. Listeners may feel an emotion when they perceive emotional expression in the music and then mimic that expression internally.
- Visual Imagery. Listeners frequently conjure up internal images to accompany the music that elicit emotional responses.
- Episodic Memory. Music may call to mind a specific remembrance of past events, along with their emotional colorations.
- Musical Expectancy. When music violates or deviates from expected patterns, the listener may feel an emotional response.
- Aesthetic Judgment. In some cases, the listener may adopt an aesthetic attitude or bring aesthetic criteria to bear on a music listening experience.

For each of these components of the model, Juslin provided extensive research evidence, including brain mechanisms. For example, in one study,[113] researchers attempted to activate four of these eight mechanisms by altering a synthesized version of Ernest Bloch's 'Prayer' from *From Jewish Life*, No. 1, for solo cello and piano.[114] ♪ The four mechanisms and their alterations were:

- *Emotional Contagion*. The basic performance was a digital version created to mimic a real human performance by including a number of expressive performance variations. Expectations were that this rendition would arouse sadness in listeners.

- *Brain stem reflex.* In this version, the cello was replaced by piano samples and sudden, sharply attacked, loud chords were inserted to arouse surprise in the listeners.
- *Episodic memory.* Here, a musical quote from the popular movie *Star Wars* was inserted in an attempt to arouse nostalgia and happiness in listeners.
- *Musical expectancy.* For the final version, the music was altered by violating melodic and harmonic expectations, while keeping the general performance intact, as a means of elicited reactions of anxiety and irritation in the listeners.

As participants listened to these four performances, they provided a self-report on their feelings and researchers monitored their facial expressions (i.e., smile and frown muscles), skin conductance, and pulse rates. There were three principal findings: (1) With one exception, each of the pieces elicited the predicted emotional response; that is, the *contagion* version aroused the most sadness, the *brain stem reflex* version the most surprise, and the *episodic* the most nostalgia and happiness. The *musical expectancy* version did arouse the most irritation, but only aroused more anxiety than two of the others, not all three. (2) Facial, skin conductance, and pulse rate measurements indicated that listeners actually experienced the emotions they reported, as opposed to merely perceiving them. (3) The results do not reflect merely surface links (i.e., slow tempo equals sadness, etc.). Rather, they are indications of the role of underlying mechanisms (i.e., contagion, brain stem reflex, etc.). In summary, the authors stated,

> Whatever its limitations, this study has provided some support for the idea that musical emotions are aroused through the ways in which musical events are processed by underlying mechanisms. What matters, ultimately, is not acoustic parameters as such, but what meaning they are given by our psychological processes, a distinction between *sound* and *significance*. By highlighting this distinction, and allowing stronger *causal* conclusions than can be drawn from field data [references omitted], the present experiment has illustrated one promising avenue towards explaining the emotional significance of music.[115]

Undoubtedly additional research is warranted and commentaries following a description of the BREVCEMA model provided numerous suggestions.[116]

Having heard from several philosophers and pondered numerous musical examples, what do you think?

1. Do you actually feel the emotions expressed in music you hear or perform?
2. Is there a difference between emotions you perceive in music and emotions you feel?
3. Do you agree with Tolstoy that great art can *infect* listeners with the feelings expressed in music?
4. What about Croce's idea that music is not a physical fact? Does music exist only in your mind?
5. Collingwood felt that there was a linkage between the composer's emotions and the emotions expressed in his or her music. Do you agree?
6. Cooke extended Collingwood's ideas when he wrote that the elements of music create an emotional vocabulary of sorts and that this is not restricted to Romantic music. If you agreed/ disagreed with Collingwood, do you feel the same about Cooke?
7. What about Kivy's and Davies's doggy or contour theories? Does music express emotions because it mimics bodily expressions?

8. Do you agree with Kivy that music can express garden-variety emotions, but not the more cognitively complex ones? If you do agree with Kivy, how do you account for research results indicating that listeners can identify a broad range of emotion words?

9. Do you think Robinson has adequately addressed the issue of pure instrumental music? Are you willing to adopt her notion, derived from Cone, that absolute music can express cognitively complex emotions because it can represent various personae?

10. Does research influence your decision to accept or reject expressionism?

Following this chapter, you may wish to head to the practice room or turn on a personal music player to hear one of your favorites. It is perfectly fine to enjoy music in the way you prefer. Do try, however, to resolve these philosophical conundrums in your own mind.

Notes

1 Aaron Ridley, "Expression in Art," in *The Oxford Handbook of Aesthetics*, ed. Jerrold Levinson (Oxford, UK: Oxford University Press, 2005), 211.

2 Edward Lippman, *A History of Western Musical Aesthetics* (Lincoln, NE: University of Nebraska Press, 1992), 83.

3 Henry Purcell, 'Dido's Lament' from *Dido and Aeneas*, performed by Janet Baker, with Charles Mackerras and the Glyndebourne Opera, http://www.youtube.com/watch?v=D_50zj7J50U.

4 Ridley, "Expression in Art," 214.

5 Gordon Graham, "Expressivism," in *The Routledge Companion to Aesthetics*, ed. Berys Gaut and Dominic Lopes (London: Routledge, 2002).

6 Leo Tolstoy, *What Is Art?*, trans. Almyer Maude (Indianapolis: Liberal Arts Press, 1896/1960), 51.

7 As quoted in Vincent Tomas, introduction to Tolstoy's *What Is Art?*, xv.

8 Tolstoy, *What Is Art?*, 134.

9 Ibid., 116.

10 Ibid., 140.

11 Frédéric Chopin, Nocturne in E Flat Major, Op. 9, No. 2, performed by Arthur Rubinstein, http://www.youtube.com/watch?v=YGRO05WcNDk.

12 Tolstoy, *What Is Art?*, 155.

13 Ibid., 157.

14 Ludwig van Beethoven, Symphony No. 9 in d minor, Op. 125, performed by Leonard Bernstein conducting the Vienna Philharmonic Orchestra, http://www.youtube.com/watch?v=3MnGfhJCK_g.

15 Charles Daniels, "Tolstoy and Corrupt Art," *Journal of Aesthetic Education* 8, no. 4 (1974): 41–49.

16 Monroe Beardsley, *Aesthetics: Problems in the Philosophy of Criticism, 2nd ed.* (Indianapolis, IN: Hackett, 1981), 318–19.

17 Gary Kemp, "Croce's Aesthetics," in *The Stanford Encyclopedia of Philosophy*, ed. Edward Zalta (2009 edition). http://plato.stanford.edu/archives/fall2009/entries/croce-aesthetics.

18 Ibid.

19 Benedetto Croce, "The Breviary of Aesthetic," *The Rice Institute Pamphlet* XLVII, no. 4 (Houston, TX: Rice University, 1961), 7.

20 Ibid., 7.

21 Ibid., 9–10.

22 Ibid., 12.

23 Ibid., 14.

24 Ibid., 52.

25 Benedetto Croce, *Guide to Aesthetics*, trans. Patrick Romanell (New York: Bobbs-Merrill, 1965), 25.

26 Croce, "The Breviary of Aesthetic," 26.

27 Ibid., 38.

28 Ibid., 41.

29 Anne Sheppard, *Aesthetics: An Introduction to the Philosophy of Art* (Oxford: Oxford University Press, 1987), 23.
30 R. G. Collingwood, *The Principles of Art* (Oxford, UK: Oxford University Press, 1958).
31 Sheppard, *Aesthetics*, 22.
32 Collingwood, *The Principles of Art*, 285.
33 Ridley, "Expression in Art," 223.
34 Collingwood, *The Principles of Art*, 314.
35 Graham, "Expressivism," 124.
36 Sheppard, *Aesthetics*, 28.
37 Deryck Cooke, *The Language of Music* (Oxford, UK: Oxford University Press, 1963), xi.
38 Ibid., 60.
39 Ibid., 64.
40 Ibid., 208.
41 Ibid., 208.
42 Ibid., 210.
43 Ludwig van Beethoven, *Missa Solemnis* in D Major, Op. 123, performed by Leonard Bernstein conducting the Hilversum Radio Chorus and the Vienna Philharmonic, https://www.youtube.com/watch?v=06PPhF2tX1g.
44 Quoted in Cooke, *The Language of Music*, 210.
45 Ibid., 273.
46 Peter Kivy, *The Corded Shell* (Princeton, NJ: Princeton University Press, 1980). This book was reprinted and expanded in Peter Kivy, *Sound Sentiment: An Essay on the Musical Emotions, Including the Complete Text of the Corded Shell* (Philadelphia: Temple University Press, 1989).
47 Peter Kivy, *Introduction to a Philosophy of Music* (Oxford, UK: Oxford University Press, 2002).
48 Peter Kivy, *Music Alone: Philosophical Reflections on the Purely Musical Experience* (Ithaca, NY: Cornell University Press, 1990).
49 Stephen Davies, *Musical Meaning and Expression* (Ithaca, NY: Cornell University Press, 1994).
50 Ibid., 228.
51 Ibid., 229.
52 Ibid., 239.
53 Jenefer Robinson, *Deeper Than Reason: Emotion and Its Role in Literature, Music, and Art* (Oxford, UK: Oxford University Press, 2005).
54 Ibid., 309–10.
55 Edward Cone, *The Composer's Voice. Ernest Bloch Lectures* (Berkeley: University of California Press, 1974).
56 Robinson, *Deeper Than Reason*, 324.
57 Ibid., 326.
58 Cone, *The Composer's Voice*, 98.
59 Ibid., 107.
60 Robinson, *Deeper than Reason*, 328.
61 Ibid., 328–29.
62 Franz Schubert, *Wanderer Fantasy*, D.760, performed by Alfred Brendel, https://www.youtube.com/watch?v=7WIVTKXb8RI.
63 Robinson, "Expression Theories," in *The Routledge Companion to Philosophy and Music*, ed. Theodore Gracyk and Andrew Kania (New York: Routledge, 2011), 209.
64 Johannes Brahms, Intermezzo in b flat minor, Op. 117, No. 2, performed by Vladimir Horowitz, http://www.youtube.com/watch?v=RooR3nsYWzw.
65 Robinson, *Deeper than Reason*, 340.
66 Ibid., 346–47.
67 Malcolm Budd, *Music and the Emotions: The Philosophical Theories* (London: Routledge and Kegan Paul, 1985).
68 Ibid., xii.
69 Noël Carroll, *Philosophy of Art* (New York: Routledge, 1999), 79.

70 Sheppard, *Aesthetics*.

71 Robinson, "Expression Theories," 207.

72 Giacomo Puccini, 'Un bel di' from *Madama Butterfly*, performed by Renata Tebaldi, http://www.youtube.com/watch?v=1woH96ROG-c.

73 Giacomo Puccini, 'Con onor muore' from *Madama Butterfly*, performed by Renata Scotto, http://www.youtube.com/watch?v=vi4n2YbQPd8.

74 Felix Mendelssohn, 'It Is Enough' from *Elijah*, performed by Dietrich Fischer-Diskau, baritone, with Rafael Frühbeck de Burgos conducting the New Philharmonia Orchestra, http://www.youtube.com/watch?v=tEkClendR3s.

75 Elton John and Bernie Taupin, 'Candle in the Wind,' performed by Elton John, http://www.youtube.com/watch?v=A8gO0Z818j4.

76 CNN Staff, "Report: Jailed Pussy Riot Members Seek Community Service in Russia," (August 23, 2013). http://www.cnn.com/2013/08/23/world/europe/russia-pussy-riot.

77 Pussy Riot, 'Punk Prayer,' performed by Pussy Riot, http://www.youtube.com/watch?v=ALS92big4TY.

78 CNN Staff, "Report."

79 Modest Mussorgsky, *Pictures at an Exhibition*, performed by Evgeny Kissin, http://www.youtube.com/watch?v=g8ei1NF0oic.

80 Modest Mussorgsky, *Pictures at an Exhibition*, orchestrated by Maurice Ravel, performed by Georg Solti conducting the Chicago Symphony Orchestra, https://www.youtube.com/watch?v=DXy50exHjes.

81 Ludwig van Beethoven, Rondo alla ingharese quasi un capriccio in G Major, *Rage Over a Lost Penny*, Op. 129, performed by Alexander Brailowsky, piano, https://www.youtube.com/watch?v=_6k_CrWBqBA.

82 Erich Hertzmann, "The Newly Discovered Autograph of Beethoven's Rondo *a capriccio*, op. 129," *The Musical Quarterly* 32, no. 2 (1946): 171–95.

83 Arnold Schoenberg, *Theme and Variations for Wind Band*, Op. 43a, performed by Gunther Schuller conducting the United States Marine Band, http://www.youtube.com/watch?v=JEVZwr8GP1s.

84 Liner notes from *The President's Own United States Marine Band: Bicentennial Collection, Vol. 10*. Altissimo: 75442262032.

85 Kate Hevner, "Experimental Studies of the Elements of Expression in Music," *The American Journal of Psychology* 48, no. 2 (1936): 246.

86 Ibid., 251.

87 Claude Debussy, 'Reflections in the Water' from *Images, Book I*, performed by Arturo Michelangeli, http://www.youtube.com/watch?v=LLbpQl1cCl8.

88 Felix Mendelssohn, Scherzo from *Midsummer Night's Dream*, Op. 21, performed by Valery Gergiev conducting the Mariinsky Theatre Orchestra, http://www.youtube.com/watch?v=hHTV3GFyHfM.

89 Franz Liszt–Ferruccio Busoni arrangement of Niccolò Paganini: *Étude* No. 2 in E Flat Major, performed by Vladimir Horowitz, http://www.youtube.com/watch?v=-Nfdve3huIA.

90 Pyotr Tchaikovsky, Symphony No. 6 in b minor, *Pathetique*, performed by Herbert von Karajan conducting the Vienna Philharmonic, http://www.youtube.com/watch?v=wHAfvUFtCIY.

91 Richard Wagner, Prelude to Act III from *Lohengrin*, performed by Arturo Toscanini conducting the NBC Symphony Orchestra, http://www.youtube.com/watch?v=InPRlxxOpOc.

92 Hevner, "Experimental Studies of the Elements of Expression in Music," 267.

93 Ibid., 252.

94 Ibid., 252.

95 Patrik Juslin and Petri Laukka, "Expression, Perception, and Induction of Musical Emotions: A Review and a Questionnaire Study of Everyday Listening," *Journal of New Music Research* 33, no. 3 (2004): 219.

96 Patrik Juslin and Sara Isaksson, "Subjective Criteria for Choice and Aesthetic Value of Music: A Comparison of Psychology and Music Students," *Research Studies in Music Education* 36, no. 2 (2014): 179–98.

97 Ibid., 189.

98 Patrik Juslin, "Five Facets of Musical Expression: A Psychologist's Perspective on Music Performance," *Psychology of Music* 31 (2003): 273–302.

99 Frédéric Chopin, *Prelude*, Op., No. 4, performed by Martha Argerich, http://www.youtube.com/watch?v=Tovh6JjaQ1A.

100 John Sloboda and Andreas Lehmann, "Tracking Performance Correlates of Changes in Perceived Intensity of Emotion During Different Interpretations of a Chopin Piano Prelude," *Music Perception* 19, no. 1 (2001): 87–120.

101 Ibid., 115.

102 B. B. King with David Ritz, *Blues All Around Me: The Autobiography of B.B. King* (New York: Avon Books, 1996), 127.

103 Ibid., 41.

104 Istvan Molnar-Szakacs and Katie Overy, "Music and Mirror Neurons: From Motion to 'E'motion," *Social Cognitive and Affective Neuroscience* 1 (2006): 235–41.

105 Katie Overy and Istvan Molnar-Szakacs, "Being Together in Time: Musical Experience and the Mirror Neuron System," *Music Perception* 26, no. 5 (2009): 492.

106 B. Haslinger, P. Erhard, E. Altenmüller, U. Schroeder, H., Boecker, and A. Ceballos-Baumann, "Transmodel Sensorimotor Networks During Action Observation in Professional Pianists," *Journal of Cognitive Neuroscience* 17, no. 2 (2005): 282–93.

107 Marc Bangert, Thomas Peschel, Gottfried Schlaug, Michael Rotte, Dieter Drescher, Hermann Hinrichs, Hans-Jochen Heinze, and Eckart Altenmüller, "Shared Networks for Auditory and Motor Processing in Professional Pianists: Evidence from fMRI Conjunction," *NeuroImage* 30 (2006): 917–26.

108 Mark Gridley and Robert Hoff, "Do Mirror Neurons Explain Misattribution of Emotions in Music?" *Perceptual and Motor Skills* 102, no. 2 (2006): 600–2.

109 Katie Overy and Istvan Molnar-Szakacs, "Being Together in Time," 489.

110 Marc Bangert et al., "Shared Networks for Auditory and Motor Processing in Professional Pianists." B. Haslinger et al., "Transmodel Sensorimotor Networks During Action Observation in Professional Pianists."

111 Istvan Molnar-Szakacs and Katie Overy, "Music and Mirror Neurons," 238.

112 Patrick Juslin, "From Everyday Emotions to Aesthetic Emotions: Towards a Unified Theory of Musical Emotions," *Physics of Life Reviews* 10, no. 3 (2013): 235–66.

113 Patrik Juslin, László Harmat, and Tuomas Eerola, "What Makes Music Emotionally Significant? Exploring the Underlying Mechanisms," *Psychology of Music* 42, no. 4 (2014): 599–623.

114 Ernst Bloch, 'Prayer' from *From Jewish Life*, No. 1, performed by Amit Peled, cello, and Stefan Petrov, piano, http://www.youtube.com/watch?v=rTso0wYH4f4.

115 Patrik Juslin et al., "What Makes Music Emotionally Significant?," 21.

116 See complete issue of *Physics of Life Reviews* 10, no. 3 (September, 2013).

13 Symbolism

The view that music is a symbol standing for something else is rooted in ancient Greek philosophies and in German Idealism. However, ardent proponents, such as Susanne Langer, Nelson Goodman, and Jean-Jacques Nattiez, took the notion further. Thus, the central importance of music was that it could symbolize something beyond itself. Before we examine specific musical examples, we will take a brief tour of philosophical ideas supporting the notion that music can refer to something outside itself and that often these meanings are symbolic.

Susanne Langer

To Langer (1895–1985), "art is the creation of forms symbolic of human feeling."[1] She wrote voluminously on philosophy, art, and music in such works as *Philosophy in a New Key*, *Feeling and Form*, *Problems of Art*, and the three-volume set *Mind: An Essay on Human Feeling*.[2] In a Prefatory Note to the third edition of *Philosophy in a New Key*, Langer says that this book should be considered a prelude to *Feeling and Form*, owing to the expansion of ideas in chapter VIII: "On Significance of Music" into a more full fledged philosophy "not only of music, but of all the arts."[3] That her ideas on music evolved over time is evidenced by her desire to "replace the unsatisfactory notion of music as an essentially ambiguous symbol by a much more precise, though somewhat difficult, concept of musical significance, involving a theory (not yet quite completed) of artistic abstraction in general."[4]

Eventually, Langer did hone her thoughts on music. Mark DeBellis succinctly stated her central thesis: "On Langer's view, music is a symbol of the 'inner life' of feeling."[5] Langer believed that "music can reveal the nature of feelings with a detail and truth that language cannot approach."[6] This is because music's significant forms "have an *ambivalence* of content which words cannot have."[7] Discursive symbols such as language denote things and provide literal meanings, but cannot adequately reflect the inner life. Presentational symbols, such as music, however, can. Music is an unconsummated symbol "because it lacks fixed dictionary denotations."[8] Langer encapsulated her conception of music as a symbolic presentation of human feeling in one of her most often quoted statements: "Music is a tonal analogue of emotive life."[9]

Langer's conception of music as a 'tonal analogue' makes it clear that music is not the raw emotion itself, nor is it a stimulus of emotion, nor a symptom of emotions; rather, it is a symbolic presentation of how we experience feelings. "Not communication but insight is the gift of music; in a very naïve phrase, a knowledge of 'how feelings go.'"[10] Thus, the patterns of music

> "One might say, perhaps, that a musical figure, besides referring to a feeling as a word does, also serves as an auditory semblance of it, and in this way reveals what it is like."
>
> (Susanne Langer)

reflect the tensions and resolutions, ebb and flow, heights and depths of the inner life. She quoted an unnamed musician who said, "music sounds as feelings feel."[11] What music expresses is "not *actual* feeling, but ideas of feeling."[12]

To Langer, the role of art in education was to educate feelings. The inner life can be chaotic and incoherent. Art experiences give shape to the inner life of feelings. "Artistic training is, therefore, the education of feeling, as our usual schooling in factual subjects . . . is the education of thought."[13] The absence of an art education allows children to experience the cheapest forms of art and this, in turn, affects the quality of life. Art education leads to a refinement of life and provides a bulwark against inner and outer chaos.

David Elliott is a severe critic of Langer's work and the impact it has had on music education philosophers, particularly Bennett Reimer.[14] He lists a number of analyses by different scholars who "shine brilliant spotlights on Langer's numerous errors of logic and false claims."[15] In his view, "a musical work is not a special type of unconsummated, presentational symbol."[16] Furthermore, he felt that she drastically misunderstood how people respond to music when she stated that music does not actually arouse emotions, but only represents how feelings go. Interestingly, Elliott used the research of neuroscientist Antonio Damasio to refute Langer's claims,[17] while Bennett Reimer uses Damasio's work to support Langer.[18]

Nelson Goodman

Goodman (1906–1998) developed "probably the most elaborately worked out and far-reaching contemporary theory of musical reference."[19] Music should not be valued as an autonomous form, but rather for "how it functions in dynamic experience."[20] He based his notion of art on a theory of symbols, tools with which we construct our reality.[21] There are two kinds of symbol systems, autographic (where there can be only one instance of a work and it lacks a notational system, such as a painting) and allographic (where there can be more than one instance of a work, such as in multiple performances of a musical composition, and there is a notational system).[22] Some symbols are representational in that they denote what the artwork refers to; music rarely denotes. Other symbols are expressive; they possess literally or metaphorically the features the artwork symbolizes.[23]

A key concept for Goodman was *exemplification*. "Exemplification is possession plus reference."[24] In other words, not only can music refer to something else, it can actually possess qualities of the referent. Thus, music may not only refer to dance, but may contain qualities of dance. The Bach French Suites, BWV 812–817,[25] ♪ for example, denote dance through the names of individual movements, such as allemande, courante, sarabande, bourreé, gavotte, minuet, or gigue. The music itself may also exemplify dance through its rhythms, tempo, and so on. In addition, exemplification links to expression. Many musical compositions do not refer to anything extramusical; however, they are expressive of forms and feelings through metaphorical exemplification. A Mozart symphony, for example, may not denote anything external, but metaphorically it may exemplify any number of expressive ideas. "A sad piece of music, according to Goodman, metaphorically possesses the property of sadness, and moreover, exemplifies that (metaphorically possessed) property."[26] Goodman believed that the arts were a means of constructing reality, or as he put it 'world-making.' As such,

> the arts must be taken no less seriously than the sciences as modes of discovery, creation, and enlargement of knowledge in the broad sense of advancement of the understanding.[27]

Music, along with the other arts, does not provide information, but it aids in our understanding of the world. Where science, broadly conceived to include a wide variety of intellectual pursuits, gives us factual information, the arts provide understandings of "human nature and the human condition" and "art can be valued for its illumination of human experience."[28]

> "The distinction between saying or representing on the one hand and showing or exemplifying on the other becomes even more evident in the case of abstract painting and music and dance that have no subject-matter but nevertheless manifest—exemplify or express—forms and feelings."
>
> (Nelson Goodman)

Monroe Beardsley

Beardsley (1915–1985) was not a symbolist, but his comments are appropriate at this juncture. He extended Goodman's use of the term 'exemplification.' As an example, he considered the first movement of Beethoven's Piano Sonata in A Major, Op. 101.[29] ♫ The first movement, according to him, was hesitant and diffident. The music exemplifies this indecisiveness of character.[30] However, he then added what he called the Exhibition Theory or Possession Theory; music does not merely exemplify, it exhibits particular properties. Thus, the final movement of Beethoven's Fifth Symphony[31] ♫ "is, so to speak, triumph-music, rather than music-referring-to-triumph."[32]

Beardsley also agreed with Goodman that "art is valuable insofar as it can produce valuable experiences."[33] However, where Goodman believed that some of the value came from the artwork referring to things outside itself, Beardsley felt that value came without referring to things external to the artwork. To Beardsley, the artwork and the person experiencing it were sealed off from any external referents. Artworks do refer, of course, but these external relationships are not a part of the aesthetic experience.

An artwork has within itself characteristics that afford an aesthetic experience.[34] Said the other way around, an aesthetic experience is controlled by the art object itself.[35] A work of art, with the twin principles of independence and autonomy, is necessary first before a person can have an aesthetic experience.[36] An aesthetic experience is intense and concentrated, and contains important aspects of unity, complexity, intensity of human regional qualities (characteristics of motives, phrases, melodies, harmonies, rhythms, etc.).[37] Regional qualities may relate to such human attitudes or behaviors as calmness, indecisiveness, or determination. Meanings of a work of art are generally stable and can be interpreted consistently based on the design.[38]

> "The sort of philosophical principle I have in mind . . . is the semiotic view of art, by which I mean, the categorization of works of art as, in the broadest sense, signs—that is, carriers of meaning and/or reference."
>
> (Monroe Beardsley)

In a later work, Beardsley said that an experience can be said to be aesthetic if it has at least four of the following five features, including the first:

1. Object-directedness: Your attention is directed by and to an art object.
2. Felt freedom: You feel a sense of harmony with the music (i.e., you are not thinking about your tax return or what is for dinner).
3. Detached affect: Although you feel the power of musical emotions, you are able to transcend them.
4. Active discovery: You exercise the constructive powers of your mind to find coherence in the musical properties.
5. A sense of wholeness: You feel restored to integration following distracting and disruptive impulses.[39]

Thus, "in Beardsley's view, works of art have instrumental value because they have the capacity to produce aesthetic experience, which in turn is valuable."[40] However, as George Dickie pointed out, Beardsley's position is incorrect, in part, because it can be shown that some works of art do refer to things outside the artwork. Aesthetic experiences are not insulated and detached from external referents.

Jean-Jacques Nattiez

In the Preface to his book *Music and Discourse*, Nattiez (1945–) began immediately with a hypothesis that music involves structures or configurations, procedures (i.e., composition), and acts of interpretation and perception.[41] He called his ensuing explanation a general theory of *musical semiology*.

> "The border between music and noise is always culturally defined—which implies that, even within a single society, this border does not always pass through the same place; in short, there is rarely a consensus."
>
> (Jean-Jacques Nattiez)

He identified two domains of referring: intrinsic (i.e., the interplay of musical form) and extramusical referring. Nattiez rejected the notion that there was a direct correspondence between music and its meanings. Different individuals do not interpret or understanding symbols uniformly. Rather, they interpret meanings individually in a myriad of ways. Musical meaning is thus fluid, dynamic, and personalized. Music is whatever people choose to recognize as such. What constitutes music is culturally defined.

Music from a Symbolist Perspective

It is abundantly clear that a great deal of music refers to things that are extramusical, that is, that music refers to things outside itself. We covered many of the relevant arguments in the previous chapter on expressionism. Here, we extend the discussion to the idea that many of these extramusical referents are symbolic in nature. Any music that has a text is automatically referential. For example, in 'Born in the USA,'[42] ♫ Bruce Springsteen sings:

I had a brother at Khe Sahn
Fighting off the Viet Cong
They're still there, he's all gone.

At a surface level, this is a clear reference to the Vietnam War. The 'Dies Irae' (Day of Wrath) portion of the Catholic Requiem Mass speaks of the day when all souls appear before God for final judgment. But it is not just the text that refers; the music can too. Verdi's *Messa da Requiem*, the music to 'Dies Irae,'[43] ♪ conveys the sense of horror and dread that one might feel in receiving his due reckoning. Even without knowing what the Latin words mean, one might get a sense of foreboding just from the music alone. An enormous amount of music from songs (both classical and popular), opera, oratorios, masses, cantatas, hymns, Broadway shows, and so on are referential in these ways.

Music can also be symbolic; that is, not only can it refer to extramusical things, it can do so in a symbolic manner. Billie Holiday sang a song entitled 'Strange Fruit,'[44] ♪ written by Lewis Allan (the pen name of Abel Meeropolo).[45] The words to the first verse are:

> Southern trees bear a strange fruit,
> Blood on the leaves and blood at the root,
> Black bodies swinging in the southern breeze,
> Strange fruit hanging from the poplar trees.

This is symbolic language portraying the brutal inhumanity of lynching. While the words are clearly symbolic, the musical elements, including the sparse piano accompaniment, the lack of rhythmic energy, and the despairing, mournful sound of Holiday's voice, also make significant contributions.

But, are words necessary, or can the music without words be symbolic, too? Certainly, in one sense, when music becomes associated with an idea over time, even without the words present, it can be symbolic. Hardly anyone knows the words to 'Hail to the Chief'[46] ♪ or to the bugle call 'Taps.'[47] ♪ Yet, there is instant recognition that one symbolizes the presidency—not just a particular president, but the office of the presidency—and the other one signifies ending, either the end of day when played at bedtime or the end of life when played at a funeral. Program music—that is, music *about* something, even if it has no text—is another way that music can be representational. There are innumerable examples, such as *Carnival of the Animals* by Camille Saint-Saëns[48] ♪ or the *Symphonie Fantastique* by Berlioz.[49] ♪ In the Berlioz, for example, the *idée fixe* (or fixed idea) is a melody that stands for his beloved, Harriet.[50] ♪ It goes through many guises as his feelings and desires change under the influence of opium. Wagner's use of leitmotivs in which a fragment of music stands to represent a person, an action, or an idea is another form of symbolic music. This symbolic usage appears in a great deal of movie music. For example, John Williams uses the Indiana Jones theme song[51] ♪ in many different iterations to symbolize Indiana Jones as hero, lover, being chased, and so on.

Critics, however, would be quick to point out that without the titles and movement headings, such as 'March to the Scaffold' from *Symphonie Fantastique*, audiences would be far less accurate in knowing what the music was about. Generations of Americans learned to associate Rossini's *William Tell Overture*[52] ♪ either with the Lone Ranger radio/television theme song or with the Mickey Mouse cartoon featuring this music. Likewise, many associate Dukas's *The Sorcerer's Apprentice*[53] ♪ with the scene from Walt Disney's movie *Fantasia*, where Mickey Mouse is the apprentice. But, for those who have never heard the radio, television, or movie versions, these explicit extramusical visual images are missing.

Richard Strauss wrote a number of tone poems, including *Don Juan*,[54] ♪ *Death and Transfiguration*,[55] ♪ *Till Eulenspiegel's Merry Pranks*,[56] ♪ *Also sprach Zarathustra*,[57] ♪ *Don Quixote*,[58] ♪

Ein Heldenleben,[59] ♪ *Sinfonia Domestica,*[60] ♪ and *An Alpine Symphony.*[61] ♪ He was so confident that he could express specific things in music that he said, "I can translate anything into sound. I can make you understand by music that I pick up my fork and spoon from this side of my plate and lay them down on the other side."[62] However, many have criticized him, taking this statement as a complete exaggeration. Rudolf Louis said, for example, that the composer "must necessarily arrive at the point where he recognizes that even the most cleverly developed tonal language is not capable of representing its object in an unambiguous way."[63]

Criticisms notwithstanding, there are undoubtedly many passages of Strauss's symphonic poems that are symbolic. As only one example from dozens that could be cited, take his symphonic poem *Also sprach Zarathustra*, Op. 30, after Friedrich Nietzsche (1896). Although there was much speculation and controversy about a musical portrayal of philosophy, Strauss claimed it was merely a musical conflict between the keys of C major and B major.[64] However, C major is to be understood as the vision of nature or world riddle and B major as human longing for a meaningful solution to the riddle or spirit. Various sections represent

> successive attempts at enlightenment through religion (a hymn in A flat major), passion (a robust Allegro in C minor), and science (a fugue in C), each followed by disappointment (returns to B minor or major); and finally a crisis (a reprise of the introduction), leading to redemption in cosmic laughter and dancing (the waltz), but no solution to the riddle (the famous 'polytonal' ending).[65]

Musically, we see the depiction of the unsolved riddle in the final measures (Fig. 13.1). Here, the piccolos, flutes, oboes, solo violin, and violins sound a B major triad very softly, high in the treble, while low in the bass, the cellos and basses sound a pizzicato C natural. "The poem ends in an unresolved conflict between the key of nature (C major) and the key of the spirit (B major)."[66]

As a final example, consider Charles Ives's *The Unanswered Question* (1908, revised 1930–1935).[67] ♪ In the Foreword to the score,[68] Ives indicates three subdivisions:

- 'The Silences of the Druids—Who Know, See and Hear Nothing' is performed by a string quartet or string orchestra *con sordini* (with mutes). "These 'Druids' would seem to be representatives of the unfathomable cosmos beyond."[69]

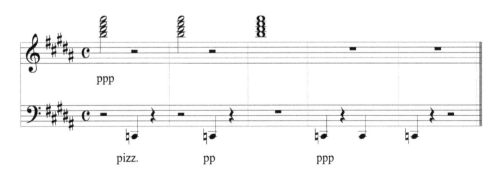

Figure 13.1 The last five measures of *Also sprach Zarathustra* by Richard Strauss

Image created by author

- 'The Perennial Question of Existence' is intoned by the trumpet, also muted.
- 'The Invisible Answer' is provided by a flute quartet.

The strings hold long, sustained chords, played very slowly and as softly as possible. Although there are chord changes, there is no 'directional movement' toward cadence points. The trumpet repeats a disjunct melody seven times throughout the piece (see Fig. 13.2). Ives described the question–answer dialogue this way:

> But the hunt for "The Invisible Answer" undertaken by the flutes and other human beings, becomes gradually more active, faster and louder through an *animando* to a *con fuoco*. "The Fighting Answers," as the time goes on, and after a "secret conference," seem to realize a futility, and begin to mock "The Question"—the strife is over for the moment. After they disappear, "The Question" is asked for the last time, and "The Silences" are heard beyond in "Undisturbed Solitude."[70]

As Matthew McDonald stated, "No doubt, we are meant to interpret this story as an allegorical representation of the existential struggles of human beings."[71]

Absolutists, of course, disagree with the notions expressed in this chapter—"Music at its best is not symbolic at all"[72] and "music, as we know and understand it, is not a representational art form."[73] Some absolutists would agree that music can sometimes represent or symbolize things. However, they would say that these extramusical references are irrelevant when considering the aesthetic value of a musical work. They argue that musical value resides solely on what happens 'inside' the music itself. Furthermore, they raise the issue of absolute or pure instrumental music. In what way can music that has no text, no program, or no past association with anything extramusical be seen to symbolize something that is extramusical? As a counterpart to all the referential musical examples listed previously, one could identify a great many sonatas, concertos, trios, quartets, and symphonies that are not referential. What about them? To what would a Bach fugue, a Haydn piano sonata, or a Mozart symphony refer, or how could they symbolize anything external?

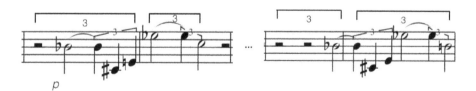

Figure 13.2 The trumpet figure representing 'The Perennial Question of Existence' from Charles Ives's *The Unanswered Question*. In the original version of 1908, the trumpet 'question' began and ended on B flat. In Ives's revised version of 1930–1935 the trumpet figure alternates between ending on C natural and B natural (shown here). In both the original and revised versions, the various iterations of the trumpet 'question' begin at different points in the measure.

Image created by author

Summary and Thought Questions

Symbolists find the meaning in music as a symbol system. To Langer, music presents how feelings go and symbolically represents the inner life. Goodman felt that music could not only represent, but could also exemplify that to which it referred. Joyful music not only points to joy, but has the properties of joy. Beardsley felt that music not only exemplifies, it exhibits or possesses particular extramusical properties. In this way, he is not a symbolist because the artwork has within itself the properties it exemplifies. Finally, Nattiez believed that there was no single interpretation or meaning of a work of art; rather, each individual could find personalized meanings.

Over the course of symbolic accounts, we find a shift from earlier to later views:[74]

Earlier accounts	Later accounts
from narrow and specific musical references	to inclusive and dynamic ones
from music as unitary and univocal	to a plural and diverse view
away from symbolism as bridging a gap between the apparent and the real	toward a creation of worlds of possibility
away from music cognition as insular and hardwired	toward one that is open, porous, malleable, and pluralistic

Those who take a symbolic view of music believe that the value of music resides in what music can symbolize. A fundamental issue is whether music's primary value lies within or outside itself. As a means toward determining whether your personal philosophy will adopt any of these points, consider the following questions:

1. Do you agree with Langer that music presents 'how feelings go,' rather than the feelings themselves?
2. What advantages or disadvantages does music have compared to language in knowing or understanding our 'inner life'? Is one medium necessarily 'better' than the other and, if so, better in what sense?
3. Goodman believed that we use symbols to construct our reality. Do you agree? What are some examples of your reality as constructed symbolically?
4. Can you give some musical examples of differences between music that exemplifies something (Goodman) and music that exhibits something (Beardsley)?
5. What do you think of Nattiez's notion that many different meanings and interpretations of a work of art are possible?
6. What effect would adopting a symbolist view have on your music teaching, performing, and listening?
7. For what reasons might you reject a view of music as symbolic?

Notes

1 Susanne Langer, *Feeling and Form* (New York: Charles Scribner's Sons, 1953), 40.
2 Susanne Langer, *Philosophy in a New Key*, 3rd ed. (Cambridge, MA: Harvard University Press, 1942/1963). Langer, *Feeling and Form*. Susanne Langer, *Problems of Art* (New York: Charles Scribner's Sons, 1957). Susanne Langer, *Mind: An Essay on Human Feeling*, *Vols. I, II, & III* (Baltimore: The Johns Hopkins Press, 1967, 1974, 1982).

3 Langer, *Philosophy in a New Key, 3rd ed.*, vii.
4 Ibid., x.
5 Marc DeBellis, "Music," in *The Routledge Companion to Aesthetics*, ed. Berys Gaut and Dominic Lopes (London: Routledge, 2002), 540.
6 Langer, *Philosophy in a New Key, 3rd ed.*, 235.
7 Ibid., 243.
8 Monroe Beardsley, *Aesthetics from Classical Greece to the Present* (Tuscaloosa, AL: The University of Alabama Press, 1966), 352.
9 Langer, *Feeling and Form*, 27.
10 Langer, *Philosophy in a New Key, 3rd ed.*, 244.
11 Langer, *Problems of Art*, 26.
12 Susanne Langer, "The Work of Art as a Symbol," in *Introductory Readings in Aesthetics*, ed. John Hospers (New York: The Free Press, 1969), 174.
13 Langer, *Feeling and Form*, 401.
14 David Elliott, "Music and Affect: The Praxial View," *Philosophy of Music Education Review* 8, no. 2 (2000): 79–88.
15 Ibid., 80.
16 Ibid., 80.
17 David Elliott and Marissa Silverman, *Music Matters: A Philosophy of Music Education, 2nd ed.* (Oxford, UK: Oxford University Press, 2015).
18 Bennett Reimer, *A Philosophy of Music Education: Advancing the Vision, 3rd ed.* (Upper Saddle River, NJ: Prentice-Hall, 2003).
19 DeBellis, "Music," 538.
20 Richard Shusterman, "Pragmatism: Dewey," in *The Routledge Companion to Aesthetics*, ed. Berys Gaut and Dominic Lopes (London: Routledge, 2002), 104.
21 Derek Mastravers, "Art, Expression and Emotion," in *The Routledge Companion to Aesthetics*, ed. Berys Gaut and Dominic Lopes (London: Routledge, 2002), 353–62.
22 Nan Stalnaker, "Fakes and Forgeries," in *The Routledge Companion to Aesthetics*, ed. Berys Gaut and Dominic Lopes (London: Routledge, 2002), 395–407.
23 Curtis Carter, "Sculpture," in *The Routledge Companion to Aesthetics*, ed. Berys Gaut and Dominic Lopes (London: Routledge, 2002), 503–17.
24 Nelson Goodman, *Languages of Art: An Approach to a Theory of Symbols* (Indianapolis: Hackett, 1976), 53.
25 J.S. Bach, French Suites, BWV 812–817, performed by Andras Schiff, piano, https://www.youtube.com/watch?v=0sDleZkIK-w.
26 DeBellis, "Music," 539.
27 Nelson Goodman, *Ways of Worldmaking* (Indianapolis: Hackett, 1978), 102.
28 Gordon Graham, *Philosophy of the Arts: An Introduction to Aesthetics, 2nd ed.* (London: Routledge, 2000), 63.
29 Ludwig van Beethoven, Piano Sonata in A Major, Op. 101, performed by Daniel Barenboim, https://www.youtube.com/watch?v=yn2CbJls2_A.
30 Edward Lippman, *A History of Western Musical Aesthetics* (Lincoln, NE: University of Nebraska Press, 1992).
31 Ludwig van Beethoven, Symphony No. 5 in c minor, Op. 67, performed by Christian Thielemann conducting the Vienna Philharmonic, http://www.youtube.com/watch?v=-VVXqNt4qU0.
32 Monroe Beardsley, "Semiotic Aesthetics and Aesthetic Education," *Journal of Aesthetic Education* 9, no. 3 (1975): 14.
33 George Dickie, *Introduction to Aesthetics: An Analytic Approach* (New York: Oxford University Press, 1997), 155.
34 Stephen Davies, "Definitions of Art," in *The Routledge Companion to Aesthetics*, ed. Berys Gaut and Dominic Lopes (London: Routledge, 2002), 169–79.
35 Alan Goldman, "The Aesthetic," in *The Routledge Companion to Aesthetics*, ed. Berys Gaut and Dominic Lopes (London: Routledge, 2002), 181–92.
36 Monroe Beardsley, *The Possibility of Criticism* (Detroit: Wayne State University Press, 1970).
37 Monroe Beardsley, *Aesthetics* (New York: Harcourt, Brace & World, 1958).

38 David Novitz, "Postmodernism: Barthes and Derrida," in *The Routledge Companion to Aesthetics*, ed. Berys Gaut and Dominic Lopes (London: Routledge, 2002), 155–65.

39 Monroe Beardsley, "In Defense of Aesthetic Value," *Proceedings and Addresses of the American Philosophical Association* 52, no. 6 (1979): 741–42.

40 Dickie, *Introduction to Aesthetics*, 149.

41 Jean-Jacques Nattiez, *Music and Discourse: Toward a Semiology of Music*, trans. Carolyn Abbate (Princeton: Princeton University Press, 1990).

42 Bruce Springsteen, 'Born in the USA,' performed by Bruce Springsteen, http://www.youtube.com/watch?v=lZD4ezDbbu4.

43 Guiseppe Verdi, 'Dies Irae' from *Messa da Requiem*, performed by Robert Shaw conducting the Atlanta Symphony Orchestra and Chorus, https://www.youtube.com/watch?v=_jBLyIQvNf0.

44 Lewis Allan, 'Strange Fruit,' performed by Billie Holiday, http://www.youtube.com/watch?v=h4ZyuULy9zs.

45 David Margolick, *Strange Fruit: The Biography of a Song* (New York: The Ecco Press, 2001).

46 James Sanderson, music; Albert Gamse, text (based on words from Sir Walter Scott's *The Lady of the Lake*), *Hail to the Chief*, performed by the United States Army Herald Trumpets, http://www.youtube.com/watch?v=JW8AJds1CzI.

47 'Taps' (arr. by Daniel Butterfield), performed by the United States Navy Band, http://www.youtube.com/watch?v=WChTqYlDjtI.

48 Camille Saint-Saëns, *Carnival of the Animals*, performed by Andrea Licata, conducting the Royal Philharmonic Orchestra, with pianists Vivian Troon and Roderick Elms, https://www.youtube.com/watch?v=5LOFhsksAYw.

49 Hector Berlioz, *Symphony Fantastique*, Op. 14, performed by Rafael Frühbeck de Burgos conducting the Denmark Radio Symphony Orchestra, http://www.youtube.com/watch?v=W9CYLAuKdtU.

50 Hector Berlioz, *idée fixe* as it first appears in the *Symphonie Fantastique* as explained by Leonard Bernstein, conductor, and Julius Baker, flautist, http://www.youtube.com/watch?v=Mvh1gpdxCv0.

51 John Williams, 'Raiders March' from *Raiders of the Lost Ark*, performed by John Williams conducting the Los Angeles Philharmonic Orchestra, http://www.youtube.com/watch?v=oKdhEWM6n_o.

52 Gioachino Rossini, *William Tell Overture*, performed by Leonard Slatkin conducting the Detroit Symphony Orchestra, http://www.youtube.com/watch?v=7TJbH0hBNyA.

53 Paul Dukas, *The Sorcerer's Apprentice*, performed by Leopold Stowkoski conducting the Philadelphia Orchestra in the Walt Disney movie *Fantasia*, https://www.youtube.com/watch?v=Gkj2QeogAsU.

54 Richard Strauss, *Don Juan*, Op. 20, performed by Fritz Reiner conducting the Chicago Symphony Orchestra, http://www.youtube.com/watch?v=obEYUa_U8sc.

55 Richard Strauss, *Death and Transfiguration*, Op. 24, performed by George Szell conducting the Cleveland Orchestra, https://www.youtube.com/watch?v=4K3E1wZWSn0.

56 Richard Strauss, *Till Eulenspiegel's Merry Pranks*, Op. 28, performed by Georg Solti conducting the Chicago Symphony Orchestra, http://www.youtube.com/watch?v=vKFKf07lIDw.

57 Richard Strauss, *Also sprach Zarathustra*, Op. 30, performed by Gustavo Dudamel conducting the Vienna Philharmonic Orchestra, https://www.youtube.com/watch?v=ETveS23djXM.

58 Richard Strauss, *Don Quixote*, Op. 34, performed by Daniel Barenboim conducting the Chicago Symphony Orchestra, http://www.youtube.com/watch?v=IdbMOkzOYaI.

59 Richard Strauss, *Ein Heldenleben*, Op. 40, performed by Richard Strauss conducting the Bavarian State Orchestra, http://www.youtube.com/watch?v=dC6t5SdQc0I.

60 Richard Strauss, *Sinfonia Domestica*, Op. 53, performed by Rudolf Kempe conducting the Staatskapelle Dresden, http://www.youtube.com/watch?v=ANmiGCLWA_w.

61 Richard Strauss, *An Alpine Symphony*, Op. 64, performed by Bernard Kaitink conducting the Vienna Philharmonic Orchestra, http://www.youtube.com/watch?v=FQhpWsRhQGs.

62 Quoted in David Bispham, *A Quaker Singer's Recollections* (New York: Macmillan, 1920), 323.

63 Rudolf Louis, "On the Tone Poems of Richard Strauss," in *Richard Strauss and His World*, ed. Bryan Gilliam, trans. Susan Gillespie (Princeton, NJ: Princeton University Press, 1992), 309.

64 Charles Youmans, "The Private Intellectual Context of Richard Strauss's 'Also sprach Zarathustra,'" *19th-Century Music* 22, no. 2 (1998): 101–26.

65 Ibid., 103.

66 Earl Moore and Theodore Heger, *The Symphony and the Symphonic Poem, 6th rev. ed.* (Ann Arbor, MI: Ulrich's Books, 1974), 261.

67 Charles Ives, *The Unanswered Question*, performed by Leonard Bernstein conducting the New York Philharmonic Orchestra, https://www.youtube.com/watch?v=vXD4tIp59L0.

68 Charles Ives, *The Unanswered Question* (New York: Southern Music Publishing Co., 1908/1930–1935).

69 Matthew McDonald, "Silent Narration? Elements of Narrative in Ives's *The Unanswered Question*," *19th-Century Music* 27, no. 3 (2004): 270–71.

70 Ives, *The Unanswered Question*, 2.

71 McDonald, "Silent Narration?," 276.

72 Carroll Pratt, "The Design of Music," *The Journal of Aesthetics and Art Criticism* 12, no. 3 (1954): 289.

73 Roger Scruton, *The Aesthetics of Music* (Oxford: The Clarendon Press, 1997), 135.

74 Wayne Bowman, *Philosophical Perspectives on Music* (New York: Oxford University Press, 1998), 252.

14 Phenomenology

In all the previous philosophical views we have surveyed so far, the center of attention has been on listening to and contemplation of a specific musical composition, such as a Beethoven symphony or a song by U2, with a determination to remain focused on the music or on that to which the music refers. Phenomenologists shift the focus away from contemplation of musical works to the lived, bodily, in-the-moment experience of engaging with music. Before we review specific philosophical viewpoints, let us remind ourselves of what it feels like to be engaged with music.

Musical Experiences

Let us begin by listing eight musical roles; feel free to add other roles:

- Composer
- Performer/Conductor
- Improviser
- Listener
- Music Theorist
- Musicologist
- Music Educator
- Music Therapist

Imagine in each case that you are engaged in that role. As a composer, we are not concerned about the finished composition, but the process of composing. If you have ever composed any music, try to recall what it felt like during moments of composition, not how you felt when you completed the work. Perhaps you had different experiences with each composition and no two were exactly alike. As a performer or improviser we are not concerned here about a remembrance or recording of your performance or improvisation, but what the experience was like when you were in the throes of creating the sounds. Whether this is singing in an opera, jamming with friends in a garage band, or conducting a middle school band, the focus is on the actual moment-by-moment performance. Note that performance scenarios can include private practice and ensemble rehearsal as well as public performances.

Previous philosophical views have not emphasized listening during a performance, but in contemplation of what was heard after the fact (past tense). No account has heretofore taken into account the moment-by-moment experience of hearing music (present tense). I encourage you to conduct a self-experiment; listen to a familiar and an unfamiliar piece. Engage in metacognition (thinking about your thinking) or stream of consciousness awareness as you do. Can you describe your listening experience?

Finally, consider the roles of music theorist, musicologist, music teacher, and music therapist. In each case, imagine that you are analyzing a composition, conducting research on a manuscript, teaching a music lesson, or working with clients in a therapy session. We are not concerned with the outcome or product (i.e., an analysis, a research paper, a student's performance, or progress in achieving therapeutic goals), but in the process of analyzing, researching and writing, teaching, or engaging with clients. Once you have spent some time reviewing which of these experiences is relevant for you, you will be ready to consider the viewpoint of phenomenology.

Edmund Husserl

Edmund Husserl (1859–1938) is credited as the father of phenomenology. He was in agreement with Descartes that the one thing we can be absolutely certain of is our conscious awareness.[1] Further, he agreed with Hegel that although we can conceptually make a distinction between our own consciousness and objects of our consciousness—that is, we are always conscious of *something*—in actual experience, however, they are indistinguishable. Critics questioned whether the objects of our consciousness have a separate existence apart from us. Husserl's original contribution was the recognition that "the objects of our consciousness do exist *as objects of consciousness for us.*"[2]

A major aspect of consciousness for Husserl was that it is always *intentional.*[3] That is to say, our consciousness is directed toward something. We think about being hungry, our work, families, plans for the future, music, beauty, and anything and everything else. To apprehend what is presented to us without prejudice or preconceptions, we must *bracket* the object of consciousness in order to experience it as it is. Bracketing is a temporary suspension of judgment to allow for a total focus on the object of consciousness.[4] The process of freeing a phenomenon from irrelevant influences is called *phenomenological reduction.* The goal is to experience the object of our consciousness (e.g., music) in all its richness and possibilities.

Husserl concerned himself with consciousness of space and time, a pursuit that has implications for musical understanding. We can only be in the *here* and *now.* Lived experiences are a series of in-the-moment events. Past and future experiences are only mental abstractions. Listening to a melody, we have a memory of the tonal past, perception of the immediate tonal now, and can make predictions of how the melody might go (e.g., expectancy theory). Another possibility is to "grasp the entire consciousness of an object as a now and say: now I seize the moment and grasp the entire consciousness as an all-together, as an all-at-once."[5] Phenomenology, then, is the way the world presents itself to our consciousness.

> "There is more wisdom in your body than in your deepest philosophy."
> (Nietzsche)

Maurice Merleau-Ponty

A major contribution of Merleau-Ponty (1908–1961) is that the body is brought more prominently into the picture. Each of us possesses a flesh, blood, and bone body with certain specific characteristics, such as height, weight, physical capabilities, and so on. This body is central to our perceptions of the world and, in fact, "it is bodily experience rather than conscious experience that is our

> "The body is our general medium for having a world."
>
> (Maurice Merleau-Ponty)

essential way of being in the world."[6] Perceptions are not inferior to reasoning and there is no world independent of our perceptions of it. Music perception, then, is an embodied activity. As Bernard Flynn put it, "According to him [Merleau-Ponty], perception is a behavior effected not by consciousness but by the body, but not by the body as a piece of the physical world, rather by the body as lived, a living body."[7]

Mikel Dufrenne

To Dufrenne (1910–1995), an aesthetic object stands out in relief from other natural and useful objects.[8] Although the aesthetic object appears *in* the world, it is not *of* the world; it is privileged. An aesthetic experience in not merely a contemplative one, rather, it is a bodily one. Speaking of the performer's role, Dufrenne said, "Thus it is still in the human body that the music becomes incarnate."[9] That aesthetic experience is tied intimately to bodily experience is captured in this brief passage:

> The aesthetic object is above all the apotheosis of the sensuous, and all its meaning is given in the sensuous. Hence the latter must be amenable to the body.[10]

That delicious phrase "apotheosis of the sensuous" is a poetic way of saying that music happens at the pinnacle of bodily experience.

To Dufrenne, aspects of space and time coalesce and turn an aesthetic object into a 'quasi-subject' in which spatiotemporal relationships are internalized. That is, time and space are held within the art object. The word he uses to describe this is 'interiority.' Thus, rhythm creates a world of time that resides within the music. Likewise, the body is drawn into the interiority of musical space. It is in this way that an aesthetic quasi-subject is not of the world. He speaks of the silence before the music begins or listening with eyes closed as means of framing a musical experience and conferring "a more palpable interiority."[11] Thus, we share the same time-space as the music and are fused into one.

> "Thus it is still in the human body that the music becomes incarnate, but in a body disciplined by the instrument, obliged to submit to long training in order to become the instrument of an instrument."
>
> (Mikel Dufrenne)

Thomas Clifton

Clifton (1935–1978) identified four core attributes of musical experiences: time, space, play, and feeling and understanding (the latter two he said are inseparable).[12]

- Musical time is felt time, not clock time; music's temporality creates its own bodily experience of time. The past and the future overlap in what we call the *present*. Our experience is one of fluidity; we live in the present but can shift our attention backward and forward in an ongoing manner.

- Musical space is inseparable from time. When we are fully, bodily engaged in music, we are in musical space, not in physical space. In effect, our personal space fuses with musical space to become one.
- Musical play involves both formal behaviors that are deliberate and purposeful and spontaneous behaviors that are acts of discovery. In contrast to others, Clifton does not find a dichotomy between play and reality. That is, play is not stepping out of or setting aside reality, rather it is "a constitution of reality"[13] and "is an irreducible element in the meaning of musical being."[14]
- Feeling is at the core of musical experiences and involves full possession of and absorption into the musical experience. At the same time, there is a constant interplay between feeling and reflective understanding. They serve as complementary restraints and enhancements, "with feeling appealing to and illuminating the path of reflection, while reflection enhances, sustains, and ratifies feeling."[15]

In sum, music has a meaning that is experienced by the body, which includes the mind, feelings, senses, will, and metabolism. Music is a humanly constructed meaning by an embodied mind. "Music is what I am when I experience it."[16] This is very similar to a line from a T. S. Elliot poem, *Four Quartets*: "You are the music, while the music lasts."[17]

David Burrows

As with other phenomenologists, Burrows (1930–) was concerned with our bodily experience in time and space. Regarding time, he said, "Music is a modeling of human temporality"[18] and

> music models the way we make ourselves up as we go along out of the discontinuities of feeling and breathing, sleeping and waking, of brain-cell firings and the heartbeat, all adding up to the macro-pulsation that is a life.[19]

Burrows felt that we live in three overlapping fields: Field 1 is the physical world of here and now, the place where our physical body moves in time and space. The view is from 'here,' the center. Field 2 is mental space and time that includes past and future, along with elsewhere (thinking of places other than where we are physically). The view is from any time or place you choose it to be. Field 3 is unbounded space and time where the spirit can move unfettered. The view is from an undifferentiated 'everywhere.'

According to Burrows, sound is inward, ambiguous, and flowing; sight is outward, particular, and fixed. Sound does not stop at the skin. It has an immediate, inward touch that cannot be kept outside the body. Sound is a unique mode of construing and constructing the world. Music has value

> "Music is narrative in the present tense: it collapses the times of narration and of what is being narrated."
> (David Burrows)

because of its ability to touch the vital center of our being. Music also allows for a synthesis of performers and listeners in a "shared present."[20]

Eleanor Stubley

One of the most significant contributions Stubley (1960–) made is the recognition that listening is not necessarily the most important way to experience music. She gives pride of place to music making. Furthermore, as a phenomenologist, she acknowledges the important role of the body. "All other things being equal, the act of performance appears to blur the sensations and perceptual boundaries distinguishing the body and mind making musical decisions and the instrument through which those decisions are heard and articulated."[21] Also, in keeping with others of like persuasion, she promotes the bodily experience of musical performance in time and space. "The performer is not merely discovering and shaping the music; he or she is also living in and through it."[22] Finally, Stubley places musical performance in a broader socio-cultural context:

> "It is as if each [musical] moment has a spatial dimension that extends between 'the here and now,' a spatial dimension that gives the musicians a bodily presence in the sounds themselves."
> (Eleanor Stubley)

Although particular to the knowledge and skill of the individual performer or ensemble, the transaction [i.e., making music] is enmeshed in an intricate web of social relationships and cultural conventions as much a part of the event as the performer's past experience, the score, and the evolving performance.[23]

Mark Johnson

Heretofore, phenomenologists have taken the position that the mind is in the body. Johnson (1949–) turned it around the other way: the body is in the mind.[24] In his view, all thinking arises from bodily experience. Through living, we develop patterns, or what Johnson calls 'image schemata.' These image schemata form the basis of later abstract thought. A corporeal basis of musical meaning explains how emotion is integral to the experience of music.

Johnson's philosophical views are bolstered by modern neuroscience. As discussed previously, in a series of books, neurologist Antonio Damasio provided evidence that the body and mind are integrated and that feelings and emotions are central to consciousness and reasoning. To reiterate, the full titles of these books provide a brief overview of his main thesis:

> "There is no (such) fully autonomous faculty of reason separate from and independent of bodily capacities such as perception and movement."
> (George Lakoff and Mark Johnson)

- *Descartes' Error: Emotion, Reason, and the Human Brain*[25]
- *The Feeling of What Happens: Body and Emotion in the Making of Consciousness*[26]
- *Looking for Spinoza: Joy, Sorrow, and the Feeling Brain*[27]

In addressing the mind–body problem, he stated categorically that "body, brain, and mind are manifestations of a single organism."[28] Feelings, that is conscious awareness of the body's emotional state, are central to judgment and decision-making.

Summary and Thought Questions

In a subsequent chapter, we will discuss praxialism, the notion that musicing (music making) is a core value of music, that builds on Stubley. For now, phenomenologists leave us with a view different from any we have discussed previously. Music is not a disembodied, rational exercise. Music is not constructed from sensory impressions that are sent to the mind. Music is not a vehicle to take us some place else. Music is a full, rich, complete, whole-body experience that is lived in the here and now.

Unlike other chapters, no musical examples are included in this one as that would invite 'after-the-fact' reflections. Rather, recall the sensations you had of 'doing' your craft from the previous section on "Musical Experiences" as you contemplate these questions:

1. How vividly can you recall the moment-to-moment thoughts and feelings you have while composing, performing, listening, and so on? Are you able to track or monitor these experiences while actually in the midst of being musically engaged?
2. Does your ability/inability to capture the essence of a transitory experience have any bearing on the value you place on a phenomenological view? That is, suppose you recall one of the most powerful experiences you have had with music, akin to Gabrielsson's strong experiences with music[29] that we have previously discussed. How is reflecting on a musical experience while it is happening different from an 'after-the-fact' recollection? In one case, the focus is on the process and the other is on the product, but is it truly possible to grasp fully the significance of an experience while you are having it?
3. If a phenomenological musical experience is a first-person account, how, then, would you account for the social nature of music? For example, if the value of an orchestra concert is that each member of the orchestra and the audience is having his or her own lived experience, does that negate the 'group dynamic' experience that seems to be so much a part of so many musical experiences?
4. Although some phenomenologists may agree with Johnson that the body is in the mind, does an emphasis on 'in-the-moment,' lived experiences negate the rich insights that can be gained by thoughtful reflection? Or, do you agree with Bowman, who said, "Revealing the bodily basis of mind enables us not only to assert, but to show how music is at once a cerebral and a bodily competence."[30]
5. How would a phenomenological view translate into your daily craft of performing, conducting, teaching, or working with therapy clients?

Notes

1 Bryan Magee, *The Great Philosophers* (Oxford: Oxford University Press, 1987).
2 Ibid., 254.
3 Peter King, *One Hundred Philosophers* (Hauppauge, NY: Barron's, 2004).
4 Monroe Beardsley, *Aesthetics from Classical Greece to the Present* (Tuscaloosa, AL: The University of Alabama Press, 1966).
5 Edmund Husserl as quoted in Edward Lippman, *A History of Western Musical Aesthetics* (Lincoln, NE: University of Nebraska Press, 1992), 439.
6 Wayne Bowman, *Philosophical Perspectives on Music* (New York: Oxford University Press, 1998), 260.
7 Bernard Flynn, "Maurice Merleau-Ponty," in *The Stanford Encyclopedia of Philosophy* (2011 edition). http://plato.stanford.edu/archives/fall2011/entries/merleau-ponty.
8 Beardsley, *Aesthetics from Classical Greece to the Present*.
9 Mikel Dufrenne, *The Phenomenology of Aesthetic Experience*, trans. Edward Casey (Evanston, IL: Northwestern University Press, 1979), 22.
10 Ibid., 339.
11 Ibid., 152.

12 Thomas Clifton, *Music as Heard: A Study in Applied Phenomenology* (New Haven, CT: Yale University Press, 1983).
13 Ibid., 73.
14 Ibid., 74.
15 Ibid., 77.
16 Ibid., 297.
17 T. S. Eliot, *Four Quartets* (Orlando, FL: Harcourt, 1968), 32.
18 David Burrows, *Time and the Warm Body: A Musical Perspective on the Construction of Time* (Leiden, The Netherlands: Brill, 2007), ix.
19 Ibid., xv.
20 Ibid., 122.
21 Eleanor Stubley, "The Performer, the Score, the Work: Musical Performance and Transactional Reading," *Journal of Aesthetic Education* 29, no. 3 (1995): 59.
22 Ibid., 61.
23 Ibid., 59–60.
24 Mark Johnson, *The Body in the Mind: The Bodily Basis of Meaning, Imagination, and Reason* (Chicago: University of Chicago Press, 1987).
25 Antonio Damasio, *Descartes' Error: Emotion, Reason, and the Human Brain* (New York: Avon Books, 1994).
26 Antonio Damasio, *The Feeling of What Happens: Body and Emotion in the Making of Consciousness* (New York: Harcourt Brace, 1999).
27 Antonio Damasio, *Looking for Spinoza: Joy, Sorrow, and the Feeling Brain* (New York: Harcourt Brace, 2003).
28 Ibid., 195.
29 Alf Gabrielsson, *Strong Experiences with Music* (Oxford, UK: Oxford University Press, 2011).
30 Bowman, *Philosophical Perspectives on Music*, 299.

15 Pragmatism

Pragmatism is "the philosophy of practical consequences."[1] Although its roots go back to Heraclitus and the Sophists in ancient Greece,[2] it is the first distinctively American school of philosophy. Its primary proponents were Charles Sanders Peirce, William James, and John Dewey. These three were sometimes called the American Pragmatists, even though they differed significantly in their views. The word *pragmatism* comes from the Greek word for a deed or action,[3] thus providing a unifying feature of all three of these viewpoints. The pragmatist's maxim might be stated: *We clarify a hypothesis by identifying its practical consequences.* Truth or meaning comes not from rational thought or opinions of authorities but from the results of an idea when tested. Thus, the scientific method is applicable—activity, awareness of the problem, observation of data, and formulation and testing of a hypothesis.[4]

All three of the American Pragmatists had a very broad range. Peirce made contributions in logic, inquiry, metaphysics, epistemology, mathematics, and science; he was called the "Leibniz of America."[5] James made major contributions in psychology as well as philosophy. Dewey had extraordinary influence on a variety of fields, including education, in addition to his philosophical writing. Peirce and James did not write about aesthetics, art, or music, and so our discussions of them will be very brief. However, their ideas influenced Dewey, who did write a significant philosophy of art.

Charles Sanders Peirce

Charles Sanders Peirce (1839–1914), pronounced *purse*,[6] is considered the founder of pragmatism.[7] He wished to distinguish between metaphysical nonsense, that is, ideas that have no observable aspects that make any practical difference, and scientific metaphysics, ideas based on experience with observable phenomena that have a practical outcome. Peirce believed that "the significance of an idea rests in the nature of its consequences."[8] In 1871 he founded the Metaphysical Club, among whose members were William James and Oliver Wendell Holmes, Jr.[9] Although Peirce was the first to be called a pragmatist, he later disagreed with James's views, so he changed the name to pragmaticism to differentiate his own ideas.[10]

> "It will sometimes strike a scientific man that the philosophers have been less intent on finding out what the facts are, than on inquiring what belief is most in harmony with their system."
>
> (Charles Sanders Peirce)

William James

William James (1842–1910) was the brother of the author Henry James (*Daisy Miller*, *The Turn of the Screw*, *The Portrait of a Lady*, etc.). "He earned his M.D. at Harvard in 1870, and taught there from 1872 to his death in 1910, at first anatomy and physiology, and then psychology, and at last philosophy."[11] He was the first person to teach psychology in the United States.[12] His book, *The Principles of Psychology*,[13] was a major contribution to the literature as it is considered "probably the best known book in all psychology."[14] His theory of emotion was also developed independently by Carl Lange and thus is called the James–Lange Theory of Emotion. This theory states that physiological changes occur first and an awareness of emotion follows.[15] The contemporary view of emotion has modified the earlier theory considerably, but it was an important idea for the better part of a century.

> "Belief creates the actual fact."
>
> (William James)

James was highly influenced by Peirce's article "How to Make Our Ideas Clear."[16] He believed that all knowledge is pragmatic; either something is right or it is wrong. In the Preface to *The Meaning of Truth*, a sequel to *Pragmatism*,[17] he wrote:

> Pragmatism asks its usual question. 'Grant an idea or belief to be true,' it says, 'what concrete difference will its being true make in any one's actual life? What experiences [may] be different from those which would obtain if the belief were false? How will the truth be realized? What, in short, is the truth's cash value in experiential terms?' The moment pragmatism asks this question, it sees the answer: TRUE IDEAS ARE THOSE THAT WE CAN ASSIMILATE, VALIDATE, CORROBORATE, AND VERIFY. FALSE IDEAS ARE THOSE THAT WE CANNOT.[18]

"James thinks our beliefs must accord with the evidence, and where the evidence for one theory is stronger than that for its competitors we have no rational choice but to prefer that theory."[19] "In other words, truth, according to the pragmatic theory, is what allows us to handle situations better, what is expedient, what 'works.'"[20]

John Dewey

In the middle of the 20th century, Bertrand Russell wrote that John Dewey (1859–1952) was "generally admitted to be the leading living philosopher of America."[21] Raised in Vermont, Dewey taught at the universities of Minnesota, Michigan, and Chicago, concluding with 25 years at Columbia University.[22] He was struck by how much progress had been made in science and technology in the past 300–400 years and he wondered whether the scientific processes that led to these successes could be applied in other areas of life.[23] Dewey's views were called Instrumentalism, sometimes Experimentalism, because ideas or knowledge were seen as tools of action; their nature was in the way they cause different effects.

Dewey was influential in democracy, religion, ethics, education, and art. In education, he stressed an active approach to learning. Practical interaction with real problems was more important than theoretical learning. He was against a spectator view of knowledge and promoted active engagement. Education was not something that was imposed from without; children should be dynamic agents in the acquisition of knowledge. They should be active learners, engaged in problem solving.

Speaking of art, Dewey said, "It is the outcome of a skilled and intelligent art of dealing with natural things for the sake of intensifying, purifying, prolonging and deepening the satisfactions which they spontaneously afford."[24] Dewey's book *Art as Experience*[25] is "by wide-spread agreement, the most valuable work on aesthetics written in English (and perhaps in any language) so far in our century."[26] Dewey recognized that art is often separated from daily life by being housed in an art gallery or museum or performed in a concert hall. He saw it as his task "to restore continuity between the refined and intensified forms of experience that are works of art and the everyday events, doings, and sufferings that are universally recognized to constitute experience."[27] This naturalistic approach drew a stronger connection between everyday and aesthetic experiences.[28]

Dewey refers to having *an* experience. By this, he meant something particular that arises out of ongoing, daily life experiences and that is marked off from what came before and after. *An* experience is seen as a consummatory experience, characterized by:

- Completeness: "when the material experienced runs its course to fulfillment."[29]
- Distinctness: an experience is not indistinct or shapeless, rather "the enduring whole is diversified by successive phases."[30]
- Identifiableness: we identify an experience by a name and may recall it with a distinctive, dominating characteristic. It "is constituted by a single *quality* that pervades the entire experience in spite of the variation of its constituent parts."[31]
- Seamlessness: "In a work of art, different acts, episodes, occurrences melt and fuse into unity, and yet do not disappear and lose their own character as they do."[32]
- Cumulativeness: there is "a sense of growing meaning conserved and accumulating toward an end that is felt as an accomplishment of a process."[33]
- Forward momentum: an experience "moves by its own urge to fulfillment."[34]

Imagine *an* experience you have had with music. For an illustration, let us take your senior recital (or a similar event if you did not perform one). This event is complete, in and of itself. It is distinct, containing the separate pieces you performed, yet these constituent parts melded into a coherent whole. You identify the experience—my senior recital—and it can be captured by a pervading quality; it was magical, it was the highlight of my undergraduate years, or however you characterize it. Even though there were individual compositions on the program, the recital can be seen as a unified experience. The recital built from beginning to end and its completion was seen as a fulfilling accomplishment. It almost seemed to take on a life of its own as the program moved toward the conclusion. Thus, your recital was *an* experience in the Deweyan sense.

Dewey believed that emotions make an experience complete and unified. Somewhat cryptically, he said, "Experience is emotional but there are no separate things called emotions in it."[35] By this he meant that the words we use to identify emotions—joy, sorrow, grief, and so on—imply discrete entities. However, emotions come and go, meld, merge, and overlap. They change as the experience unfolds. *An* experience is a dynamic occurrence.

An aesthetic experience, or esthetic as Dewey preferred it, is "the clarified and intensified development of traits that belong to every normally complete experience."[36] The word 'artistic' implies doing, making, or creating; the word 'esthetic' denotes perception and enjoyment. Because there is no word in the English language that conjoins the two, Dewey

> "Art is not the possession of the few who are recognized writers, painters, musicians; it is the authentic expression of any and all individuality."
>
> (John Dewey)

felt that this artificially separates an aesthetic experience from an artistic experience. To him, doing and undergoing are strongly related. He characterized an aesthetic experience this way:

> An object is peculiarly and dominantly esthetic, yielding the enjoyment characteristic of esthetic perception, when the factors that determine anything which can be called *an* experience are lifted high above the threshold of perception and are made manifest for its own sake.[37]

Using these words, we might compare an everyday session in the practice room with a recital. The daily practice regimen shares many characteristics with the recital, but during the recital those same actions are intensified and clarified such that the recital transcends the regular practice time and becomes *an* aesthetic experience.

Throughout *Art as Experience*, Dewey mostly wrote about art in general and not too frequently about music. However, he did have some particular things to say about music. Because sound expresses emotions in a direct, intimate way, music is considered both the lowest and the highest form of art. It is the lowest because of its origins in animal sounds and because nearly everyone can appreciate music without special training. "On the other side, there are types of music, those most prized by connoisseurs, that demand special training to be perceived and enjoyed, and its devotees form a cult, so that *their* art is the most esoteric of all arts."[38]

He felt that art is an important humanizing force; it transcends barriers of culture and language. In this regard, music deserves special mention.

> The power of music in particular to merge different individualities in a common surrender, loyalty and inspiration, a power utilized in religion and in warfare alike, testifies to the relative universality of the language of art.[39]

We began this short description of Dewey's ideas with the understanding that his interests were wide-ranging and highly influential in a number of fields. However,

> It may be seriously argued that for Dewey, therefore, surprising as this may seem to those who think of him in terms of his pragmatism, his instrumentalism in logic, his liberalism in politics, and progressivism in education, it is art and the aesthetic in experience which ultimately constitutes the kernel of genuine philosophy.[40]

As highly regarded as *Art as Experience* is, there are, as one might expect, critics. Arnold Isenberg, for example, said, "This book is a hodgepodge of conflicting methods and undisciplined speculations."[41] In spite of such a harsh comment, Isenberg did admire the book. However, he felt that it needed something else. His suggestion was analytic philosophy, an approach developed by Bertrand Russell and Ludwig Wittgenstein. Mathematical logic was used to analyze philosophical statements or concepts. "Philosophical aesthetics is *an analysis of the concepts and principles of criticism* and other aesthetic studies, such as the psychology of art."[42] Richard Shusterman agreed that Dewey's definition of aesthetic experience is "hopelessly inadequate"[43] and that he "creates considerable confusion"[44] by his lack of clarity. "Hence analytic philosophers typically dismiss his whole idea of aesthetic experience as a disastrous muddle."[45] Pragmatism can also be faulted for its over-reliance on the scientific method.[46] Some questions or issues are simply not amenable to experimental investigation.

A Utilitarian View

Dewey's term Instrumentalism has acquired another meaning that, while it bears some relation to his usage, has quite a different connotation. Going all the way back to the ancient Greeks' notion that music had the power to influence human thought and behavior for good or for ill, there are those who find the utilitarian value of music to be primary. Whether called instrumentalism, functionalism, or utilitarianism, the thrust of this view is that music gains value as it serves nonmusical aims. For instance, we might value teaching and learning certain songs in elementary school as a means of inculcating patriotism. [Note that this usage is not to be confused with the Utilitarianism espoused by Jeremy Bentham, John Stuart Mill, and others as a philosophy of normative ethics.]

In American education, Lowell Mason predicated the inclusion of music in the curriculum on the basis of its intellectual nature, referring back to the placement of music along with arithmetic, geometry, and astronomy in the Upper Quadrivium of the seven liberal arts, on the basis of its moral influence, and on the physical effects of singing and the improvement of health.[47] Nearly 150 years later, utilitarian values were promoted on the basis of music's role in "character education and the development of better citizenship."[48] Even today, the National Association for Music Education promotes the benefits conveyed by music education as consisting of: success in society, success in school and learning, success in developing intelligence, and success in life.[49]

Because few serious philosophers have developed utilitarianism into a valid philosophical view regarding music, more will be said on this topic in Chapter 22: Advocacy. The issue is not so much whether music can increase school attendance, whether the presence of a community orchestra can improve the local economy, or whether music plays a vital role in such ceremonies as weddings and funerals. There are data to support all these outcomes and many more besides. Rather, the philosophical question is whether utilitarian outcomes constitute the primary value of music.

> "Vocal music tends to produce social order and happiness in a family."
> (Lowell Mason)

Summary and Thought Questions

In sum, pragmatists value music when it provides *an* aesthetic experience, during which normal perceptions and actions are intensified and clarified. Music has the power to bring people together by crossing linguistic and cultural lines. Consider these questions as you determine whether pragmatism will find a place in your philosophy of music.

1. Do you agree with the American Pragmatists that truth is what works or what can be validated?
2. Do you agree with Dewey's naturalistic approach in which aesthetic experiences are resonant with everyday experiences only with clarified and intensified perceptions and actions? If so, what aspects of musical aesthetic experiences you have had (such as your senior recital) were clarified and intensified?
3. In thinking about a musical episode that was *an* experience for you, discuss each of the following characteristics:

   - Completeness
   - Distinctness

- Identifiableness
- Seamlessness
- Cumulativeness
- Forward momentum

4. Do you agree that music is both the lowest and highest art form?
5. How do you respond to the criticisms that Dewey's ideas are inadequate, confusing, full of undisciplined speculations, and a disastrous muddle?
6. If you were to adopt Dewey's pragmatic philosophy, how would we see its influence in your musical decisions and actions?
7. What practical or functional uses of music do you experience on a regular basis? Are these sufficiently important to raise them to a level of primary values?

Notes

1 William Sahakian and Mabel Sahakian, *Ideas of the Great Philosophers* (New York: Fall River Press, 2005), 150.
2 Harold Abeles, Charles Hoffer, and Robert Klotman, *Foundations of Music Education, 2nd ed.* (New York: Schirmer Books, 1994).
3 Bryan Magee, *The Great Philosophers* (Oxford: Oxford University Press, 1987), 283.
4 John Dewey, *How We Think* (Boston: D.C. Heath, 1910).
5 Magee, *The Great Philosophers*, 291.
6 Samuel Stumpf and James Fieser, *Philosophy: History and Problems, 6th ed.* (New York: McGraw-Hill, 2003), 394.
7 Philip Stokes, *Philosophy: The World's Greatest Thinkers* (London: Arcturus, 2007).
8 Sahakian and Sahakian, *Ideas of the Great Philosophers*, 153.
9 Peter King, *One Hundred Philosophers* (Hauppauge, NY: Barron's, 2004).
10 Robert Solomon, *Introduction to Philosophy, 8th ed.* (New York: Oxford University Press, 2005).
11 Will Durant, *The Story of Philosophy* (New York: Simon and Schuster, 1953), 382.
12 King, *One Hundred Philosophers*, 130.
13 William James, *The Principles of Psychology* (New York: Henry Holt and Co., 1890).
14 Ian Hunter, "James, William," in *The Oxford Companion to the Mind*, ed. Richard Gregory (Oxford, UK: Oxford University Press, 2004), 492.
15 Morten Kringlebach, "Emotion," in *The Oxford Companion to the Mind*, ed. Richard Gregory (Oxford, UK: Oxford University Press, 2004), 287–90.
16 Charles Peirce, "How to Make Our Ideas Clear," *Popular Science Monthly* 12 (1878): 286–302.
17 William James, *Pragmatism* (New York: Longmans, Green and Co., 1907).
18 William James, *The Meaning of Truth* (New York: Longmans Green, and Co., 1909), v–vi.
19 Magee, *The Great Philosophers*, 289.
20 Solomon, *Introduction to Philosophy*, 279.
21 Bertrand Russell, *The History of Western Philosophy* (New York: Simon and Schuster, 1945), 819.
22 Stumpf and Fieser, *Philosophy: History and Problems*, 403.
23 Magee, *The Great Philosophers*, 291.
24 John Dewey, *Experience and Nature* (London: George Allen & Unwin, 1929), 389.
25 John Dewey, *Art as Experience* (New York: Perigree Books, 1934/1980).
26 Monroe Beardsley, *Aesthetics from Classical Greece to the Present* (Tuscaloosa, AL: The University of Alabama Press, 1966), 332.
27 Dewey, *Art as Experience*, 3.
28 Lauri Väkevä, "Philosophy of Music Education: As Art of Life: A Deweyian View," in *The Oxford Handbook of Philosophy in Music Education*, ed. Wayne Bowman and Ana Lucía Frega (New York: Oxford University Press, 2012).

29 Dewey, *Art as Experience*, 35.
30 Ibid., 36.
31 Ibid., 37.
32 Ibid., 36.
33 Ibid., 39.
34 Ibid., 39.
35 Ibid., 42.
36 Ibid., 46.
37 Ibid., 57.
38 Ibid., 238.
39 Ibid., 335.
40 Albert Hofstadter and Richard Kuhns, eds., *Philosophies of Art & Beauty: Selected Readings in Aesthetics from Plato to Heidegger* (Chicago: University of Chicago Press, 1976), 578.
41 Arnold Isenberg, "Analytical Philosophy and the Study of Art," *The Journal of Aesthetics and Art Criticism* 46 (1987): 128.
42 Ibid., 128.
43 Richard Shusterman, "The End of Aesthetic Experience," *The Journal of Aesthetic Experience* 55, no. 1 (1997): 33.
44 Ibid., 34.
45 Ibid., 34.
46 Abeles, Hoffer, and Klotman, *Foundations of Music Education*.
47 Edward Birge, *History of Public School Music in the United States* (Washington, DC: Music Educators National Conference, 1928).
48 Michael Mark, *Contemporary Music Education, 3rd ed.* (New York: Schirmer Books, 1996), 59.
49 "Facts and Insights on the Benefits of Music Study," National Association for Music Education, 2007. http://musiced.nafme.org/resources/why-music-education-2007/.

16 Social Philosophy

The thrust of this philosophical view is summarized neatly in the following statement: "Music is an inherently social phenomenon: the patterns and regularities that exist in physical sounds only take on musical meaning when they are interpreted as such by groups of people."[1] In a previous chapter, we saw that Eleanor Stubley placed music in a social context. A generation before her, Theodor Adorno and Jacques Attali used this idea as a cornerstone of their philosophies. In this view, we can only understand music in the social context in which it is heard and experienced. Furthermore, music is an important agent of social change.

Theodor Adorno

Adorno (1903–1969) was highly influenced by modernist movements in music. Throughout the latter part of the 19th century, the music of Wagner, Strauss, Debussy, and Mahler featured increasing chromaticism, dissonance, and movement away from the grounding in tonality that had dominated the so-called 'common-practice' era for the past several centuries. Following these composers, Stravinsky, Hindemith, Milhaud, and others continued to use tonal centers, albeit in significantly different ways from before. Bartók, with his use of bitonality (e.g., in the *Mikrokosmos*)[2] ♫ represents something of a halfway point between these composers and composers of the Second Viennese School, notably Schoenberg, Berg, and Webern, who explored atonality, the complete dissolution of a tonal center. In *Philosophy of Modern Music*,[3] Adorno presented studies of Stravinsky and Schoenberg, portraying Stravinsky as a representative of reactionary forces, particularly in his neoclassic compositions such as *Pulcinella* (1920)[4] ♫ and *Symphony of Psalms* (1930).[5] ♫ "The folkloristic neo-classic and collectivistic schools all have but one desire: to remain in the haven of safety and herald the pre-formed."[6] Adorno was highly influenced by his composition studies with Alban Berg from 1925–1928;[7] thus he sees Schoenberg as a representative of progressive forces. He was also highly influenced by Karl Marx's criticisms of capitalism.[8] These two factors played a significant role in the development of his philosophy of music.

> "Art is the social antithesis of society, not directly deducible from it."
>
> (Theodor Adorno)

Adorno wrote in opposition to the idealist's notion of universal truths. Idealists believed that the perception of beauty in music is not an individual preference. Rather, with the proper use of cognitive faculties such as imagination and free play, anyone could discover an underlying unity, a universal property of beauty. Adorno felt that individuals were capable of deriving their own particular conceptions from their interactions with music. He used three terms that are important to define if we are to understand his philosophical ideas concerning music:

- *Reification* is the treatment of abstract values as things. For example, beauty may be considered a commodity. It is packaged and marketed. Consider the way music is advertised. In the classical world, performers are often promoted as personalities over the aesthetic qualities of their performances. In commercial music, the packaging and marketing of music is axiomatic.
- *Commodification* means that things are valued for their status as abstract units for exchange; use value becomes less important than exchange value. To Adorno, music had become a product to be bought and sold, rather than an art form.
- *Fetishization* means that impersonal things have value on their own. For example, developing and maintaining a complete music collection takes on a value in and of itself, independent of the artistic or aesthetic merits of the collection. A person who has recordings of 12 of Shostakovich's 15 symphonies may obtain the other three just to have a complete collection.

Adorno believed that the role of music was to promote social progress. When people become comfortable with the music they listen to, it no longer challenges them. Music that caters to familiarity, comfort, and easy listening dulls social consciousness and serves as a tool of the forces of domination. Music that provokes, startles, and challenges is music that has value. What kind of music does this? Adorno gives the atonal music of Schoenberg as an example of good music because it resists the status quo. Unfortunately, the kind of music that challenges social structures is the very kind of music that society tends to ignore and reject.

The culture industry's control of music negates discussions of value. Popular music is so generic, so mindless, that it stifles social discourse.

> The frame of mind to which popular music originally appealed, on which it feeds, and which it perpetually reinforces, is simultaneously one of distraction and inattention. Listeners are distracted from the demands of reality by entertainment which does not demand attention either.[9]

This vacuous approach to music turns people into what Adorno calls 'culture consumers.'

Many classical audiences are also culture consumers in that symphony orchestras must program standards such as Mozart and Beethoven symphonies; too much challenging contemporary music decreases attendance, and perhaps more importantly fund raising. Unfortunately, the very music that is most likely to foster social progress (e.g., Schoenberg) is exactly the kind of music that audiences are least likely to demand.

Many readers find Adorno unduly pessimistic and elitist. For example, Jay Bernstein identified three lines of criticism leveled at Adorno's philosophy:

> (1) it is unduly pessimistic about the emancipatory potential of modern liberal societies; (2) it turns its face against the call for praxis indigenous to the Marxist tradition; (3) it provides only an aesthetic alternative to current problems and conceptions of reason.[10]

While many of his trenchant comments have a ring of truth, Adorno has not provided a viable means of escape from the evils of capitalism that he deplores. If the good music is only that which provokes and challenges the status quo and that very music is listened to by only a very small minority, there does not seem to be a positive way forward. Nevertheless, Adorno's conception of music as an agent of social relevance and change is a point well taken.

Jacques Attali

Attali (1943–) believed that music is a means of creating and understanding the social and political world. "Music is more than an object of study; it is a way of perceiving the world. A tool of understanding."[11] The world is filled with noise and this noise has negative consequences. However, music can forge cohesion from chaos, order from randomness. Attali posited three historical modes of relationship between music and society, and a fourth one that he felt was about to emerge:

- *Ritual*: Music is a tool of ritual power to make people forget the fear of violence.
- *Representation*: Music is a tool of representative power when it makes people believe in order and harmony.
- *Repetition*: Music is a tool of bureaucratic power when it is used to silence people.
- *Composition*: Freedom in the future will come when people are directly engaged in creating and making music for the pleasure of it.

Attali wrote the following in 1985:

> Fetishized as a commodity, music is illustrative of the evolution of our entire society: deritualize a social form, repress an activity of the body, specialize its practice, sell it as a spectacle, generalize its consumption, then see to it that it is stockpiled until it loses its meaning. Today, music heralds . . . the establishment of a society of repetition in which nothing will happen anymore. But at the same time, it heralds the emergence of a formidable subversion, one leading to a radically new organization never yet theorized, of which self-management is but a distant echo.[12]

In the foreword to Attali's book *Noise: The Political Economy of Music*, Frederic Jameson wrote:

> The argument of *Noise* is that music . . . has precisely this annunciatory vocation [i.e., to anticipate historical developments]; and that the music of today stands both as a promise of a new, liberating mode of production, and as the menace of a dystopian possibility which is that mode of production's baleful mirror image.[13]

> "And today, whenever there is music, there is money. Looking only at the numbers, in certain countries more money is spent on music than on reading, drinking, or keeping clean. Music, an immaterial pleasure turned commodity, now heralds a society of the sign, of the immaterial up for sale, of the social relation unified in money."
> (Jacques Attali)

In an afterword, Susan McClary expressed her concern that Attali's stridency against received music scholarship might fall on deaf ears. "It is, therefore, quite conceivable that those trained in music will perceive the book's content also as noise—that is, as nonsense—and dismiss it out of hand."[14] Nevertheless, "*Noise*, by accounting theoretically for these new ways of articulating possible worlds through sound and by demonstrating the crucial role music plays in the transformation of societies, encourages and legitimates these efforts."[15]

Music in a Social Context

If we move beyond the particulars of Adorno and Attali and instead think of music's value as derived from its power to raise human consciousness and promote social progress, we can recall several positive examples. For example, during the Civil Rights Movement of the 1960s in America, singing the anthem 'We Shall Overcome'[16] ♫ emboldened civil rights activists to persevere in the face of fire hoses, nightsticks, and snarling dogs. Public sentiment about the war in Vietnam changed dramatically when Bob Dylan, Joan Baez, Pete Seeger, and Peter, Paul, and Mary began singing about the futility of war. More recent examples include orchestra programs in Venezuela, Paraguay, and the Middle East.

> "Music can change the world because it can change people."
>
> (Bono)

El Sistema (the System) was founded by Jose Antonio Abreu in 1975 as the National System of Youth and Children's Orchestras of Venezuela. It has provided training in the music of Bach, Mozart, Beethoven, and Brahms to hundreds of thousands of children.[17] These youngsters come from the poorest shanty-towns and barrios, and music has saved them from lives of poverty, abuse, drug addiction, and crime. One of the most famous products of El Sistema is Gustavo Dudamel, the conductor of the Los Angeles Philharmonic. In one video, Dudamel is heard conducting a Venezuelan youth orchestra performing Shostakovich's Symphony No. 10 in the Royal Albert Hall in London.[18] ♫ To Venezuelans, music is a social savior, which is represented in El Sistema's motto 'to play and to fight.' To these young musicians, this means "undertaking music as a collective experience which also involves individual effort: it entails a relentless pursuit of excellence and, above all, it means persevering until dreams become reality."[19]

> "Involvement becomes a weapon against poverty and inequality, violence and drug abuse."
>
> (José Antonio Abreu)

What is happening in Venezuela is paralleled by a movement in Paraguay called the Landfill Harmonic. Cateura is a slum built on a landfill. Amazingly, children play musical instruments built of trash pulled from the rubbish. Says one small girl, "My life would be worthless without music."[20] In another video, a young man can be heard performing Bach on a cello made from a discarded oilcan and wood pulled from the trash heap.[21] Clearly, the quality of music making is important, but perhaps more important is the use of music to help children escape lives of futility and to live life on a plane that far transcends their meager circumstances.

Yet another example is the West-Eastern Divan Orchestra.[22] Based in Seville, Spain, orchestra members come from Egypt, Iran, Israel, Jordan, Lebanon, Palestine, Syria, Turkey, and Spain. The orchestra was founded by Daniel Barenboim,[23] an Argentine-born Israeli, and Edward Said, a Palestinian literary critic, "to perform music and promote mutual understanding, non-violence and reconciliation" among Middle-Eastern people.[24] According to a journalist who was embedded in one of their tours:

> "Perhaps music will save the world."
>
> (Pablo Casals)

The West-Eastern Divan is not an 'orchestra for peace,' as it is so often dubbed, but an 'orchestra against ignorance'—mine, too. It is a singular space in which human beings who are otherwise forcibly kept apart can come together to exchange ideas and views, learn about each other and, above all, listen to each other in a world that would otherwise keep them silent.[25]

Statements made by the musicians reinforce this notion. A Lebanese/Palestinian violinist in the orchestra commented, "Here we're not in a situation where there is an oppressed and an oppressor. It's different. We are by default all equal, which makes it possible—and beautiful—to see human relationships and friendships grow day after day."[26] An Israeli trumpeter said, "The first time I was talking to an Arab musician. . . . We were fighting, struggling. . . . Little by little, I started seeing other sides, other aspects, and a fuller picture of the thing."[27]

In America, music in the schools plays a significant social role. Essays written by over a thousand teenagers about the meaning of music in their lives were organized around five central themes: (a) identity formation in and through music, (b) emotional benefits, (c) music's life benefits, including character-building and life skills, (d) social benefits, and (e) positive and negative impressions of school music programs.[28] Numerous comments in these essays referred to the important role music played in helping them work through their struggles and challenges. For example, one young man wrote how music helped him and his sister cope with the loss of their parents. Others

> "The West-Eastern Divan Orchestra is a humanitarian idea. . . . [It] may not change the world, but it is a step forward."
>
> (Daniel Barenboim)

spoke of music's social benefits in relation to its function as a distraction from involvement in spurious activity such as drugs, alcohol, smoking (cigarettes), gang life, and promiscuous sex—in their own lives or in the lives of adolescents in general.[29]

Music may also find its meaning in a social context in more general terms. That is, as Eleanor Stubley stated in Chapter 14, social interactions among performers and audiences are a significant part of the musical experience. Social meanings could include representation of culture as in nationalistic music (e.g., Sibelius's *Finlandia*)[30] ♫ or genres such as Irish music. It can include social interactions among performers on stage or social behaviors among audience members. Consider, for example, differences in deportment among attendees at a classical concert, a stadium rock concert, or a pub. In each case, the musical experience does not reside outside the social context.

Summary and Thought Questions

"Art can reveal to us new modes of perception and feeling which jolt us out of our habitual ways; it can make us aware of possibilities of alternative societies whose existence is not yet."[31] Let us grant a tacit agreement with this statement for now. The question then becomes what kind of music can do this. Can all types of music bring about social changes or can only music of a specific kind? Consider this as you ponder your answers to the following questions:

1. Do you subscribe to Adorno's rather restrictive view that classical music, for the most part, along with jazz and popular music, has become too tame and too regressive to challenge the status quo?
2. Do you think music has been "fetishized as a commodity"? In other words, has music become a product that has value on its own (i.e., independent of the act of making music) and is something to be bought and sold?

3. Even if you reject Adorno's narrower stance and Attali's somewhat broader position, would you agree that music derives a great deal of its value from the social context in which it is encountered?

4. Can you give examples other than the ones given here—the Civil Rights Movement, the Vietnam era, El Sistema, the Landfill Harmonic, the West-Eastern Divan Orchestra, American music education—where music has had a significant social impact?

5. What implications does a social philosophy of music have for your life in music? How would it change the way you compose, perform, teach, or listen?

Notes

1 Adrian North, David Hargreaves, and Mike Tarrant, "Social Psychology and Music Education," in *The New Handbook of Research on Music Teaching and Learning*, ed. Richard Colwell and Carol Richardson (New York: Oxford University Press, 2002), 604.

2 Béla Bartók, *Mikrokosmos*, performed by Béla Bartók, http://www.youtube.com/watch?v=DPZX4YAcFKI.

3 Theodor Adorno, *Philosophy of Modern Music*, trans. Anne Mitchell and Wesley Blomster (New York: Continuum International Publishing, 1948/2004).

4 Igor Stravinksy, *Pulcinella Suite*, performed by the Netherlands Radio Chamber Orchestra conducted by Jaap van Zweden, https://www.youtube.com/watch?v=VwongNsp1RA.

5 Igor Stravinsky, *Symphony of Psalms*, performed by Lukas Foss conducting the Milwaukee Symphony and the Wisconsin Conservatory Symphony Chorus, http://www.youtube.com/watch?v=LUGyAtcEFy8.

6 Adorno, *Philosophy of Modern Music*, 106.

7 Andy Hamilton, "Adorno," in *The Routledge Companion to Philosophy and Music*, ed. Theodore Gracyk and Andrew Kania (New York: Routledge, 2011).

8 Jay Bernstein, "Adorno, Theodor Wiesengrund (1903–69)," in *Routledge Encyclopedia of Philosophy, Version 1.0*, ed. Edward Craig (London and New York: Routledge, 1998), 48–52.

9 Theodor Adorno, *Essays on Music*, selected, with introduction and notes, by Richard Leppert, trans. Susan Gillespie (Berkeley, CA: University of California Press, 2002), 458.

10 Bernstein, "Adorno, Theodor Wiesengrund (1903–69)," 51.

11 Jacques Attali, *Noise: The Political Economy of Music*, trans. Brian Massumi (Manchester, UK: Manchester University Press, 1985), 4.

12 Ibid., 5.

13 Ibid., xi.

14 Ibid., 149.

15 Ibid., 158.

16 'We Shall Overcome,' sung by Mahalia Jackson, http://www.youtube.com/watch?v=TmR1YvfIGng.

17 Ed Vulliamy, "Orchestral Manoeuvres," *The Observer* (July 29, 2007). http://www.guardian.co.uk/music/2007/jul/29/classicalmusicandopera1.

18 Dmitri Shostakovich, Symphony No. 10, performed by Gustavo Dudamel conducting an El Sistema Orchestra from Venezuela, https://www.youtube.com/watch?v=XKXQzs6Y5BY.

19 "About El Sistema," Cal Performances, University of California, Berkeley, SchoolTime Study Guide, 2012–2013 Season. https://calperformances.org/learn/k-12/pdf/2012/Dudamel_SBOoV_Study_Guide_Revised_4.pdf.

20 Anastasia Tsioulcas, "The Landfill Harmonic: An Orchestra Built from Trash, 2012." http://www.npr.org/blogs/deceptivecadence/2012/12/19/167539764/the-landfill-harmonic-an-orchestra-built-from-trash.

21 Ibid.

22 Elena Cheah, *An Orchestra Beyond Borders: Voices of the West-Eastern Divan Orchestra* (London: Verso Books, 2009).

23 Daniel Barenboim, *Music Quickens Time* (London: Verso Books, 2008).

24 West-Eastern Divan Orchestra, 2015. http://www.west-eastern-divan.org/news/.

25 Clemency Burton-Hill, "West-Eastern Divan Orchestra: Uniting Arabs, Israelis," *BBC Culture* (August 22, 2014). http://www.bbc.com/culture/story/20140822-music-uniting-arabs-and-israelis.

26 West-Eastern Divan Orchestra, 2015.

27 Ibid.
28 Patricia Campbell, Claire Connell, and Amy Beegle, "Adolescents' Expressed Meanings of Music In and Out of School," *Journal of Research in Music Education* 55, no. 3 (2007): 220–36.
29 Ibid., 230.
30 Jan Sibelius: *Finlandia*, performed by Vasily Petrenko conducting the Royal Liverpool Orchestra, http://www.youtube.com/watch?v=L6P3cIJHWjw.
31 Christopher Small, *Music-Society-Education* (New York: Schirmer, 1977), 2.

17 Praxialism

Praxialism is not a term generally used in philosophy. That is, the word does not appear in *The Oxford Guide to Philosophy, The Routledge Companion to Aesthetics, The Internet Encyclopedia of Philosophy, The Stanford Encyclopedia of Philosophy*, or similar compendia in philosophy.[1] However, praxialism has gained prominence in music education, especially, such that it deserves consideration in a study of music philosophy. Although the ensuing discussions will come largely from the fields of education and music education, the roots of praxialism lie in music philosophy. Praxialism, thus, may be a valid viewpoint for performers, therapists, and so on, as well as for music educators.

A first step is to understand the meaning of the term *praxialism*. The root of the term comes from the Greek *praxis*, meaning to do. Several dictionaries give examples having to do with the practical side of a profession or discipline as opposed to the theoretical side. Paulo Freire, known in education circles for his ideas on critical pedagogy, said that praxis is "reflection and action upon the world in order to transform it."[2] Praxis "cannot be purely intellectual but must involve action; nor can it be limited to mere activism, but must include serious reflection."[3]

If we lift the term out of the context in which Freire used it and apply it to music philosophy, we might say that a full understanding of the value of music cannot merely arise from thinking about it; one must be actively involved in music—composing, performing, conducting, listening, teaching, and so on. However, engaging in any of these activities without serious reflection is insufficient as well. From a praxialist viewpoint, music is valued prop-

> "What the educator does in teaching is to make it possible for the students to become themselves."
>
> (Paulo Freire)

erly as we understand it intellectually, engage in it actively, and reflect on our musical experiences thoughtfully. From the time of Plato until today, there has too often been a separation between *thinkers* (i.e., philosophers) and *doers* (i.e., musicians). Similar schisms occur when conductors become the thinkers and ensemble members merely doers, or students blindly do whatever music teachers tell them to do, and so on. Praxialism calls for a more comprehensive, coherent approach. In support of this notion, Freire insists that "praxis implies no dichotomy by which this praxis could be divided into a prior stage of reflection and a subsequent stage of action. Action and reflection occur simultaneously."[4]

Francis Sparshott and Christopher Small provided antecedents to current praxial accounts. Sparshott questioned an aesthetic approach by challenging the assumption that music exists to be appreciated. He provided examples from around the world to illustrate the concept that music is much broader and more complicated than an artwork conceived as an object of contemplation.

> In fact, if we take music as a kind of human praxis (what musicians do), which after all is a standpoint we cannot dispense with, we have to suppose that every interest that could find expression in that activity will actually find it there.[5]

He found that of all the different ways of musical understanding, none could be privileged as being better than the others.

Small wrote to expand Westerners' concept of music.[6] He presented numerous examples to illustrate the notion that for many people around the world, music does not exist to be listened to for itself. Rather, music is integrated into the fabric of living. Everyone participates, young and old, male and female. Later, he coined the term *musicking* to reflect this broadened view of music and gave it this definition: "*To music is to take part, in any capacity, in a musical performance, whether by performing, by listening, by rehearsing or practicing, by providing materials for performance (what is called composing), or by dancing.*"[7] Philosophers who later wrote more specifically about a praxial philosophy of music education were highly influenced by Sparshott and Small.

> "Generation after generation of musicians have been so conditioned by the neat arrangement of black dots on the stave that they can think of music only in those terms."
>
> (Christopher Small)

Phillip Alperson

Phillip Alperson (1946–), a student of Sparshott, wrote one of the first influential articles promoting a praxial view of music education. In the article, he contrasted praxialism with two prevailing views:

- Aesthetic formalism: creating and responding to music with attention to the aesthetic qualities of form. What we have previously called 'absolute formalism,' Alperson called a strict form of aesthetic formalism. "The first of these strategies, however, construes the notion of form in a relatively narrow way as perceptual properties of a certain sort: the sensual, syntactic, and structural properties of the works themselves."[8] An example of aesthetic formalism in the music classroom is a listening lesson wherein the students follow and anticipate the design of a musical composition.
- Enhanced aesthetic formalism, also referred to as the aesthetic cognitivist view (where he reserves the term cognitivism to refer to the fact that "musical properties and features provide *extramusical* knowledge),"[9] is what we have previously called absolute expressionism. Enhanced aesthetic formalism allows for "a wider range of expressive and representational meaning."[10] Here we are concerned with how expression or representation occurs through an apprehension of form. Expressive aesthetic cognitivism is the education of feeling. For example, members of a high school band learning to perform *An American Elegy* might explore how the composer Frank Ticheli used musical language to express the thoughts and feelings encapsulated in the dedication—"composed in memory of those who lost their lives at Columbine High School on April 20, 1999, and to honor the survivors."[11] ♫

As an alternative to these two approaches, Alperson proffered a third view—praxialism. Rather than focusing on universal or absolute features of the music as found in either strict or enhanced formalism, praxialists attempt "to understand art in terms of the variety of meaning and values evidenced in actual practice in particular cultures."[12] Praxialists place aesthetic aspects of music alongside other non-aesthetic functions as found in musical practices of particular societies.

> The basic aim of a praxial philosophy of music is to understand, from a philosophical point of view, just what music has meant to people, an endeavor that includes but is not limited to a consideration of the function of music in aesthetic contexts.[13]

Taking a praxial view does not limit one to a consideration of aesthetic properties, whether strict or enhanced, but also includes

> thinking of music in the context of social rituals, the function of music as a heuristic device for scientific and philosophical theories, the use of music for the communication or enforcement of social norms, the use of music in music therapy, and so on.[14]

Alperson provided examples of the interconnections between aesthetic and non-aesthetic functions. He gave an extended description of how jazz has many formal features that can be appreciated from an aesthetic viewpoint. In addition, there are many social aspects of jazz, such as the lives of Black musicians in a discriminatory society. We will return to Alperson subsequently, as he responded to other views of praxialism.

"For, as Aristotle long ago observed, it is not an easy matter to determine the nature of music or the exact purpose for which music ought to be studied, but it is only when the philosophy of music confronts musical practice in all its complexity that it will approach anything like a comprehensive understanding of music as a human practice."

(Philip Alperson)

David Elliott

Beginning with his book *Music Matters*,[15] David Elliott has been an important advocate for praxialism in music education.

> The first time Elliott (1995) uses the term he states that "praxial emphasizes that 'music' ought to be understood in relation to the meanings and values evidenced in actual music making and music listening in specific cultural contexts" (p. 14). In other words, says Elliott, the *starting* point of PME [praxial music education] is that music involves at least *four* interlocking dimensions: musical doers or "agents" (music makers and listeners of any kind), musical doing (music making of all kinds, and listening), something done (musical products, including compositions, improvisations, and arrangements), and the contexts—artistic, historical, social, cultural, educational, ethical, political, and so forth—in which musicing, listening, and the products of these take place (pp. 39–45). An important point, then, is that "without some form

of intentional human activity, there can be neither musical sounds nor works of musical sound. In short, *what music is, at root, is a human activity"* (p. 39).[16]

Elliott's central thesis is that developing musicianship and listenership in all students depends on a wide variety of musical activities, including performing, improvising, composing, arranging, and conducting—each activity to be paired with listening, as well as listening to recordings and live performances. Music making and music listening should be at the core of all music education programs.[17] Furthermore, students should be engaged in *"active reflection and critically reflective action* dedicated to supporting and advancing *human flourishing and well-being*, the *ethical care* of others, and the positive *transformation* of people's everyday lives."[18] Music teaching and learning should integrate people, processes, products, and ethical concerns in social-cultural contexts, or what he calls social praxis.

> "One of the first things we notice about music is the innumerable ways societies and individuals create, use, value, teach, learn, and conceptualize 'music' and 'musical' products, processes, experiences, and so forth."
> (David Elliott and Marissa Silverman)

Several authors, including those who are generally supportive of praxialism, have criticized Elliott's views. Constantijn Koopman wrote that Elliott made a significant contribution to music education philosophy, but that there were also deficiencies.[19] For example, he felt that the framework was 'empty,' lacking a substantive view of the nature of music. He wrote,

> Elliott fails to establish a distinctive value for music. The values he takes music to provide can be found in a large number of other activities. Elliott looks for value at the wrong place. The distinctive values of music are to be discovered in the specific characteristics of music itself, rather than in its presenting cognitive challenges.[20]

Koopman also felt that cognition was privileged and feelings neglected.

Others have found issues to disagree with as well. Several have criticized what they perceive to be Elliott's narrow stance that performance is the only way to develop musicianship, musical understanding, or listening skills.[21] They feel that performance is *an* important means to these goals, but not *the* only important one. As Robert Cutietta and Sandra Stauffer pointed out, there is no evidence that performing a piece necessarily improves one's comprehension of it and, in contrast, there is evidence that repeated listening experiences can lead to differences.[22]

In advancing his own views, Elliott has consistently attacked the predominant view during the second half of the 20th century, music education as aesthetic education (MEAE).[23] This approach was promoted by Harry Broudy,[24] Charles Leonhard,[25] Leonhard and Robert House,[26] and especially Elliott's former mentor,[27] Bennett Reimer.[28] Elliott listed three primary concerns:[29]

- First, he was concerned with MEAE's focus on musical works rather than on musicing as a process.
- Second, he objected to what he perceived as MEAE's narrow and restricted approach to music perception, that is, a focus on aesthetic elements to the exclusion of "religious, moral, social, cultural, historical, political, practical or otherwise nonstructural"[30] aspects.

- Finally, he resisted the notion that the aesthetic experience is the only or even the primary outcome of value.

Elliott[31] and Reimer[32] exchanged criticisms in a series of publications. Subsequently, Alperson provided a bridge between the two philosophical views, if not between the two proponents; we will examine his views in the next section.

Since the time most of these criticisms were published, Elliott and Marissa Silverman published a second edition of *Music Matters* in 2015.[33] In this book, they stated that a praxial philosophy rests on five premises:

- 1 & 2: the natures of music education and community music depend on the natures of music and the natures of education.
- 3 & 4: the values of music education and community music depend on the values of music and education.
- 5: the natures and values of music, education, and school music and community music depend on the nature of human personhood.[34]

The goals of a praxial music education are to enable students to live a well-lived and self-fulfilling life, and to foster personal and communal well-being and happiness, in short to promote human flourishing.[35]

Alperson Revisited

In 2010, Alperson introduced the term *robust praxialism*.[36] He felt that an anti-aesthetic position was not only unnecessary, but also inconsistent with a praxial view.

> Let me say at the outset that there is, as far as I can see, no principled reason why, on a praxial view, the creation, performance, or appreciation of music undertaken with respect to aesthetic properties should be excluded or devalued. In fact, I believe that such a move is inadvisable and that it runs contrary to the principle tenets of praxialism, as least as I understand the position.[37]

Alperson goes on to describe praxialism as a very broad viewpoint that incorporates personal, cultural, and social aspects. He includes aesthetic responses among the important reasons why people respond to music so strongly. "There are, I submit, musical practices in which the creation, performance, and appreciation of aesthetically rich music routinely take center stage."[38] He felt that those who excluded or discounted aesthetic experiences were contradicting the inclusiveness of robust praxialism. "To ignore what many people take to be a central feature of musical production and gratification seriously diminishes the explanatory reach of the praxial position."[39]

> " . . . the philosophy of music should take as its subject not only the specifically aesthetic values of music deriving from the sensuous, structural, and referential aspects of music, but also the artistic values of music pertaining to the larger cultural and social significance that have been a part of musical practice since antiquity."
> (Philip Alperson)

According to Alperson, aesthetic aspects can remain alongside non-aesthetic aspects without one disturbing the other. That is, to value the social aspects of a musicing experience does not mean that aesthetic aspects have to be ignored.

> But I will say this. For those of us who love music and who wish to engender that love of music in our students, for those of us who wish to foster the range of musical skills, creativity, and understanding to deepen that love, it is essential that we embrace the full measure of musical meaning and value. This is what I mean by "robust" praxialism.[40]

Robust praxialism, thus, affirms the critical role that aesthetic aspects can and do play in human musical experiences. There is no need to choose between aesthetic education and praxialism.

Thomas Regelski

Ah, but it is never that easy in the philosophical world. Thomas Regelski, who had earlier criticized the music-education-as-aesthetic-education (MEAE) approach, remained unconvinced. In an article written prior to Alperson's presentation of robust praxialism, Regelski said that in contrast to an aesthetic approach, a praxial music education was designed to make a difference in students' lives and in society.[41] Following Alperson's article, he continued to believe that aesthetic aspects were unnecessary.[42] "Praxialism does not *need* aesthetic speculations to be robust . . ."[43] "Music education should thus continue to move 'beyond aesthetics.' . . . Un-burdened by unnecessary aesthetic this, aesthetic that, aesthetic whatever, the 'praxial turn' in music education continues to point in newly beneficial directions."[44]

> The praxial theory I advance includes, then, in addition to the kinds of traditional musical practices Elliott seems to focus on, all manner of down-to-earth and everyday musical "doings" that bring about "right results" of all kinds for all kinds of people, whether or not educated musically in performance.[45]

Regelski wanted to include amateur and recreational uses of music. He felt that "music is not only for experts or an elite few connoisseurs, it is also of and for the down-to-earth conditions of everyday life and life well lived in terms of the 'good time' thus created."[46]

Regelski extended this notion in a new book, whose title provides a clue to his orientation: *A Brief Introduction to a Philosophy of Music and Music Education as Social Praxis*.[47] In it, he continues his argument against music as aesthetic education and, instead, promotes music as social praxis. By this he means that music has value for social and ethical reasons. Human beings are social creatures and just as language facilitates human interactions, so does music. Rather than finding primary value in the aesthetic contemplation of great works of music, Regelski finds it in how people expedite and enhance their dealings with one another through musical experiences of all kinds. "More broadly speaking, musicking, in all its forms, is a key source of social harmony that creates and reinforces vital social meanings and cultural realities."[48]

Musical Examples

Because of some praxialists' aversion to musical works, a list of composers and compositions is not the best way to illustrate their philosophy. Rather, in this case, musical examples should come in the guise of various ways of musicing, such as singing in a church choir, jamming in a garage band, performing with a symphony orchestra, strumming a guitar and singing with friends, participating in a drum circle, practicing the piano, improvising on Orff instruments, and on and on. Not only is each of these musical engagements to be valued, but the social, cultural, political, religious, and historical contexts in which they occur are to be valued as well.

A similar situation exists with regard to listening. To provide illustrations of listening in praxialism, one would describe various listening situations: listening 'across' the ensemble while performing in a band, orchestra, or choir, listening to a classmate improvise during a jazz ensemble rehearsal, listening to the car radio, listening to the organ during a wedding, and so on.

Summary and Thought Questions

Sparshott and Small promoted precursors to a praxial philosophy of music; Alperson, Elliott, Regelski, and others have more sharply focused on praxialism as a philosophy of music education. A central concept is the balance found between action and reflection as simultaneous processes. A second key concept is that praxialism is a comprehensive approach in which all the ways of engaging with music, or musicing, are valid. Furthermore, musicing is absorbed and integrated into the fabric of living. It does not exist separate and apart from everyday life.

A third major concept has to do with the role of aesthetics. Some praxialists prefer to dispense with the notion of aesthetics altogether. Others are more willing to include aesthetic concerns under the umbrella of robust praxialism. Prominence is given to direct engagement with music rather than contemplation of musical works. In addition, the social context, the role of music in political and cultural dialogue, and musicing in everyday life by amateurs as well as trained musicians, receive their due. As you ponder whether praxialism is a viewpoint you want to espouse, consider these questions:

1. What are the strengths and weaknesses of praxialism as you understand the viewpoint?
2. Who makes the stronger case: Alperson and his robust praxialism, or those praxialists, such as Elliott and Regelski, who exclude or at least greatly diminish aesthetic concerns?
3. In a similar vein, is a focus on product (i.e., musical works) antithetical to a focus on process (i.e., musicing), or can they co-exist in a more balanced approach?
4. Do you think that self-growth, self-knowledge, optimal experience (flow), and enjoyment are the primary outcomes of musical experiences? What additional outcomes might you wish to add to this list?
5. If you were to adopt a praxial view, what influence would this have on your musical activities, both personal and professional?

Notes

1 Ted Honderich, ed., *The Oxford Guide to Philosophy* (Oxford, UK: Oxford University Press, 2005). The word 'praxis' does appear in this encyclopedia (p. 751), but only in relation to a definition of the Greek word (i.e., 'action' or 'doing') and the Marxist Praxis Group, not in relation to a fully developed philosophy or anything having to do with music or the arts. Berys Gaut and Dominic Lopes, eds., *The Routledge Companion to Aesthetics* (New York: Routledge, 2001). James Fieser and Bradley Dowden, eds., *Internet Encyclopedia of Philosophy*, 2015. http://www.iep.utm.edu. Edward Zalta, ed., *Stanford Encyclopedia of Philosophy* (2015 edition). http://plato.stanford.edu.

2 Paulo Freire, *Pedagogy of the Oppressed, 30th Anniversary Edition*, trans. Myra Ramos (New York: Continuum, 2005), 51.

3 Ibid., 65.

4 Ibid., 128.

5 Francis Sparshott, "Aesthetics of Music: Limits and Grounds," in *What Is Music? An Introduction to the Philosophy of Music*, ed. Philip Alperson (University Park, PA: The Pennsylvania State University Press, 1994), 53.

6 Christopher Small, *Music-Society-Education* (New York: Schirmer, 1977).

7 Christopher Small, *Musicking* (Middletown, CT: Wesleyan University Press, 1998), 9.

8 Philip Alperson, "What Should One Expect from a Philosophy of Music Education?" *Journal of Aesthetic Education* 25, no. 3 (1991): 220.

9 Ibid., 227.

10 Ibid., 225.

11 Frank Ticheli, *An American Elegy*, performed by Eugene Corporan conducting the North Texas Wind Symphony, https://www.youtube.com/watch?v=YIIKdBYfmlo.

12 Alperson, "What Should One Expect from a Philosophy of Music Education?," 233.

13 Ibid., 234.

14 Ibid., 234.

15 David Elliott, *Music Matters: A New Philosophy of Music Education* (New York: Oxford University Press, 1995).

16 Marissa Silverman, Susan Davis, and David Elliott, "Praxial Music Education: A Critical Analysis of Critical Commentaries," *International Journal of Music Education* 32, no. 1 (2013): 55–56. Note: the page numbers in parentheses refer to pages in David Elliott, *Music Matters*.

17 David Elliott, introduction to *Praxial Music Education: Reflections and Dialogues*, ed. David Elliott (New York: Oxford University Press, 2005).

18 David Elliott and Marissa Silverman, *Music Matters: A Philosophy of Music Education, 2nd ed.* (New York: Oxford University Press, 2015), 52.

19 Constantijn Koopman, "The Nature of Music and Musical Works," in *Praxial Music Education*, ed. David Elliott (Oxford, UK: Oxford University Press, 2005), 79–97.

20 Ibid., 84.

21 Wayne Bowman, "The Limits and Grounds of Musical Praxialism," in *Praxial Music Education*, ed. David Elliott (Oxford, UK: Oxford University Press, 2005), 52–78. Wayne Bowman, "Why Musical Performance?", in *Praxial Music Education*, ed. David Elliott (Oxford, UK: Oxford University Press, 2005), 142–64. C.K. Szego, "Praxial Foundations of Multicultural Music Education," in *Praxial Music Education*, ed. David Elliott (Oxford, UK: Oxford University Press, 2005), 196–218.

22 Robert Cutietta and Sandra Stauffer, "Listening Reconsidered," in *Praxial Music Education*, ed. David Elliott (Oxford, UK: Oxford University Press, 2005), 123–41.

23 Michael Mark, "The Evolution of Music Education Philosophy from Utilitarian to Aesthetic," *Journal of Research in Music Education* 30, no. 1 (1982): 15–21.

24 Harry Broudy, "A Realistic Philosophy of Music Education," in *Basic Concepts in Music Education: The Fifty-Seventh Yearbook of the National Society for the Study of Education*, ed. Nelson Henry (Chicago: University of Chicago Press, 1958), 62–87.

25 Charles Leonhard, "Music Education—Aesthetic Education," *Education* 74, no. 1 (1953): 23–26. Charles Leonhard, *A Realistic Rationale for Teaching Music* (Reston, VA: Music Educators National Conference, 1985).

26 Charles Leonhard and Robert House, *Foundations and Principles of Music Education* (New York: McGraw-Hill, 1959).

27 Marie McCarthy and J. Scott Goble, "The Praxial Philosophy in Historical Perspective," in *Praxial Music Education*, ed. David Elliott (New York: Oxford University Press, 2005), 19–51.

28 Bennett Reimer, *A Philosophy of Music Education* (Englewood Cliffs, NJ: Prentice-Hall, 1970).

29 Elliott, *Music Matters*, 29–38.

30 Ibid., 33.

31 David Elliott, "A Philosophy of Music Education (Second Edition) by Bennett Reimer," *Philosophy of Music Education Newsletter* 2, no. 1 (1989): 5–9. David Elliott, "Music Education as Aesthetic Education:

A Critical Inquiry," *Quarterly Journal of Music Teaching and Learning* 2 (1991): 48–66. Elliott, *Music Matters*. David Elliott, ed., *Praxial Music Education* (New York: Oxford University Press, 2005). David Elliott and Marissa Silverman, "Rethinking Philosophy, Re-viewing Musical-Emotional Experiences," in *The Oxford Handbook of Philosophy in Music Education*, ed. Wayne Bowman and Ana Lucía Frega (Oxford, UK: Oxford University Press, 2012), 37–62.

32 Bennett Reimer, "Reflections on David Elliott's Critique of *A Philosophy of Music Education*," *Philosophy of Music Education Newsletter* 2, no. 2 (1990): 1–8. Bennett Reimer, "Reimer Responds to Elliott," *Quarterly Journal of Music Teaching and Learning* 2 (1991): 67–75. Bennett Reimer, "David Elliott's 'New' Philosophy of Music Education: Music for Performers Only," *Council for Research in Music Education* 128 (1996): 59–89. Bennett Reimer, *A Philosophy of Music Education: Advancing the Vision, 3rd ed.* (Upper Saddle River, NJ: Prentice-Hall, 2003).

33 David Elliott and Marissa Silverman, *Music Matters, 2nd ed.* (New York: Oxford University Press, 2015).

34 Ibid., 15.

35 Ibid., 18.

36 Philip Alperson, "Robust Praxialism and the Anti-aesthetic Turn," *Philosophy of Music Education Review* 18, no. 2 (2010): 171–93.

37 Ibid., 184.

38 Ibid., 185.

39 Ibid., 185.

40 Ibid., 191.

41 Thomas Regelski, "Music and Music Education: Theory and Praxis for 'Making a Difference,'" *Educational Philosophy and Theory* 37, no. 1 (2005): 7–27.

42 Thomas Regelski, "Response to Philip Alperson, 'Robust Praxialism and the Anti-aesthetic Turn,'" *Philosophy of Music Education Review* 19, no. 2 (2010): 196–203.

43 Ibid., 199.

44 Ibid., 200.

45 Thomas Regelski, "Curriculum: Implications of Aesthetic versus Praxial Philosophies," in *Praxial Music Education*, ed. David Elliott (Oxford, UK: Oxford University Press, 2005), 233.

46 Ibid., 235.

47 Thomas Regelski, *A Brief Introduction to a Philosophy of Music and Music Education as Social Praxis* (New York: Routledge, 2015).

48 Ibid., 65.

18 Feminism

The role of women throughout music history is largely unfamiliar to many. Examined in some detail, however, there is a rich heritage of pioneering and visionary women who have made significant contributions. Even so, there is no question that women have been systematically denied equal opportunity to explore, develop, and share their musical gifts. Largely absent from philosophical discussions for many centuries, women in the 20th and 21st centuries have made significant contributions. In particular, women have offered a uniquely feminine approach to understanding music. Before examining some of the feminist philosophical views, we will take a brief look at some of the major female figures in music.

Women in Music History

The Greek Muses, patron goddesses of music and poetry (where poets were also musicians) included Calliope, muse of heroic or epic poetry; Erato, muse of lyric and love poetry; Euterpe, muse of music or flutes; Polyhymnia, muse of sacred poetry; Terpsichore, muse of dancing and choral song; and Melpomene, muse of singing and, later, tragedy.[1] During the 12th–13th centuries, there were 20 known women troubadours in the Provençal region of France. These troubadours, daughters and wives of noblemen, were poets who wrote and sang about courtly love. "Although they wrote about love, the women's language and the situations they describe are strikingly different from those of their male counterparts."[2] The poems of these women are critically important because they provide us with some of the few, if not only, female witnesses of courtly life during this period. The remainder of this section contains selected, brief biographical sketches of important female personages in music history. More extensive accounts can be found in a number of excellent sources.[3]

Hildegard von Bingen (1098–1179), a Benedictine nun, was a prolific writer penning works in theology, medicine, biographies of saints, and sacred visionary works, as well as music and at least one dramatic play.[4] Her music consisted of nearly 80 chants.[5] ♫ In defending the role of music in worship, she wrote:

> "There is the Music of Heaven in all things and we have forgotten how to hear it until we sing."
>
> (Hildegard of Bingen)

Therefore, those of the Church who have imposed silence on the singing of the chants for the praise of God without well-considered weight of reason so that they have unjustly stripped God of the grace and comeliness of His own praise, unless they will have freed themselves from their errors here on earth, will be without the company of the angelic songs of praise in heaven.[6]

Maria Anna Mozart (1751–1829), known as Nannerl, was Wolfgang's older sister. She toured with her brother as a brilliant pianist and performed alongside him for the crowned heads of Europe.[7] Although the records are sketchy, it is more than likely, in fact probable, that the young Wolfgang was musically influenced by his sister. She may have tutored him, as a sort of assistant teacher to her father, and undoubtedly Wolfgang looked up to her and did his best to emulate her. "In 1769, when she was 18 years old and eligible to marry, her father ended her days on the road,"[8] effectively curtailing her musical career although she did not marry until 1789. We do know that she composed—as witnessed by this quote from Wolfgang: "My dear sister! I am in awe that you can compose so well, in a word, the song you wrote is beautiful"[9]—but none of her manuscripts have survived. One naturally wonders what she might have produced if she had been allowed the same opportunities as her brother.

> "My brother was a rather pretty child."
> (Maria Anna Mozart)

Fanny Mendelssohn Hensel (1805–1847) was the sister of the composer Felix Mendelssohn. She studied piano with her mother and received an excellent music education.[10] Although Felix was supportive, he had a conflicted attitude about the publication of Fanny's music.

> I hope I don't need to say that if she decides to publish anything, I will help her all I can and alleviate any difficulties arising from it. But I cannot persuade her to publish anything, because it is against my views and convictions.[11]

He clearly felt that attempting to publish her compositions would interfere with her domestic duties. Their father agreed. When she was only 15, her father wrote, "Music will perhaps become his [Felix's] profession, while for *you* it can and must only be an ornament, never the root of your being and doing."[12] In spite of their admonitions, Fanny was able to compose more than 400 works, though few were published in her lifetime. Ironically, Felix did perform some of her works. In fact, even more ironically, at one point he had to admit to Queen Victoria that the song she had just sung with Prince Albert at the organ—'Italien,'[13] ♫ from *Twelve Songs*, Op. 8, No. 3—actually was written by Fanny! It appears, then, that Felix did honestly appreciate Fanny's talent and "his reluctance for her to publish stemmed more from societal and familial attitudes than from a lack of confidence in the quality of her works."[14]

> "It must be a sign of talent that I do not give up, though I can get nobody to take an interest in my efforts."
> (Fanny Mendelssohn Hensel)

Clara Wieck Schumann (1819–1896), the wife of Robert Schumann and friend of Johannes Brahms, gained fame as a brilliant concert pianist and as a composer. Her compositions were admired by the likes of Mendelssohn, Chopin, and Liszt.[15] Before her marriage to Robert, she composed mostly for performances at her own concerts. "Almost all of the 182 programs she gave between 1828 and 1840 boasted at least one work by the young Clara Wieck."[16] During her marriage, she and Robert often consulted each other on their compositions and some of the notes on the autograph score of her Piano Trio in g minor, Op. 17[17] ♫ seem to be in Robert's hand. After her husband's death in 1856 she stopped composing, focusing her energies on her seven remaining children (an eighth child had died previously), performing, teaching, and editing Robert's works. Although her father was not only her teacher and a very strong supporter, it is a sign of the times to recognize that from the time she began her diary at the age of seven until she was 18, nearly every entry was written or dictated by her father.[18] Nevertheless, when he died she wrote the following in her diary, "Although we had many disagreements it never affected my love for him, a love which all my life long has been heightened by gratitude."[19] Programs exist for 1,299 concerts and assuming others may have been lost or that there were recitals in homes without programs, the number is likely to be considerably higher.

> "My imagination can picture no fairer happiness than to continue living for art."
> (Clara Schumann)

Alma Schindler Mahler's (1879–1964) primary interest was composition in her younger years before her marriage to Gustav Mahler. "By the time she became engaged to Mahler, she had already produced more than 100 lieder, some instrumental music, and a sketch for an opera."[20] During her marriage, her husband forbad her to compose. "Not until the marriage came to a crises point in 1910, causing Mahler to consult with Freud, did Mahler realize what he had done and encouraged her, out of fear of losing her, to resume her composition."[21] Subsequently, he helped her publish some songs, only 14 of which survive.[22] ♫

> "I composed a song and believe it's not bad."
> (Alma Mahler)

Nadia Boulanger (1887–1979) was a French composer whose music did not gain much recognition.[23] ♫ Although she won second place in the 1908 *Prix de Rome* composition competition,[24] it was as a teacher that she gained lasting fame. The stellar roster of 20th century composers, performers, and conductors who were her pupils is impressive, including Robert Russell Bennett, Marc Blitzstein, Elliott Carter, Aaron Copland, Ingolf Dahl, David Diamond, Donald Erb, Ross Lee Finney, Arthur Frackenphol, John Eliot Gardiner, Roy Harris, Karel Husa, Quincy Jones, John Kirkpatrick, Dinu Lipatti, Quinto Maganini, Douglas Moore, Thea Musgrave, Daniel Pinkham, Philip Glass, Ástor Piazolla, Stanislaw Skrowaczewski, Larry Smith, Serge Tcherepnin, David Ward-Steinman, and dozens of others.[25] "By early 1931, Boulanger had become so friendly with Stravinsky that he sent her copies of his newest works long before their public premières,"[26] and she conducted the first performance of his *Dumbarton Oaks Concerto*.[27] ♫ She also conducted the BBC Symphony, New York Philharmonic, and Philadelphia Orchestra, and was the first woman to conduct the Boston Symphony Orchestra and the Royal Philharmonic Orchestra.

> "I've been a woman for a little over 50 years and have gotten over my initial astonishment. As for conducting an orchestra, that's a job where I don't think sex plays much part."
> (Nadia Boulanger)

Of course, there are many more justly renowned women composers, conductors, and performers today. Although it is tempting to provide a list, either it would have to be too long to be practical or it would have to leave out too many deserving musicians. Perhaps a more appropriate way to set the stage for the feminist philosophical views upcoming is to present some additional facts and figures that illustrate that no matter how much progress has been made, there is still a long way to go to reach full parity between men and women in the professional musical world:

- Women were not allowed to earn a degree in music from Oxford University until 1921.[28]
- "As late as 1969, applications from women musicians for a position in the Berlin Philharmonic were returned with the answer: 'Following an old tradition, the Berlin Philharmonic does not accept any women musicians.' The Berlin Philharmonic first accepted women in 1982."[29] Today's roster includes 19 women out of 126 musicians (15%).[30] Sabine Meyer, a clarinetist, was invited by the conductor Herbert van Karajan to become the first woman to join the orchestra in 1982 at the age of 23. After a probationary period, the orchestra voted overwhelmingly against her permanent appointment.[31] She left after only nine months to pursue a solo career, subsequently performing with many major orchestras around the world.[32]
- According to a survey taken at the BBC Proms in 2013, the largest music festival in the world, only 5.4% of the composers represented on the programs of 61 orchestral and 8 chamber music concerts were women.[33] Furthermore, when Marin Alsop conducted on the Last Night concert, it was the first time a woman had done so since the inception of the Proms in 1895.
- Details from the New York Philharmonic website support both sides of the argument that there is progress on the one hand and sufficient gaps remaining on the other:[34]

    - Of five conductors listed, including Leonard Bernstein who died in 1990, all are male.
    - 20 of 31 violinists are female.
    - 7 of 11 violists are female.
    - 6 of 12 cellists are female.
    - 1 of 9 bassists is female.
    - 3 of 4 flutists are female.
    - 1 of 4 oboists is female.
    - 2 of 4 clarinetists are female.
    - 2 of 4 bassoonists are female.
    - 1 of 5 hornists is female.
    - None of the 4 trumpeters is female.
    - None of the 3 trombonists is female.
    - The lone tubist is male.
    - None of the 4 timpanists or percussionists is female.
    - The lone harpist is female.
    - None of the three keyboardists (harpsichord, piano, organ) is female.
    - The total, including conductors and all musicians, is 44 females out of 104 musicians or 42 percent.

- Kathleen McKeage found gender associations for instruments among 628 college band students (e.g., more females played flute and more males played trombone).[35] Of this group, fewer females participated in jazz ensembles, largely because they less frequently played instruments found in such groups. In 1978, Harold Abeles and Susan Porter collected data demonstrating that gender associations were evident; boys preferred so-called masculine instruments (e.g., brass and percussion instruments) but females had a wider preference range.[36] More than

30 years later, Abeles conducted follow-up studies confirming that little had changed in the intervening three decades.[37]

- In an article posted October 9, 2013, Anastasia Tsioulcas reported recent interviews in which three male conductors—Bruno Mantovani, Director of the Paris Conservatory; Yuri Temirkanov, Music Director and Chief Conductor of the Saint Petersburg Philharmonic; and Vasily Petrenko, Conductor of the Royal Liverpool Philharmonic—all made statements to the effect that women do not belong on the podium in front of symphony orchestras. Their reasons ranged from child-bearing and rearing to lack of strength to stand up to the physical rigors of the job.[38]

This sketchy and necessarily brief overview of women in music provides a context for the feminist philosophies that follow. Regardless of one's view of these philosophies, it is perhaps understandable why some women have taken these stances in light of centuries of exclusion and marginalization.

A Musical Example

Several examples of compositions by women composers were given in the previous brief biographies. Many more contemporary works could be added, such as Joan Tower's *Fanfares for the Uncommon Woman*,[39] ♫ Pauline Oliveros's 'Bottoms Up 1,'[40] ♫ or Tania León's *Inura*.[41] ♫ Women composers' voices are being heard more prominently, too, as in the recently released book of interviews with 25 contemporary American women composers.[42] Ironically, however, we are going to explore a work of a male composer as a means of providing a context for the feminist philosophical views that follow.

Robert Schumann's song cycle, *Frauenliebe und -leben*, Op. 42[43] ♫ (A Woman's Love and Life) has received much attention from traditional and feminist scholars alike. Schumann set these poems of Adelbert von Chamisso in 1840, during his 'year of song' in which he wrote 138 of them.[44] He completed the cycle in two days[45] and intended it, along with *Myrthen*, Op. 25,[46] ♫ as a wedding present;[47] however, the first public performance did not occur until 1862.[48] Although the songs are presented from the woman's point of view, both text and music were written by men. "The cycle has been criticized on several counts. Chamisso's poetry is not of the highest quality and more importantly, when viewed in contemporary social light, the idea of a woman's entire being revolving only around her husband and her position as a wife goes against the grain for many."[49] Others, however, disagree and find that Schumann not only intended but, indeed, succeeded in honoring his beloved Clara.

The eight poems that Schumann set—a ninth poem of Chamisso is not included in his cycle—tell the story of a woman who falls in love and marries, has a child, then mourns her husband after his death. This work may be somewhat autobiographical in that Chamisso had just married a much younger woman when he wrote the poems and Robert married Clara, who was nine years younger, several months after composing the work.[50] Table 18.1 presents a brief outline.

According to Kristina Muxfeldt, "Schumann's song cycle has kept these texts alive in the present, but our appreciation of the songs has also been tempered by a sensitivity to the outmoded social values reflected in Schumann's (and, residually, Chamisso's) portrayal of the life of an abstract figure of woman."[52] Ruth Solie stated that

> all the songs of the first half . . . are actually about him: his image, his character, his choice of her, his ring. It is only after her enclosure within established patriarchal rules that she is entitled to the events unquestionably her own, pregnancy and childbirth.[53]

Table 18.1 Outline of Robert Schumann's *Frauenliebe und -leben*[51]

Original title	English translation	Storyline
1. Seit ich ihn gesehen	Since I saw him	She has seen him for the first time, and now he is the only thing she can see.
2. Er, der Herrlichste von allen	He, the most glorious of all	She describes his many perfections, and her own lowliness.
3. Ich kann's nicht fassen, nicht glauben	I can't understand it, I don't believe it	He has chosen her, and she cannot believe it.
4. Du Ring an meinem Finger	You, ring on my finger	She sings to his ring, which she now wears, and promises to belong to him totally.
5. Helft mir, ihr Schwestern	Help me, O sisters	She asks her sisters to help her prepare for the wedding; at the end she takes leave of them.
6. Süsser Freund, du blickest	Sweet friend	She confides to him the reason for her happy tears, and shows him where she will put the cradle.
7. An meinem Herzen, an meiner Brust	At my heart, at my breast	She rocks and plays with the baby.
8. Nun hast du mir den ersten Schmerz getan	Now you have hurt me for the first time	His death, she says, is the first wrong he has ever done her, and she can no longer live.

Her conclusion is that a feminist interpretation is among those that present alternatives to a traditional formalist approach.

Mary Andrew, while acknowledging that many find both the poetry and music express outmoded ideas about male–female relationships, nevertheless contended that Schumann portrayed "a very strong female persona" by "his choice of poetry, the formal structure he used, the tonal relationships among the songs, and musical elements within the songs."[54] For example, where the first five songs are strongly linked in terms of key relationships (B flat, E flat, c minor, E flat, and B flat)—at a time in the storyline when the woman is infatuated, being courted and married, and the personality "not yet independent"[55]—numbers 6 and 7 explore more distant keys (G and D), "where the character feels to be at her strongest and most fulfilled, experiencing what a man can never hope to attain."[56] In the eighth and final song, the key is d minor, a partial return to the opening key, which the piano alone brings full circle to B Flat Major in the postlude. In this concluding passage, the piano restates an entire stanza from the first song, perhaps representing the widow recalling her first moments of falling in love.

> "Once Schumann decided on the poetry to honor his beloved Clara, he set about to design the strongest, most tightly organized song cycle of all his vocal works."
>
> (Mary Andrew)

Andrew also found that, "Schumann continually strengthened the female image throughout the cycle" in the way that the piano avoids the masculine style of accompaniment of other song-cycles and instead supplies a "more subtle and refined treatment, in which the piano is given equal importance but never allowed to overpower . . . a symbol of the relationship being portrayed: The woman is never dominated."[57]

> In conclusion, it can be seen that Schumann created in *Frauenliebe und -leben* a musical portrait truly worthy of the strong woman he loved. He chose poetry that spoke directly to his heart; he used a form that provided a vehicle for unity, inner connection, and dramatic growth of character; he arranged a tonal plan to reinforce this inner growth; and he used musical gestures throughout the cycle to portray a vivid and lively woman who was equal to his own beloved Clara.[58]

Suzanne Cusick is among those who disagree with this positive view of what she called Schumann's beautiful and hateful song cycle.[59] In traditional scholarship, meaning is found "in the music itself," where music's meanings are closed and fixed and "musical works will always have an enormous (and insidious) power to force either submission to their image of gender or complete refusal to participate in it."[60] She imagined a performance of *Frauenliebe und -leben* by the internationally recognized singer Jessye Norman and speculated that Norman's persona could be completely submerged into Schumann's conception of womanhood, or that she might choose to insert her own, individual personality. "Either way, my pleasure in her performance and my sense of closure at the end of it partly derives from the public display of her temporary obedience to someone else's idea of who she should be."[61]

> "A problem that I think bedevils all of us engaged in [feminist critique is] the deciphering and demystification of gender messages in our repertoire's canonic works."
>
> (Suzanne Cusick)

Cusick next provided a lengthy description of the process whereby, according to formalists, performers should subjugate their personae to the music itself. In reacting to a passage of Edward T. Cone, in which he portrayed a good performance in hegemonic masculine terms, she asked a series of questions:

> So . . . a good performance is one which subordinates parts to the whole: and one which achieves a sense of unity by performing closure events so that the last one will sound "if not precisely masculine, at least . . . strong"? So . . . if it is masculine closure that makes the *persona* of a work whole (by suppressing its parts), then the desirable *persona* of even an "incorrigibly feminine" piece is gendered masculine? So . . . the performed submission of parts to the whole performs the submission of the feminine to the masculine?[62]

By this reasoning, Cusick arrived at the position that these same processes occur in absolute music as in program music. A singer would thus be adhering to gender roles even in singing Rachmaninov's *Vocalise*,[63] ♪ a song without text, as well as *Frauenliebe und -leben*. She contended that even when performers are performing absolute classical music, one is performing "discourses of hegemony and gender."[64]

However, what Cusick calls a 'resisting performance' is possible. She discussed a recording of Schumann's song cycle by Jessye Norman, rather than the imagined one. This performance

> brilliantly exceeds my speculations about how musical performance might teach resistance to discourse and that demonstrates, as well, that a resisting performance need not seem

'unmusical.' Indeed, this is a performance that teaches us how resistance, rather than submission, may be beautifully performed.[65]

Thus, Norman

> denies us both the luxury of hearing this song as Schumann's 'music itself' (freed from the time-bound ideology of its text, hearable as having an essential character like absolute music) *and* the luxury of hearing it as primarily *voice*.[66]

Cusick adds: "Neither faithful nor faithless but something more complex, Jessye Norman's recorded performance of *Frauenliebe und -leben* might be understood to provide us with a politically useful model of how we all might perform cultural resistance rather than cultural disobedience."[67] Ironically, in liner notes to a Jessye Norman recording of *Frauenliebe und -leben*, presumably the one to which Cusick refers and which is regrettably out of print, Klaus Vokura stated that, " 'the woman is only too plainly allotted a role subordinate to the man's' and points out that such sentiments stir great uneasiness in this postfeminist era."[68]

In a powerful, closing passage, Cusick asked important and disturbing questions about deciphering classical music from a feminist perspective:

> Our instinct to flee the implied misogyny of so much classical music is thus an instinct that threatens us with wrenching and self-inflicted psychic pain; yet how can we justify to ourselves a continued sanctioning (through listening, teaching, performance) of objectionable repertoire? *Can* we listen to this music again, now that we can no longer romanticize it?[69]

She decides, "We *can* listen to music again."[70] However,

> we must listen a little less reverently to the patterns (so powerful and pure as to be proposed to us as timeless and true) formed by pitches and rhythms, and a little more attentively to the subtle but powerful ways those patterns may be continually transformed by the displacements of endlessly proliferating resistant performances.[71]

Using this discussion to provide a context, let us now turn to feminist philosophies of music.

Feminist Philosophies of Music

In preceding chapters we have encountered few women so far, Susanne Langer, Jenefer Robinson, and Eleanor Stubley being three primary exceptions. However, in recent years more women have added their voices to the dialogue. What follows are brief discussions of the ideas of three who have been proponents of a feminist philosophy of music: Heide Göttner-Abendroth, Susan McClary, and Marcia Citron.

Heide Göttner-Abendroth

Göttner-Abendroth (1941–) proposed a matriarchal aesthetic in contrast to a patriarchal one. She defined patriarchy as "domination of the fathers."[72] However, matriarchal societies are not the reverse of patriarchal; that is, they do not infer that women rule over men. Rather "they are,

> "Despite all the hostility directed against Modern Matriarchal Studies, it is not possible to disregard its findings."
> (Heide Göttner-Abendroth)

without exception, egalitarian societies. . . . They are societies that are free of domination, but they still have their guidelines and codes."[73]

Göttner-Abendroth based her aesthetic theories on ethnological investigations of matriarchal societies. Whether these matriarchal societies actually existed or are mythological is controversial. Here are two statements contradicting the actual existence of matriarchies: "What is known about the past and present conditions of primitive and early peoples does not augur well for any future discovery of a clear-cut and indisputable case of matriarchy."[74] "Theoretically, prehistory could have been matriarchal, but it probably wasn't, and nothing offered up in support of the matriarchal thesis is especially persuasive."[75] Nevertheless, Göttner-Abendroth contended that not only were there matriarchal societies in prehistory, there are current examples today on every continent except Europe.[76] To her, any society that is not overtly patriarchal is to be considered matriarchal.

> Some of these still existing societies are the Mosuo, Yao, Miao, and Tan peoples in China, the Chiang people of Tibet, the Minangkabau of Sumatra, the Ainu of Japan, the Trobrianders of Melanesia in the Pacific, the Khasi, Garo and Nayar of India, the Bantu, Akan, and Ashanti peoples in Africa, the Berbers and Tuareg of North Africa, the Arawak peoples of South America, the Cuna and Juchitanians of Central America, the Hopi and Pueblo peoples as well as the Iroquois peoples of North America, just to name the main ones.[77]

Göttner-Abendroth bases her matriarchal aesthetic on nine principles:[78]

1. Matriarchal art is located beyond the fictional.
2. Matriarchal art has an enduring and predetermined framework: the structure of matriarchal mythology.
3. Matriarchal art transcends the traditional mode of communication that consists of: author-text (art product)-reader.
4. Matriarchal art demands the total commitment of all participants.
5. Matriarchal art does not correspond to an extended model of communication with the elements: author-text-dealer-agent-audience.
6. Matriarchal art cannot be subdivided into genres because it cannot be objectified.
7. As matriarchal art derives from the structure of matriarchal mythology that has a completely different value system—and not merely a reversed or contradictory one—from that of patriarchy, it too shares this different system of values.
8. The social changes which matriarchal art brings about override the divisions in the aesthetic sphere.
9. Matriarchal art is not 'art.'

As a result, to her a matriarchal aesthetic is one that is more inclusive and egalitarian than a patriarchal aesthetic.

> My definition of *matriarchal art* is radical because it neutralizes the conventional separation of the artistic genres; the division of the traditional domains of 'art,' 'science,' 'religion,' 'economics,' and 'politics'; and the dichotomy between the spheres of 'art' and 'life.'[79]

Matriarchal art

> is precisely that matriarchal cult, in which, in the magical ritual festivals, people were completely integrated into the symbolic fulfillment of their complex practices; in which dance, music, language, and gesture coalesced into one; in which art was a continuum that included the body, sensuality, and the cosmically experienced world.[80]

In a passage reminiscent of the opening section of this chapter, Göttner-Abendroth wrote, "Even today, women must present their works in a society whose value system is fundamentally patriarchal and whose cultural institutions (publishing houses, book markets, fairs, academies, conservatories, universities—even the ministry of culture) are controlled by men."[81] Thus, through her scholarship, Göttner-Abendroth invites us to re-consider gender roles in music.

Susan McClary

Is the "vast majority of music consumed in the Western world . . . concerned with articulating, in a variety of different ways, male hegemonic processes"?[82] Is sonata-allegro form an example of male dominance? Is tonality itself laden with sexual imagery (e.g., withholding promised fulfillment until climax, patterns of tension and repose, arousing and channeling desire, etc.)? To McClary (1946–), the answer to these questions is 'yes.'

> To be sure, music's beauty is often overwhelming, its formal order magisterial. But the structures graphed by theorists and the beauty celebrated by aestheticians are often stained with such things as violence, misogyny, and racism. And perhaps more disturbing still to those who would present music as autonomous and invulnerable, it also frequently betrays fear—fear of women, fear of the body.[83]

As presented in her highly influential book, *Feminine Endings*, McClary's research has focused on five topics:[84]

- Musical construction of gender and sexuality.
- Gendered aspects of traditional music theory.
- Gender and sexuality in musical narrative.
- Music as a gendered discourse.
- Discursive strategies of women musicians.

In terms of minute musical details, McClary points out that cadences ending on a strong beat are identified as masculine, while those ending on a weak beat are termed feminine.[85] On a much larger scale, she considers opera. There are strong and dignified female characters, such as the Countess in Mozart's *The Marriage of Figaro*, as exemplified in her arias 'Porgi amor'[86] ♫ and 'Dove sono.'[87] ♫ However, these are among the exceptions. Far more frequent are hurtful, negative, or stereotypical portrayals of women as weak, passive, and dutiful. Consider, for example, Leporello's infamous catalog aria from Mozart's *Don Giovanni*, 'Madamina, il catalogo è questo,'[88] ♫ in which he lists Don Giovianni's numerous conquests:

> in Italy, 640 . . . in Spain 1003! . . . women of every rank, of every shape and age. . . . It's not about whether she's rich, or ugly or beautiful; just so long as she wears a skirt, you know what happens then![89]

> "To the large extent that music can organize our perceptions of our own bodies and emotions, it can tell us things about history that are not accessible through any other medium."
>
> (Susan McClary)

The fact that this is presented comically and in engaging music makes the hurtful messages all the more insidious. Consider one final example of a female character the opposite of the Countess. Carmen, the central female lead in Bizet's opera of the same name, is the epitome of a sexually charged siren who uses her feminine wiles to ensnare men.[90] Her persona of sexuality and promiscuity is exemplified in the aria 'Habañera,'[91] ♪ which exudes exoticism. "Carmen's number is further marked by chromatic excess, as her melodic line teases and taunts, forcing the attention to dwell on the moment—on the erogenous zones of her inflections."[92]

Beyond music with text, McClary points out that many of the same ideas persist in instrumental music. In a detailed analysis of the second movement of Mozart's Piano Concerto in G Major, K. 453,[93] ♪ she explores how,

> The Mozart of 'pure order' currently serves as an icon of the old cultural order for purposes of warding off—or at least institutionally marginalizing—the increasingly successful encroachments of new, previously disenfranchised producers (ethnic minorities, members of the working class, women) and forms of culture.[94]

This is an idea developed further by Marcia Citron, as we shall see in the next section. In the meantime, we leave McClary with the words of Suzanne Cusick, who described her work as mainly focused on "constructions of gender and sexuality in canonical works by men and on resistances to those constructions in non-canonical works by women."[95] By so doing, "McClary's feminist scholarship promises a kind of liberation for all of us."[96]

Marcia Citron

Citron (1945–) explored the role of gender in the musical canon.[97] As seen in music, literature, and other fields, the notion of a privileged list of works is highly problematic. "No mere list of books, the literary canon has signified a field of struggle over vital social issues."[98] There is a power contest over whose ideology will prevail. In art music, for example, one may legitimately ask why the music of white (mostly) European males (who are mostly dead) should assume place of honor over works by people of color, from elsewhere in the world, and from females. Of course, there is also the ethnomusicological concern over the notion of works altogether.[99]

Citron wrote about the 'sonata aesthetic' as a symbol of Western patriarchal values.[100] Here, she included sonata form and the genres that incorporate it, such as symphonies, chamber music, solo sonatas, and sometimes concertos. Scholars and music critics often view sonata form as the epitome of compositional skill, as exemplified in the works of Beethoven. First themes are identified as principal themes or masculine and are most often energetic and powerful. Second themes, subsidiary or feminine, are often tender and lyrical. As an affirmation

> "Which music is deemed canonic says a great deal about the image a society has of itself."
>
> (Marcia Citron)

of masculine triumph, principal themes prevail as the second theme migrates to the tonal key of the first theme in the recapitulation. The "feminine theme symbolized women's subordination in society, while the principal, masculine theme reflected male hegemony."[101] Thus, male dominance is found in pure or absolute music, as well as in music with text.

As a contrast to male-composed sonata form, Citron analyzed Cécile Chaminade's Piano Sonata, Op. 21.[102] ♪ Published in 1895, "the first movement, the longest and most complex, features a flexible treatment of sonata form. Often ambiguous, the structure may result from a mixture of three conventions: sonata form, character piece, and prelude and fugue."[103] In a detailed analysis, Citron explained why, in her mind, this movement is resistant to traditional hierarchical relationships between men and women:

> Overall, what we may have in this movement is a resistance to the hierarchical relationship between masculine and feminine as articulated in the gendered codes of sonata form and even more importantly in the ideologies they represent. This is expressed through a reconceptualization of the feminine: not an obliteration of the feminine, and not an inversion of power relations, but in a sense a refusal to play by the rules laid out in ideology.[104]

Summary and Thought Questions

Perhaps most people would agree that women have made significant progress in music in recent decades. There are more women with doctorates teaching music at universities, more female composers and conductors, and numerous female performers in both classical and popular genres. However, just as readily, most anyone who spends any time at all thinking about this issue would have to say that there are still significant barriers and glass ceilings that preclude women from having an equal opportunity with men. Moreover, it is perhaps in prevailing attitudes and thought patterns that the real problems lie, especially in the realm of music philosophy. Carolyn Korsmeyer stated that "virtually all the areas of the discipline [aesthetics] bear the mark of gender in their basic conceptual frameworks."[105] Because art is linked to social position and power and there is always disparity in the employment of power, "art is an enterprise where sex and sexuality, gender and social position, and cultural authority all have formidable roles."[106] Mary Devereaux agreed when she described feminist aesthetics as "a diverse family of theories, approaches, and models of criticism united by resistance to 'male' privilege and domination in the sphere of art and aesthetic experience."[107] Perhaps more substantial progress will be made in providing everyone equal opportunity—not just women, but people of color, and all others who have been disenfranchised—when our collective philosophical worldview has become more inclusive.

Ponder your responses to the following questions as a way of determining how and to what extent the ideas presented in this chapter will inform your own philosophy of music:

1. From your perspective, how do you view the current status of women in professional music careers? What aspects seem to be improving and what aspects need to be changed?
2. What personal experiences have you had that lend credence to the view that women in music are disenfranchised in comparison to males?
3. If you had to make a 'guesstimate,' how much music by women composers have you performed or heard on concert and recital programs? If you eliminate special programs devoted to the music of female composers, is there much female representation left on other programs?

4. Do you consider certain aspects of music composition—full cadences seen as masculine and half cadences seen as feminine; first theme in sonata form masculine, second theme feminine; and so on—indicative of male domination?

5. How would you characterize patriarchal and matriarchal views of music? Or do you contend that these labels are arbitrary and artificial, with no actual significance in the 'real' musical world (i.e., the musical world as experienced in schools, concert halls, daily life, and the like, in opposition to the theoretical world of philosophy).

6. Do you agree with the notion that a feminist approach to aesthetics is ultimately liberating for all—not just women and others who have been disenfranchised, but for men as well? How could adopting the ideas of feminist philosophers be beneficial for men? What do men have to gain from a 'resistant' perspective?

7. How does your understanding of feminist aesthetics affect your philosophy of music; or, does it?

Notes

1   Eric Havelock, *The Muse Learns to Write* (New Haven, CT: Yale University Press, 1986).
2   Magda Bogin, *The Women Troubadours* (New York: W.W. Norton, 1980), 13.
3   James Briscoe, ed., *New Historical Anthology of Music by Women* (Bloomington, IN: Indiana University Press, 2004). Anne Gray, *The World of Women in Classical Music* (San Diego: WordWorld, 2007). Jennifer Kelly, *In Her Own Words: Conversations with Composers in the United States* (Champaign-Urbana, IL: University of Illinois Press, 2013). Carol Neuls-Bates, ed., *Women in Music: An Anthology of Source Readings from the Middle Ages to the Present* (New York: Harper & Row, 1982). Karin Pendle and Melinda Boyd, eds., *Women in Music: A Research and Information Guide, 2d ed.* (New York: Routledge, 2005). Julie Sadie and Rhian Samuel, eds., *Norton/Grove Dictionary of Women Composers* (London: The Macmillan Press, 1995).
4   Michael Klaper, "Hildegard von Bingen," in *New Historical Anthology of Music by Women*, ed. James Briscoe (Bloomington, IN: Indiana University Press, 2004).
5   Hildegard von Bingen, *11000 Virgins*, Chants for St. Ursula, performed by Anonymous 4, http://www.youtube.com/watch?v=n9uMd1ap51A.
6   Hildegard von Bingen quoted in *Women in Music*, ed. Carol Neuls-Bates, 20.
7   *Mozart's Sister* (2010), a film by René Féret. http://www.youtube.com/watch?v=AQQtqfWA2gk.
8   Elizabeth Rusch, "Maria Anna Mozart: The Family's First Prodigy," *Smithsonian.com*, 2011 http://www.smithsonianmag.com/arts-culture/Maria-Anna-Mozart-The-Familys-First-Prodigy.html#ixzz2OqUxVUHG, 1.
9   Wolfgang Mozart quoted in Rusch, "Maria Anna Mozart," 2.
10 Marcia Citron, "Gender and the Field of Musicology," *Current Musicology* 53 (1993): 66–75.
11 Marcia Citron, *Gender and the Musical Canon* (Cambridge, UK: Press Syndicate, 1993), 110.
12 Abraham Mendelssohn quoted in Marcia Citron, "Felix Mendelssohn's Influence on Fanny Mendelssohn Hensel as a Professional Composer," *Current Musicology* 37, no. 8 (1984): 10.
13 The song 'Italien' was originally published by Felix Mendelssohn: 'Italien' from *Twelve Songs*, Op. 8, No. 3; however, it was actually composed by his sister Fanny. Here it is performed by Akiko Ogawa, alto, and Hiroaki Yamada, piano: http://www.youtube.com/watch?v=OSA029AGsY8.
14 Citron, "Felix Mendelssohn's Influence on Fanny Mendelssohn Hensel as a Professional Composer," 17.
15 Nancy Reich, "Clara Wieck Schumann," in *New Historical Anthology of Music by Women*, ed. James Briscoe (Bloomington, IN: Indiana University Press, 2004).
16 Ibid., 140.
17 Clara Schumann, Piano Trio in g minor, Op. 17, performed by the Galos Piano Trio, https://www.youtube.com/watch?v=C5dBOpy0_zg.
18 Nancy Reich, *Clara Schumann: The Artist and the Woman* (Ithaca, NY: Cornell University Press, 2001).
19 Clara Schumann quoted in Susanna Reich, *Clara Schumann: Piano Virtuoso* (New York: Clarion Books, 1999), 77.

20 Sally Macarthur, *Feminist Aesthetics in Music* (Westport, CT: Greenwood Publishing Co, 2002), 67.

21 Ibid., 67.

22 Alma Mahler, *Lieder*, performed by Hiroaki Yamada, alto, and Hiroaki Yamada, piano, http://www.youtube.com/watch?v=M9CYlOU_SJU.

23 Nadia Boulanger, *Trois pièces*, performed by Dora Kuzmin, cello, and Petra Gilming, piano, http://www.youtube.com/watch?v=YfcUkVbyy9M.

24 Neuls-Bates, *Women in Music*, 239.

25 Leonie Rosenstiel, *Nadia Boulanger: A Life in Music* (New York: W.W. Norton, 1982).

26 Ibid., 237. See also: Kimberly Francis, "A Dialogue Begins: Nadia Boulanger, Igor Stravinsky, and the Symphonie de Psaumes," *Women & Music* 14 (2010): 22–44.

27 Igor Stravinsky, *Dumbarton Oaks Concerto*, performed by Igor Stravinsky conducting the Orchestra della Radiotelevisione della Svizzera Italiana, https://www.youtube.com/watch?v=C-8fr2QRFGI.

28 Dawn Bennett, *Understanding the Classical Music Profession: The Past, the Present and Strategies for the Future* (Burlington, VT: Ashgate Publishing, 2008), 53.

29 Ibid., 53.

30 Berlin Philharmonic, accessed January 25, 2014, http://www.berliner-philharmoniker.de/en/orchestra/.

31 Serge Schmemann, "Karajan Leaves Berlin Philharmonic," *New York Times* (April 25, 1989). http://www.nytimes.com/1989/04/25/arts/karajan-leaves-berlin-philharmonic.html?pagewanted=all&src=pm.

32 "Sabine Meyer Biographie," *Sabine Meyer*, 2013. http://www.sabine-meyer.com/index.php/21/articles/biographie-en.html.

33 "Women in Music," BBC Proms Survey 2013. http://www.womeninmusic.org.uk/proms-survey.htm.

34 *New York Philharmonic Orchestra*, accessed January 25, 2014, http://nyphil.org/about-us/the-orchestra/musicians-of-the-orchestra.

35 Kathleen McKeage, "Gender and Participation in High School and College Instrumental Jazz Ensembles," *Journal of Research in Music Education* 52, no. 4 (2004): 343–56.

36 Harold Abeles and Susan Porter, "The Sex-Stereotyping of Musical Instruments," *Journal of Research in Music Education* 26, no. 2 (1978): 65–75.

37 Harold Abeles, "Are Musical Instrument Gender Associations Changing?" *Journal of Research in Music Education* 57, no. 2 (2009): 127–39.

38 Anastasia Tsioulcas, "What Is Classical Music's Women Problem?" *Deceptive Cadence* from NPR Classical, 2013. http://www.npr.org/blogs/deceptivecadence/2013/10/09/230751348/what-is-classical-musics-women-problem.

39 Joan Tower, *Fanfares for the Uncommon Woman*, performed by Octavio Mas-Arocas conducting the Interlochen Arts Academy Orchestra, http://www.youtube.com/watch?v=hm8EZj5skY8.

40 Pauline Oliveros, 'Bottoms Up 1' from *Reverberations: Tape and Electronic Music*, http://www.youtube.com/watch?v=UbKMdszoY_Y.

41 Tania León, *Inura*, performed by Tania León, conducting Son Sonora Voices, Son Sonora Ensemble, and DanceBrazil Percussion, http://www.youtube.com/watch?v=gFN05rFPxTA.

42 Jennifer Kelly, *In Her Own Words: Conversations with Composers in the United States* (Champaign-Urbana, IL: University of Illinois Press, 2013).

43 Robert Schumann, *Frauenliebe und -Leben*, Op. 42, performed by Jessye Norman, soprano, and Irwin Gage, piano, https://www.youtube.com/watch?v=1KEgm9DV70o.

44 Alfred Einstein, *Music in the Romantic Era* (New York: W.W. Norton, 1947), 187.

45 David Ferris, *Schumann's Eichendorff Liederkreis and the Genre of the Romantic Cycle* (Oxford: Oxford University Press, 2000).

46 Robert Schumann, *Myrthen*, Op. 25, performed by Mitsuko Shirai, soprano, and Harmut Höll, piano, https://www.youtube.com/watch?v=MpfnWGH1xRY.

47 Carol Kimball, *Song: A Guide to Art Song Style and Literature* (Milwaukee, WI: Hal Leonard, 2005), 80.

48 Phillip Huscher, "Robert Schumann: *Frauenliebe und –Leben*, Op. 42." Program notes for the Chicago Symphony Orchestra (2015). http://cso.org/uploadedFiles/1_Tickets_and_Events/Program_Notes/ProgramNotes_Uchida_Plays_Mozart.pdf.

49 Kimball, *Song*, 80.

50 Richard Stokes, *The Book of Lieder: The Original Texts of Over 1000 Songs* (London: Faber and Faber, 2005).

51 Ruth Solie, "Whose Life? The Gendered Self in Schumann's *Frauenliebe* Songs," in *Music and Text: Critical Inquiries*, ed. Steven Scher (New York: Cambridge University Press, 1992), 200.

52 Kristina Muxfeldt, "*Frauenliebe und -Leben* Now and Then," *19th-Century Music* 25, no. 1 (2001): 29.

53 Solie, *Whose Life?*, 233.

54 Mary Andrew, "Schumann's *Frauenliebe und -Leben*: A Feminist Dilemma?" *Journal of Singing—The Official Journal of the National Association of Teachers of Singing* 54, no. 1 (1997): 7.

55 Ibid., 8.

56 Ibid., 8.

57 Ibid., 8.

58 Ibid., 9.

59 Suzanne Cusick, "Gender and the Cultural Work of a Classical Music Performance," *Repercussions* 3, no. 1 (1994): 80.

60 Ibid., 80.

61 Ibid., 83.

62 Ibid., 96.

63 Sergei Rachmaninov, *Vocalise*, Op. 34, No. 14, performed by Kiri Te Kanawa, soprano, at the Royal Opera House in Covent Garden, Stephen Barlow conducting, http://www.youtube.com/watch?v=fW630zFA93Y.

64 Cusick, "Gender and the Cultural Work of a Classical Music Performance," 93.

65 Ibid., 100–101.

66 Ibid., 106.

67 Ibid., 108.

68 Klaus Vokura, booklet notes for Schumann: *Frauenliebe und -Leben*. Jessye Norman, soprano, with Irwin Gage, piano, 1975 (Phillips CD 420 784–2), quoted in Andrew, "Schumann's *Frauenliebe und -Leben*: A Feminist Dilemma?," 7.

69 Cusick, "Gender and the Cultural Work of a Classical Music Performance," 78.

70 Ibid., 109.

71 Ibid., 109–10.

72 Heide Göttner-Abendroth, "Matriarchal Society: Definition and Theory," in *The Gift, a Feminist Analysis*, ed. G. Vaughan, trans. Solveig Göttner and Karen Smith (London: Meltemi Press, 2004). http://www.matriarchiv.info/uploads/HGA-E-Matriarchal-Society-Definition-and-Theory.pdf.

73 Heide Göttner-Abendroth, "Modern Matriarchal Studies. Definitions, Scope and Topicality," *Societies of Peace: 2nd World Congress on Matriarchal Studies*, 2003. http://www.second-congress-matriarchal-studies.com/goettnerabendroth.html.

74 Joan Bamberger, "The Myth of Matriarchy: Why Men Rule in Primitive Society," in *Women, Culture and Society*, ed. Michelle Rosaldo and Louise Lamphere (Stanford, CA: Stanford University Press, 1974), 264–65.

75 Cynthia Eller, *The Myth of Matriarchal Prehistory: Why an Invented Past Won't Give Women a Future* (Boston: Beacon Press, 2001), 6.

76 Göttner-Abendroth, "Matriarchal Society: Definition and Theory."

77 Göttner-Abendroth, "Modern Matriarchal Studies. Definitions, Scope and Topicality."

78 Heide Göttner-Abendroth, "Nine Principles of a Matriarchal Aesthetic," in *Feminist Aesthetics*, ed. Gisela Ecker, trans. Harriet Anderson (Boston: Beacon Press, 1985), 81–84.

79 Heide Göttner-Abendroth, *The Dancing Goddess: Principles of a Matriarchal Aesthetic*, trans. Maureen Krause (Boston: Beacon Press, 2001), 10.

80 Ibid., 28.

81 Ibid., 22–23.

82 John Shepherd, "Music and Male Hegemony," in *Music as Social Text*, ed. John Shepherd (Cambridge: Polity Press, 1991), 171.

83 Susan McClary, *Feminine Endings: Music, Gender, & Sexuality* (Minneapolis: University of Minnesota Press, 2002), 4.

84 Ibid.

85 Susan McClary, "Towards a Feminist Criticism of Music," *Canadian University Music Review* 10, no. 2 (1990): 9–17.

86 Wolfgang Mozart, 'Porgi amor' from *The Marriage of Figaro*, performed by Renee Fleming at the Metropolitan Opera, http://www.youtube.com/watch?v=NToJ2phG7Qk.

87 Wolfgang Mozart, 'Dove sono' from *The Marriage of Figaro*, performed by Leontyne Price at the Metropolitan Opera, http://www.youtube.com/watch?v=WXEENQoiy_s.
88 Wolfgang Mozart, 'Madamina, il catalogo è questo' from *Don Giovanni*, performed by Ferrucio Furlanetto at the Metropolitan Opera, conducted by James Levine, https://www.youtube.com/watch?v=INF9r5jju0A.
89 Translation from Opera in English (July 30, 2011). http://operainenglish.blogspot.com/2011/07/madamina-il-catalogo-e-questo-don.html.
90 Susan McClary, "Paradigm Dissonances: Music Theory, Cultural Studies, Feminist Criticism," *Perspectives of New Music* 32, no. 1 (1994): 68–85.
91 Georges Bizet, 'Habañera' from *Carmen*, performed by Grace Bumbry in a movie version directed by Herbert von Karajan, http://www.youtube.com/watch?v=Qs0E2CufQ7c.
92 Susan McClary, *Georges Bizet: Carmen* (Cambridge, UK: Cambridge University Press, 1992), 75.
93 Wolfgang Mozart, Piano Concerto in G Major, K. 453, 2nd movement, performed by Leonard Bernstein, pianist and conductor with the Vienna Philharmonic, http://www.youtube.com/watch?v=itiY352hgjM.
94 Susan McClary, "A Musical Dialectic from the Enlightenment: Mozart's 'Piano Concerto in G Major, K. 453, movement 2,' " *Cultural Critique* 4 (1999): 164.
95 Suzanne Cusick, "Gender, Musicology, and Feminism," in *Rethinking Music*, ed. Nick Cook and Mark Everist (New York: Oxford University Press, 1999), 489.
96 Ibid., 487.
97 Marcia Citron, *Gender and the Musical Canon* (Cambridge, UK: Cambridge University Press, 1993).
98 Ibid., 1.
99 An enormous amount of the world's music is not experienced in 'works' *per se*, but through the act of making music or musicing. See the comments of Christopher Small and others on musicing in Chapter 17: Praxialism.
100 Marcia Citron, "Feminist Approaches to Musicology," in *Cecilia Reclaimed: Feminist Perspectives on Gender and Music*, ed. Susan Cook and Judy Sou (Urbana, IL: University of Illinois Press, 1994), 15–34.
101 Ibid., 21–22.
102 Cécile Chaminade, Piano Sonata in c minor, Op. 21, performed by Peter Basil Murdock-Saint, https://www.youtube.com/watch?v=Tg3Sa7oppis.
103 Citron, *Gender and the Musical Canon*, 147.
104 Ibid., 154.
105 Carolyn Korsmeyer, "Feminist Aesthetics," in *The Stanford Encyclopedia of Philosophy* (2012 edition), ed. Edward Zalta. http://plato.stanford.edu/archives/win2012/entries/feminism-aesthetics/.
106 Carolyn Korsmeyer, *Gender and Aesthetics: An Introduction* (New York: Routledge, 2004), 1.
107 Mary Devereaux, "Feminist Aesthetics," in *The Oxford Handbook of Aesthetics*, ed. Jerrold Levinson (Oxford, UK: Oxford University Press, 2003), 647.

19 Postmodernism

The term *postmodernism* had already been used in art and certainly there were postmodernist ideas in philosophy before it became a formal term.[1] However, "the term 'postmodernism' first entered the philosophical lexicon in 1979, with the publication of *The Postmodern Condition* by Jean-François Lyotard."[2] Postmodernism is so-named in reaction to the period of modernism that began with Kant and extends through the early 20th century. Postmodernism is "deeply suspicious of things like essences, absolutes, timeless truths, and universals."[3] "In philosophy, in the arts, in science, in political theory and in sociology, postmodernism challenges the entire culture of realism, representation, humanism and empiricism."[4]

> "A work can become modern only if it is first postmodern. Thus, understood, postmodernism is not modernism at its end, but in the nascent state, and this state is recurrent."
>
> (Jean-François Lyotard)

According to Elizabeth Ermarth, there are two basic assumptions that underpin an understanding of postmodernism:

> First, the assumption that there is no common denominator—in 'nature' or 'truth' or 'God' or 'the future'—that guarantees either the One-ness of the world or the possibility of neutral or objective thought. Second, the assumption that all human systems operate like language, being self-reflexive rather than referential systems—systems of differential function which are powerful but finite, and which construct and maintain meaning and value.[5]

The second assumption implies that it is impossible to determine Truth; instead, postmodernists ask questions such as 'whose reality?' and 'which truth'?

Friedrich Nietzsche (1844–1900) was highly influential on later postmodernist philosophers such as Jacques Derrida and Richard Rorty. One of his ideas that has particular relevance for music philosophy is the notion of nihilism, as it was "one of the most powerful influences in the arts."[6] According to Nietzsche, nihilism is "the radical repudiation of value, meaning, and desirability."[7] Scientific discoveries—for example, Einstein's theory of relativity[8]—were also highly influential. After all, if even time is relative, not absolute, we should be free to question all truths and all value systems. Ironically, in spite of the prevailing impression that nihilism is an inherently pessimistic view,

> Nietzsche actually was a profoundly positive thinker, concerned above all to discover a way beyond the nihilistic reaction he believed to be the inevitable consequence of the impending

collapse of traditional values and modes of interpretation to a new 'affirmation' and 'enhancement' of life.'[9]

> "Without music, life would be a mistake."
> (Friedrich Nietzsche)

Postmodernism in Music

As with other uses of the term, postmodernism in music refers to a rejection of universals such as tonality and an embracement of fragmentation, pluralism, and difference.[10] Previously, in the chapter on Social Philosophy (Chapter 16), we read about Adorno's view of Stravinsky, Hindemith, and Milhaud as reactionary and Schoenberg, Berg, and Webern as progressive. Atonality would certainly be included in a postmodernist view, but it would also include other contemporary musical approaches such as aleatoric or chance music, minimalism, or performance art in classical music, as well as heavy metal, punk rock, ska, emo, rap/hip-hop, and a host of popular and commercial music styles.

Music has been ubiquitous around the world for many thousands of years, but 'world music' as a contemporary genre is also a postmodernist phenomenon in that the label recognizes that much of the world's music does not conform to Western notions of tonality, meter, timbres, and so on. It should also be noted that there is still a great deal of modern music (i.e., music based on tonality and other aspects of the common-practice period) in parallel with postmodern music.

There are many, many postmodern composers whose music bears discussion (e.g., Milton Babbitt, Pauline Oliveros, Krzysztof Penderecki, Terry Riley, Karlheinz Stockhausen, and on and on). However, we will consider briefly three works by the composer John Cage that will stand as exemplars of postmodernism.

4'33"[11] ♫

In 1952 pianist David Tudor gave the premiere performance of *4'33"*. He began by closing the keyboard lid and focusing on a stopwatch. Twice he raised and lowered the lid to indicate the ends of movements and turned the pages of the score, which contained no notes. Rather than hearing musical sounds from the piano, the audience heard wind noises outside the open-air concert hall, rain drops pattering during the second and third movements, and audience noises.[12]

0'0" (Zero Minutes, Zero Seconds or *4'33"* No. 2)[13] ♫

The score for this 1962 piece contains the following instruction: "In a situation provided with maximum amplification (no feedback), perform a disciplined action."[14] This action can be interrupted, should not repeat the same action in another performance, and should not be the performance of a musical composition. As a piece to be performed "in any way by anyone,"[15] performances have included Cage preparing, slicing, juicing, and drinking vegetables. There is actually a recording that contains no tracks, no music, no noise. It contains nothing at all.[16]

Organ2/ASLSP (As Slow as Possible)[17] ♫

Cage wrote *ASLSP* (As SLow aS Possible) in 1985 for piano; initial performances and recordings ranged from six minutes to eight hours.[18] Two years later, he adapted it for organ and gave it the name *Organ2/ASLSP*. In 2001, the John Cage Organ Foundation in Halberstadt, Germany, initiated a project to perform the piece over a period of 639 years. The length of the performance was not chosen arbitrarily. An early 12-tone keyboard was built for an organ in the St. Burchardi chapel in Halberstadt in 1361, 639 years before the year 2000. Today, a specially designed organ sustains each tone for the specified length of time; for example, the note change that occurred in October, 2013, will be sustained until September, 2020.

There are numerous discussions of whether these works are even music;[19] however, that is not the immediate point I want you to consider.[20] Rather, take these three works, and the many others you can identify, as exemplars of a postmodernist approach. Clearly, these pieces defy the notions most people have of what constitutes music. Taken as a whole, with the many differing compositional techniques notwithstanding, this music requires an approach described in a book title: *Beyond Structural Listening? Postmodern Modes of Hearing*.[21] In other words, one must forego a formalist listening approach in which each piece is conceived as an autonomous unity and attention is paid primarily to formal relationships within a given composition. According to Rose Subotnik, listeners must be freed up to pay attention to aspects other than a composition's structural integrity.

> Such emphasis does require a constant effort to recognize and interpret relationships between the elements of a musical configuration and history, conventions, technology, social conditions, characteristic patterns, responses, and values of the various cultures involved in that music.[22]

Andrew Dell'Antonio adds elements of "incoherence, discontinuity, situatedness, alienation, and subjectivity as features of the listening experience."[23] In actuality, however, what Dell'Antonio and Subotnik are proposing is a postmodernist listening approach that applies to all music, not just postmodern music. The music of Cage and other postmodernists may make the same kind of 'structural listening' that is often employed in listening to Bach and Beethoven more apparently irrelevant. But, a postmodernist view is that all music is situated within socio-cultural contexts and that there is much more to the musical experience than the notes themselves.

Postmodernism as a Music Philosophy

A postmodernist view is unwilling to privilege any particular philosophical or aesthetic view over others. There is no rationale for claiming that one style of music is better than another or that one aesthetic stance (e.g., formalism, referentialism, phenomenology, etc.) is the correct, only, or 'better' one. This multifaceted, pluralistic approach rejects singular or universal views and instead embraces all possibilities.

Consider the aspect of beauty. An extreme postmodernist position challenges conventional notions of beauty, throwing out the term altogether. "Beauty—once defined by idealization, regularity, harmony, balance, fidelity to the appearance of the world—is no longer the exclusive or even the primary calling card of the arts."[24] Beauty is less a concern than whether an art object is interesting, memorable, or inviting of further encounters.

A positive aspect of postmodernism is that all music philosophies and all musical styles have an opportunity to be heard. Music of women composers, music of minority composers, music that is difficult, confusing, challenging, or offensive—all now have a chance not only to be heard, but to be validated as legitimate members of musical society. Contrarily, one of the difficulties with this position is that if everything has value, nothing has value, a position which taken in the extreme leads to nihilism. "Nihilism is the belief that all values are baseless and that nothing can be known or communicated."[25] Roger Scruton makes the point that great art affirms the actual:

> Postmodernist irony is simply a more sophisticated way of avoiding the question of modern life—the question of what we are to affirm in it, and what to deny. If art ceases to affirm life, then it loses its point: after all, life is all that we have.[26]

Stated more simply, "if everything counts, then nothing counts."[27] "Because all music is equally valuable, any will do!"[28] Robert Walker particularized the argument by comparing Beethoven's song cycle *To the Distant Beloved*[29] ♫ with Britney Spears's 'I'm a Slave 4 U'[30] ♫ or 'Baby One More Time':[31] ♫

> Postmodern arguments suggest that all music is valuable. Thus, the argument often goes, Beethoven's music is no more musically or educationally valuable than, say, that of Britney Spears: just different. . . . [This argument] is disingenuous and dissembling because it ignores content.[32]

He contended that not all music is equally valuable. Following an analysis, he went on to say that Beethoven is "valuable precisely because it is the product of generations of Western musicians attempting to express the human condition in all its complexity, requiring reflection on human tragedy, sorrow, happiness, and triumph."[33]

> Britney's songs, in contrast, present little or no challenge, technically or intellectually, concerning the content (romantic relationships), while Beethoven offers complex, intricate, and imaginative insights into the issues and problems of relationships, manifest in the sophisticated vocal sounds, expressive performance practices, and challenging semantic content. Britney's are childlike in their simplicity, while Beethoven's require maturity of thought and consideration.[34]

Of course, it is important to realize that Walker was writing about musical values. Harkening back to the discussion in Chapter 6 of the ring analogy, one could say that determinations of personal and functional values might lead to different conclusions. Certainly, everyone has the right to like and dislike whatever music he or she chooses. Furthermore, given particular circumstances such as a college fraternity party or a senior voice recital, either Beethoven or Spears would be more or less appropriate.

For the purposes of determining your musical value system, postmodernism may appear to be an appealing choice. Certainly, the inclusiveness of the approach may be appealing. However, at least according to some scholars, declaring that all music is equally valuable leads to nihilism. If everything has value, then nothing has value and in that case, it makes no difference what music is being listened to, performed, or studied.

Music education philosopher Bennett Reimer proffered a way out of this dilemma. He stated that modernism and postmodernism do not have to exist in extremes. He criticized the polar opposites of philosophical unitarianism (there is one correct view) and pluralism (all views are equally valid).[35] Instead, he proposed a synergistic view in an attempt to temper extremes and find ways of combining them or allowing them to work together.[36] For example, he provided a synergistic proposal for form, practice, social agency, the boundaries of music, and utilitarian values.

- Music as form. Formalism values an intellectual appreciation of structure and internal relationships. At its extreme, formalism devalues emotions; external references to people, places, things; symbolism; political-social context; and so on. Extreme formalism leads to elitism; that is, only the most educated can follow the form. On the other hand, even untrained listeners who like music they can 'follow' (i.e., follow what's going on in the music or the form) can be formalists of a different sort. Thus, Reimer argues that those who throw out formalism because of its extreme position are missing the fact that many people gain meaningful musical experiences through apprehension of the form and the 'work' itself (i.e., the creation and performance of it fades into the background).
- Music as practice. The value of music is in the doing of it. The word praxial means action, and the focus is on the process, not the product (or autonomous form). Process and product do not have to be oppositional; that is, the emphasis does not have to be on one or the other. One can value both the work of art and at the same time value the process that created the product. Each depends on the other. A synergistic approach recognizes a balance, with emphasis shifting from one to the other as the occasion demands.
- Music as social agency. Music has value as it serves socio-political purposes. Formalist (art for art's sake) and contextualist (the social and political significance) positions each contribute something to the other. The synergistic approach finds value in each and recognizes that balances can shift depending on circumstances.
- Musical boundaries. One view is that music exists in and as its own world, unlike anything else. On the other hand, music for many people is connected to life, including all of human experience—politics, religion, health, nationhood, commerce, sociology, psychology, science, and so on. An insular, sealed (hermetic) world contrasts with an experience embedded in the totality of life and living. A synergistic approach moves from hard boundaries to soft boundaries. One can preserve the integrity of music and yet recognize that it meets us wherever we are and whatever we are doing (weddings, political rallies, listening quietly at home, etc.).
- Music and utilitarian values. What is music good for? Some contend that it is good for raising test scores, making people 'smarter,' instilling discipline, improving social skills, developing leadership, and any number of things. These are frequently used in advocacy positions. In a synergistic approach, philosophy and advocacy can complement each other. There is a need to balance both.

One could continue Reimer's list by seeking a synergistic balance among:

- functional values versus disinterested values (i.e., art for art's sake)
- beauty versus a lack of concern for beauty
- thinking versus feeling versus experiencing (rationalism versus empiricism versus phenomenology)
- music in the foreground (e.g., at a concert) versus music in the background (e.g., in a store or restaurant)
- individual versus group responses

In each case, a balanced or synergistic view takes the position that any view of music's value when taken at an extreme is untenable. Rather, the synergistic view recognizes that insights can be gained from a variety of viewpoints. The individual involved and the particular circumstances in which music is encountered can cause shifting priorities.

A critic might respond that a person adopting such a transitory, shifting view is avoiding the deep thinking required to establish bedrock principles. She is left without a core to her philosophy, a guiding principle that provides a solid footing on which she can stand firmly. Much as situational ethics rejects an understanding of universal right and wrong, situational aesthetics leaves one adrift, moving facilely from one musical experience to the next. What is the meaning and value of music? It depends. Furthermore, David Elliott and Marissa Silverman contend that a synergistic philosophy, at least as espoused by Reimer, is based on flawed understandings of emotions and feelings.[37]

Possible Solution?

Some of you may be attracted by the notion of a pluralistic approach to your music philosophy, but are also concerned about the lack of a core value. Perhaps you are neither prepared to say that any one view such as formalism or phenomenology is adequate for accounting for all the values of music, nor are you willing to agree that all views are equally acceptable. Is there a way out of this conundrum? Let us propose a possible solution, recognizing that just as no view given throughout this book has been immune from criticism, neither is this one.

Recall from previous discussions the number of times various philosophers have stated that music provides insights into the human condition. As shorthand for this idea, let us call this 'the Sister Wendy philosophy of music,' using a slightly amended version of her concise statement as the core value: "Music helps us to become more fully human." Stated in a nutshell, any musical experience or musical work has value to the extent that it enhances and enriches the human experience. Contrarily, musical experiences or musical works that diminish or weaken the human experience have limited or no value.

What does it mean to become more fully human or to have a humanizing experience? Just as we used 'anesthetic' to define 'aesthetic,' we can begin with the word 'dehumanizing.' We have only to hear or read the daily news to be aware of so many instances where individuals are bullied, harassed, or victimized in many ways. These experiences can cause people to feel marginalized, disenfranchised, or like second-class citizens—in other words, less than fully human. In contrast, humanizing experiences are those that empower the individual by enhancing opportunities for growth, thoughts and feelings, learning, love, joy, and all other aspects affecting quality of life. "Music can be perceived as mirroring what it means to be a human being, the conditions for life in its various phases, what life can offer, and how one ought/can take advantage of its possibilities."[38] For example, here's what one young man said about a Bruce Springsteen concert:

> For me, the concert was an expression of what it means to be human. The difficulties, love, joy, drivel, playing, seriousness, guilt, hopelessness. [It was] a drama that fills all of life, all those parts that make up what it means to be human.[39]

A core aspect of the human experience is being in community with others. Here is a woman's comment after hearing a powerful performance of Mahler's Symphony No. 8:[40] ♪

> A very important part of this was the feeling that the music united us all in a wordless understanding that all of us had been part of a unique *shared experience*. . . . The music conveyed

a clear message, the tones as well as the words, that gave rise to the thoughts and associations around the existential issues that were extremely topical for me just then.[41]

Of course, these powerful experiences also occur in musical engagements other than listening. Following an experience of participating with Maasai dancers, a middle-aged woman said, "It all connected into a total experience: the smells, the dance, the singing, the sandy beach, the drum on the other side of the lake, the mist, and the sunrise. It was an intense experience of being present."[42] In short, all three of these individuals became, in Sister Wendy's words, more fully human as a result of these musical experiences.

Let us illustrate the Sister Wendy philosophy by following the musical experiences of Sue, a doctoral piano major, for a few days. In the mornings and evenings, she croons lullabies to her newborn. The focus is not on the song as an artwork to be contemplated for its structural elegance nor its profundity of referential content. Rather, it is a moment of shared intimacy with her infant daughter. Later, during her daughter's nap, Sue studies and practices the piano pieces she will play in a recital next month. At the moment, she is working to understand the harmonic and rhythmic complexities of the Prokofiev Sonata No. 7 in B Flat.[43] ♫ She does not want to play from note to note without understanding the inner relationships that make the movement into a coherent whole. She marks critical places in the score, rehearsing sections as she goes, and will later create an analytic outline of the piece.

Sue is excited about the big weekend coming up. Her husband bought prime tickets for them and some of their best friends to attend a concert of her favorite rock group that is on tour in her town. She is already planning to wear a tour t-shirt she bought the first time she heard them when she and her husband were dating in college. Saturday night, the university she attends is presenting *The Magic Flute*.[44] ♫ A large group of her classmates are attending together because they have been studying the opera in one of their classes. In particular, she is eager to see if she can identify some of the Masonic and political references Mozart has embedded in the score. Sunday morning the church choir in which she sings is performing a 'sung service' in which the message will be presented via a variety of musical styles, including praise choruses, traditional hymns, a selection from Mendelssohn's oratorio *Elijah*,[45] ♫ and a bring-down-the-roof arrangement of the gospel song 'Ride on King Jesus.'[46] ♫

From a pluralistic perspective, Sue might find different values in every one of these musical situations. Furthermore, the musical experiences, works, and ways she approaches each one provide many humanizing experiences. As her attention swings from a shared moment with her daughter to understanding a musical score to an event suffused with nostalgia to a revered artwork noted for its extramusical references to a shared, religious experience, she might also find shifting, overlapping, and contradictory values coming to the fore. If she were to adopt a fixed, rigid modernist perspective, she would be faced with the daunting task of trying to force each experience into a constricting, compartmentalized box. Adopting an extreme postmodernist view would mean that all these experiences were equally valuable.

While Sue can recognize that there is value in all these experiences, each important in their own way, they are not valuable for the same philosophical reasons. Furthermore, she is free to find multiple values in the same experience. For example, when she is analyzing the Prokofiev score, she might be a formalist and then immediately take a phenomenological perspective as she rehearses the passages just analyzed. At the rock concert she might be simultaneously feeling especially close to her husband, while somehow sharing a different sense of community with her friends. This is not to suggest that Sue is consciously and intentionally switching philosophical positions, but rather that there is fluidity in her experience. In different circumstances, any of the philosophical positions discussed in this book can be valued, as long as they lead to a humanizing experience.

This picture seems rosy: so far every musical experience Sue has had is leading her to become more fully human. What are some examples of dehumanizing experiences? Here are two examples: (1) Suppose after analyzing and practicing the Prokofiev, Sue goes to her lesson and her teacher is harshly critical. At one point, Sue makes a slight mistake and the teacher, with dripping condescension, says, "You *do* read music, don't you?" (2) The rock concert Sue attended with her husband was a wonderful evening. She had such a good time with him and with her friends. The concert was a blending of in-the-moment fun with many happy memories stimulated by the songs they sang along and danced to. However, some of the songs contained coarse language, inappropriate subject matter, and gross stage antics that Sue found distasteful and chose to overlook. Since her college days, Sue has matured and no longer takes pleasure in some things that originally attracted her to the group. In short, dehumanizing aspects of a musical experience or work are devalued, just as humanizing aspects are valued. To reiterate, these can happen in rapidly shifting, simultaneously occurring, and contradictory patterns.

Recall the discussion of Schumann's *Frauenliebe und -leben* in Chapter 18: Feminism. Some writers found positive values in the work, others found it hurtful and distasteful, and others were conflicted. Thus, in the Sister Wendy philosophical view, the same work or same musical experience can be valued in different ways by different people. A heavy metal song with 'hard core' expressions may be dehumanizing to some and of significant value to others.[47] In a similar fashion, different genres can be appreciated and valued for different reasons as they lead one to become more fully human.

The Sister Wendy statement is by no means the only core value one could use for a pluralistic view. What other core value statements can you identify? As previously stated, this is not presented as a 'perfect' solution, a perfect philosophy of music. What deficiencies, limitations, or problems can you identify?

Summary and Thought Questions

Seen in a positive light, postmodernism both in music and in music philosophy provides a fresh, unfettered approach where rigid strictures are no longer in favor. Composers are not bound by long-standing confines such as tonality. Those whose music has been marginalized for centuries now have the opportunity to be heard and appreciated. New and bold approaches to creating and making music are not only allowed but encouraged.

In similar fashion, philosophers no longer take a unitary approach, but view the world from any and all perspectives. Postmodernists have opened the way for unencumbered access, allowing each person to appreciate and enjoy all kinds of music and musical experiences for all kinds of reasons.

Critics, however, are concerned that a cardinal principle of postmodernists—that no perspective is privileged over others—when taken at the extreme, leads to nihilism. Reimer offered a synergistic approach, striking a balance between modernist and postmodernist perspectives. Thus, for example, musicing and contemplation of the outcomes of musicing can co-exist; rather than focusing exclusively on process or product, it is possible to consider both aspects simultaneously or in subtly shifting balances. Another possibility is a pluralistic approach in which a variety of perspectives are subsumed under an overarching core principle. Different musical experiences in different circumstances can be valued for a variety of reasons, all of which support a fundamental organizing principle that provides stability. Here are some questions to help you sort through these options:

1. Do you believe that philosophical modernism is finished and that it no longer has useful ideas to contribute to a dialogue on the nature, meaning, and value of music?
2. Does the lack of a unitary, core value of music, as seen in postmodernism—that is, the concept that all views of music's value are viable—pose any particular problems?
3. What challenges and advantages does pluralism pose?
4. Does Reimer's synergistic approach appeal to you?
5. Can you imagine a pluralistic view in which all the disparate ideas are bound to a 'first among equals' core statement? For example, what about the Sister Wendy approach—"music makes us more fully human"—as a core principle? Does it seem tenable to say that any musical experience has value to the extent that it is humanizing, while dehumanizing musical experiences have lesser or no value? What other core principles might you use to provide an anchor for a pluralistic approach?
6. If you were to adopt a postmodernist position, or any of the alternatives, how would it affect your composing, performing, listening, and teaching?

Notes

1 David Novitz, "Postmodernism: Barthes and Derrida," in *The Routledge Companion to Aesthetics*, ed. Berys Gaut and Dominic Lopes (London: Routledge, 2002), 155–65.
2 Gary Aylesworth, "Postmodernism," in *The Stanford Encyclopedia of Philosophy* (2015 edition), ed. Edward Zalta. http://plato.stanford.edu/archives/win2010/entries/postmodernism/.
3 Wayne Bowman, *Philosophical Perspectives on Music* (New York: Oxford University Press, 1998), 359.
4 Elizabeth Ermarth, "Postmodernism," in *Routledge Encyclopedia of Philosophy, Version 1.0*, ed. Edward Craig (London and New York: Routledge, 1998), 6743.
5 Ibid., 6742.
6 Robert Walker, "Avoiding the Dangers of Postmodern Nihilist Curricula in Music Education," in *The Oxford Handbook of Philosophy in Music Education*, ed. Wayne Bowman and Ana Lucía Frega (Oxford, UK: Oxford University Press, 2011), 391.
7 Friedrich Nietzsche, *The Will to Power*, ed. Walter Kaufmann, trans. Walter Kaufmann and R. J. Hollingdale (New York: Vintage Books, 1968), 7.
8 Stephen Hawking, *A Brief History of Time* (New York: Bantam Books, 1998).
9 Richard Schacht, "Nietzsche, Friedrich Wilhelm," in *The Oxford Guide to Philosophy*, ed. Ted Honderich (Oxford, UK: Oxford University Press, 2005), 655–56.
10 Kenneth Gloag, *Postmodernism in Music* (Cambridge, UK: Cambridge University Press, 2012).
11 John Cage, *4'33"*, performed by William Marx, http://www.youtube.com/watch?v=JTEFKFiXSx4.
12 Kyle Gann, *No Such Thing as Silence. John Cage's 4'33"* (Yale University Press, 2010).
13 John Cage, *0'00"*, performed by Haco, https://www.youtube.com/watch?v=6I1gfOlNNo4.
14 Database of John Cage Works: johncage.org. http://johncage.org/pp/John-Cage-Works.cfm.
15 Gilbert Chase, "John Cage," in *The International Cyclopedia of Music and Musicians, 11th ed.*, ed. Oscar Thompson (New York: Dodd, Mead & Co., 1989), 337.
16 Database of John Cage Works: johncage.org. http://johncage.org/pp/John-Cage-Works.cfm.
17 John Cage, *Organ2/ASLSP*, performed by Christoph Bossert, organ, https://www.youtube.com/watch?v=ZYnEWbL6yao.
18 Jeffrey Byrd and John Fritch, "Forever Ephemeral: John Cage's ASLSP," *Performance Research: A Journal of the Performing Arts* 17, no. 5 (2012): 5. Terez Mertes, "As Slow as Possible," *Violin Blogs*, 2008. http://www.violinist.com/blog/Terez/20088/9005.

19 Stephen Davies, "John Cage's 4'33": Is It Music?" in *Themes in the Philosophy of Music*, ed. Stephen Davies (Oxford, UK: Oxford University Press, 2003), 11–29.

20 See discussions such as: Andrew Kania, "Definition," in *The Routledge Companion to Philosophy and Music*, eds. Theodore Gracyk and Andrew Kania (New York: Routledge, 2011), 3–13. Jennifer Judkins, "Silence, Sound, Noise, and Music," in *The Routledge Companion to Philosophy and Music*, ed. Theodore Gracyk and Andrew Kania (New York: Routledge, 2011), 14–23.

21 Andrew Dell'Antonio, ed., *Beyond Structural Listening? Postmodern Modes of Hearing* (Berkeley, CA: University of California Press, 2004).

22 Rose Subotnik, *Deconstructive Variations: Music and Reason in Western Society* (Minneapolis, MN: University of Minnesota Press, 1996), 172.

23 Dell'Antonio, *Beyond Structural Listening?*, 11.

24 Howard Gardner, *Truth, Beauty, and Goodness Reframed* (New York: Basic Books, 2011), 49.

25 Alan Pratt, "Nihilism," *Internet Encyclopedia of Philosophy*, 2005. http://www.iep.utm.edu/nihilism/.

26 Roger Scruton, *The Aesthetics of Music* (Oxford: The Clarendon Press, 1997), 493.

27 David Elliott, "Music Education Philosophy," in *The Oxford Handbook of Music Education*, ed. Gary McPherson and Graham Welch (Oxford, UK: Oxford University Press, 2011), 68.

28 Robert Walker, "Avoiding the Dangers of Postmodern Nihilist Curricula in Music Education," 390.

29 Ludwig van Beethoven, *An die Ferne Geliebte*, Op. 98, performed by Dietrich Fischer-Dieskau, voice, and Gerald Moore, piano, https://youtu.be/KOk7EWYbyqk.

30 Britney Spears, 'I'm a Slave 4 U,' performed by Britney Spears, https://youtu.be/Mzybwwf2HoQ.

31 Britney Spears, 'Baby One More Time,' performed by Britney Spears, https://youtu.be/C-u5WLJ9Yk4.

32 Walker, "Avoiding the Dangers of Postmodern Nihilist Curricula in Music Education," 397.

33 Ibid., 388.

34 Ibid., 388.

35 Bennett Reimer, "Once More with Feeling: Reconciling Discrepant Accounts of Musical Affect," *Philosophy of Music Education Review* 12, no. 1 (2004): 4–16.

36 Bennett Reimer, *A Philosophy of Music Education: Advancing the Vision, 3rd ed.* (Upper Saddle River, NJ: Prentice-Hall, 2003).

37 David Elliott and Marissa Silverman, *Music Matters: A Philosophy of Music Education, 2nd ed:* (New York: Oxford University Press, 2015).

38 Alf Gabrielsson, *Strong Experiences with Music*, trans. Rod Bradury (Oxford, UK: Oxford University Press, 2011), 149.

39 Ibid., 150.

40 Gustav Mahler, Symphony No. 8, performed by Leonard Bernstein conducting the Vienna Philharmonic Orchestra, https://www.youtube.com/watch?v=NSYEOLwVfU8.

41 Gabrielsson, *Strong Experiences with Music*, 152.

42 Ibid., 154.

43 Sergei Prokofiev, Sonata No. 7 in B Flat Major, Op. 33, performed by Sviatoslav Richter, https://www.youtube.com/watch?v=NNb1qYqWP0E.

44 Wolfgang Mozart, *The Magic Flute*, performed by Riccardo Muti conducting the Vienna Philharmonic at the 2006 Salzburg Festival, https://www.youtube.com/watch?v=w9zwQNib-h4.

45 Felix Mendelssohn, *Elijah*, performed by Ann Howard Jones, conductor, and the Boston University Chorus and Orchestra, https://www.youtube.com/watch?v=iBMTzryAnrk.

46 'Ride On King Jesus,' performed by the In HIS Presence Gospel Choir, https://youtu.be/etGrFu6dyAE.

47 Deena Weinstein, *Heavy Metal: The Music and Its Culture*, revised edition (Cambridge, MA: Da Capo Press, 2000).

Section III

Making It Your Own

20 Articulating a Philosophy of Music

If you have read the preceding 19 chapters, you have encountered many different views on philosophy in general, on core aspects of art (e.g., beauty, emotion, and aesthetics), and a wide range of specific music philosophies. Ideally, you have also taken the time to read some of the writings of the many philosophers cited throughout, or at least those with whose views you agree. At this point you may be feeling confused by so many choices or you may be gaining some ground on formulating your own thoughts. Either way, the purpose of this chapter is to help you express your music philosophy in as clear and unambiguous language as you can. To do this most effectively requires feedback, something a book cannot do. Therefore, it will be most helpful if you work with an instructor or friends and colleagues who can respond to your ideas with constructive feedback.

Writing and speaking are the two primary ways you will share your philosophy. Fortunately, the two inform each other, so it will be helpful to move back and forth between writing your ideas and saying them. Reading aloud what you have written is an effective technique, as is giving a formal speech or presentation. However, neither should be emphasized to the exclusion of talking spontaneously about your philosophy. Strive for being so secure in your thoughts that you can carry on a casual conversation about your philosophy in which you explain your ideas in a dialogue that is not scripted. When you can be involved in a free exchange of ideas in which you represent your ideas faithfully and accurately without resorting to notes or prepared remarks, you will have arrived at a high level of confidence and security in your approach.

> "I must study politics and war, that my sons may have the liberty to study mathematics and philosophy, natural history and naval architecture, in order to give their children a right to study painting, poetry, music, architecture, tapestry, and porcelain."
>
> (John Adams)

How to begin? As noted, you already have begun if you have read all the chapters to this point. If you have not done so already, I would highly recommend answering as many of the thought questions at the end of each chapter as you can; writing down your responses, while more time consuming, is likely to require more precise and thoughtful responses than simply thinking up a quick, internal response. Collate your written responses and organize them into categories. A simple filing system would be to place all of the responses in which you express agreement with an idea into one folder, responses in which you disagree into another, and responses in which you are undecided into a third. Responses to the exercises in this chapter can be added to the folders you create.

Exercises

Here are some hints before you begin the following exercises:

- As indicated, spend time articulating your responses in both spoken and written form. Because we normally write and speak differently, do not restrict your verbalized responses to reading a written statement. Also, saying something aloud is very different from ruminating internally. If you can, say your response to someone else. If not, record your response.
- Also, as previously indicated, file your responses to these exercises in the folders you have already created or into new ones. The goal is that at some point you will have a folder of 'things I believe about the nature, meaning, and value of music' that will eventually form the core of your music philosophy.
- In reviewing the folder containing ideas with which you resonate, identify the generating authors and read some of their original works.
- Many of these exercises are presented in a polarized or dichotomous fashion. For example, you are asked to consider whether you are an absolutist or referentialist or a formalist/expressionist. Do not automatically default to an 'I think both are important' position. If you truly think that whatever positions being presented are equivalent, put your response into a 'Pluralism' folder for further consideration. Although pluralism can be a viable position, as discussed in Chapter 19, it comes with its own set of issues to resolve. Do not use a pluralistic approach as an easy way out because you simply cannot decide. Rather, use it if you truly are convinced that this is the position you want to promote.
- Recognize that choosing one position over another does not mean that you find no value in the other position. For example, say you decide expressionism most closely resonates with your own thoughts. That does not mean that you find no value in the internal structures of music (formalism). Rather, it means that, for you, the expression of feelings and emotions takes precedence over an intellectual appreciation of the formal properties of music.
- Whenever possible in the exercises that follow, provide a musical example. If you choose to illustrate with a musical work, be specific. Do not give 'piano sonatas' as an example; provide composer and title for a specific piano sonata. Likewise, if you do not wish to give a musical work, but prefer to use a musical activity instead, do not say 'improvising.' Be specific about what improvisational circumstances illustrate the choice you have made. Provide as many details as possible to provide as rich a description as you can.
- It can also be helpful to think of music (either works or activities) that, for you, have less musical value. If everything has value, nothing has value. If you say that all music has equal value, you are saying that there is no such thing as artistic standards. For example, if you believe that music's greatest value lies in its ability to effect or influence social change, you must ask yourself whether all music is equally capable of doing that. Adorno was clear about what music had this value. If you ascribe to the general idea of music as a social change agent, but not to Adorno's particular exemplars, what music is and is not effective in bringing about changes in social behaviors and circumstances?
- Some of these exercises are intentionally provocative. That is, by asking you to take positions that on the surface seem outrageous or unfair, you are actually being given the opportunity to produce a counter argument. Regardless of where you fall in the matter, attempting to answer these questions honestly and clearly will help sharpen the focus of your philosophy. Try not

to respond solely out of emotion or personal preference. That is, emotional responses and personal preferences may give you strong hints about your values system, but use a logical thought process to provide a coherent answer.

> "There's a difference between a philosophy and a bumper sticker."
> (Charles M. Schulz)

Exercise 1: Do you think the *primary* value or meaning of music comes from within the music itself or from what the music points to outside itself? In other words, are you an absolutist or a referentialist? Give one or more musical examples that support your position.

Again, note that if you say 'I am an absolutist,' you are not denying that some value may come from extramusical references; rather, you are saying that, in general, extramusical references are secondary to the music itself. Likewise, if you say 'I am a referentialist,' you could still recognize that the music itself does have value, but that it is superseded by where the music takes us.

Exercise 2: Is the *primary* value of music intellectual or emotional? Illustrate by choosing at least one musical example that is programmatic and one that is pure, instrumental music.

Exercise 3: If you had trouble making choices in Exercises 1 and 2, does the viewpoint of absolute expressionism provide a viable alternative? If so, how would you illustrate this position musically, with both programmatic and absolute musical examples?

Exercise 4: Beauty

4a. What are the attributes of musical beauty (e.g., something rare or original, something pleasurable, something with 'good' shape or form, something moving or expressive, etc.)?

4b. In *Ode on a Grecian Urn*, John Keats concludes the poem with these lines:

> "Beauty is truth, truth beauty—that is all
> Ye know on earth, and all ye need to know."

What do you think he meant by this?

4c. Describe why you agree or disagree with the statement that 'beauty is in the eye of the beholder.'

4d. The ancient Latin aphorism '*degustibus non disputandem est*' means there is no disputing about taste, or we might say that everyone is entitled to his opinion. Do you agree with this in reference to beauty?

4e. What things influence our perception of beauty (e.g., upbringing, socioeconomic status, gender, ethnicity, culture, symmetry, proportion, etc.)?

4f. What is the role of beauty in the human experience? Do human beings have a need for beauty? Can you think of nonmusical examples that illustrate the importance of beauty for human beings? What implications does this concept have for music?

The point of the next three exercises is to help you think through and articulate your values system. Often, making comparisons is frustrating and seemingly unnecessary. However, an inability to do so may mean that there is no such thing as artistic standards. Anything, no matter how trite or trivial, or no matter how poorly produced (out of tune, wrong notes, etc.) is just as good as anything else. Creativity, quality, and excellence count for nothing. If Exercises 5, 6, and 7 seem to push you into making decisions or statements with which you do not feel comfortable, provide a defense for an alternative position, one that argues for the validity of any artistic expression.

Exercise 5: Setting aside issues of 'better' or 'worse' for a moment, and using admittedly artificial and simplistic dichotomies, identify artworks or experiences in two extremes: Category 1 includes artworks and experiences that are transitory, superficial, banal, or trite. Category 2 contains profound artworks or experiences that plumb the depths of the human experience, that challenge us to contemplate the meaning of life, our role—both as an individual and as a species—in the universe. As an example, consider two poems:

Trick or Treat

Trick or Treat, smell my feet.
Give me something good to eat.
If you don't, I don't care.
I'll pull down your underwear.
Anonymous childhood rhyme

The Night Has a Thousand Eyes

The night has a thousand eyes,
   And the day but one;
Yet the light of the bright world dies
   With the dying sun.
The mind has a thousand eyes,
   And the heart but one;
Yet the light of a whole life dies
   When love is done.
F. W. Bourdillon[1]

What implications do these 'categories' have for music? If you are uncomfortable polarizing music in this way, how could you argue that no distinctions can be made between trivial and profound music? Note that we still have not said that one is necessarily *better* than another, only that they are different. Here are two musical examples similar to the poems, except in this case the Dolly Parton example can hardly be called trivial. Rather let us say that these two examples represent very different styles or approaches. Do we have any basis for placing one 'above' the other? If so, what is that basis?

Dolly Parton: 'Two Doors Down'

Two doors down
They're laughing and drinkin' and having a party

Two doors down
They're not aware that I'm around.[2] ♫

Strauss: Four Last Songs, *IV: 'Im Abendrot' (At Sunset).*

We have through sorrow and joy
gone hand in hand;
From our wanderings, let's now rest
in this quiet land.

Around us, the valleys bow
as the sun goes down.
Two larks soar upwards
dreamily into the light air.

Come close, and let them fly.
Soon it will be time for sleep.
Let's not lose our way
in this solitude.

O vast, tranquil peace,
so deep in the evening's glow!
How weary we are of wandering—
Is this perhaps a hint of death?[3] ♫
Poem by Joseph von Eichendorff

In this case, it is absolutely critical to listen to the music. For it is the musical portrayal of the text with which we are concerned. I would encourage you not to take the easy way out by taking a polarized view at either end of a continuum. At one end: 'Of course, these two are not comparable in any way. One is decidedly more profound in its treatment of a serious subject than the other.' At the other end: 'There is no basis for judging one superior to the other. All music has equal value.' You may, indeed, wish to stake your claim at either end of the continuum, or anywhere in between; however, do so on the basis of a solid, logical rationale. Do not respond out of passion or strong personal preference.

Exercise 6: Suppose we were to ask a thousand English literature professors and a thousand art history professors to identify great works in Western art. The works listed below are intentionally conservative and intended only to prime your thinking. They are 'safe' works from the older, established canon. Begin by creating your own list of literature and visual art that might include contemporary, female, and minority creators. Then, do the same for the music column by thinking of what composers and what specific pieces of music represent the greatest contributions to the repertoire of Western music. No ethnocentric bias is intended here, simply that most of us would not have the expertise to evaluate artworks from non-Western cultures. If you do have the background and expertise to list non-Western examples in all three columns, feel free to do so.

Books/Plays/Poems	Paintings/Sculptures	Music
Shakespeare: *Hamlet, King Lear, Macbeth, Othello*	Michelangelo: *David, Pietà,* Ceiling of the Sistine Chapel	
Hugo: *Les Misérables*	Da Vinci: *Mona Lisa*	
Dickens: *Tale of Two Cities, Oliver Twist, David Copperfield, Great Expectations*	Van Gogh: *Starry Night, Self-Portrait, The Potato Eaters, Sunflowers*	
Austen: *Pride and Prejudice, Sense and Sensibility, Emma*	Kahlo: *Frida and Diego Rivera, The Two Fridas*	
Tolstoy: *War and Peace, Anna Karenina*	Picasso: *Les damoiselles d'Avignon, Guernica*	
Poems by Wordsworth, Dickinson, Keats, Shelly, Byron	Rodin: *The Thinker, The Kiss*	

Now that you have identified sample works, think about why they merit such a lofty status. Are there commonalities among the works in each column? Are there commonalities among the three columns? In other words, can we say anything meaningful about the value of 'great' art? Are Shakespeare, Michelangelo, and Beethoven (or whomever you would place in the third column) striving to express some of the same things? If so, what is this that they are after?

Exercise 7:   Thinking now about musical engagements or activities as opposed to specific musical works, describe how one musical activity might have more artistic integrity, authenticity, or artistic value than another. For example, suppose Jack and Pete are in the basements of their respective homes. Both are playing guitar. Jack is idly passing time with no particular motivation. He is not being careful about what he is doing; rather he is mindlessly noodling or 'messing around.' Pete, on the other hand, is struggling to compose a song about his younger sister who is going through chemotherapy treatments. He wants to express his love for her and how much she means to him. Can you find a basis for evaluating musicing, as opposed to musical works?

Exercise 8:   What is the point of 'great art'? That is, what do people get from reading great literature, viewing great artworks, or listening to great music? What do we find when we engage ourselves in great art? Why is it not only important, but ideal (perhaps even necessary) for everyone to seek out and participate in 'great art' experiences? It is probably necessary for you to articulate your concept of 'great art' as part of your answer.

Exercise 9:   What are the relative strengths and weakness of large, formal ensemble experiences, such as band, orchestra, and choir, and relatively smaller, informal performance groups such as a jazz combo, a garage band, or an old-time ensemble?

Exercise 10:   On what basis could you argue that art music, classical music (or however you want to label the music of Bach, Beethoven, and Brahms) is inherently superior to music of other styles (pop, rock, folk, emo, ska, rap/hip-hop, and on and on)? If you cannot make that argument, how would you argue the case that singing 'The Coo Coo Bird' (traditional), while accompanying yourself on the banjo, is the equivalent of singing in the chorus of the Brahms *Requiem*?

Exercise 11: Similar to Exercise 9, how do you account for world music? Do you wish to exclude world music from your philosophy? If so, on what basis? If you wish to acknowledge and incorporate world music into your philosophy, what level of expertise do you have for doing so? Can you say that a Peruvian wedding song has artistic value without knowing the first thing about Peruvian music?

Exercise 12: What is an aesthetic experience? Can you describe one or more aesthetic experiences you have had in music? How do aesthetic experiences in music occur for you most often—when listening, performing, or in other ways? Are aesthetic concerns an important reason for you to value music?

Exercise 13: For this exercise, rate each of the following according to this scale:

0 = I do not have enough information to give this viewpoint a rating.
1 = My views are in complete opposition to this viewpoint.
2 = My views are somewhat in opposition to this viewpoint.
3 = I am ambivalent on this viewpoint.
4 = My views are somewhat in agreement with this viewpoint.
5 = My views are in complete agreement with this viewpoint.

Although you should take some time to consider each viewpoint, err on the side of first impressions rather than a belabored contemplation. Do not worry at the moment whether your choices lead to contradictions; these can be resolved at a later date. Choose one or more musical works or experiences that illustrate the choices you make.

a. Music has value primarily because of its mathematical, scientific basis.

0 1 2 3 4 5

b. Music has value primarily because it imitates absolute ideals such as truth and beauty.

0 1 2 3 4 5

c. Music has value primarily because it can influence human character, morals, and ethical behavior.

0 1 2 3 4 5

d. Music has value primarily because it represents a blend of Plato's rationalism with your faith beliefs.

0 1 2 3 4 5

e. Music has value primarily because of its central role in religious worship.

0 1 2 3 4 5

f. Music has value primarily because it appeals to the rational mind.

0 1 2 3 4 5

g. Music has value primarily because of its rich sensory experiences.

0 1 2 3 4 5

h.   Music has value primarily because it is a means of bringing together thought and feeling, mind and body.

0 1 2 3 4 5

i.   Music has value primarily because the interrelationships of musical elements are intellectually stimulating and satisfying.

0 1 2 3 4 5

j.   Music has value primarily because of how it makes me feel.

0 1 2 3 4 5

k.   Music has value primarily because of what it refers to outside itself.

0 1 2 3 4 5

l.   Music has value primarily because it symbolically represents things that are important to me.

0 1 2 3 4 5

m.   Music has value primarily because of the in-the-moment, lived bodily experience it affords.

0 1 2 3 4 5

n.   Music has value primarily because it affords *an* experience that connects to daily living.

0 1 2 3 4 5

o.   Music has value primarily because of the functional role it plays in my life.

0 1 2 3 4 5

p.   Music has value primarily because the consequences of musical experiences are positive and pleasurable.

0 1 2 3 4 5

q.   Music has value primarily because it is a vehicle for social progress.

0 1 2 3 4 5

r.   Music has value primarily because of the role it plays in social interactions.

0 1 2 3 4 5

s.   Music has value primarily because it is a multifaceted experience that affects my personal self-growth.

0 1 2 3 4 5

t.   Music has value primarily because it gives voice to marginalized and disenfranchised groups.

0 1 2 3 4 5

u.   Music has value primarily because it allows for a wide array of viewpoints, each of which has equal merit.

0   1   2   3   4   5

v.   Music has value primarily because it allows one to become more fully human.

0   1   2   3   4   5

If none of the foregoing statements represent your views exactly, you will have the opportunity to construct your own in Exercise 15.

Exercise 14:   Do you see any connection between music and this statement of Socrates—"The unexamined life is not worth living"? That is, can music be a vehicle for examining your life? What examples can you provide?

Exercise 15:   Try to capture your philosophy in one sentence. Start with a stem such as one of the following:

I believe that the nature, value, and meaning of music is found in . . .
For me, the core value of music is . . .
Music has meaning and value to human beings because . . .

Exercise 16:   Once you have written one sentence, turn that into a paragraph. Illustrate your thesis with several musical examples. Pick at least one programmatic piece of music and one absolute instrumental work. Provide specifics, including composer and title. Continue by providing two more examples in which you do not find value according to this philosophy. As always, you may substitute musical activities or musical engagements for works, or mix and match them.

Enough exercises! At some point, you have to begin to commit to your own thoughts and ideas. In the extended quote that follows, Estelle Jorgensen provides a clear rationale for finding your own voice. Under a heading called 'A Personal Perspective,' she wrote:

> Here, I speak of the necessity of making one's own philosophical voice heard. In the reading that one does, it is possible to become so caught up in the ideas of other writers that one forgets about the importance of articulating one's own perspective. When this happens, one's argument may too easily dissolve into a literature review of what others have written or even into an argument by quoting authority. One may expect that others should have the same respect for a particular authority one admires, that they should agree that invoking the name of this authority suffices to make the argument. This is not how philosophy should work. There comes a point when it is necessary to put away one's books and the writing of others, and develop one's own argument. An authority's comments or conceptions maybe helpful tools in making a point, but they should remain just that. . . . This experience [a project she worked on] reinforced for me the idea that one may become so seduced by the ideas of others that one's entire frame of reference can become theirs, and even one's language is borrowed from them. At that point, it must be time to ask: Enough of other's [*sic*] views and words: what are my own?[4]

We have arrived at the point where you need to stake your own claim. To reiterate and expand upon comments made at the beginning of Chapter 1, my suggestion is that you put yourself into one of the following three categories:

- Category 1. If much of this material is new to you and you have little formal experience in philosophy (either in general or specifically in music), then I encourage you to find one of the philosophical views presented in Chapters 8–19 and latch onto it. You can certainly color it with your own experiences and musical examples, but you may want to stay rather close to the arguments presented by a recognized philosopher.
- Category 2. If you have had some previous experiences with music philosophy, you may feel a little more freedom toward modifying one of the philosopher's views that you have read about in this book or in another publication. You may agree with the general tenets of this philosopher but prefer to amend, modernize, or otherwise adjust the language.
- Category 3. If you have had considerable experience with music philosophy and are willing to make a serious commitment toward reading deeply in the literature and spending sufficient time and energy, you may feel the need to develop an 'original' philosophy. This is not for the faint hearted! Some of the greatest minds over several thousand years of Western history have struggled with the creation of a music philosophy. Join them if you dare!

Perhaps there is little more to be said at this point. Now it comes down to talking and writing. And revising, revising, revising. Be patient with yourself. Try not to set about this task with fear and trepidation. Rather, celebrate the fact that you have come this far. Remember, too, that this is just a beginning. Likely, you will want/need to revisit and revise your philosophy several times over the course of your career. Challenge yourself to find the bedrock on which your music philosophy rests.

Notes

1 Francis Bourdillon, "The Night Has a Thousand Eyes," in *A Victorian Anthology, 1837–1895*, ed. Edmund Stedman (Cambridge: Riverside Press, 1895), 533.
2 Dolly Parton, 'Two Doors Down,' performed by Dolly Parton, https://youtu.be/9w3WHYFohCM.
3 Jane Jones, "Richard Strauss: *Four Last Songs* – A Swansong of Sublime Beauty," *Classic fM*, accessed on June 24, 2016, http://www.classicfm.com/composers/strauss/guides/richard-strauss-four-last-songs/#GgsdPct0fmo5RYFg.97. Richard Strauss, 'Im Abendrot' (At Sunset) from *Vier Letzte Liederi* (*Four Last Songs*), performed by Kiri Te Kanawa, soprano, and Georg Solti conducting the BBC Philharmonic Orchestra, https://www.youtube.com/watch?v=co61XmUu-tc.
4 Estelle Jorgensen, "Values and Philosophizing about Music Education," *Philosophy of Music Education Review* 22, no. 1 (2014): 10–11.

21 Applying Your Philosophy

Whatever philosophical view you espouse, if it does not affect your musical life it will not be much good. The way you listen, perform, teach, or compose music is a reflection of your beliefs about music's value and meaning. What you believe about music should make a difference.

The purpose of this chapter is to help you get started in applying your philosophy to what you do musically on a daily basis. What follows are a series of brief stories, one per chapter for Chapters 8–19. Because there are numerous ideas in each of these chapters, each vignette serves as only one example among many that could be given. Each is intentionally brief because to be more detailed would move the chapter closer to being prescriptive. Rather than considering the vignettes as models, think of them as ideas to stimulate your own thinking. Pondering how your philosophy impacts your musical life is also a good way to sharpen your philosophy. Move back and forth between articulating and applying your philosophy; each will clarify the other and will ensure a consistent approach.

Chapter 8: Contributions to Music Philosophy from the Ancient Greeks

Music's moral influence.

As mothers of teenagers, Molly and Sharon are members of a parent group organized to monitor media content such as movies, books, magazines, and music. Group members are sensitive to issues of censorship; however, they feel strongly that their children should not be exposed to certain negative influences. Molly and Sharon chair the music section and, along with other parents, they feel that there is much popular music that is perfectly fine for their children to listen to and perform. Their concern is with the lyrics of some types of music and with other performance aspects. Lyrics that promote mistreatment of women, violence, substance abuse, or aggressive anti-social behaviors are a constant worry. They also do not condone stage and video antics that are highly suggestive or ultra inflammatory. These parents realize that they cannot control everything their children are exposed to, and they do not want to. They simply wish to support positive influences in their children's lives and mitigate negative and deleterious pressures.

Chapter 9: From Classical Antiquity to the Renaissance

Music's rational basis.

Matthew is a middle-aged man who has been building his music library throughout most of his life. He started with LPs, added cassette tapes, moved somewhat reluctantly to CDs due to the expense, and now downloads almost everything off the Internet. His tastes are very eclectic, ranging from classical and jazz to country, popular, and world music. Once, when a visiting friend was perusing Matthew's collection, he casually asked, "How do you decide what to buy?" Matthew's immediate response was, "I just buy whatever I like." However, when he thought more about it, he realized there was a basis for what he liked. Put simply, he liked music that made sense. Not having studied music philosophy or music theory formally, Matthew would not have used rationalistic terminology to explain his selection process. But he was a musician, and he understood how things worked aurally. Once he realized this, he planned to spend some time with a local university music theory professor who could give him the language to express what he already understood from many years of careful listening.

Chapter 10: Rationalism, Empiricism, and Idealism

Finding musical beauty by balancing thoughts and feelings.

Carl is a high school band director. Early in his career he was intently focused on his own teaching and conducting skills. As he matured, his attention shifted to his students and what they ought to be getting from their time in band. He found himself wavering back and forth between wanting his students to learn *about* music—that is, to become musically literate—and wanting them to be touched *by* the music. About this time he took a music philosophy course as part of his summers-only master's program. In this course he encountered the writing and thoughts of Friedrich Schiller. Two ideas struck him in particular. First, he was convinced by Schiller's notion of the importance of beauty. Second, he appreciated how Schiller united reason (formal drive) with feelings (sensuous drive) in creating artistic beauty (play drive). Putting these ideas into practice, Carl worked to ensure that his rehearsals combined instruction in facts and knowledge about composers and the music the band was learning with opportunities for students to express their feelings and sense of pleasure in performing, all with the goal of expressing beauty in an artistic way.

Chapter 11: Formalism

Structure has meaning.

Antoinette is a university music theory professor. She has published a number of papers on different theories of how listeners cognitively organize the music they hear. In her student days, she completed advanced work in Heinrich Schenker's analytic approach[1] and in Fred Lerdahl and Ray Jackendoff's *Generative Theory of Tonal Music*.[2] Her goal is to better understand how we make sense of music. What 'rules' might be inherent in the human mind (e.g., Gestalt laws of cognitive organization) and what are culturally based (e.g., tonality)? Even when she is teaching or writing about programmatic repertoire, such as a Strauss tone poem or an operatic aria, her focus is on how the music is structured and how various musical elements interact with each other to create a coherent whole. Just as physicists gain meaning by gradually understanding the structure of the universe, Antoinette finds meaning—and experiences deep pleasure—by unraveling the mysteries of musical structure and how the human mind makes sense of it.

Chapter 12: Expressionism

To sing is to express feelings.

Arturo is a tenor who has sung in opera houses all over the world. The amount of preparation necessary to learn an opera role is daunting and demanding and in preparing for his career, Arturo spends untold hours in the practice room learning the art of singing. He mastered vocal technique and understands enough vocal pedagogy and voice science to monitor his vocal health. He studied a number of languages and is keenly aware that he cannot just sing the words; he has to understand what he is singing. In addition, he studied acting and learned stagecraft. Arturo struggled early in his career because he was so caught up in the mechanics of his performances that he lost sight of his purpose. Finally, an older répétiteur with whom he was preparing a role took him aside and asked him some direct questions about his motivation for singing. What was he trying to accomplish? What did he want his audiences to experience? Suddenly, Arturo realized that all the vocal technique and diction work were merely means to a greater end. Once he realized that his overarching goal was give voice to the character's feelings, he was freed up to give thrilling performances. Now, conductors, critics, colleagues, and audiences marvel at his ability to express the most profound emotions in a dramatic and compelling way. Arturo trusts his preparation and confidently steps on stage, clear-minded about his goal to let his voice become a powerful mode of expression.

Chapter 13: Symbolism

Music symbolizes feelings.

Jane is a music therapist who believes that music has the power to represent aspects of life that are important to individual clients with whom she works. For example, she works with Sam, a 16-year-old boy who his teachers suspect is being verbally abused by his father. Sam harbors much anger, but when his school counselor attempts to discuss this with him, he is unable to articulate his thoughts and feelings. As a means of allowing Sam to express himself nonverbally, Jane asks Sam to have an imaginary conversation with his father by playing on some percussion instruments she has set up. She encourages him to express in music what he cannot say in words. After a hesitant beginning, Sam is soon vigorously striking drums and cymbals as a way of unleashing his feelings of anger and resentment. The music he creates allows him to symbolize his feelings and this is a step toward his eventually being able to articulate these deeply personal feelings in words. As a means of nonverbal communication, music therapy has made it possible for Sam to begin sharing verbally that which was initially expressed symbolically in music.

Chapter 14: Phenomenology

The joy is in performing.

Seth is a classical guitarist. He teaches a wide variety of private students and performs recitals regularly. As much as he loves and values classical guitar repertoire, Seth's deeper passion is playing folk music on guitar, banjo, and ukulele with old-time ensembles every chance he gets. For him, the greatest value of music is not in the songs themselves, but in the active participation of both performers and audience members in a shared musical experience. He relishes the opportunity to 'get lost' in the music, when he is so into the experience that he loses track of time. Musicing, for Seth, is a whole-body experience. His feet tap the beat, his body sways, and his entire being is engaged in creating musical sounds. When the performance is over and Seth is on the way home, he can bask in the glow of an evening well spent. But for him, no 'after-the-fact' rumination can ever match those moments of pure ecstasy when he becomes one with his instrument and the music pours out effortlessly.

Chapter 15: Pragmatism

Having *an* experience.

"How was it, Mom and Dad?" Bill asked his parents, 74-year-old Pete and 68-year-old Greta. "Oh, it was the most wonderful experience," his mom answered. All the way from the airport to the coffee shop, Pete and Greta burbled on about the trip they had just taken with the New Horizons Band. This concert band, whose members are primarily senior citizens, with some younger adults and a few teenagers scattered among the ensemble, had just returned from performing a concert at a national AARP convention in Chicago. Weekly rehearsals, individual practice sessions at home, social bonding with old and new friends, planning sessions, traveling to the big city, eating out at fancy restaurants, staying in a huge downtown hotel, and, of course, the concert itself, all coalesced into a memorable, lifetime experience. In describing their adventure, it was hard for Pete and Greta to identify individual components that were more important than others. They viewed this special time as a singular event in their lives.

Chapter 16: Social Philosophy

Music saves people.

Kim is a violin major at the local university and Jeremy is a music education major. They assist several faculty members in an after-school music program held in a disadvantaged neighborhood. Students at this school are provided instruments and instruction for free. There are programs for beginners, intermediates, and advanced students, generally, but not always, consisting of elementary, middle school, and high school students, respectively. School administrators, teachers, and parents are excited about the program because during the five years since the program's inception they have seen absenteeism and behavioral programs decrease, and test scores and grades go up. Kim and Jeremy appreciate this, but they are even more impressed with what this is doing to the students' perceptions of self-worth and their belief in what they can accomplish with their lives. Historically, very few of the children from this neighborhood have gone to college. Even though the current program has only been in existence for a few years, several students have already gone on to college and many more are planning to do so. Making beautiful music is important and the teachers strive to help the students achieve musical excellence. But Kim and Jeremy are among those who see the real value of the program as a way to save lives. Even those who do not go to college will gain lifelong benefits from the experience of participating in the music program.

Chapter 17: Praxialism

Reflective musicing leads to self-growth.

Anna is a middle school choral and general music teacher. She loves her job and relishes each opportunity she has to work with her students. Her approach to the general music class is one of active music making. Students sing, play on classroom instruments, and listen to a wide variety of music. She is particularly proud of the special program she has developed using computers to teach composition. Her choirs, of course, are busy singing a wide variety of repertoire as well. One of the hallmarks of Anna's approach is the attention she pays to reflective thinking. To her, music-ing without reflection smacks of training more than education. She requires each student, both in classes and in ensembles, to keep a journal. Some of what students write is open-ended or free choice, but a significant portion is directed by rubrics. In addition to rubrics concerned with aspects of the music, students are encouraged to keep a log of their personal growth. In what ways do they see themselves changing? What new insights have they gained from the current classroom/rehearsal activities? Parents and other teachers have confirmed what the students themselves say: music has led them to a deeper awareness of themselves and others.

Chapter 18: Feminism

Half the world's population has something worthwhile to offer.

As a musicologist, LaTania's scholarly pursuit is on music composed and performed by women. She was unhappy in her previous position because she felt marginalized. The only time music of female composers appeared on recitals and concerts was either as a brief nod to allow token representation or on 'special' concerts featuring music composed and primarily performed by women. LaTania was thrilled when she assumed her new position and met Brad, a fellow musicologist. Brad shared her convictions and together they forged a strong alliance. Over time, music of women composers began to appear more frequently on programs simply because it was music that deserved to be heard. Their first breakthrough came when music submitted for a new music festival was blind reviewed. Several compositions by women composers were chosen solely on the basis of the quality of the music. From there, the concept spread and now the band, choir, orchestra, and jazz ensemble, as well as faculty and student recitalists, regularly perform the music of women composers on an equal footing with music written by the other half of the population.

Chapter 19: Postmodernism

All music has value.

Mark is a concert promoter and radio program announcer. He manages a number of venues in the community that collectively present a wide variety of concerts and programs. In the past year, he sponsored a summertime jazz series at a lakeside shed, a classical chamber music series with each concert in a different church or synagogue, an African gospel choir on a tour of the United States, an Indonesian gamelan ensemble, a Mexican Mariachi group, and four popular and country music groups. His radio show is called *Music for All* and in similar fashion features an eclectic mix of musical genres and styles. Each week's program focuses on a different type of music and includes live performances, interviews with artists, and recordings. A cynic might say that Mark's eclecticism is economically driven; that is, it is a purely a marketing strategy calculated to bring in the most dollars. Admittedly, Mark started out that way; he had no philosophical worldview, he was just out to make a living. In time, however, based on his own experiences and the feedback he has received from hundreds of patrons and listeners, he has come to understand that all music has value. Even if there are particular styles he is less keen on, he supports the notion that there are others who do respond passionately to that music, and who is he to deny their right to find pleasure in the music of their choice?

To reiterate, these vignettes are only intended to stimulate your thinking. How would you apply what you believe about the nature, meaning, and value of music to your own situation? Unlike the brevity of these examples, work for a rich, in-depth description of what difference your views will make as you perform, compose, teach, or listen to music. Imagine you could follow yourself around for a few days, taking notes on what you observe. Would any of your actions reflect your philosophical beliefs? Write your statement in first-person.

Notes

1 Felix Salzer, *Structural Hearing: Tonal Coherence in Music* (Mineola, NY: Dover, 1962).
2 Fred Lerdahl and Ray Jackendoff, *A Generative Theory of Tonal Music* (Cambridge, MA: The MIT Press, 1983).

22 Advocacy

Suppose you were asked to speak to the City Council about why they should vote to support the local symphony with public funds. If so, would you respond with an argument based on the fact that having a symphony is economically advantageous to the city because of increased parking revenues, restaurant receipts, and so on? Or, suppose local music teachers pleaded with you to speak to the school board about why they should vote 'no' on a proposal to cut funding for music in the schools. In this instance, would you respond by saying that student attendance rates are higher in schools with high-quality music programs? It just so happens that both arguments are based on evidence.[1] But does either argument rely on the kinds of values that are found in a music philosophy?

Although there can be, and often is, a relationship between music philosophy and music advocacy, they are not the same thing. Philosophy has been characterized as a search for truth, and advocacy as a means of persuading others to a particular point of view.[2] In this chapter, we will explore the role of advocacy and why you might or might not choose to rely on your philosophy when called upon to advocate for music.

What Is Advocacy?

Michael Mark said that

> Advocacy is the way that we as music educators can explain to policy makers, as well as to the general public, the reasons why our profession is important and why we need their support to continue serving the needs of society.[3]

Although this definition is particularized for music education, it can apply more broadly simply by changing the phrase 'music educators' to 'musicians.' In other words, any time we explain the value of music (of an opera company, of a church choir, of a community band, of a music program for a nursing home) to anyone (local, state, and federal agencies, administrators, or policy makers), we are advocating for music. We are trying to persuade others to understand the value of music in such a way that they will support our particular interests.

Why Is Advocacy Necessary?

Twenty-first century America seems oddly polarized when it comes to music. On the one hand, pop artists and even some classical musicians command amazingly high fees for their performances.

According to one website, the pop singer Beyoncé earns $54 million dollars per year[4] and Renée Fleming makes up to $20,000 per opera performance.[5] Even if these figures are to be taken with a grain of salt as approximations rather than certified figures, and understanding that such figures can fluctuate dramatically, it is probably a safe assumption to say that some musicians do extremely well from the standpoint of fame and fortune.

Another example of the way in which music is highly regarded in our society is the prevalence and popularity of music shows on television. *Glee*, a highly rated television show centered on a high school glee club, and the similar *High School Musical*, are two examples, along with such reality shows as *American Idol* and *The Voice*. Given the faddish nature of television show popularity, these shows may not be popular for long, but they have each had enormous popularity during their time.

That music has enormous popularity in our country is reflected in the overwhelming positive responses to various music surveys.

> According to a recent Gallup Poll conducted for NAMM, the International Music Products Association, 95% of Americans consider music to be part of a well-rounded education, and 93% feel that schools should offer music education as part of the regular curriculum. Nearly four in five (79%) even say that music education should be *mandated* for every student in school.[6]

In the same report, 88% of Americans said that music was a very important part of their lives. In another Gallup poll, 85% of Americans who do not play a musical instrument wish they did.[7] Overall, consumer arts spending, not specifically for music, was $150 billion in 2010 and music instrument sales amounted to $6.3 billion.[8]

The preceding examples will stand as support for the commonsense notion that music is extremely popular in the United States. This rosy picture is counterbalanced by dismal news at the other end of the spectrum. Many school districts have seen their music programs curtailed and professional orchestras and opera companies are struggling. According to a news report dated April 10, 2013, high school music programs in Ft. Collins, Colorado were in danger of being downsized. "Under a former and recent budget proposal, the school's music department was to lose one part-time choir teacher, all jazz and barbershop choirs and other opportunities. Public outcry over the 'devastating' cuts lead to discussions about what could be salvaged."[9] The famed Chicago Symphony Orchestra went on strike in 2012 and "the Philadelphia Orchestra emerged from Chapter 11 in July [2012]. Strikes and lockouts have lingered in Atlanta and Detroit. Others, like Boston and New York, have seen costs outpace revenues."[10] Also in 2012, Seattle Opera announced a million dollar shortfall in their operating budget.[11]

If music programs—amateur, non-profit, professional, public, and private—were thriving, there would be little or no need for advocacy. Quite simply, advocacy is necessary because even major high profile programs are facing severe financial challenges. Even where programs are flourishing or holding their own, advocacy efforts are necessary to avoid future problems. In the next few sections we will examine what not to do and what to do to promote music.

What Not to Do

One example of music advocacy gone awry is the 'music makes you smarter' movement of the 1990s. The precipitating event was the publication of a brief letter in *Nature* in 1993.[12] The authors described an experiment in which 36 college students completed spatial reasoning tasks following three different conditions: (1) after listening to ten minutes of Mozart's Sonata for Two Pianos in D major, K. 448;[13] ♪ (2) after listening to ten minutes of a relaxation tape; and (3) after ten minutes of silence. IQ scores following the Mozart condition were 119, compared to 111 for the relaxation tape and 110 in the silence condition. Because of the music used, this also became known as 'the Mozart Effect.'

From this study, and a few others, there was a flurry of activities promoting the influence of music on intelligence. For example, at one point, the governor of Georgia wanted the legislature to buy classical music CDs to give to all newborn babies to stimulate brain development.[14] In an article by Temple Grandin, Matthew Peterson, and one of the authors of the original study, Gordon Shaw, the authors drew the following conclusion:

> We strongly suggest that music education be present in our schools, preferably starting in preschool, to develop "hardware" for ST [spatial-temporal] reasoning in the child's brain. The absolutely crucial, but now neglected, role of ST reasoning in learning difficult math and science concepts must be explored and exploited.[15]

Note that the reason that music should be taught in schools is to develop nonmusical intellectual capacities. So egregious were some of these claims that another one of the authors of the original study refuted them, under a heading entitled "The Myth of the Mozart Effect."[16] A number of review articles have debunked the notion that simply listening to music, let alone one specific composition, will improve intelligence in any meaningful way.[17] The issue is much more nuanced than that.

In spite of the exaggerated claims of the 'music makes you smarter' movement, some research studies do indicate that music has a positive influence on nonmusical cognitive domains. So as not to get too far afield from the topic of advocacy, we will review only two of these studies. In one experiment, children who had completed three years of instrumental music training ($n = 41$) were compared to children in a control group ($n = 18$) who received general music instruction but neither instrumental training nor one-on-one music instruction.[18] The Instrumental Music (IM) group obtained higher scores on two near-transfer tasks closely related to music (melodic discrimination and fine motor skills in both hands) and two far-transfer tasks distantly related to music (vocabulary and nonverbal reasoning skills). The IM group did not outperform controls in tests of phonemic awareness or spatial skills.

In another study, elementary school students enrolled in exemplary music programs had higher English and mathematics standardized test scores than students enrolled in weaker music programs.[19] At the middle school level, music students (whether enrolled in exemplary or deficient music programs) fared better on standardized academic achievement tests than students who were not involved in music classes. From these results and those of others (e.g., see Kraus and colleagues),[20] it is clear that positions at either extreme—that music instruction has no effect on nonmusical domains or that music instruction ensures higher grades and test scores—are untenable. Those who wish to advocate for music need to provide a more nuanced picture of the effects of music instruction. Otherwise, the risk is that hyperbole will backfire and lead to a reduction in support from important constituents.

In 2012, the National Association for Music Education website posted this information (italics added):[21]

> The benefits of a high-quality classroom music experience are boundless:
>
> - The intellectual and technical skills developed through music education lead to more comprehensive brain development, which contributes to academic achievement in *other* areas, such as math and reading;
> - The honing of self expression and creativity, which not only helps keep students in school but also motivates them to work harder in *other* classes and assists them with becoming more actively involved in the community as adults;
> - Performance opportunities that encourage and nurture lifelong connections and an appreciation for the arts;
> - Enhanced *teamwork prowess, discipline, and problem solving skills*, all of which aid in molding better *employees* and *citizens*; and
> - A profoundly positive influence on students in disadvantaged communities.

Notice how frequently the role of music appears to be in support of nonmusical benefits and academic areas.

Even though the preceding information is not currently on the NAfME website, the current campaign called Broader Minded lists arguments in support of music education such as brain development, academic achievement (e.g., higher grade point averages, attendance, and graduation rates), inherent benefits (e.g., decision-making, grit, and multiple ways of knowing), and 21st-century skills (e.g., creativity, collaboration, and communication). Again, the argument is not that these are false statements or even that they should not be used in advocacy situations. Rather, the concern is for balance.

Bennett Reimer wrote about primary and secondary reasons for having music education in the schools.[22] Here, we will broaden his language slightly to include musical experiences of all kinds, such as symphony orchestras, opera companies, classical music radio stations, and church choirs. Primary reasons are those supporting the contention that music occupies a unique place in the human experience and that it is necessary for all human beings to be involved in music.

Secondary reasons include all the benefits of musical experiences that are not unique to music, such as developing self-confidence, leadership skills, school, church, or civic pride, and so on. In a school setting, students can develop leadership skills through many activities such as sports, the debate team, working on the yearbook, or serving in student government. For example, students in Harlem gained significant social and academic benefits from a newly instituted chess program.[23] Therefore, it is a weak argument to say that we need a music program in order for students to develop leadership skills. On the contrary, if we promote the value of a music program for primary reasons (i.e., based on your philosophy), secondary reasons can be included as value-added items.

Outside of school, some might encourage parents to enroll their children in private piano lessons so that the children will learn good time management skills. Others might encourage adults to join a church choir or a New Horizons Band because of the opportunity to forge strong social bonds. Some business people attend symphony concerts or opera performances because it is good to be seen in those settings. Likewise, they may support the local classical radio station because it is good advertising. However, we probably don't view time management, socializing, and advertising as the

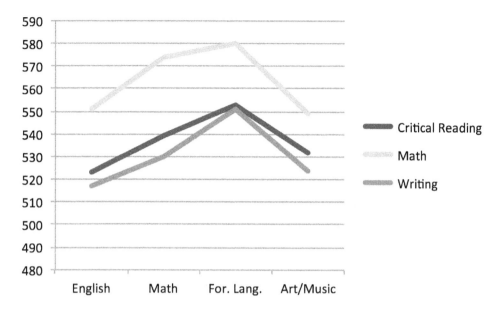

Figure 22.1 SAT scores among students with more than four years of study in English, mathematics, foreign language, or art/music

Image created by author

primary reasons why we should be involved in any of these musical activities. Thinking of as many items as possible to put on a 'secondary' list is a good strategy for advocacy, as long as primary reasons are kept in mind.

One should be aware, however, of creating a false basis for garnering support. Once it is shown that a particular claim is false (e.g., Music Makes You Smarter), support for music can be lost. Also, if the premise is that music is good for improving nonmusical aspects, then music is placed in a secondary position. Suppose, for example, we want to say that music improves math scores. Even if it did, students can improve math scores much more effectively by spending more time on math. Figure 22.1, for example, indicates that among students who have had more than four years of study in English, mathematics, foreign language, or art/music, SAT scores for art/music students were next to lowest in critical reading and writing, and lowest in math.[24] Total SAT scores placed art and music students (1,605) behind foreign language students (1,684), math (1,643), and ahead of English (1,591).

Strategies and Resources for Music Advocacy

In the opening paragraph, two advocacy rationales were given, along with the statement that there is evidence to support them. These rationales were based on economics and improved test scores. We will examine several economic arguments, followed by some examples of perceived benefits of music education.

Prevention Not Cure

Perhaps one of the best ways to promote music in any situation is to be ever vigilant and on the lookout for ways to secure support. Music advocates are like lobbyists.[25] In Washington, DC, lobbyists are constantly sniffing the prevailing political winds, monitoring the latest moods of Congress with regard to their particular interest. They do not wait until trouble arises; they constantly scan the far horizons and work to ensure that problems do not even have a chance to occur. They establish good working relationships with those who have power and influence over their interest.

Actually, there are music lobbyists. Many representatives from a broad cross section of arts organizations attend the national Arts Advocacy Day in Washington, DC.[26] One of the major efforts over the past few years has been garnering support to change STEM (science, technology, engineering, and math) into STEAM (science, technology, engineering, arts, and math). Currently, the co-chairs of the Congressional STEAM caucus are Rep. Suzanne Bonamici (D-OR) and Rep. Elise Stefanik (R-NY). In efforts such as these, music lobbyists aim to build relationships and support for music.

Music advocacy does not have to happen at the national level. In fact, since "all politics is local" (a phrase coined by former Speaker of the House Tip O'Neill), it is imperative that arts advocacy begins at home. A general strategy that has proved to be very beneficial is to get stake-holders involved in music. This could include such things as inviting a local sports figure or dignitary to conduct the community orchestra, giving the mayor a small, 'spear-carrying' role in an opera, or asking the school board president, superintendent, or principal to be involved in a musical production of some kind.

Economic Rationales in Music Advocacy

In 2008, the United States Conference of Mayors produced a report that contained this statement:

> The arts, humanities, and museums are critical to the quality of life and livability of America's cities. It has been shown that the nonprofit arts and culture industry generates over $166 billion in economic activity annually, supports over 5.7 million full time jobs, and returns over $12 billion in federal income taxes annually. Governments which support the arts on average see a return on investment of over $7 in taxes for every $1 that the government appropriates.[27]

More specific to music education, Dr. John Benham has developed the idea of Reverse Economics in which he uses district-wide numbers to show that eliminating music teachers actually increases costs.[28] This is because additional classroom teachers have to be hired to monitor the students who can no longer be accommodated in music classes. In one particular school district, for example, a proposal was made to eliminate instrumental music positions. Over 2,500 students were enrolled in bands and orchestras, grades 4–12. If the school district were to cut the music budget by $156,000, all the 4–6 instrumental students would be eliminated, with new students now beginning in the 7th grade.

As these students are no longer in band and orchestra (dropping to zero in year 5), new teachers would have to be hired to teach classes the students must now take. At the end of five years, 63 new classes would have to be added at a cost of $378,000. Thus, eliminating music teachers would not save the school district money; it more than doubles the expense. "Added to the anticipated savings of $156,000 this would have amounted to an annual budget miscalculation (reverse economic effect) of $534,000."[29] Based on these figures, the school board did not approve the proposal and none of the instrumental music positions were eliminated.

Economics certainly plays a major role in other music situations, such as professional orchestras. The presence of orchestras in local communities is financially beneficial. The three major orchestras in Chicago—the Chicago Symphony, Lyric Opera, and Grant Park—contributed a significant portion of the $2.3 billion generated by arts organizations in the city in 2012.[30] In 2008, the Boston Symphony, Boston Pops, and Tanglewood collectively contributed $166.7 million to the economy of Massachusetts.[31] On this basis, James Shanahan wrote an article in which he attempted to integrate the role of aesthetics in music and economics.[32]

Additional Resources

There are many sources for music advocacy, including articles and websites. Those listed here are a few samplings. Because websites change frequently, some of these may not be available, but it should be easy to search for additional sites.

Illustrative Articles for Music Advocacy:

Susan Hallam, "How to Advocate for Music: Personal Stories of Music Education Advocacy: The Power of Music," *International Journal of Music Education* 23, no. 2 (2005): 144–48.

W. Luksetich, "A Simultaneous Model of Nonprofit Symphony Orchestra Behavior," *Journal of Cultural Economics* 19, no. 1 (1995): 49–68.

Linda Lyons, "Americans Want Music Students to Play On," *Gallup*, 2003. http://www.gallup.com/poll/8434/Americans-Want-Music-Students-Play.aspx.

Marie McCarthy and J. Scott Goble, "Music Education Philosophy: Changing Times," *Music Educators Journal* 89 (2002): 19–26.

Bennett Reimer, "The Danger of Music Education Advocacy," *International Journal of Music Education* 23, no. 2 (2005): 139–42.

Selected Websites for Arts/Music Advocacy:

Americans for the Arts: http://ww3.artsusa.org
Arts Education Partnership: http://www.aep-arts.org
California Alliance for Arts Education: http://www.artsed411.org
Children's Music Workshop: http://www.childrensmusicworkshop.com/advocacy/
International Society for Music Education: http://www.isme.org/advocacy-articles
League of American Orchestras: http://americanorchestras.org
Mr. Holland's Opus Foundation: http://www.mhopus.org
Music Australia: http://musicaustralia.org.au/advocacy/
NAMM Foundation (National Association of Music Merchants): http://nammfoundation.org
National Association for Music Education (NA*f*ME): http://www.nafme.org/take-action/
NA*f*ME Broader Minded: http://www.broaderminded.com
VH1 Save the Music Foundation: http://www.vh1.com/partners/save_the_music/

Summary and Thought Questions

Music advocacy can be based strongly on a music philosophy or it may rely more on expedient issues. There are several risks associated with advocating strictly on the basis of a philosophical view, including: (a) Explaining a philosophy completely may take too long. You may lose your audience. (b) A fully developed philosophy may be too difficult and complicated for a lay audience to grasp in a relatively short presentation. You may confuse your constituents. (c) Relying solely on primary reasons and leaving out secondary ones may rob you of some persuasive arguments. You may end up 'cutting off your nose to spite your face.'

There are also risks associated with abandoning your philosophy and advocating solely on the basis of secondary reasons: (a) If you are successful in advocating on the basis of secondary reasons, your primary reasons may have no credibility with your stake-holders. For example, a school music program that gains support because of a promise that it will raise test scores may not be perceived as having any value in and of itself. (b) If a secondary reason turns out not to be true, then there is no support for the unstated primary values. For example, if a financial study indicates that the presence of the local symphony did not increase sales revenues among area restaurants, some could make the argument that it is not necessary to support the symphony.

The most effective strategy should be to ground your argument on primary reasons but to incorporate secondary ones whenever they might be useful. Be aware of your stake-holders and plan your presentation, whether given verbally or in writing, to clarify the most important reasons why they should support your program. To help you do this, here are some thought questions:

1. In your mind, what are the main differences between a music philosophy and a music advocacy position?
2. Thinking about the need for advocacy, do you think the position of music is generally improving in American society, weakening, or holding its own?
3. More specifically than the previous question, what is the status of music in your particular domain (e.g., professional orchestra, opera company, private lessons, university teacher, public school music educator, church choir director, music therapist, and so on)? Strong and thriving? Weak and in danger of disappearing?
4. Based on the 'what not to do' section, can you think of anything you have been doing or done in the past that you might want to stop or modify?
5. Based on prevention suggestions, can you identify some advocacy approaches you have taken that have been effective in enhancing your professional success?
6. What are the economic realities of your particular musical domain? How do you see the long-term future in terms of economic viability for your current professional career path?
7. List the top three primary and top three secondary reasons why someone should support your music program or endeavor.
8. An elevator speech is a brief summary of a sales pitch that typically lasts only 30 seconds or at the most only a minute or two. Craft an elevator speech that emphasizes the main points you would want your audience to grasp.

Final Comments

The journey from the first chapter to here has been filled with a very large number of thoughts coming from almost every direction conceivable. At this point, you may feel that the fog is lifting and that you are beginning to have a firm grasp on your music philosophy. Contrarily, you may still feel overwhelmed with all the choices and possibilities. Either way, it will be important for you to continue to read, think, write, and talk about these issues throughout your career. A philosophy should be a 'living' thing, not static. As you grow and change and your circumstances change, your philosophy will need to stay abreast of those changes.

Now that you have done all this work, please do not let your philosophy sit on a shelf gathering dust. Use it. Let it help you make thoughtful decisions. Let it help you remember why you do what you do. Having a clearly articulated philosophy will help you withstand the inevitable stresses and strains that we all go through from time to time. Ideally, it will also be a source of joy as you remember why music has value for you and those with whom you work.

Notes

1 Americans for the Arts. Arts & Economic Prosperity IV, 2015. http://www.americansforthearts.org/by-program/reports-and-data/research-studies-publications/arts-economic-prosperity-iv/national-findings. National Association for Music Education. Music Education and Successful Schools, 2015. http://www.nafme.org/take-action/what-to-know/all-research/.

2 Wayne Bowman, "To What Question(s) Is Music Education Advocacy the Answer?" *International Journal of Music Education* 23, no. 2 (2005): 125–29.

3 Michael Mark, "A History of Music Education Advocacy," *Music Educators Journal* 89, no. 1 (2002): 44.

4 "Beyoncé Knowles," *Mywage.org*, 2015. http://www.mywage.org/zimbabwe/main/salary/vip-celebrities-pay/musicians-pay.

5 "Opera Singers' Income," *Opera Lively* (September 2, 2012). http://operalively.com/forums/showthread.php/1190-Opera-singers-income.

6 Linda Lyons, "Americans Want Music Students to Play On," *Gallup*, 2003. http://www.gallup.com/poll/8434/Americans-Want-Music-Students-Play.aspx.

7 "New Gallup Survey by NAMM Reflects Majority of Americans Agree with Many Benefits of Playing Musical Instruments," National Association of Music Merchants, 2009. https://www.namm.org/news/press-releases/new-gallup-survey-namm-reflects-majority-americans.

8 Arts Index. National Arts Index, 2013. http://www.artsindexusa.org/national-arts-index.

9 Madeline Novey, "FCHS Cuts a Symptom of Bigger Challenges," Coloradoan.com (April 10, 2013). http://www.coloradoan.com/article/20130409/NEWS01/304090045/Fort-Collins-High-School-cuts-symptom-bigger-budget-challenges.

10 Heather Gillers and Jason Grotto, "Chicago Symphony Orchestra Strike Reflects Deeper Financial Woes," *Chicago Tribune* (October 17, 2012). http://articles.chicagotribune.com/2012-10-17/news/ct-met-cso-finances-20121007_1_cso-bass-player-chicago-symphony-orchestra-riccardo-muti.

11 Brendan Kiley, "Seattle Opera Anticipates $1 Million Budget Shortfall," *SLOG News and Arts* (June 26, 2012). http://slog.thestranger.com/slog/archives/2012/06/26/seattle-opera-anticipates-1-million-budget-shortfall.

12 Frances Rauscher, Gordon Shaw, and Catherine Ky, "Music and Spatial Task Performance," *Nature* 365 (1993): 611.

13 Wolfgang Mozart, Sonata for Two Pianos in D Major, K. 448, performed by Murray Perahia and Radu Lupu, https://www.youtube.com/watch?v=v58mf-PB8as.

14 Kevin Sack, "Georgia's Governor Seeks Musical Start for Babies," *The New York Times* (January 15, 1998). http://www.nytimes.com/1998/01/15/us/georgia-s-governor-seeks-musical-start-for-babies.html.

15 Temple Grandin, Matthew Peterson, and Gordon Shaw, "Spatial-Temporal versus Language-Analytic Reasoning: The Role of Music Training," *Arts Education Policy Review* 99, no. 6 (1998): 13.

16 James Catterall and Frances Rauscher, "Unpacking the Impact of Music on Intelligence," in *Neurosciences in Music Pedagogy*, ed. Wilfried Gruhn and Frances Rauscher (New York: Nova Biomedical Books, 2007), 169–98.

17 Steven Demorest and Steven Morrison, "Does Music Make You Smarter?" *Music Educators Journal* 87, no. 2 (2000): 17–22. Donald Hodges, "Does Music *Really* Make You Smarter?" *Southwestern Musician* 67, no. 9 (1999): 28–33. E. Glenn Schellenberg and Michael Weiss, "Music and Cognitive Abilities," in *The Psychology of Music, 3rd ed.*, ed. Diana Deutsch (Amsterdam: Elsevier, 2013), 499–550.

18 Marie Forgeard, Ellen Winner, Andrea Norton, and Gottfried Schlaug, "Practicing a Musical Instrument in Childhood Is Associated with Enhanced Verbal Ability and Nonverbal Reasoning," *PLoS ONE* 3, no. 10 (2008): 1–8.

19 Christopher Johnson and Jenny Memmott, "Examination of Relationships between Participation in School Music Programs of Differing Quality and Standardized Test Results," *Journal of Research in Music Education* 54, no. 4 (2006): 293–307.

20 Nina Kraus and colleagues at Northwestern University have published a number of studies concerning the effects of music instruction on language skills. Available from http://www.brainvolts.northwestern.edu/projects/music/index.php.

21 "Music Education: Core to Orchestrating Success." *American Orff-Schulwerk Association*, accessed on June 24, 2016, http://aosa.org/resources/music-education-policy-roundtable/music-education-core-to-orchestrating-success/.

22 Bennett Reimer, *A Philosophy of Music Education, 2nd ed.* (Englewood Cliffs, NJ: Prentice-Hall, 1989).

23 Jo Coudert, "From Street Kids to Royal Knights," *Reader's Digest* (June 1989). https://www.chesshouse.com/from_street_kids_to_royal_knights_a/110.htm.

24 "College-Bound Seniors Total Group Profile Report, 2014," *The College Board*. https://secure-media.collegeboard.org/digitalServices/pdf/sat/TotalGroup-2014.pdf.

25 Michael Mark, "Why Does Our Profession Need Advocacy?" *International Journal of Music Education* 23, no. 2 (2005): 95–98.

26 "Arts Advocacy Day," *Americans for the Arts* (2015). http://www.americansforthearts.org/events/arts-advocacy-day.

27 "Strong Cities . . . Strong Families . . . For a Strong America. Mayors' 10-point Plan," *League of American Orchestras* (2008). http://usmayors.org/pressreleases/documents/10-PointPlan_1107.pdf.

28 John Benham, *Music Advocacy: Moving from Survival to Vision* (Lanham, MD: Rowman and Littlefield Education, 2011).

29 Ibid., 156.

30 John von Rhein, "Message to Symphony Orchestras in Troubled Times: Think Positive," *Chicago Tribune* (August 22, 2012). http://articles.chicagotribune.com/2012–08–22/entertainment/ct-ent-0822-classical-icsom-20120822_1_orchestras-symphony-musicians-opera-musicians.

31 "Boston Symphony Orchestra Generates More Than $166 Million Annually in Statewide Economic Activity, According to New Study by Mount Auburn Associations," *BusinesWire* (June 6, 2008). http://www.businesswire.com/news/home/20080606005632/en/Boston-Symphony-Orchestra-Generates-166-Million-Annually.

32 James Shanahan, "The Consumption of Music: Integrating Aesthetics and Economics," *Journal of Cultural Economics* 29, no. 2 (1978): 13–26.

Bibliography

Aarden, Bret. "Dynamic Melodic Expectancy." Ph.D. dissertation, Ohio State University, 2003. http://rave.ohiolink.edu/etdc/view?acc_num=osu1060969388.

Abeles, Harold. "Are Musical Instrument Gender Associations Changing?" *Journal of Research in Music Education* 57, no. 2 (2009): 127–39.

Abeles, Harold, Charles Hoffer, and Robert Klotman. *Foundations of Music Education, 2nd ed*. New York: Schirmer Books, 1994.

Abeles, Harold, and Susan Porter. "The Sex-Stereotyping of Musical Instruments." *Journal of Research in Music Education* 26, no. 2 (1978): 65–75.

Abell, Arthur. *Talks with Great Composers*. New York: Philosophical Library, 1955.

"About El Sistema." Cal Performances, University of California, Berkeley, SchoolTime Study Guide, 2012–2013 Season: https://calperformances.org/learn/k-12/pdf/2012/Dudamel_SBOoV_Study_Guide_Revised_4.pdf.

Abraham, Gerald. *The Concise Oxford History of Music*. Oxford: Oxford University Press, 1985.

Abril, Carlos. "Toward a More Culturally Responsive General Music Education." *General Music Today* 27, no. 1 (2013): 6–11.

Adorno, Theodor. *Philosophy of Modern Music*. Translated by Anne Mitchell and Wesley Blomster. New York: Continuum International Publishing, 1948/2004.

———. *Essays on Music*. Selected, with introduction and notes by Richard Leppert. Translated by Susan Gillespie. Berkeley, CA: University of California Press, 2002.

Allen, Michael, John Geringer, and Rebecca MacLeod. "Performance Practice of Violin Vibrato: An Artist-Level Case Study." *Journal of String Research* 4 (2009): 27–38.

Alperson, Philip. "What Should One Expect from a Philosophy of Music Education?" *Journal of Aesthetic Education* 25, no. 3 (1991): 215–42.

———. "Robust Praxialism and the Anti-aesthetic Turn." *Philosophy of Music Education Review* 18, no. 2 (2010): 171–93.

Americans for the Arts, 2015. http://ww3.artsusa.org.

Americans for the Arts. Arts & Economic Prosperity IV, 2015. http://www.americansforthearts.org/by-program/reports-and-data/research-studies-publications/arts-economic-prosperity-iv/national-findings.

Anderson, Richard. "From Calliope's Sisters." In *Aesthetics: The Big Questions*, Edited by Carolyn Korsmeyer, 19–33. Malden, MA: Blackwell, 1998.

Andrew, Mary. "Schumann's *Frauenliebe und -Leben*: A Feminist Dilemma?" *Journal of Singing—The Official Journal of the National Association of Teachers of Singing* 54, no. 1 (1997): 7–10.

Anselm, St. *Proslogion (Discourse on the Existence of God)*. Translated by Sidney Deane, 1078/1903. http://www.fordham.edu/halsall/basis/anselm-proslogium.asp#CHAPTER%20XV.

Aquinas, Thomas. *Summa Contra Gentiles, Book I*. Translated by Joseph Rickaby, 1264. http://www.basilica.org/pages/ebooks/St.%20Thomas%20Aquinas-The%20Summa%20Contra%20Gentiles.pdf.

———. *Summa Theologica*, Translated by Fathers of the English Dominican Province, 1265–75/1947. http://www.basilica.org/pages/ebooks/St.%20Thomas%20Aquinas-Summa%20Theologica.pdf.

Aristotle. *Politics: A Treatise on Government*. Translated by William Ellis. New York: E.P. Dutton, 350 BC/1928.

Armstrong, Louis. "Jazz is a Language." In *They Talk about Music, Vol. 2*, Edited by Robert Cumming, 128–29. Rockville Centre, NY: Belwin/Mills, 1971.

"Arts Advocacy Day." Americans for the Arts (2015). http://www.americansforthearts.org/events/arts-advocacy-day.

Arts Education Partnership, 2015. http://www.aep-arts.org.

Arts Index. 2013 National Arts Index. www.artsindexusa.org/national-arts-index.

Attali, Jacques. *Noise: The Political Economy of Music*. Translated by Brian Massumi. Manchester, UK: Manchester University Press, 1985.

Augustine, St. *Confessions*. Translated by Albert Outler, 398/1994. http://www.fordham.edu/halsall/basis/confessions-bod.asp.

———. *The City of God*. Translated by Marcus Dods. New York: C. Scribner, 413/1871.

Ausubel, David. "The Use of Advance Organizers in the Learning and Retention of Meaningful Verbal Material." *Journal of Educational Psychology* 51, no. 1 (1960): 267–72.

Aylesworth, Gary. "Postmodernism." *The Stanford Encyclopedia of Philosophy* (2015 edition), Edited by Edward Zalta. http://plato.stanford.edu/archives/win2010/entries/postmodernism/.

Bamberger, Joan. "The Myth of Matriarchy: Why Men Rule in Primitive Society." In *Women, Culture and Society*, Edited by Michelle Rosaldo and Louise Lamphere, 263–80. Stanford, CA: Stanford University Press, 1974.

Bangert, Marc, Thomas Peschel, Gottfried Schlaug, Michael Rotte, Dieter Drescher, Hermann Hinrichs, Hans-Jochen Heinze, and Eckart Altenmüller. "Shared Networks for Auditory and Motor Processing in Professional Pianists: Evidence from fMRI Conjunction." *NeuroImage* 30 (2006): 917–26.

Barenboim, Daniel. *Music Quickens Time*. London: Verso Books, 2008.

Batteux, Abbé. "The Fine Arts Reduced to a Single Principle." In *Aesthetics*, Edited by Susan Feagin and Patrick Maynard and Translated by Robert Walters, 102–4. Oxford: Oxford University Press, 1746/1997.

Baugh, Bruce. "Prolegomena to Any Aesthetics of Rock Music." *The Journal of Aesthetics and Art Criticism* 51, no. 1 (1993): 23–29.

———. "Music for the Young at Heart." *The Journal of Aesthetics and Art Criticism* 53, no. 1 (1995): 81–83.

Beardsley, Monroe. *Aesthetics*. New York: Harcourt, Brace & World, 1958.

———. *Aesthetics from Classical Greece to the Present*. Tuscaloosa, AL: The University of Alabama Press, 1966.

———. "The Instrumentalist Theory of Aesthetic Value." In *Introductory Readings in Aesthetics*, Edited by John Hospers, 308–19. New York: The Free Press, 1969.

———. *The Possibility of Criticism*. Detroit: Wayne State University, 1970.

———. "Semiotic Aesthetics and Aesthetic Education." *Journal of Aesthetic Education* 9, no. 3 (1975): 5–26.

———. "In Defense of Aesthetic Value." *Proceedings and Addresses of the American Philosophical Association* 52, no. 6 (1979): 723–49.

———. *Aesthetics: Problems in the Philosophy of Criticism, 2nd ed.* Indianapolis: Hackett, 1981.

Bélis, Annie. "Aulos." In *Grove Music Online. Oxford Music Online*, 2012. http://www.oxfordmusiconline.com/subscriber/article/grove/music/01532.

Bell, Clive. *Art*. New York: Frederick A. Stokes Co., 1913.

———. "Significant Form." In *Introductory Readings in Aesthetics*, Edited by John Hospers, 87–99. New York: The Free Press, 1913/1969.

Benham, John. *Music Advocacy: Moving from Survival to Vision*. Lanham, MD: Rowman and Littlefield Education, 2011.

Bennett, Dawn. *Understanding the Classical Music Profession: The Past, the Present and Strategies for the Future*. Burlington, VT: Ashgate Publishing, 2008.

Bentley, Eric, Editor. *Shaw on Music: A Selection from the Music Criticism of Bernard Shaw*. Garden City, NY: Doubleday, 1955.

Bergonzi, Louis. "Sexual Orientation and Music Education: Continuing a Tradition." *Music Educators Journal* 96, no. 2 (2009): 21–25.

Berlin Philharmonic Roster, accessed January 25, 2014. http://www.berliner-philharmoniker.de/en/orchestra/.

Berlyne, Daniel. *Aesthetics and Psychobiology*. New York: Appleton-Century-Crofts, 1971.

———, Editor. *Studies in the New Experimental Aesthetics: Steps Toward an Objective Psychology of Aesthetic Appreciation*. Washington, DC: Hemisphere Publishing, 1974.

Bernstein, Jay. "Adorno, Theodor Wiesengrund (1903–69)." In *Routledge Encyclopedia of Philosophy, Version 1.0*, Edited by Edward Craig, 48–52. London and New York: Routledge, 1998.

Bernstein, Leonard. *The Infinite Variety of Music*. New York: Simon and Schuster, 1966.

Besmer, Fremont. *Horses, Musicians, & Gods: The Hausa Cult of Possession-Trance*. Zaria, Nigeria: Ahmadu Bello University Press, 1983.

Bigand, Emmanuel, and Bénédicte Poulin-Charronat. "Tonal Cognition." In *The Oxford Handbook of Music Psychology*, Edited by Susan Hallam, Ian Cross, and Michael Thaut, 59–71. Oxford, UK: Oxford University Press, 2009.

Birge, Edward. *History of Public School Music in the United States*. Washington, DC: Music Educators National Conference, 1928.

Birkhoff, George. *Aesthetic Measure*. Cambridge, MA: Harvard University Press, 1933.

Bispham, David. *A Quaker Singer's Recollections*. New York: Macmillan, 1920.

Blacking, John. *How Musical Is Man?* Seattle: University of Washington Press, 1973.

Boethius, Anicius. *Fundamentals of Music*. Edited by Claude Palisca and Translated by Calvin Bower. New Haven, CT: Yale University Press, 1989.

Bogin, Magda. *The Women Troubadours*. New York: W.W. Norton, 1980.

Bonner, Stanley. *Education in Ancient Rome*. New York: Routledge, 2012.

Borges, Jorge. *The Aleph and Other Stories*. New York: Penguin Books, 2004.

Bosanquet, Bernard. *The Introduction to Hegel's Philosophy of Fine Art*, Translated by Bernard Bosanquet. London: Kegan Paul, Trench, Trübner, 1905.

"Boston Symphony Orchestra Generates More Than $166 Million Annually in Statewide Economic Activity, According to New Study by Mount Auburn Associations." *Business Wire* (June 6, 2008). http://www.busnesswire.com/news/home/20080606005632/en/Boston-Symphony-Orchestra-Generates-166-Million-Annually.

Bourdillon, Francis. "The Night Has a Thousand Eyes." In *A Victorian Anthology, 1837–1895*, Edited by Edmund Stedman, 533. Cambridge: Riverside Press, 1895.

Bower, Calvin. *Boethius' The Principles of Music: An Introduction, Translation, and Commentary*. Nashville, TN: George Peabody College for Teachers, 1966.

Bowman, Wayne. *Philosophical Perspectives on Music*. New York: Oxford University Press, 1998.

———. "The Limits and Grounds of Musical Praxialism." In *Praxial Music Education*, Edited by David Elliott, 52–78. Oxford, UK: Oxford University Press, 2005.

———. "Why Musical Performance?" In *Praxial Music Education*, Edited by David Elliott, 142–64. Oxford, UK: Oxford University Press, 2005.

———. "To What Question(s) Is Music Education Advocacy the Answer?" *International Journal of Music Education* 23, no. 2 (2005): 125–29.

———. "Music's Place in Education." In *The Oxford Handbook of Music Education*, Edited by Gary McPherson and Graham Welch, 21–39. Oxford, UK: Oxford University Press, 2012.

Bradley, Deborah. "Good for What, Good for Whom?: Decolonizing Music Education Philosophies." In *The Oxford Handbook of Philosophy in Music Education*, Edited by Wayne Bowman and Ana Lucía Frega, 409–33. New York: Oxford University Press, 2012.

Brand, Manny. "Relationship Between Home Musical Environment and Selected Musical Attributes of Second-Grade Children." *Journal of Research in Music Education* 34, no. 2 (1986): 112–20.

Brennan, Brian. "Augustine's *De Musica*." *Vigiliae Christianae* 42, no. 3 (1988) 267–81.

Briscoe, James, Editor. *New Historical Anthology of Music by Women*. Bloomington, IN: Indiana University Press, 2004.

Broadie, Alexander. "Aquinas, St. Thomas." In *The Oxford Guide to Philosophy*, Edited by Ted Honderich, 45–48. Oxford, UK: Oxford University Press, 2005.

Broudy, Harry. "A Realistic Philosophy of Music Education." In *Basic Concepts in Music Education: The Fifty-seventh Yearbook of the National Society for the Study of Education*, Edited by Nelson Henry, 62–87. Chicago: University of Chicago Press, 1958.

Broyd, Samantha, Charmaine Demanuele, Stefan Debener, Suzannah Helps, Christopher James, and Edmund Sonuga-Barke. "Default-mode Brain Dysfunction in Mental Disorders: A Systematic Review." *Neuroscience & Biobehavioral Reviews* 33, no. 3 (2009): 279–96.

Bruner, Jerome. *On Knowing: Essays for the Left Hand*. New York: Atheneum, 1969.

Bryant, David. "The 'cori spezzati' of St. Mark's: Myth and Reality." *Early Music History* 1 (1981): 165–86.

Budd, Malcolm. *Music and the Emotions: The Philosophical Theories*. London: Routledge and Kegan Paul, 1985.

Budiansky, Stephen. "The Kids Play Great, but That Music . . ." *Washington Post* (Saturday, January 30, 2005); Page B03. http://www.washingtonpost.com/wp-dyn/articles/A46383–2005Jan29.html.

———. "The Repertoire *Is* the Curriculum: Getting Back to the Basics in Music Education." Paper based on a talk presented to the World Association of Symphonic Bands and Ensembles, Cincinnati, OH (July 10, 2009). http://www.budiansky.com/MUSIC.html.

———. *Talk to the College Band Directors National Association, Eastern Division*. West Chester, PA (March 13, 2010). http://www.budiansky.com/MUSIC.html.

Budiansky, Stephen, and Timothy Foley. "The Quality of Repertoire in School Music Programs: Literature Review, Analysis, and Discussion." *Journal of the World Association for Symphonic Bands and Ensembles* 12 (2005): 17–39.

Bukhofzer, Manfred. *Music in the Barqoque Era*. New York: W. W. Norton, 1947.

Bullmore, Ed, and Olaf Sporns. "Complex Brain Networks: Graph Theoretical Analysis of Structural and Functional Systems." *Nature Reviews Neuroscience* 10 (2009): 186–98.

Burkholder, J. Peter, Donald Grout, and Claude Palisca. *A History of Western Music, 7th ed.* New York: W.W. Norton, 2006.

Burn, Andrew. *Niceta of Remesiana: His Life and Works*. Cambridge, UK: Cambridge University Press, 1905.

Burnham, Douglas. "Immanuel Kant: Aesthetics." *Internet Encyclopedia of Philosophy* (2005). http://www.iep.utm.edu/kantaest/.

Burrows, David. *Time and the Warm Body: A Musical Perspective on the Construction of Time*. Leiden, The Netherlands: Brill, 2007.

Burt, Cyril, Editor. *How the Mind Works*. New York: D. Appleton-Century Co., 1934.

Burton-Hill, Clemency. "West-Eastern Divan Orchestra: Uniting Arabs, Israelis." *BBC Culture* (August 22, 2014). http://www.bbc.com/culture/story/20140822-music-uniting-arabs-and-israelis.

Buszin, Walter. "Luther on Music." *The Musical Quarterly* 32, no. 1 (1946): 80–97.

Butler, Abigail, Vicki Lind, and Constance McKoy. "Equity and Access in Music Education: Conceptualizing Culture as Barriers to and Supports for Music Learning." *Music Education Research* 9, no. 2 (2007): 241–53.

Byong-ki, Hwang. "Aesthetic Characteristics of Korean Music in Theory and in Practice." *Asian Music* 9, no. 2 (1978): 29–40.

Byrd, Jeffrey, and John Fritch. "Forever Ephemeral: John Cage's ASLSP." *Performance Research: A Journal of the Performing Arts* 17, no 5 (2012): 5–8.

California Alliance for Arts Education, 2011: http://www.artsed411.org

Campbell, Patricia, Claire Connell, and Amy Beegle. "Adolescents' Expressed Meanings of Music in and out of School." *Journal of Research in Music Education* 55, no. 3 (2007): 220–36.

Carroll, Noël. *A Philosophy of Mass Art*. Oxford, UK: Clarendon Press, 1998.

———. *Philosophy of Art*. New York: Routledge, 1999.

———. "Formalism." In *The Routledge Companion to Aesthetics*, Edited by Berys Gaut and Dominic Lopes, 87–96. London: Routledge, 2002.

Carter, Curtis. "Sculpture." In *The Routledge Companion to Aesthetics*, Edited by Berys Gaut and Dominic Lopes, 503–17. London: Routledge, 2002.

Catterall, James, and Frances Rauscher. "Unpacking the Impact of Music on Intelligence." In *Neurosciences in Music Pedagogy*, Edited by Wilfried Gruhn and Frances Rauscher, 169–98. New York: Nova Biomedical Books, 2007.

Chamberlain, David. "Philosophy of Music in the *Consolatio* of Boethius." *Speculum* 45, no. 1 (1970): 80–97.

Chase, Gilbert. "John Cage." In *The International Cyclopedia of Music and Musicians, 11th ed.*, Edited by Oscar Thompson, 336–38. New York: Dodd, Mead and Co., 1989.

Cheah, Elena. *An Orchestra Beyond Borders: Voices of the West-Eastern Divan Orchestra*. London: Verso Books, 2009.

Cheslock, L. "An Introductory Study of the Violin Vibrato." *Research Studies in Music* 1 (1931). Baltimore: Peabody Conservatory.

Child, Jr., William. "Monroe Beardsley's Three Criteria for Aesthetic Value: A Neglected Resource in the Evaluation of Recent Music." *Journal of Aesthetic Education* 34, no. 2 (2000): 49–63.

Children's Music Workshop, accessed December 20, 2015. http://www.childrensmusicworkshop.com/advocacy/.

Choate, Robert, Editor. *Documentary Report of the Tanglewood Symposium: Music in American Society*. Washington, DC: Music Educators National Conference, 1968.

Chomsky, Noam. *Chomsky on Miseducation*. Edited by Donaldo Macdeo. Lanham, MD: Rowman & Littlefield, 2000.

Churchland, Paul. *Neurophilosophy at Work*. Cambridge: Cambridge University Press, 2007.

Citron, Marcia. "Felix Mendelssohn's Influence on Fanny Mendelssohn Hensel as a Professional Composer." *Current Musicology* 37, no. 8 (1984): 9–17.

———. "Gender and the Field of Musicology." *Current Musicology* 53 (1993): 66–75.

———. *Gender and the Musical Canon*. Cambridge, UK: Press Syndicate, 1993.

———. "Feminist Approaches to Musicology." In *Cecilia Reclaimed: Feminist Perspectives on Gender and Music*, Edited by Susan Cook and Judy Tsou, 15–34. Urbana, IL: University of Illinois Press, 1994.

Clifton, Thomas. *Music as Heard: A Study in Applied Phenomenology*. New Haven, CT: Yale University Press, 1983.

CNN Staff. "Report: Jailed Pussy Riot Members Seek Community Service in Russia" (August 23, 2013). http://www.cnn.com/2013/08/23/world/europe/russia-pussy-riot.

Cochrane, Tom. "Music, Emotions and the Influence of the Cognitive Sciences." *Philosophy Compass* 5, no. 11 (2010): 978–88.

Cohen, L. Jonathan. "Philosophy and Science." In *The Oxford Companion to Philosophy*, Edited by Ted Honderich, 674–78. Oxford: Oxford University Press, 1995.

"College-Bound Seniors Total Group Profile Report, 2014." *The College Board*. https://secure-media.college-board.org/digitalServices/pdf/sat/TotalGroup-2014.pdf.

Collier, Geoffrey. "Beyond Valence and Activity in the Emotional Connotations of Music." *Psychology of Music* 35, no. 1 (2007): 110–31.

Collingwood, R. G. *The Principles of Art*. Oxford, UK: Oxford University Press, 1958.

Cone, Edward. *The Composer's Voice. Ernest Bloch Lectures*. Berkeley: University of California Press, 1974.

Cook, Nicholas. "Theorizing Musical Meaning." *Music Theory Spectrum* 23, no. 2 (2001): 170–95.

Cook, Scott. "'Yue Ji' 樂記—*Record of Music*: Introduction, Translation, Notes, and Commentary." *Asian Music* 26, no. 2 (1995): 1–96.

Cooke, Deryck. *The Language of Music*. Oxford: Oxford University Press, 1963.

Cottingham, John. "Faith." In *Western Philosophy*, Edited by David Papineau, 108–31. New York: Metro Books, 2009.

Coudert, Jo. "From Street Kids to Royal Knights." *Reader's Digest* (June 1989). https://www.chesshouse.com/from_street_kids_to_royal_knights_a/110.htm.

Crane, Tim. "Hegel." In *Western Philosophy*, Edited by David Papineau, 30. New York: Metro Books, 2009.

Crispino, Enrica. *Michelangelo*. Translated by Silvia Silvestri. Florence: Giunti, 2001.

Croce, Benedetto. "The Breviary of Aesthetic." *The Rice Institute Pamphlet* XLVII, no. 4 (Houston, TX: Rice University, 1961).

———. *Guide to Aesthetics*. Translated by Patrick Romanell. New York: Bobbs-Merrill, 1965.

Cross, Ian. "The Evolutionary Nature of Musical Meaning." *Musicae Scientiae*, Special Issue: Music and Evolution (2009): 179–200.

Cross, Ian, and Elizabeth Tolbert. "Music and Meaning." In *The Oxford Handbook of Music Psychology*, Edited by Susan Hallam, Ian Cross, and Michael Thaut, 24–34. Oxford: Oxford University Press, 2009.

Curd, Martin, and J. A. Cover. *Philosophy of Science: The Central Issues*. New York: W.W. Norton, 1998.

Currie, Gregory. "Aesthetics and Cognitive Science." In *The Oxford Handbook of Aesthetics*, Edited by Jerrold Levinson, 706–21. Oxford UK: Oxford University Press, 2003.

Cusick, Suzanne. "Gender and the Cultural Work of a Classical Music Performance." *Repercussions* 3, no. 1 (1994): 77–110.

———. "Gender, Musicology, and Feminism." In *Rethinking Music*, Edited by Nick Cook and Mark Everist, 471–98. New York: Oxford University Press, 1999.

Cutietta, Robert, and Sandra Stauffer. "Listening Reconsidered." In *Praxial Music Education*, Edited by David Elliott, 123–41. Oxford, UK: Oxford University Press, 2005.

Damasio, Antonio. *Descartes' Error: Emotion, Reason, and the Human Brain*. New York: Avon Books, 1994.

———. *The Feeling of What Happens: Body and Emotion in the Making of Consciousness*. New York: Harcourt Brace, 1999.

———. *Looking for Spinoza: Joy, Sorrow, and the Feeling Brain*. New York: Harcourt Brace, 2003.

Daniels, Charles. "Tolstoy and Corrupt Art." *Journal of Aesthetic Education* 8, no. 4 (1974): 41–49.

Darrow, Alice-Ann. "Culturally Responsive Teaching: Understanding Disability Culture." *General Music Today* 26, no. 3 (2013): 32–34.

Davidson, George. "Introduction." In *Philosophy: The World's Great Thinkers*, Edited by Philip Stokes, 4–5. London: Arcturus Publishing, 2011.

Davies, Stephen. *Musical Meaning and Expression*. Ithaca, NY: Cornell University Press, 1994.

———. "Rock versus Classical Music." *The Journal of Aesthetics and Art Criticism* 57, no. 2 (1999): 193–204.

———. "Definitions of Art." In *The Routledge Companion to Aesthetics*, Edited by Berys Gaut and Dominic Lopes, 169–79. London: Routledge, 2002.

———. "Profundity in Instrumental Music." *British Journal of Aesthetics* 42, no. 4 (2002): 343–56.

———. "'John Cage's 4'33': Is It Music?" In *Themes in the Philosophy of Music*, Edited by Stephen Davies, 11–29. Oxford, UK: Oxford University Press, 2003.

———. "Emotions Expressed and Aroused by Music: Philosophical Perspectives." In *Oxford Handbook of Music and Emotion: Theory, Research, Applications*, Edited by Patrik Juslin and John Sloboda, 15–43. Oxford: Oxford University Press, 2010.

DeBellis, Mark. "Music." In *The Routledge Companion to Aesthetics*, Edited by Berys Gaut and Dominic Lopes, 531–44. London: Routledge, 2002.

De Clercq, Rafael. "Aesthetic Properties." In *The Routledge Companion to Philosophy and Music*, Edited by Theodore Gracyk and Andrew Kania, 144–54. London: Routledge, 2011.

Dell'Antonio, Andrew, Editor. *Beyond Structural Listening? Postmodern Modes of Hearing*. Berkeley, CA: University of California Press, 2004.

Demorest, Steven, and Steven Morrison. "Does Music Make You Smarter?" *Music Educators Journal* 87, no. 2 (2000): 17–22.

Dennett, Daniel. *Freedom Evolves*. New York: Penguin Books, 2003.

Descartes, René. "Chapter 4." In *Discourse on the Method of Rightly Conducting the Reason, and Seeking Truth in the Sciences*. Project Gutenberg, 1637/1996. http://www.literature.org/authors/descartes-rene/reason-discourse/chapter-04.html.

———. *Passions of the Soul*. Translated by Jonathan Bennett, 1649/2015. http://www.earlymoderntexts.com/assets/pdfs/descartes1649part2.pdf.

Devereaux, Mary. "Feminist Aesthetics." In *The Oxford Handbook of Aesthetics*, Edited by Jerrold Levinson, 647–66. Oxford, UK: Oxford University Press, 2003.

Dewey, John. *How We Think*. Boston: D.C. Heath, 1910.

———. *Experience and Nature*. London: George Allen and Unwin, 1929.

———. *Art as Experience*. New York: Perigree Books, 1934/1980.

Dickie, George. "The Myth of the Aesthetic Attitude." *American Philosophical Quarterly* 1, no. 1 (1964): 56–65.

———. *Introduction to Aesthetics: An Analytic Approach*. New York: Oxford University Press, 1997.

Dufrenne, Mikel. *The Phenomenology of Aesthetic Experience*. Translated by Edward Casey. Evanston, IL: Northwestern University Press, 1979.

Duignan, Brian. "George Berkeley." *The Encyclopedia Britannica* (July 31, 2014). http://www.britannica.com/biography/George-Berkeley.

Dupré, Ben. *50 Philosophy Ideas You Really Need to Know*. London: Quercus, 2007.

Durant, Will. *The Story of Philosophy*. New York: Simon and Schuster, 1953.

Dutton, Blake. "Benedict de Spinoza." *Internet Encyclopedia of Philosophy*, 2005. http://www.iep.utm.edu/spinoza/

Dutton, Denis. *The Art Instinct*. Oxford: Oxford University Press, 2009.

Eagleman, David. *Incognito: The Secret Lives of the Brain*. New York: Pantheon Books, 2011.

———. *The Brain: The Story of You*. New York: Pantheon Books, 2015.

Eco, Umberto, Editor. *History of Beauty*. Translated by Alastair McEwen. New York: Rizzoli, 2002.

———, Editor. *On Ugliness*. New York: Rizzoli, 2007.

Einstein, Alfred. *Music in the Romantic Era*. New York: W.W. Norton, 1947.

Eisner, Elliot. "Aesthetic Modes of Knowing." In *Learning and Teaching: The Ways of Knowing. Eighty-fourth Yearbook of the National Society for the Study of Education*, Edited by Elliot Eisner, 22–36. Chicago: University of Chicago Press, 1985.

Eliot, T. S. *Four Quartets*. Orlando, FL: Harcourt, 1968.

Eller, Cynthia. *The Myth of Matriarchal Prehistory: Why an Invented Past Won't Give Women a Future*. Boston: Beacon Press, 2001.

David Elliott, "Music Education Philosophy," in *The Oxford Handbook of Music Education*, ed. Gary McPherson and Graham Welch (Oxford, UK: Oxford University Press, 2011), 68.

Elliott, David. "A Philosophy of Music Education (Second Edition) by Bennett Reimer." *Philosophy of Music Education Newsletter* 2, no. 1 (1989): 5–9.

———. "Music Education as Aesthetic Education: A Critical Inquiry." *Quarterly Journal of Music Teaching and Learning* 2 (1991): 48–66.

———. *Music Matters: A New Philosophy of Music Education*. New York: Oxford University Press, 1995.

———. "Music and Affect: The Praxial View." *Philosophy of Music Education Review* 8, no. 2 (2000): 79–88.

———, Editor. *Praxial Music Education: Reflections and Dialogues*. New York: Oxford University Press, 2005.

———. Introduction to *Praxial Music Education: Reflections and Dialogues*. Edited by David Elliott. New York: Oxford University Press, 2005.

———. "Music Education Philosophy," in *The Oxford Handbook of Music Education*, Edited by Gary McPherson and Graham Welch. Oxford, UK: Oxford University Press, 2011.

Elliott, David, and Marissa Silverman. "Rethinking Philosophy, Re-viewing Musical-emotional Experiences." In *The Oxford Handbook of Philosophy in Music Education*, Edited by Wayne Bowman and Anna Lucía Frega, 37–62. Oxford, UK: Oxford University Press, 2012.

———. *Music Matters: A Philosophy of Music Education, 2nd ed.* New York: Oxford University Press, 2015.

Ermarth, Elizabeth. "Postmodernism." In *Routledge Encyclopedia of Philosophy, Version 1.0*, Edited by Edward Craig, 6742–46. London and New York: Routledge, 1998.

Erskine, Noel. "Rap, Reggae, and Religion: Sounds of Cultural Dissonance." In *Noise and Spirit: The Religious and Spiritual Sensibilities of Rap Music*, Edited by Anthony Pinn, 71–84. New York: New York University Press, 2003.

"Facts and Insights on the Benefits of Music Study." National Association for Music Education, 2007. http://musiced.nafme.org/resources/why-music-education-2007/.

Farnsworth, Paul. *The Social Psychology of Music*. Ames, IA: The Iowa State University Press, 1969.

Feagin, Susan, and Patrick Maynard. *Aesthetics*. Oxford: Oxford University Press, 1997.

Ferris, David. *Schumann's Eichendorff Liederkreis and the Genre of the Romantic Cycle*. Oxford: Oxford University Press, 2000.

Fieser, James, and Bradley Dowden, Editors. *Internet Encyclopedia of Philosophy*, 2015. http://www.iep.utm.edu.

Fisher, John. "Popular Music." In *Routledge Companion to Philosophy and Music*, Edited by Theodore Gracyk and Andrew Kania, 405–15. London and New York: Routledge, 2011.

Flage, Daniel. "George Berkeley (1685–1753)," *The Internet Encyclopedia of Philosophy*, http://www.iep.utm.edu

Flynn, Bernard. "Maurice Merleau-Ponty." *The Stanford Encyclopedia of Philosophy* (2011 edition), Edited by Edward Zalta. http://plato.stanford.edu/archives/fall2011/entries/merleau-ponty.

Forbes, Guy. "The Repertoire Selection Practices of High School Choral Directors." *Journal of Research in Music Education* 49, no. 2 (2001): 102–21.

Forgeard, Marie, Ellen Winner, Andrea Norton, and Gottfried Schlaug. "Practicing a Musical Instrument in Childhood Is Associated with Enhanced Verbal Ability and Nonverbal Reasoning." *PLoS ONE* 3, no. 10 (2008): 1–8.

Francis, Kimberly. "A Dialogue Begins: Nadia Boulanger, Igor Stravinsky, and the Symphonie de Psaumes." *Women & Music* 14 (2010): 22–44.

Fransson, Peter, and Guillaume Marrelec. "The Precuneus/Posterior Cingulate Cortex Plays a Pivotal Role in the Default Mode Network: Evidence from a Partial Correlation Network Analysis." *Neuroimage* 42 (2008): 1178–84.

Freire, Paulo. *Pedagogy of the Oppressed, 30th Anniversary Edition*. Translated by Myra Ramos. New York: Continuum, 2005.

Freire, Paulo, and Donaldo Macedo. "A Dialogue: Culture, Language and Race." *Harvard Educational Review* 65, no. 3 (1995): 377–402.

Fried, Itzhak, Roy Mukamel, and Gabriel Kreiman. "Internally Generated Preactivation of Single Neurons in Human Medial Frontal Cortex Predicts Volition." *Neuron* 69, no. 3 (2011): 548–62.

Froebel, Friedrich. *The Education of Man*. Translated by W. N. Hailmann. Mineola, NY: Dover, 1826/2005.

Fux, Johann. *The Study of Counterpoint from Johann Joseph Fux's Gradus ad Parnassum*. Edited and Translated by Alfred Mann. New York: W.W. Norton, 1965.

Gabrielsson, Alf. "Emotions in Strong Experiences with Music." In *Music and Emotion: Theory and Research*, Edited by Patrik Juslin and John Sloboda, 431–49. New York: Oxford University Press, 2001.

———. "Strong Experiences with Music." In *Handbook of Music and Emotion*, Edited by Patrik Juslin and John Sloboda, 547–74. Oxford: Oxford University Press, 2010.

———. *Strong Experiences with Music*. Oxford, UK: Oxford University Press, 2011.

Gabrielsson, Alf, and Siv Wik. "Strong Experiences Related to Music: A Descriptive System." *Musicae Scientiae* 7, no. 2 (2003): 157–217.

Gadalla, Moustafa. *The Ancient Egyptian Culture Revealed.* Greensboro, NC: Tehuti Research Foundation, 2007.

Gann, Kyle. *No Such Thing as Silence. John Cage's 4'33."* New Haven, CT: Yale University Press, 2010.

Gardner, Howard. *Intelligence Reframed: Multiple Intelligences for the 21st Century.* New York: Basic Books, 1999.

———. *Truth, Beauty, and Goodness Reframed.* New York: Basic Books, 2011.

Gaut, Berys, and Dominic Lopes, Editors. *The Routledge Companion to Aesthetics.* New York: Routledge, 2001.

Gay, Geneva. "Preparing for Culturally Responsive Teaching." *Journal of Teacher Education* 53, no. 2 (2002): 106–16.

Gazzaniga, Michael. *Who's in Charge? Free Will and the Science of the Brain.* New York: HarperCollins, 2011.

Geringer, John, Michael Allen, and Rebecca MacLeod. "Initial Movement and Continuity of Vibrato Among High School and University String Players." *Journal of Research in Music Education* 53, no. 3 (2005): 248–59.

———. "String Vibrato: Research Related to Performance and Perception." *String Research Journal* 1 (2010): 7–23.

———. "Perceived Pitch of Violin and Cello Vibrato Tones among Music Majors." *Journal of Research in Music Education* 57, no. 4 (2010): 351–63.

Gettier, Edmund. "Is Justified Belief True Knowledge?" *Analysis* 23, no. 6 (1963): 121–23.

Gillers, Heather, and Jason Grotto. "Chicago Symphony Orchestra Strike Reflects Deeper Financial Woes." *Chicago Tribune* (October 17, 2012). http://articles.chicagotribune.com/2012–10–17/news/ct-met-cso-finances-20121007_1_cso-bass-player-chicago-symphony-orchestra-riccardo-muti.

Gloag, Kenneth. *Postmodernism in Music.* Cambridge, UK: Cambridge University Press, 2012.

Göttner-Abendroth, Heide. "Nine Principles of a Matriarchal Aesthetic." In *Feminist Aesthetics*, Edited by Gisela Ecker, Translated by Harriet Anderson, 81–94. Boston: Beacon Press, 1985.

———. *The Dancing Goddess: Principles of a Matriarchal Aesthetic.* Translated by Maureen Krause. Boston: Beacon Press, 2001.

———. "Modern Matriarchal Studies. Definitions, Scope and Topicality." Societies of Peace: 2nd World Congress on Matriarchal Studies, 2003. http://www.second-congress-matriarchal-studies.com/goettnerabendroth.html.

———. "Matriarchal Society: Definition and Theory." In *The Gift, a Feminist Analysis.* Edited by Genevieve Vaughan, Translated by Solveig Göttner and Karen Smith. London: Meltemi Press, 2004. http://www.matriarchiv.info/uploads/HGA-E-Matriarchal-Society-Definition-and-Theory.pdf.

Goldman, Alan. "The Aesthetic." In *The Routledge Companion to Aesthetics*, Edited by Berys Gaut and Dominic Lopes, 181–92. London: Routledge, 2002.

———. "Value." In *The Routledge Companion to Philosophy and Music*, Edited by Theodore Gracyk and Andrew Kania, 155–64. London: Routledge, 2011.

Goldstein, Avram. "Thrills in Response to Music and Other Stimuli." *Physiological Psychology* 8, no. 1 (1980): 126–29.

Goodman, Nelson. *Languages of Art: An Approach to a Theory of Symbols.* Indianapolis: Hackett, 1976.

———. *Ways of Worldmaking.* Indianapolis: Hackett, 1978.

Gracyk, Theodore. "Valuing and Evaluating Popular Music." *The Journal of Aesthetics and Art Criticism* 57, no. 2 (1999): 205–20.

Graham, Gordon. *Philosophy of the Arts: An Introduction to Aesthetics, 2nd ed.* London: Routledge, 2000.

———. "Expressivism." In *The Routledge Companion to Aesthetics*, Edited by Berys Gaut and Dominic Lopes, 119–30. London: Routledge, 2002.

———. *Philosophy of the Arts: An Introduction to Aesthetics, 3rd ed.* London: Routledge, 2005.

Grandin, Temple, Matthew Peterson, and Gordon Shaw. "Spatial-temporal Versus Language-analytic Reasoning: The Role of Music Training." *Arts Education Policy Review* 99, no. 6 (1998): 11–14.

Gray, Anne. *The World of Women in Classical Music.* San Diego: WordWorld, 2007.

Greene, Maxine. "Teaching for Aesthetic Experience." In *Toward an Aesthetic Education*, 21–43. Washington, DC: Music Educators National Conference, 1971.

Gridley, Mark, and Robert Hoff. "Do Mirror Neurons Explain Misattribution of Emotions in Music?" *Perceptual and Motor Skills* 102, no. 2 (2006): 600–2.

Grillparzer, Franz. "Quotation by Franz Grillparzer." *Columbia World of Quotations.* http://quotes.dictionary.com/What_is_the_use_of_aesthetics_if_they.

Guerrant, Mary. "Three Aspects of Music in Ancient China and Greece." *College Music Symposium* 20 (1980). http://symposium.music.org/index.php?option=com_k2&view=item&id=1870:three-aspects-of-music-in-ancient-china-and-greece&Itemid=124.

Gurney, Edmund. "On Some Disputed Points in Music." *Fortnightly Review* 20, no. 115 (1876): 106–30.

———. *The Power of Sound.* London: Smith, Elder, & Co, 1880.

Gusnard, Debra, Erbil Akbudak, Gordon Shulman, and Marcus Raichle. "Medial Prefrontal Cortex and Self-Referential Mental Activity: Relation to a Default Mode of Brain Function." *Proceedings of the National Academy of Sciences* 98 (2001): 4259–64.

Guyer, Paul. "18th Century German Aesthetics." *The Stanford Encyclopedia of Philosophy* (2008 edition), Edited by Edward Zalta. http://plato.stanford.edu/archives/fall2008/entries/aesthetics-18th-german/

———. "History of Modern Aesthetics." In *The Oxford Handbook of Aesthetics*, Edited by Jerrold Levinson, 25–60. Oxford, UK: Oxford University Press, 2005.

Hall, G. Stanley. "The Psychology of Music and the Light It Throws upon Musical Education." *The Pedagogical Seminary* 15, no. 3 (1908), 358–64.

"Hall, G. Stanley." *Encylopædia Britannica Online*, November 10, 2015. http://www.britannica.com/biography/G-Stanley-Hall.

Hallam, Susan. "How to Advocate for Music: Personal Stories of Music Education Advocacy: The Power of Music." *International Journal of Music Education* 23, No. 2 (2005): 144–48.

Hamilton, Andy. "Adorno." In *The Routledge Companion to Philosophy and Music*, Edited by Theodore Gracyk and Andrew Kania, 391–402. New York: Routledge, 2011.

Hanslick, Eduard. *The Beautiful in Music.* Edited by Morris Weitz. Translated by Gustav Cohen. New York: Bobbs-Merrill, 1854/1957.

———. *Music Criticisms (1846–99).* Edited and Translated by Henry Pleasants. Baltimore: Penguin Books, 1950.

Haslinger, B., P. Erhard, E. Altenmüller, U. Schroeder, H. Boecker, and A. Ceballos-Baumann. "Transmodel Sensorimotor Networks During Action Observation in Professional Pianists." *Journal of Cognitive Neuroscience* 17, no. 2 (2005): 282–93.

Havelock, Eric. *The Music Learns to Write.* New Haven, CT: Yale University Press, 1986.

Hawking, Stephen. *A Brief History of Time.* New York: Bantam Books, 1998.

Hawking, Stephen and Leonard Mlodinow. *The Grand Design.* New York: Random House, 2010.

Hegel, Georg. "Philosophy of Mind." In *The Encyclopaedia of the Philosophical Sciences with Five Introductory Essays.* Translated by William Wallace. Project Gutenberg EBook. (1830/1894/2012). http://www.gutenberg.org/files/39064/39064-h/39064-h.html#toc37

———. *Aesthetics. Lectures on Fine Art, 2 Volumes.* Translated by T. Malcolm Knox. Oxford, UK: Clarendon Press, 1835/1975.

———. *The Philosophy of History.* Translated by J. Sibree. Kitchener, Ontario, CA: Batoche Books, 1837/2001.

Hemingway, Colette, and Seán Hemingway. "Music in Ancient Greece." In *Heilbrunn Timeline of Art History.* New York: The Metropolitan Museum of Art, October 2001. http://www.metmuseum.org/toah/hd/grmu/hd_grmu.htm.

Herrer, G., and H. Harrer. "Music, Emotion, and Autonomous Function." In *Music and the Brain*, Edited by Macdonald Critchley and R. Henson, 202–16. London: William Heinemann Medical Books, 1977.

Hertzmann, Erich. "The Newly Discovered Autograph of Beethoven's Rondo *a capriccio*, op. 129." *The Musical Quarterly* 32, no. 2 (1946): 171–95.

Hevner, Kate. "Experimental Studies of the Elements of Expression in Music." *The American Journal of Psychology* 48, no. 2 (1936): 246–68.

Hindemith, Paul. *A Composer's World: Horizons and Limitations.* Cambridge, MA: Harvard University Press, 1952.

Hodges, Donald. "Does Music *Really* Make You Smarter?" *Southwestern Musician* 67, no. 9 (1999): 28–33.

———, Editor. *Sounds of Learning: The Impact of Music Education*, 2005. http://performingarts.uncg.edu/mri/research-areas/music-education#impact.

———. *Music in the Human Experience: An Introduction to Music Psychology.* New York: Routledge, 2011.

Hodges, Donald, Jonathan Burdette, and David Hairston. "Aspects of Multisensory Perception: The Integration of Visual and Auditory Information Processing in Musical Experiences." In *The Neurosciences and Music II: From Perception to Performance*, Edited by Giuliano Avanzini, Luisa Lopez, Stefan Koelsch, and Maria Majno. *Annals of the New York Academy of Sciences* 1060 (2005): 175–85.

Hoffer, Charles. "Some Thoughts on the Final Report of the Yale Seminar." *Bulletin of the Council for Research in Music Education* 60 (1979): 25–30.

Hofstadter, Albert, and Richard Kuhns, Editors. *Philosophies of Art & Beauty: Selected Readings in Aesthetics from Plato to Heidegger.* Chicago: University of Chicago Press, 1976.

Honderich, Ted, Editor. *The Oxford Guide to Philosophy.* Oxford, UK: Oxford University Press, 2005.

Horovitz, Silvina, Allen Braun, Walter Carr, Dante Picchioni, Thomas Balkin, Masaki Fukunaga, and Jeff Duyn. "Decoupling of the Brain's Default Mode Network During Sleep." *Proceedings of the National Academy of Sciences* 106, no. 27 (2009): 11376–81.

Houlgate, Stephen. "Hegel's Aesthetics." In *The Stanford Encyclopedia of Philosophy* (2014 edition), Edited by Edward Zalta. http://plato.stanford.edu/archives/spr2014/entries/hegel-aesthetics/.

Howard, Jay, and John Streck. *Apostles of Rock: The Splintered World of Contemporary Christian Music.* Lexington, KY: University Press of Kentucky, 1999.

Huffman, Carl. "Pythagoras." In *The Stanford Encyclopedia of Philosophy* (2011 edition), Edited by Edward Zalta. http://plato.stanford.edu/archives/fall2011/entries/pythagoras/.

Hume, David. "Of the Standard of Taste." In *Aesthetics: The Big Questions*, Edited by Carolyn Korsmeyer, 137–50. Malden, MA: Blackwell, 1757/1998.

Humphreys, Jere, "The Child-Study Movement and Public School Music Education." *Journal of Research in Music Education* 33, no. 2 (1985), 79–86.

Hunter, Ian. "James, William." In *The Oxford Companion to the Mind*, Edited by Richard Gregory, 492–4. Oxford, UK: Oxford University Press, 2004.

Huron, David. *Sweet Anticipation: Music and the Psychology of Expectation.* Cambridge, MA: The MIT Press, 2006.

———. "Aesthetics." In *The Oxford Handbook of Music Psychology*, Edited by Susan Hallam, Ian Cross, and Michael Thaut, 151–59. Oxford, UK: Oxford University Press, 2009.

Huscher, Phillip. "Robert Schumann: *Frauenliebe und –Leben*, Op. 42." Program notes for the Chicago Symphony Orchestra, 2015. http://cso.org/uploadedFiles/1_Tickets_and_Events/Program_Notes/Program Notes_Uchida_Plays_Mozart.pdf.

International Society for Music Education, 2014. http://www.isme.org/advocacy-articles.

Internet Encyclopedia of Philosophy, 2016. http://www.iep.utm.edu.

Inwood, Michael. "Hegel." In *The Routledge Companion to Aesthetics*, Edited by Berys Gaut and Dominic Lopes, 65–74. London: Routledge, 2002.

————. "Schiller, Johann Christoph Freidrich von." In *The Oxford Guide to Philosophy*, Edited by Ted Honderich, 844–5. Oxford, UK: Oxford University Press, 2005.

Isenberg, Arnold. "Analytical Philosophy and the Study of Art." *The Journal of Aesthetics and Art Criticism* 46 (1987): 125–36.

Istók, Eva, Elvira Brattico, Thomas Jacobsen, Kaisu Krohn, Mira Müller, and Mari Tervaniemi. "Aesthetic Responses to Music: A Questionnaire Study." *Musicae Scientiae* 13, no. 2 (2009): 183–206.

Ives, Charles. *The Unanswered Question*. New York: Southern Music Publishing Co., 1908/1930–1935.

James, William. *The Principles of Psychology*. New York: Henry Holt and Co., 1890.

————. *Pragmatism*. New York: Longmans, Green and Co., 1907.

————. *The Meaning of Truth*. New York: Longmans Green, and Co., 1909.

Janaway, Christopher. "Beauty." In *The Oxford Companion to Philosophy*, Edited by Ted Honderich, 80–81. Oxford: Oxford University Press, 1995.

————. "Plato." In *The Routledge Companion to Aesthetics*, Edited by Berys Gaut and Dominic Lopes, 3–13. London: Routledge, 2002.

Joad, Cyril. *Guide to Philosophy*. Toronto: General Publishing Co., 1936/1957.

John, Eileen. "Art and Knowledge." In *The Routledge Companion to Aesthetics*, Edited by Berys Gaut and Dominic Lopes, 329–40. London: Routledge, 2002.

Johnson, Christopher, and Jenny Memmott. "Examination of Relationships between Participation in School Music Programs of Differing Quality and Standardized Test Results." *Journal of Research in Music Education* 54, no. 4 (2006): 293–307.

Johnson, Mark. *The Body in the Mind: The Bodily Basis of Meaning, Imagination, and Reason*. Chicago: University of Chicago Press, 1987.

Jones, Jane. "Richard Strauss: Four Last Songs – A Swansong of Sublime Beauty." *Classic fM*, accessed on June 24, 2016, http://www.classicfm.com/composers/strauss/guides/richard-strauss-four-last-songs/#GgsdPct0fmo5RYFg.97.

Jorgensen, Estelle. "Concerning Justice and Music Education." *Music Education Research* 9, no. 2 (2007): 169–89.

————. "Values and Philosophizing about Music Education." *Philosophy of Music Education Review* 22, no. 1 (2014): 5–21.

Judkins, Jennifer. "Silence, Sound, Noise, and Music." In *The Routledge Companion to Philosophy and Music*, Edited by Theodore Gracyk and Andrew Kania, 14–23. New York: Routledge, 2011.

Juilliard Repertory Library. *Juilliard Repertory Library: Reference/Library Edition*. Cincinnati, OH: Canyon Press, 1970.

Junda, Mary. "Broadside Ballads: Social Consciousness in Song." *General Music Today* 26, no. 3 (2013): 18–24.

Juslin, Patrik. "Five Facets of Musical Expression: A Psychologist's Perspective on Music Performance." *Psychology of Music* 31 (2003): 273–302.

————. "From Everyday Emotions to Aesthetic Emotions: Towards a Unified Theory of Musical Emotions." *Physics of Life Reviews* 10 (2013): 235–66.

Juslin, Patrik, László Harmat, and Tuomas Eerola. "What Makes Music Emotionally Significant? Exploring the Underlying Mechanisms." *Psychology of Music* 42, no. 4 (2014): 599–623.

Juslin, Patrik, and Sara Isaksson. "Subjective Criteria for Choice and Aesthetic Value of Music: A Comparison of Psychology and Music Students." *Research Studies in Music Education* 36, no. 2 (2014): 179–98.

Juslin, Patrik, and Petri Laukka. "Expression, Perception, and Induction of Musical Emotions: A Review and a Questionnaire Study of Everyday Listening." *Journal of New Music Research* 33, no. 3 (2004): 217–38.

Juslin, Patrik, Simon Liljeström, Daniel Västfjäll, Gonçalo Barradas, and Ana Silva. "An Experience Sampling Study of Emotional Reactions to Music: Listener, Music, and Situation." *Emotion* 8, no. 5 (2008): 668–83.

Juslin, Patrik, and Daniel Västfjäll. "Emotional Responses to Music: The Need to Consider Underlying Mechanisms." *Behavioral and Brain Sciences* 31, no. 5 (2008): 559–621.

Kania, Andrew. "Definition." In *The Routledge Companion to Philosophy and Music*, Edited by Theodore Gracyk and Andrew Kania, 3–13. London: Routledge, 2011.

Kant, Immanuel. *Critique of Pure Reason*. Translated by J. Meiklejohn, 1781. http://philosophy.eserver.org/kant/critique-of-pure-reason.txt

———. "Critique of Aesthetic Judgment." In *Critique of Judgment*. Translated by James Meredith, 1790. http://philosophy.eserver.org/kant/critique-of-judgment.txt.

Kaplan, Max, Page Bailey, William Cornog, Alvin Eurich, Freda Goldman, William Hartshorn, Warner Lawson, Father Normal O'Connor, and Ralph Tyler. "A Philosophy of the Arts for an Emerging Society." In *Documentary Report of the Tanglewood Symposium*, Edited by Robert Choate, 110–21. Washington, DC: Music Educators National Conference, 1968.

Kauffman, Robert. "Some Aspects of Aesthetics in the Shona Music of Rhodesia." *Ethnomusicology* 13, no. 3 (1969): 507–11.

Keats, John. "Ode on a Grecian Urn." In *One Hundred and One Famous Poems*, Edited by Roy Cook, 140–141. Chicago: The Cable Co., 1820/1929.

Kelly, Jennifer. *In Her Own Words: Conversations with Composers in the United States*. Champaign-Urbana, IL: University of Illinois Press, 2013.

Kemp, Gary. "Croce's Aesthetics." In *The Stanford Encyclopedia of Philosophy* (2009 edition), Edited by Edward Zalta. http://plato.stanford.edu/archives/fall2009/entries/croce-aesthetics/.

Kerman, Joseph, and Alan Tyson. *The New Grove Beethoven*. New York: W.W. Norton, 1983.

Kiley, Brendan. "Seattle Opera Anticipates $1 Million Budget Shortfall." *SLOG News and Arts* (June 26, 2012). http://slog.thestranger.com/slog/archives/2012/06/26/seattle-opera-anticipates-1-million-budget-shortfall.

Kimball, Carol. *Song: A Guide to Art Song Style and Literature*. Milwaukee, WI: Hal Leonard, 2005.

King, B.B. with David Ritz. *Blues All Around Me: The Autobiography of B.B. King*. New York: Avon Books, 1996.

King, Peter. *One Hundred Philosophers*. Hauppauge, NY: Barron's, 2004.

Kirwan, Christopher. "Augustine: City of God." In *Central Works in Philosophy, 1: Ancient and Medieval*, Edited by John Shand, 140–68. Montreal: McGill-Queen's University Press, 2005.

Kivy, Peter. *The Corded Shell*. Princeton, NJ: Princeton University Press, 1980.

———. *Sound Sentiment: An Essay on the Musical Emotions*. Philadelphia: Temple University Press, 1989.

———. *Music Alone: Philosophical Reflections on the Purely Musical Experience*. Ithaca, NY: Cornell University Press, 1990.

———. *Introduction to a Philosophy of Music*. Oxford, UK: Oxford University Press, 2002.

———. "Another Go at Musical Profundity: Stephen Davies and the Game of Chess." *British Journal of Aesthetics* 43, no. 4 (2003): 401–11.

———. "Moodology: A Response to Laura Sizer." *Journal of Aesthetics and Art Criticism* 65, no. 3 (2007): 312–18.

Klaper, Michael. "Hildegard von Bingen." In *New Historical Anthology of Music by Women*, Edited by James Briscoe, 14–20. Bloomington, IN: Indiana University Press, 2004.

Klein, Peter. "Skepticism." In *The Stanford Encyclopedia of Philosophy* (2011 edition), Edited by Edward Zalta. http://plato.stanford.edu/archives/sum2011/entries/skepticism/.

Klemm, W. "Free Will Debates: Simple Experiments Are Not So Simple." *Advances in Cognitive Psychology* 6, no. 6 (2010): 47–65.

Kneiter, Gerard. "The Nature of Aesthetic Education." In *Toward an Aesthetic Education*, 3–19. Washington, DC: Music Educators National Conference, 1971.

Knowles, Beyoncé. *Mywage.org*, 2015. http://www.mywage.org/zimbabwe/main/salary/vip-celebrities-pay/musicians-pay.

Konečni, Vladimir. "The Aesthetic Trinity: Awe, Being Moved, Thrills." *Bulletin of Psychology and the Arts* 5, no. 2 (2005): 27–44.

———. "Does Music Induce Emotion? A Theoretical and Methodological Analysis." *Psychology of Aesthetics, Creativity, and the Arts* 2 (2008): 115–29.

———. "Aesthetic Trinity Theory and the Sublime." *Philosophy Today* 55, no. 1 (2011): 64–73.

———. "Music, Affect, Method, Data: Reflections on the Carroll v. Kivy Debate." *American Journal of Psychology* 126, no. 2 (2013): 179–95.

Konečni, Vladimir, Amber Brown, and Rebekah Wanic. "Comparative Effects of Music and Recalled Life-events on Emotional State." *Psychology of Music* 36, no. 3 (2008): 289–308.

Konečni, Vladimir, Rebekah Wanic, and Amber Brown. "Emotional and Aesthetic Antecedents and Consequences of Music-Induced Thrills." *American Journal of Psychology* 120, no. 4 (2007): 619–43.

Koopman, Constantijn. "The Nature of Music and Musical Works." In *Praxial Music Education*, Edited by David Elliott, 79–97. Oxford, UK: Oxford University Press, 2005.

Korsmeyer, Carolyn. *Aesthetics: The Big Questions*. Malden, MA: Blackwell, 1998.

———. *Gender and Aesthetics: An Introduction*. New York: Routledge, 2004.

———. "Feminist Aesthetics." In *The Stanford Encyclopedia of Philosophy* (2012 edition), Edited by Edward Zalta. http://plato.stanford.edu/archives/win2012/entries/feminism-aesthetics/.

Kramer, Jonathan. "The Fibonacci Series in Twentieth-century Music." *Journal of Music Theory* 17, no. 1 (1973): 110–48.

Kringlebach, Morten. "Emotion." In *The Oxford Companion to the Mind*, Edited by Richard Gregory, 287–90. Oxford, UK: Oxford University Press, 2004.

Krumhansl, Carol. *Cognitive Foundations of Musical Pitch*. New York: Oxford University Press, 1990.

Lacey, A. *A Dictionary of Philosophy*. London: Routledge, 1986.

Landels, John. *Music in Ancient Greece and Rome*. New York: Routledge, 1999.

Langer, Susanne. *Philosophy in a New Key, 3rd ed.* Cambridge, MA: Harvard University Press, 1942/1963.

———. *Feeling and Form*. New York: Charles Scribner's Sons, 1953.

———. *Problems of Art*. New York: Charles Scribner's Sons, 1957.

———. *Mind: An Essay on Human Feeling, Vols. I, II, & III*. Baltimore: The Johns Hopkins Press, 1967, 1974, 1982.

———. "The Work of Art as a Symbol." In *Introductory Readings in Aesthetics*, Edited by John Hospers, 171–84. New York: The Free Press, 1969.

Law, Stephen. *Philosophy*. New York: Metro Books, 2007.

League of American Orchestras, 2008. http://www.americanorchestras.org/advocacy-government/music-education/music-education-advocacy-tools/orchestras-in-advocacy.html.

League of American Orchestras, 2015. http://americanorchestras.org.

Leaver, Robin. "Luther on Music." In *The Pastoral Luther: Essays on Martin Luther's Practical Theology*, Edited by Timothy Wengert, 271–91. Grand Rapids, MI: Wm. B. Eerdmans, 2009.

Ledo-Regal, Luis Manuel. "What Is Scientific Philosophy?" *Scientific Philosophy* (May 15, 2008). http://scientific-philosophy.blogspot.com.

Lehman, Paul. "Advocacy for Music Education: Ten Tips to Protect and Strengthen Your Music Program." *International Journal of Music Education* 23, no. 2 (2005): 175–78.

Leibniz, Gottfried. *Principles of Nature and Grace Based on Reason*. Translated by Jonathan Bennett (1714/2006). http://www.earlymoderntexts.com/assets/pdfs/leibniz1714a.pdf.

Leonhard, Charles. "Music Education—Aesthetic Education." *Education* 74, no. 1 (1953): 23–26.

———. "Was the Yale Seminar Worthwhile?" *Bulletin of the Council for Research in Music Education* 60 (1979): 61–64.

———. *A Realistic Rationale for Teaching Music*. Reston, VA: Music Educators National Conference, 1985.

Leonhard, Charles, and Robert House. *Foundations and Principles of Music Education*. New York: McGraw-Hill, 1959.

Lerdahl, Fred, and Ray Jackendoff. *A Generative Theory of Tonal Music.* Cambridge, MA: The MIT Press, 1983.

Levinson, Jerrold. "Musical Profundity Misplaced." *Journal of Aesthetics and Art Criticism* 50, no. 1 (1992): 58–60.

———. *The Pleasures of Aesthetics: Philosophical Essays.* Ithaca, NY: Cornell University Press, 1996.

———. "Music and Negative Emotion." In *Music and Meaning*, Edited by Jenefer Robinson, 215–41. Ithaca, NY: Cornell University Press, 1997.

Lewis, C. S. *The Four Loves.* New York: Harcourt, Brace, 1960.

Libet, Benjamin, Anthony Freeman, and Keith Sutherland, Editors. *The Volitional Brain: Towards a Neuroscience of Free Will.* Exeter, UK: Imprint Academic, 2004.

Liebert, Robert. "Michelangelo's Mutilation of the Florence *Pietà*: A Psychoanalytic Inquiry." *Art Bulletin* 59, no. 1 (1977): 47–54.

Lind, Vicki, and Constance McKoy. *Culturally Responsive Teaching in Music Education: From Understanding to Application.* New York: Routledge, 2016.

Lippman, Edward. *A History of Western Musical Aesthetics.* Lincoln, NE: University of Nebraska Press, 1992.

Lorand, Ruth. "In Defense of Beauty." *American Society of Aesthetics*, 2007. http://aesthetics-online.org/?page=LorandBeauty&hhSearchTerms=%22Lorand%22.

Louis, Rudolf. "On the Tone Poems of Richard Strauss." In *Richard Strauss and His World*, Edited by Bryan Gilliam, Translated by Susan Gillespie, 305–10. Princeton, NJ: Princeton University Press, 1992.

Luksetich, W. "A Simultaneous Model of Nonprofit Symphony Orchestra Behavior." *Journal of Cultural Economics* 19, no. 1 (1995): 49–68.

Lyons, Linda. "Americans Want Music Students to Play On." *Gallup*, 2003. http://www.gallup.com/poll/8434/Americans-Want-Music-Students-Play.aspx.

Maas, Martha. "Kithara." *Grove Music Online. Oxford Music Online*, 2012. http://www.oxfordmusiconline.com/subscriber/article/grove/music/15077.

Maas, Martha, and Jane Synder. *Stringed Instruments of Ancient Greece.* New Haven, CT: Yale University Press, 1989.

Macarthur, Sally. *Feminist Aesthetics in Music.* Westport, CT: Greenwood Publishing Co., 2002.

Mace, Sandra, Cynthia Wagoner, David Teachout, and Donald Hodges. "Genre Identification of Very Brief Musical Excerpts." *Psychology of Music* 40, no. 1 (2011): 112–28.

MacLeod, Rebecca. "Influences of Dynamic Level and Pitch Register on the Vibrato Rates and Widths of Violin and Viola Players." *Journal of Research in Music Education* 56, no. 1 (2008): 43–54.

———. "A Pilot Study of Relationships Between Pitch Register and Dynamic Level and Vibrato Rate and Width in Professional Violinists." *String Research Journal* 1 (2010): 75–83.

Madsen, Clifford. "Emotion versus Tension in Haydn's Symphony No. 104 as Measured by the Two-dimensional Continuous Response Digital Interface." *Journal of Research in Music Education* 46, no. 4 (1998): 546–54.

Madsen, Clifford, Ruth Brittin, and Deborah Capperella-Sheldon. "An Empirical Method for Measuring the Aesthetic Experience to Music." *Journal of Research in Music Education* 41, no. 1 (1993): 57–69.

Magee, Bryan. *The Great Philosophers.* Oxford: Oxford University Press, 1987.

Mainwaring, James. "An Examination of the Value of the Empirical Approach to Aesthetics." *British Journal of Psychology* 32, no. 2 (1941): 114–30.

Manuel, Peter. "Ethnomusicology." In *Routledge Companion to Philosophy and Music*, Edited by Theodore Gracyk and Andrew Kania, 535–45. London and New York: Routledge, 2011.

Manuel, Peter, and Stephen Blum. "Classical Aesthetic Traditions of India, China, and the Middle East." In *Routledge Companion to Philosophy and Music*, Edited by Theodore Gracyk and Andrew Kania, 245–56. London and New York: Routledge, 2011.

Margolick, David. *Strange Fruit: The Biography of a Song.* New York: The Ecco Press. 2001.

Margolis, Joseph. "Medieval Aesthetics." In *The Routledge Companion to Aesthetics*, Edited by Berys Gaut and Dominic Lopes, 27–36. London: Routledge, 2002.

Mark, Michael. "The Evolution of Music Education Philosophy from Utilitarian to Aesthetic." *Journal of Research in Music Education* 30, no. 1 (1982): 15–21.

———. *Contemporary Music Education, 3rd ed.* New York: Schirmer Books, 1996.

———. "A History of Music Education Advocacy." *Music Educators Journal* 89, no. 1 (2002): 44–48.

———. "Why Does Our Profession Need Advocacy?" *International Journal of Music Education* 23, no. 2 (2005): 95–98.

———, Editor. *Music Education: Source Readings from Ancient Greece to Today, 4th ed.* New York: Routledge, 2013.

Martindale, Colin, and Kathleen Moore. "Priming, Prototypicality, and Preference." *Journal of Experimental Psychology: Human Perception and Performance* 14, no. 4 (1988): 661–70.

Maslow, Abraham. "A Theory of Human Motivation." *Psychological Review* 50, no. 4 (1943): 370–96.

———. "Music, Education, and Peak Experiences." In *Documentary Report of the Tanglewood Symposium*, Edited by Robert Choate, 68–75. Washington, DC: Music Educators National Conference, 1968.

———. *Toward a Psychology of Being, 2nd ed.* New York: Van Nostrand Reinhold Co, 1968.

———. *Motivation and Personality, 2nd ed.* New York: Harper and Row, 1970.

———. *The Farther Reaches of Human Nature.* New York: Penguin Books, 1971.

Mastravers, Derek. "Art, Expression and Emotion." In *The Routledge Companion to Aesthetics*, Edited by Berys Gaut and Dominic Lopes, 353–62. London: Routledge, 2002.

Mathiesen, Thomas, Dimitri Conomos, George Leotsakos, Sotirios Chianis, and Rudolph Brandi. "Greece." In *Grove Music Online. Oxford Music Online*, 2012. http://www.oxfordmusiconline.com/subscriber/article/grove/music/11694pg1.

Mattheson, Johann. *Der vollkommene Capellmeister.* A revised translation with critical commentary by Ernest Harriss. Ann Arbor, MI: UMI Press, 1739/1981.

McAnally, Elizabeth. "General Music and Children Living in Poverty." *General Music Today* 26, no. 3 (2013): 25–31.

McCarthy, Marie and J. Scott Goble, "Music Education Philosophy: Changing Times." *Music Educators Journal* 89 (2002): 19–26.

———. "The Praxial Philosophy in Historical Perspective." In *Praxial Music Education*, Edited by David Elliott, 19–51. New York: Oxford University Press, 2005.

McClary, Susan. "Towards a Feminist Criticism of Music." *Canadian University Music Review* 10, no. 2 (1990): 9–17.

———. *Georges Bizet: Carmen.* Cambridge, UK: Cambridge University Press, 1992.

———. "Paradigm Dissonances: Music Theory, Cultural Studies, Feminist Criticism." *Perspectives of New Music* 32, no. 1 (1994): 68–85.

———. "A Musical Dialectic from the Enlightenment: Mozart's 'Piano Concerto in G Major, K. 453, Movement 2.'" *Cultural Critique* 4 (1999): 129–69.

———. *Feminine Endings: Music, Gender, & Sexuality.* Minneapolis: University of Minnesota Press, 2002.

McDonald, Matthew. "Silent Narration? Elements of Narrative in Ives's *The Unanswered Question*." *19th-Century Music* 27, no. 3 (2004): 263–86.

McDonald, William. "Søren Kierkegaard." In *The Stanford Encyclopedia of Philosophy* (2012 edition), Edited by Edward Zalta. http://plato.stanford.edu/archives/fall2012/entries/kierkegaard/.

McKeage, Kathleen. "Gender and Participation in High School and College Instrumental Jazz Ensembles." *Journal of Research in Music Education* 52, no. 4 (2004): 343–56.

McMahon, Jennifer. "Beauty." In *The Routledge Companion to Aesthetics*, Edited by Berys Gaut and Dominic Lopes, 227–38. London: Routledge, 2002.

McMurray, Foster. "Pragmatism in Music Education." In *Basic Concepts in Music Education: The Fifty-seventh Yearbook of the National Society for the Study of Education*, Edited by Nelson Henry, 30–61. Chicago: University of Chicago Press, 1958.

McWhinnie, Harold. "A Review of Research on Aesthetic Measure." *Acta Psychologia* 28 (1968): 363–75.

Mendelson, Michael. "Saint Augustine." In *The Stanford Encyclopedia of Philosophy* (2012 edition), Edited by Edward Zalta. http://plato.stanford.edu/archives/win2010/entries/augustine/.

Merriam, Alan. *The Anthropology of Music.* Chicago: Northwestern University Press, 1964.

Merriam-Webster Dictionary, 2015. http://www.merriam-webster.com/dictionary/aesthetics.

Mertes, Terez. "As Slow as Possible." *Violin Blogs*, 2008. www.violinist.com/blog/Terez/20088/9005

Meyer, Leonard. *Emotion and Meaning in Music.* Chicago: The University of Chicago Press, 1956.

———. *Music, the Arts, and Ideas.* Chicago: The University of Chicago Press, 1967.

———. *Explaining Music.* Chicago: The University of Chicago Press, 1973.

———. "Music and Emotion: Distinction and Uncertainties." In *Music and Emotion*, Edited by Patrik Juslin and John Sloboda, 341–60. New York: Oxford University Press, 2001.

Molnar-Szakacs, Istvan, and Katie Overy. "Music and Mirror Neurons: From Motion to 'E'motion." *Social Cognitive and Affective Neuroscience* 1 (2006): 235–41.

Moore, Allan. "Rock." In *Routledge Companion to Philosophy and Music*, Edited by Theodore Gracyk and Andrew Kania, 416–25. London and New York: Routledge, 2011.

Moore, Earl, and Theodore Heger. *The Symphony and the Symphonic Poem, 6th rev. ed.* Ann Arbor, MI: Ulrich's Books, 1974.

Morton, Adam. "Knowledge." In *Western Philosophy*, Edited by David Papineau, 72–105. New York: Metro Books, 2009.

Morucci, Valerio. "Reconsidering *cori spezzati*: A New Source from Central Italy." *Acta Musicologica* 84, no. 1 (2013): 21–41.

Mr. Holland's Opus Foundation, 2015. http://www.mhopus.org.

Music Australia, accessed December 20, 2015. http://musicaustralia.org.au/advocacy/.

"Music Education: Core to Orchestrating Success." American Orff-Schulwerk Association, accessed June 24, 2016. http://aosa.org/resources/music-education-policy-roundtable/music-education-core-to-orchestrating-success/.

Muxfeldt, Kristina. "*Frauenliebe und -Leben* Now and Then." *19th-Century Music* 25, no. 1 (2001): 27–48.

NAfME Broader Minded, accessed December 20, 2015. http://www.broaderminded.com.

NAMM Foundation (National Association of Music Merchants), 2014. http://nammfoundation.org.

Narmour, Eugene. *The Analysis and Cognition of Melodic Complexity: The Implication-realization Model.* Chicago: The University of Chicago Press, 1992.

National Association for Music Education (NAfME), 2015. http://www.nafme.org/take-action/.

National Association for Music Education. Music Education and Successful Schools, 2015. http://www.nafme.org/take-action/what-to-know/all-research/.

Nattiez, Jean-Jacques. *Music and Discourse: Toward a Semiology of Music.* Translated by Carolyn Abbate. Princeton: Princeton University Press, 1990.

Nehamas, Alexander. "An Essay on Beauty and Judgment." *The Threepenny Review* 80 (Winter, 2000). http://www.threepennyreview.com.

Neuls-Bates, Carol, Editor. *Women in Music: An Anthology of Source Readings from the Middle Ages to the Present.* New York: Harper and Row, 1982.

"New Gallup Survey by NAMM Reflects Majority of Americans Agree with Many Benefits of Playing Musical Instruments." National Association of Music Merchants, 2009. https://www.namm.org/news/press-releases/new-gallup-survey-namm-reflects-majority-americans.

New York Philharmonic Orchestra, 2011. http://nyphil.org/about-us/the-orchestra/musicians-of-the-orchestra.

"Niceta of Remesiana." *Encyclopedia Britannica*, 2015. http://www.britannica.com/biography/Nicetas-of-Remesiana.

Nieminen, Sirke, Eva Istók, Elvira Brattico, and Mari Tervaniemi. "The Development of the Aesthetic Experience of Music: Preference, Emotions, and Beauty." *Musicae Scientiae* 16, no. 3 (2012): 372–91.

Nietzsche, Friedrich. *The Gay Science.* Translated by Josefine Nauckhoff. Cambridge: Cambridge University Press, 1882/2001.

———. *The Will to Power.* Edited by Walter Kaufmann. Translated by Walter Kaufmann and R. J. Hollingdale. New York: Vintage Books, 1968.

North, Adrian, and David Hargreaves. *The Social and Applied Psychology of Music.* Oxford: Oxford University Press, 2008.

North, Adrian, David Hargreaves, and Mark Tarrant. "Social Psychology and Music Education." In *The New Handbook of Research on Music Teaching and Learning,* Edited by Richard Colwell and Carol Richardson, 604–625. New York: Oxford University Press, 2002.

Novey, Madeline. "FCHS Cuts a Symptom of Bigger Challenges." Coloradoan.com (April 10, 2013). http://www.coloradoan.com/article/20130409/NEWS01/304090045/Fort-Collins-High-School-cuts-symptom-bigger-budget-challenges.

Novitz, David. "Postmodernism: Barthes and Derrida." In *The Routledge Companion to Aesthetics,* Edited by Berys Gaut and Dominic Lopes, 155–65. London: Routledge, 2002.

Nusbaum, Emily, Paul Silvia, Roger Beaty, Chris Burgin, Donald Hodges, and Thomas Kwapil. "Listening Between the Notes: Aesthetic Chills in Everyday Music Listening." *Psychology of Aesthetics, Creativity, and the Arts* 8, no. 1 (2014): 104–9.

Nussbaum, Charles. *The Musical Representation: Meaning, Ontology, and Emotion.* Cambridge, MA: MIT Press, 2007.

"The Odeion of Ephesus." *Ephesus,* 2010–2015. http://www.ephesus.ws/the-odeion-of-ephesus.html.

O'Hear, Anthony. "Education, the History of the Philosophy of." In *The Oxford Guide to Philosophy,* Edited by Ted Honderich, 228–31. Oxford, UK: Oxford University Press, 2005.

———. "Luther, Martin." In *The Oxford Guide to Philosophy,* Edited by Ted Honderich, 547–48. Oxford, UK: Oxford University Press, 2005.

O'Neill, William. *Educational Ideologies: Contemporary Expressions of Educational Philosophy.* Santa Monica, CA: Goodyear Publishing, 1981.

Overy, Katie, and Istvan Molnar-Szakacs. "Being Together in Time: Musical Experience and the Mirror Neuron System." *Music Perception* 26, no. 5 (2009): 489–504.

Palisca, Claude. *Seminar in Music Education.* ERIC document ED003429. New Haven, CT: Yale University, 1963.

———. *Music in Our Schools: A Search for Improvement. Report of the Yale Seminar on Music Education.* Washington, DC: U.S. Department of Health, Education and Welfare, Office of Education, OE-33033, Bulletin 1964, No. 28.

———. *Baroque Music.* Englewood-Cliffs, NJ: Prentice-Hall, 1968.

Parsons, Lawrence, Justine Sergent, Donald Hodges, and Peter Fox. "The Brain Basis of Piano Performance." *Neuropsychologia* 43, no. 2 (2005): 199–215.

Peirce, Charles. "How to Make Our Ideas Clear." *Popular Science Monthly* 12 (1878): 286–302.

Pendle, Karin and Melinda Boyd, Editors. *Women in Music: A Research and Information Guide, 2d ed.* New York: Routledge, 2005.

Peretz, Isabelle, and Robert Zatorre, Editor. *The Cognitive Neuroscience of Music.* Oxford: Oxford University Press, 2003.

Peter Kivy, *Philosophies of Arts: An Essay in Differences.* Cambridge, UK: Cambridge University Press, 1997.

Plato. *Republic.* Translated by Benjamin Jowett. The Project Gutenberg Ebook #1497, 2012. http://www.gutenberg.org/ebooks/1497.

———. *Apology.* Translated by Benjamin Jowett. The Project Gutenberg Ebook #1656, 2013. http://www.gutenberg.org/files/1656/1656-h/1656-h.htm.

———. *Timaeus.* Translated by Benjamin Jowett. The Project Gutenberg Ebook #1572, 2013. http://www.gutenberg.org/ebooks/1572.

Plotinus. *The Six Enneads.* Translated by Stephen MacKenna and B. S. Page, 250/1917–1930. http://www.sacred-texts.com/cla/plotenn/enn502.htm.

Portnoy, Julius. *The Philosopher and Music: A Historical Outline*. New York: Da Capo Press, 1954.

Powell, Newman. "Fibonacci and the Golden Mean: Rabbits, Rumbas, and Rondeaux." *Journal of Music Theory* 23, no. 2 (1979): 227–73.

Pratt, Alan. "Nihilism." *Internet Encyclopedia of Philosophy*, 2005. http://www.iep.utm.edu/nihilism/.

Pratt, Carroll. *Music as the Language of Emotion: A Lecture Delivered in the Whittall Pavilion of the Library of Congress* (December 21, 1950). http://www.questia.com/PM.qst?a=o&d=6090173.

———. "The Design of Music." *The Journal of Aesthetics and Art Criticism* 12, no. 3 (1954): 289–300.

Pratt, Rosalie, and Ralph Spintge, Editors. *MusicMedicine2*. St. Louis: MMB Music, 1995.

Priest, Stephen. *The British Empiricists, 2d ed.* New York: Routledge, 2007.

Prieto, Carlos. *The Adventures of a Cello*. Translated by Elena Murray. Austin, TX: University of Texas Press, 2006.

Quinton, Anthony. "Philosophy." In *The Oxford Companion to Philosophy*, Edited by Ted Honderich, 666–70. Oxford: Oxford University Press, 1995.

Rader, Melvin. *A Modern Book of Esthetics*. New York: Holt, Rinehart and Winston, 1960.

Raichle, Marcus, Ann MacLeod, Abraham Snyder, Wiliam Powers, Debra Gusnard, and Gordon Shulman. "A Default Mode of Brain Function." *Proceedings of the National Academy of Sciences USA* 98, no. 2 (2001): 676–82.

Ramachandran, V., and William Hirstein. "The Science of Art: A Neurological Theory of Aesthetic Experience." *Journal of Consciousness Studies* 6, nos. 6–7 (1999): 15–51.

Rameau, Jean-Phillippe. *Treatise on Harmony: Reduced to Its Natural Principles Divided into Four Books*. Translated with an introduction and notes by Philip Gossett. Mineola, NY: Dover Books, 1722/1971.

Rauscher, Frances, Gordon Shaw, and Catherine Ky. "Music and Spatial Task Performance." *Nature* 365 (1993): 611.

Reagan, Timothy. *Non-Western Educational Traditions: Indigenous Approaches to Educational Thought and Practice, 3rd ed.* Mahwah, NJ: Lawrence Erlbaum Associates, 2005.

Reed, Edward. *From Soul to Mind: The Emergence of Psychology, from Erasmus Darwin to William James*. New Haven: Yale University Press, 1997.

Regelski, Thomas. "Curriculum: Implications of Aesthetic versus Praxial Philosophies." In *Praxial Music Education*, Edited by David Elliott, 219–48. Oxford, UK: Oxford University Press, 2005.

———. "Music and Music Education: Theory and Praxis for 'Making a Difference.'" *Educational Philosophy and Theory* 37, no. 1 (2005): 7–27.

———. "Response to Philip Alperson, 'Robust Praxialism and the Anti-aesthetic Turn.'" *Philosophy of Music Education Review* 19, no. 2 (2010): 196–203.

———. *A Brief Introduction to a Philosophy of Music and Music Education as Social Praxis*. New York: Routledge, 2015.

Reich, Nancy. *Clara Schumann: The Artist and the Woman*. Ithaca, NY: Cornell University Press, 2001.

———. "Clara Wieck Schumann." In *New Historical Anthology of Music by Women*, Edited by James Briscoe, 140–69. Bloomington, IN: Indiana University Press, 2004.

Reich, Susanna. *Clara Schumann: Piano Virtuoso*. New York: Clarion Books, 1999.

Reichenbach, Hans. *The Rise of Scientific Philosophy*. Berkeley: University of California Press, 1951.

Reid, Louis. "Greatness." In *A Modern Book of Esthetics: An Anthology, 3rd ed.*, Edited by Melvin Rader, 481–85. New York: Holt, Rinehart, and Winston, 1960.

Reilly, Maureen. *Music, a Cognitive Behavioral Intervention for Anxiety and Acute Pain Control in the Elder Cataract Patient*. Unpublished doctoral dissertation: The University of Texas Graduate School of Biomedical Sciences at San Antonio, School of Nursing, 1999.

Reimer, Bennett. *A Philosophy of Music Education*. Englewood-Cliffs, NJ: Prentice-Hall, 1970.

———. "The Yale Conference: A Critical Review." *Bulletin of the Council for Research in Music Education* 60 (1979): 5–14.

———. *A Philosophy of Music Education, 2nd ed.* Englewood-Cliffs, NJ: Prentice-Hall, 1989.

———. "Reflections on David Elliott's Critique of *A Philosophy of Music Education.*" *Philosophy of Music Education Newsletter* 2, no. 2 (1990): 1–8.

———. "Reimer Responds to Elliott." *Quarterly Journal of Music Teaching and Learning* 2 (1991): 67–75.

———. "David Elliott's 'New' Philosophy of Music Education: Music for Performers Only." *Council for Research in Music Education* 128 (1996): 59–89.

———. *A Philosophy of Music Education: Advancing the Vision, 3rd ed.* Upper Saddle River, NJ: Prentice-Hall, 2003.

———. "Once More with Feeling: Reconciling Discrepant Accounts of Musical Affect." *Philosophy of Music Education Review* 12, no. 1 (2004): 4–16.

———. "The Danger of Music Education Advocacy." *International Journal of Music Education* 23, no. 2 (2005): 139–42.

Repp, Bruno. "The Aesthetic Quality of a Quantitatively Average Music Performance: Two Preliminary Experiments." *Music Perception* 14 (1997): 419–44.

Ridley, Aaron. "Expression in Art." In *The Oxford Handbook of Aesthetics*, Edited by Jerrold Levinson, 211–27. Oxford, UK: Oxford University Press, 2005.

Riedel, Johannes. "The Function of Sociability in the Sociology of Music and Music Education." *Journal of Research in Music Education* 12, no. 2 (1964), 149–58.

Riis, Jacob. *The Making of an American.* Project Gutenberg EBook, 1901/2004. http://www.gutenberg.org/cache/epub/6125/pg6125.html.

Robinson, Jenefer, Editor. *Music and Meaning.* Ithaca, NY: Cornell University Press, 1997.

———. *Deeper than Reason: Emotion and Its Role in Literature, Music, and Art.* Oxford, UK: Oxford University Press, 2005.

———. "Expression Theories." In *The Routledge Companion to Philosophy and Music*, Edited by Theodore Gracyk and Andrew Kania, 201–11. New York: Routledge, 2011.

Robinson, Sharon, and Jane West. "Preparing Inclusive Educators: A Call to Action." *Journal of Teacher Education* 63, no. 4 (2012): 291–93.

Rodríguez, Luis. "Education in Latin American Music Schools: A Philosophical Perspective." In *The Oxford Handbook of Philosophy in Music Education*, Edited by Wayne Bowman and Ana Lucía Frega, 231–48. New York: Oxford University Press, 2012.

Rosenberg, Alex. *Philosophy of Science: A Contemporary Introduction, 3rd ed.* New York: Routledge, 2012.

Rosenstiel, Leonie. *Nadia Boulanger: A Life in Music.* New York: W.W. Norton, 1982.

Rubin, Jeanne. "Montessorian Music Method: Unpublished Works." *Journal of Research in Music Education* 31, no. 3 (1983), 215–26.

Rubinov, Mikail, and Olaf Sporns. "Complex Network Measures of Brain Connectivity: Uses and Interpretations." *Neuroimage* 52 (2010): 1059–69.

Rusch, Elizabeth. "Maria Anna Mozart: The Family's First Prodigy." *Smithsonian.com*, 2011. http://www.smithsonianmag.com/arts-culture/Maria-Anna-Mozart-The-Familys-First-Prodigy.html#ixzz2OqUxVUHG.

Russell, Bertrand. *The Problems of Philosophy.* Oxford: Oxford University Press, 1912.

———. *The History of Western Philosophy.* New York: Simon and Schuster, 1945.

———. *Wisdom of the West.* London: Rathbone Books, 1959.

Saarikallio, Suvi, Sirke Nieminen, and Elvira Brattico. "Affective Reactions to Musical Stimuli Reflect Emotional Use of Music in Everyday Life." *Musicae Scientiae* 17, no. 1 (2012): 27–39.

"Sabine Meyer Biographie." *Sabine Meyer.* http://www.sabine-meyer.com/index.php/21/articles/biographie-en.html.

Sachs, Curt. *Our Musical Heritage, 2d ed.* Englewood Cliffs, NJ: Prentice-Hall, 1955.

Sack, Kevin. "Georgia's Governor Seeks Musical Start for Babies." *The New York Times* (January 15, 1998). http://www.nytimes.com/1998/01/15/us/georgia-s-governor-seeks-musical-start-for-babies.html.

Sacks, Oliver. "The Power of Music." *Brain* 129 (2006): 2528–32.

Sadie, Julie, and Rhian Samuel, Editors. *Norton/Grove Dictionary of Women Composers*. London: The Macmillan Press, 1995.

Sahakian, William, and Mabel Sahakian. *Ideas of the Great Philosophers*. New York: Fall River Press, 2005.

Salzer, Felix. *Structural Hearing: Tonal Coherence in Music*. Mineola, NY: Dover, 1962.

Sams, Eric. *The Songs of Johannes Brahms*. Bolton, UK: Biddles, Guildford and King's Lynn, 2000.

Sandresky, Margaret. "The Golden Section in Three Byzantine Motets of Dufay." *Journal of Music Theory* 25, no. 2 (1981): 291–306.

Santayana, George. *The Sense of Beauty: Being the Outline of Aesthetic Theory*. New York: Dover, 1896.

———. *The Life of Reason*. Amherst, NY: Prometheus Books, 1905/1998.

Schacht, Richard. "Nietzsche, Friedrich Wilhelm." In *The Oxford Guide to Philosophy*, Edited by Ted Honderich, 655–59. Oxford, UK: Oxford University Press, 2005.

Schellenberg, E. Glenn, and Michael Weiss. "Music and Cognitive Abilities." In *The Psychology of Music, 3rd ed.*, Edited by Diana Deutsch, 499–550. Amsterdam: Elsevier, 2013.

Scherer, Klaus. "The Singer's Paradox: On Authenticity in Emotional Expression on the Opera Stage." In *The Emotional Power of Music: Multidisciplinary Perspectives on Musical Arousal, Expression, and Social Control*, Edited by Tom Cochrane, Bernardino Fantini, and Klaus Scherer, 55–73. Oxford, UK: Oxford University Press, 2013.

Schiller, Friedrich. *On the Aesthetic Education of Man in a Series of Letters*. Translated by Reginald Snell. New York: Continuum, 1795/1990.

Schlaug, Gottfried, Andrea Norton, Katie Overy, and Ellen Winner, E. "Effects of Music Training on the Child's Brain and Cognitive Development." In *The Neurosciences and Music II; From Perception to Performance*, Edited by Giuliano Avanzini, Luisa Lopez, Stefan Koelsch, and Maria Majno. *Annals of the New York Academy of Sciences* 1060 (2005): 219–30.

Schliesser, Eric. "Hume's Newtonianism and Anti-Newtonianism." In *The Stanford Encyclopedia of Philosophy* (2008 edition), Edited by Edward Zalta. http://plato.stanford.edu/archives/win2008/entries/hume-newton/.

Schmemann, Serge. "Karajan Leaves Berlin Philharmonic." *New York Times* (April 25, 1989). http://www.nytimes.com/1989/04/25/arts/karajan-leaves-berlin-philharmonic.html?pagewanted=all&src=pm.

Schopenhauer, Arthur. *The World as Will and Representation, Vol. 1*. In *The Cambridge Edition of the Works of Schopenhauer*, Edited by Christopher Janaway, Translated by Judith Norman and Alistair Welchman. Cambridge, UK: Cambridge University Press, 1819/2010.

Schweitzer, Albert. *J.S. Bach*. Translated by Ernest Newman. London: Adam and Charles Black, 1923.

Scruton, Roger. *The Aesthetics of Music*. Oxford, UK: The Clarendon Press, 1997.

———. *Understanding Music: Philosophy and Interpretation*. London: Continuum UK, 2009.

———. *Beauty: A Very Short Introduction*. Oxford, UK: Oxford University Press, 2011.

Seashore, Carl. "In Search of Beauty in Music." *The Musical Quarterly* 28, no. 3 (1942): 302–8.

———. *In Search of Beauty in Music: A Scientific Approach to Musical Aesthetics*. New York: The Ronald Press, 1947.

Sendrey, Alfred. *Music in Ancient Israel*. New York: Philosophical Library, 1968.

Shanahan, James. "The Consumption of Music: Integrating Aesthetics and Economics." *Journal of Cultural Economics* 29, no. 2 (1978): 13–26.

Shapshay, Sandra. "Schopenhauer's Aesthetics." In *The Stanford Encyclopedia of Philosophy* (2012 edition), Edited by Edward Zalta. http://plato.stanford.edu/archives/sum2012/entries/schopenhauer-aesthetics/.

Shepherd, John. "Music and Male Hegemony." In *Music as Social Text*, Edited by John Shepherd, 152–73. Cambridge: Polity Press, 1991.

Sheppard, Anne. *Aesthetics: An Introduction to the Philosophy of Art*. Oxford: Oxford University Press, 1987.

Shusterman, Richard. "The End of Aesthetic Experience." *The Journal of Aesthetic Experience* 55, no. 1 (1997): 29–41.

———. "Moving Truth: Affect and Authenticity in Country Musicals." *The Journal of Aesthetics and Art Criticism* 57, no. 2 (1999): 221–33.

———. "Pragmatism: Dewey." In *The Routledge Companion to Aesthetics*, Edited by Berys Gaut and Dominic Lopes, 97–100. London: Routledge, 2002.

Silber, Kate. "Johann Heinrich Pestalozzi." *Encyclopædia Britannica Online* (May 13, 2014). http://www.britannica.com/biography/Johann-Heinrich-Pestalozzi.

Silverman, Marissa, Susan Davis, and David Elliott. "Praxial Music Education: A Critical Analysis of Critical Commentaries." *International Journal of Music Education* 32, no. 1 (2013): 53–69.

Silvia, Paul, and Emily Nusbaum. "On Personality and Piloerection: Individual Differences in Aesthetic Chills and Other Unusual Aesthetic Experiences." *Psychology of Aesthetics, Creativity, and the Arts* 5 (2011): 208–14.

Singer, Peter. "Hegel, Georg Wilhelm Friedrich." In *The Oxford Guide to Philosophy*, Edited by Ted Honderich, 365–69. Oxford, UK: Oxford University Press, 2005.

Sister Wendy Beckett. *Sister Wendy: The Complete Collection*. BBC Video E1690, 1992.

Skov, Martin, and Oshin Vartanian, Editors. *Neuroaesthetics*. Amityville, NY: Baywood, 2009.

Sloboda, John. "Music Structure and Emotional Response: Some Empirical Findings." *Psychology of Music* 19 (1991): 110–20.

Sloboda, John, and Andreas Lehmann. "Tracking Performance Correlates of Changes in Perceived Intensity of Emotion During Different Interpretations of a Chopin Piano Prelude." *Music Perception* 19, no. 1 (2001): 87–120.

Small, Christopher. *Music-Society-Education*. New York: Schirmer, 1977.

———. *Musicking*. Middletown, CT: Wesleyan University Press, 1998.

Smith, J. David, and Robert Melara. "Aesthetic Preference and Syntactic Prototypicality in Music: 'Tis the Gift to be Simple." *Cognition* 34 (1990): 279–98.

Snell, Reginald. Introduction to *On the Aesthetic Education of Man in a Series of Letters* by Friedrich Schiller. Translated by Reginald Snell. New York: Continuum, 1795/1990.

Solie, Ruth. "Whose Life? The Gendered Self in Schumann's *Frauenliebe* Songs." In *Music and Text: Critical Inquiries*, Edited by Steven Scher, 219–40. New York: Cambridge University Press, 1992.

Solomon, Robert. *Introduction to Philosophy, 8th ed.* New York: Oxford University Press, 2005.

Sparshott, Francis. "Aesthetics of Music: Limits and Grounds." In *What is Music? An Introduction to the Philosophy of Music*, Edited by Philip Alperson, 33–98. University Park, PA: The Pennsylvania State University Press, 1994.

Spencer, Herbert. *Education: Intellectual, Moral, and Physical*. London: Williams and Norgate, 1861.

Spinte, Ralph, and Roland Droh, Editors. *Music Medicine*. St. Louis: MMB Music, 1992.

Stalnaker, Nan. "Fakes and Forgeries." In *The Routledge Companion to Aesthetics*, Edited by Berys Gaut and Dominic Lopes, 395–407. London: Routledge, 2002.

Stapert, Calvin. *A New Song for an Old World. Musical Thought in the Early Church*. Grand Rapids, MI: Wm. B. Eerdmans, 2007.

Steed, Janna. *Duke Ellington: A Spiritual Biography*. New York: Crossroad Publishing Co, 1999.

Stokes, Dustin. "Aesthetics and Cognitive Science." *Philosophy Compass* 4, no. 5 (2009): 715–733.

Stokes, Philip. *Philosophy: The World's Greatest Thinkers*. London: Arcturus, 2007.

Stokes, Richard. *The Book of Lieder: The Original Texts of Over 1000 Songs*. London: Faber and Faber, 2005.

Stolnitz, Jerome. "Beauty: Some Stages in the History of an Idea." *Journal of the History of Ideas* 22, no. 2 (1961): 185–204.

———. "The Aesthetic Attitude." In *Aesthetics: The Big Questions*, Edited by Carolyn Korsmeyer, 78–83. Malden, MA: Blackwell, 1998.

Stowe, David. *How Sweet the Sound: Music in the Spiritual Lives of Americans*. Cambridge, MA: Harvard University Press, 2004.

Stravinsky, Igor. *Poetics of Music in the Form of Six Lessons*. Translated by Arthur Knodel and Ingolf Dahl. New York: Vintage Books, 1960.

"Strong Cities . . . Strong Families . . . For a Strong America. Mayors' 10-point Plan," League of American Orchestras (2008). http://usmayors.org/pressreleases/documents/10-PointPlan_1107.pdf.

Strunk, Oliver. *Source Readings in Music History: The Baroque Era*. New York: W. W. Norton, 1722/1965.

Stubley, Eleanor. "Philosophical Foundations." In *Handbook of Research on Music Teaching and Learning*, Edited by Richard Colwell, 3–20. New York: Schirmer, 1992.

———. "The Performer, the Score, the Work: Musical Performance and Transactional Reading." *Journal of Aesthetic Education* 29, no. 3 (1995): 55–69.

Stumpf, Samuel, and James Fieser. *Philosophy: History and Problems, 6th ed.* New York: McGraw-Hill, 2003.

Subotnik, Rose. *Deconstructive Variations: Music and Reason in Western Society*. Minneapolis, MN: University of Minnesota Press, 1996.

Sullivan, J. *Beethoven: His Spiritual Development*. New York: Vintage Books, 1927.

Sundram, Jason. "Vier Letzte Lieder by Richard Strauss." Program Notes (2004). http://jsundram.freeshell.org/ProgramNotes/Strauss_Leider.html.

Sweet, William. "Herbert Spencer." *Internet Encyclopedia of Philosophy*, accessed November 10, 2015. http://www.iep.utm.edu/spencer/.

Szego, C. K. "Praxial Foundations of Multicultural Music Education." In *Praxial Music Education*, Edited by David Elliott, 196–218. Oxford, UK: Oxford University Press, 2005.

Tellstrom, A. Theodore. *Music in American Education: Past and Present*. New York: Holt, Rinehart, and Winston, 1971.

Tervaniemi, Mari. "Musical Sounds in the Human Brain." In *Neuroaesthetics*, Edited by Martin Skov and Oshin Vartanian, 221–31. Amityville, NY: Baywood, 2009.

Tichi, Cecelia. *High Lonesome: The American Culture of Country Music*. Chapel Hill, NC: University of North Carolina Press, 1994.

Tillich, Paul. *Dynamics of Faith*. New York: HarperCollins, 1957/2001.

Tolstoy, Leo. *What is Art?* Translated by Almyer Maude. Indianapolis: Liberal Arts Press, 1896/1960.

Tomas, Vincent. Introduction to Tolstoy's *What is Art?* (vii–xvii). Indianapolis: Liberal Arts Press, 1960.

Tsioulcas, Anastasia. "The Landfill Harmonic: An Orchestra Built from Trash," 2012. http://www.npr.org/blogs/deceptivecadence/2012/12/19/167539764/the-landfill-harmonic-an-orchestra-built-from-trash.

———. "What Is Classical Music's Women Problem?" *Deceptive Cadence* from NPR Classical, 2013. http://www.npr.org/blogs/deceptivecadence/2013/10/09/230751348/what-is-classical-musics-women-problem

Tucker, Mark, Editor. *The Duke Ellington Reader*. Oxford, UK: Oxford University Press, 1993.

Urban, W. M. "The Driving Force of Idealism." In *Perspectives in Philosophy*, Edited by Robert Beck, 144–49. New York: Holt, Rinehart and Winston, 1961.

Väkevä, Lauri. "Philosophy of Music Education: As Art of Life: A Deweyian View." In *The Oxford Handbook of Philosophy in Music Education*, Edited by Wayne Bowman and Ana Lucía Frega, 86–110. New York: Oxford University Press, 2012.

Valsiner, Jaan. "Introduction to the Transaction Edition." In *The Montessori Method*, Edited by Maria Montessori, xi–xx. New Brunswick, NJ: Transaction Publishers, 2014.

VandenBos, Gary. *APA Dictionary of Psychology*. Washington, DC: American Psychological Association, 2007.

VH1 Save the Music Foundation, 2013. http://www.vh1.com/partners/save_the_music/.

Voloshinov, Alexander. "Symmetry as a Superprinciple of Science and Art." *Leonardo* 29, no. 2 (1996): 109–113.

Von Rhein, John. "Message to Symphony Orchestras in Troubled Times: Think Positive." *Chicago Tribune* (August 22, 2012). http://articles.chicagotribune.com/2012–08–22/entertainment/ct-ent-0822-classical-icsom-20120822_1_orchestras-symphony-musicians-opera-musicians.

Vulliamy, Ed. "Orchestral Manoeuvres." *The Observer* (July 29, 2007). http://www.guardian.co.uk/music/2007/jul/29/classicalmusicandopera1.

Wachsmann, Klaus, Bo Lawergren, Ulrich Wegner, and John Clark. "Lyre." In *Grove Music Online. Oxford Music Online* (2012). http://www.oxfordmusiconline.com/subscriber/article/grove/music/50534.

Wade, Bonnie. *Thinking Musically, 2nd ed.* New York: Oxford University Press, 2009.

Walker, Robert. "Avoiding the Dangers of Postmodern Nihilist Curricula in Music Education." In *The Oxford Handbook of Philosophy in Music Education*, Edited by Wayne Bowman and Ana Lucía Frega, 386–405. Oxford, UK: Oxford University Press, 2011.

Walters, Barbara. "The Feast and Its Founders." In *The Feast of Corpus Christi*, Edited by Barbara Walters, Vincent Corrigan, and Peter Ricketts, 3–56. University Park, PA: The Pennsylvania State University Press, 2006.

Walton, Susan. "Aesthetic and Spiritual Correlations in Javanese Gamelan Music." *Journal of Aesthetics and Art Criticism* 65, no. 1 (2007): 31–41.

Wang, Yuhwen. "Cultivating Virtuous Character: The Chinese Traditional Perspective of Music Education." In *The Oxford Handbook of Philosophy in Music Education*, Edited by Wayne Bowman and Ana Lucía Frega, 263–83. New York: Oxford University Press, 2012.

Warburton, Nigel. *Philosophy: The Basics, 3rd ed.* London: Routledge, 1999.

Warren, Charles. "Brunelleschi's Dome and Dufay's Motet." *The Musical Quarterly* 59, no. 1 (1973): 92–105.

Weber, William. "Mass Culture and the Reshaping of European Musical Taste, 1770–1870." *International Review of the Aesthetics and Sociology of Music* 25, nos. 1/2 (1994): 175–190.

Weinstein, David. "Herbert Spencer." In *The Stanford Encyclopedia of Philosophy* (2012 edition), Edited by Edward Zalta. http://plato.stanford.edu/archives/fall2012/entries/spencer/.

Weinstein, Deena. *Heavy Metal: The Music and Its Culture*, revised edition. Cambridge, MA: Da Capo Press, 2000.

West, Martin. *Ancient Greek Music.* New York: Oxford University Press, 1992.

West-Eastern Divan Orchestra, 2015. http://www.west-eastern-divan.org/news/.

White, David. "Toward a Theory of Profundity in Music." *The Journal of Aesthetics and Art Criticism* 50, no. 1 (1992): 23–34.

White, John. "Education, Problems of the Philosophy of." In *The Oxford Guide to Philosophy*, Edited by Ted Honderich, 231–34. Oxford, UK: Oxford University Press, 2005.

Whitford, David. "Martin Luther (1483–1546)." *Internet Encyclopedia of Philosophy* (2005). http://www.iep.utm.edu/luther/.

Whitwell, David. *Ancient Views on Music and Religion.* Austin, TX: Whitwell Publishing, 2013.

Wicks, Robert. "Arthur Schopenhauer." In *The Stanford Encyclopedia of Philosophy* (2012 edition), Edited by Edward Zalta. http://plato.stanford.edu/archives/win2011/entries/schopenhauer/.

Wilczek, Frank. *A Beautiful Question: Finding Nature's Deep Design.* New York: Penguin Press, 2015.

Wilkins, Robin, Donald Hodges, Paul Laurienti, Matthew Steen, and Jonathan Burdette. "Network Science: A New Method for Investigating the Complexity of Musical Experiences in the Brain." *Leonardo* 45, no. 3 (2012): 282–83.

———. "Network Science and the Effects of Music Preference on Functional Brain Connectivity: From Beethoven to Eminem." *Nature Scientific Reports* 4 (2014): 6130. DOI: 10.1038/srep06130.

Wirtz, Rolf. *Art and Architecture of Florence.* Florence: Könemann, 2005.

Wittgenstein, Ludwig. *Lectures and Conversations on Aesthetics, Psychology and Religious Beliefs.* Berkeley, CA: University of California Press, 1967.

"Women in Music." BBC Proms Survey 2013. http://www.womeninmusic.org.uk/proms-survey.htm.

Youmans, Charles. "The Private Intellectual Context of Richard Strauss's 'Also Sprach Zarathustra.'" *19th-Century Music* 22, no. 2 (1998): 101–26.

Young, James. "Between Rock and a Harp Place." *The Journal of Aesthetics and Criticism* 53, no. 1 (1995): 78–81.

———. "The Cognitive Value of Music." *The Journal of Aesthetics and Art Criticism* 57, no. 1 (1999): 41–54.

Zalta, Edward, Editor. *Stanford Encyclopedia of Philosophy* (2015 edition). http://plato.stanford.edu/.

Index

Note: Italicized page numbers indicate a figure on the corresponding page. Page numbers in bold indicate a table on the corresponding page.

Abeles, Harold 212–13
Abreu, José Antonio 197
Abril, Carlos 33
absolute expressionism 56, 84, 85, 87–9, 88, 91, 143, 144, 148, 202
Absolute Idea 130–1
absolute music 138–9
absolutism 56, 81, 84
active discovery 172
active reflection 204
Adams, John 239
Adorno, Theodor 4, 194–6
advocacy *see* music advocacy
aesthetic awe 58
aesthetic formalism 202
aesthetic judgment 128–9, 163
aesthetics and music: aesthetic, defined 64–5; aesthetic experience 65–6; art and music, defined 62–4; Berlyne's Arousal Theory 72; bodily experiences and 182; BRECVEMA model 74; chills, as aesthetic indicator 73–4; determination of value 69–70; experimental aesthetics 70–5; Golden Mean ratio 72; introduction 4, 8, 62; neuroaesthetics 74–5; popular music 93–5; Preference for Prototype Theory 72–3, 73; school music 95–8; summary and thought questions 75–6; values of 66–8; world music 98–100
Aesthetic Trinity Theory (ATT) 58
affect, defined 54
affect principle 65
Age of Enlightenment 126
Age of Reason 126
Alperson, Phillip 202–3, 205–6
An American in Paris (Gershwin) 89, 89
anarchism and education 30

Ancient Greeks, music philosophy: Aristotle, thoughts on music 111–12; expression of emotion 152; harmonious balance in music 109–10; introduction 90, 107; music as mathematics 108–9; overview 107–8; personal application 249; summary and thought questions 112–13
Ancient Rome, music in 115–16
Andrew, Mary 215–16
Anselm of Canterbury (St. Anselm) 18
anthropology and music 18
Aquinas, Thomas 18, 119–20
Arban, Jean-Baptiste 89
Aristotle (Greek philosopher) 25, 42, 111–12
Armstrong, Louis 64
Arousal Theory 72
Art as Experience (Dewey) 189–90
art traditions/institutions 63
Attali, Jacques 196
Augustinus, Aurelius *see* St. Augustine of Hippo
aulos instrument 108

Bach, J. S. 20, 55, 82, 139, 153, 158, 170
background emotions 55
Bacon, Francis 17
Bandini Pietà (Michelangelo) 43, 44–5
Barenboim, Daniel 198
Batteaux, Abbé 62
Baugh, Bruce 94–5
Baumgarten, Alexander 64, 127
Beardsley, Monroe 64, 154, 171–2
beauty and music: beauty, defined 39, 40; beauty in art 39–45; introduction 8, 39; opinions on 41; overview 46–8; perception and 41; research on 48–9; subjective judgments 42; summary and thought questions 49; truth, goodness, and morals 42; ugliness and 43, 43–5

Beckett, Wendy *see* Sister Wendy
Beethoven, Ludwig van 130, 139, 155–6
being moved state 58
Bell, Clive 141–2
Bergonzi, Louis 33
Berkeley, George 125, 127
Berlioz, Hector 139
Berlyne's Arousal Theory 72
Bernstein, Jay 195
Bernstein, Leonard 53, 59
biology and music 18
Birkhoff, George 62
Boethius (Roman philosopher) 15, 17, 118–19
Bono (Paul David Hewson) 197
Borges, Jorge Luis 18
Boulanger, Nadia 212
Bowman, Wayne 30
Brahms, Johannes 68, 139
brain stem reflex 163, 164
Braun, Wernher von 19
BRECVEMA model 74, 163–4
Britten, Benjamin 49
Brittin, Ruth 62, 70, 71
Broudy, Harry 204
Browning, Robert 27
Bruckner, Anton 139
Bruner, Jerome 28
Bryant, David 133
Budd, Malcolm 140–1, 158
Budiansky, Stephen 97–8
Burrows, David 183
Butler, Abby 34

Cage, John 145
Capperella-Sheldon, Deborah 62, 70, 71
Carroll, Noël 57, 93–4, 144–5, 148
Cartesian principles 64
Chaminade, Cécile 221
Charles, Ray 34
chelys-lyre (tortoise lyre) 107–8
childhood notion of beauty in music 48–9
Child-Study Movement 31–2
chills, as aesthetic indicator 73–4
Chomsky, Noam 33
Cicero (Roman politician) 4
Citron, Marcia 220–1
classical antiquity to the Renaissance: Ancient Rome 115–16; early church writings 117; introduction 90–1, 115; Middle Ages 118–21; personal application 249–50; Plotinus writings on music 116–17; summary and thought questions 121–2
Clifton, Thomas 182–3

closure strategy 142–3
cognition principle 65
Collier, Geoffrey 56
Collingwood, R.G. 154–5
commodification, defined 195
common denominator argument 144–5
common sense and knowledge 25
compositional power of music 196
Cone, Edward 157–8
Confucius (Chinese philosopher) 9, 41
conservatism and education 30
Continuous Response Digital Interface (CRDI) 62, 71
Cook, Nicholas 27
Cooke, Deryck 56, 91, 155–6
creativity, defined 63
critically reflective action 204
criticism, defined 63
Critique of Pure Reason (Kant) 19, 128
Croce, Benedetto 91, 154
Cross, Ian 64
culturally responsive teaching (CRT) 33–4
cultural matrix principle 65
Cusick, Suzanne 216–17
Cutietta, Robert 204

Damasio, Antonio 54–5, 170, 184
Daniels, Charles 153
Darrow, Alice-Ann 33
David (Michelangelo) 39, *40*, 41, 42
Davies, Stephen 68, 94–5, 157
DeBellis, Mark 169
De Clercq, Rafael 64
deep emotion 58
Default Mode Network (DMN) 75
De institutione musica (Boethius) 118
delineation, defined 58
Dell'Antonio, Andrew 228
Dennett, Daniel 16
Descartes, René 15, 54, 126, 135
Desmond, Paul 85, *86*
detached affect 172
Devereaux, Mary 221
Dewey, John 32, 64, 132, 188–90
Dickie, George 65
Dickinson, Emily 39
direct pleasure 62–3
discursive symbols 169
Disraeli, Benjamin 48
Dohnanyi, Ernst von 46
Dudamel, Gustavo 197
Dufay, Guillaume 132–3
Dufrenne, Mikel 92, 182

Durant, William 5, 15, 128
Dutton, Denis 62

Eagleman, David 19
early church writings 117
Eco, Umberto 43
education and music: introduction 7; music
    education, defined 6–7; music education as
    aesthetic education 204–5; 'music makes you
    smarter' movement 256–9, 259; overview 29–34;
    philosophy of 30–2; social justice and CRT 33–4;
    summary 34–5; understand beauty through
    139
Eichendorff, Joseph von 68
Einstein, Albert 17, 226
Eisner, Elliot 28
Ellington, Duke 20
Elliott, David 170, 203–5, 231
emotional saturation 63
emotion and music: Ancient Greeks and 152;
    emotion, defined 54–5; introduction 8, 53–4;
    philosophical thought about 55–6; provoked by
    artworks 141; psychological research on 56–8;
    research on 160–3; role in philosophy 58–9;
    summary and thought questions 59–60
empiricism: introduction 91, 125; musical examples
    132–3; music philosophy, personal application
    250; overview 127; summary and thought
    questions 133–4
episodic memory 163, 164
epistemology 4, 24–6
Ermarth, Elizabeth 226
Erskine, Noel 20
ethics 4
evaluative conditioning 163
evidentialism 25
exemplification concept 170–1
Exhibition Theory 171
Expectancy Theory 91, 142–3, 147–8
experience and knowledge 25
Experience Sampling Methods (ESM) 74
experimental aesthetics 70–5
experimentalism 188
expressionism: Collingwood, R.G. 154–5; Cooke,
    Deryk 155–6; Croce, Benedetto 91, 154; Davies,
    Stephen 157; introduction 91, 152; Kivy, Peter
    156, 157; musical examples 158–60; music
    emotions, research 160–3; music philosophy,
    personal application 250–1; overview 55, 58;
    Robinson, Jenefer 157–8; summary and thought
    questions 163–5; Tolstoy, Leo 153
expressive individuality 63
extrinsic learning 28

Fantaisie and Variations on *The Carnival of Venice*
    (Arban) 89
Farnsworth, Paul 71
Fechner, Gustav 71
feelings, defined 54
felt freedom 172
Feminine Endings (McClary) 219
feminism: Citron, Marcia 220–1;
    Göttner-Abendroth, Heide 217–19; introduction
    92–3, 210; McClary, Susan 219–20; musical
    examples 214–17, 215; music philosophy,
    personal application 253; philosophies of music
    217–21; summary and thought questions 221–2;
    women in music history 210–14
fetishization, defined 195
figure-ground relationships 142
floating intentionality concept 64
focus principle 65
Foley, Timothy 97
Forbes, Guy 97
formal drive *(formtrieb*: Schiller) 130; *see also* play
    drive, sensuous drive
formalism: aesthetic formalism 202; Bell, Clive
    141–2; evaluation of 144–5; Gurney, Edmund
    140–1; Hanslick, Eduard 138–40; introduction
    91, 138; musical examples 145–6; music
    philosophy, personal application 250; music
    psychology research 146–7; overview 58, 85, 86;
    summary and thought questions 147–8
formal *vs.* informal learning 29–30
Freire, Paulo 33, 201
Frobel, Friedrich 31
functional harmony 147
function argument 145
fundamentalism and education 30

Gabrieli, Giovanni 132
Gabrielsson, Alf 29, 58, 83, 185
Gardner, Howard 27–8
Gazzaniga, Michael 16
Gemütsbewegungen movement 26
genres and styles of music 8
German Idealism *see* idealism
GERMS model in expressionism 161–2
Gershwin, George 89, *89*
Gestalt psychology 142
Gettier, Edmund 25
Goethe, Johann Wolfgang von 142
Golden Mean ratio 72
Goldman, Alan 66
Goldman, Edwin Franko 89
Goldstein, Avram 73
good continuation strategy 142

294   *Index*

Goodman, Nelson 27, 92, 170–1
goodness and beauty 42
'goodness-of-fit' 146
Göttner-Abendroth, Heide 217–19
Graham, Gordon 67, 155
Grand Canyon Suite (Grofé) 82, 82
Greek melodies 108
Greene, Maxine 64
Grofé, Ferde 82, 82–3
Gurney, Edmund 56, 140–1

Hall, G. Stanley 31–2
Hanslick, Eduard 53, 55, 138–40, 147
Harmonices Mundi (Kepler) 109
harmonious balance in music 109–10
Hartmann, Viktor 159
Hawking, Stephen 15
Haydn, Joseph *143*
Hegel, Georg 53, 130–1
Heidegger, Martin 5
Hendrix, Jimi 20, 25
Hensel, Fanny Mendelssohn 211
Hevner, Kate 160–1
Hevner Adjective Cycle 160
Hildegard of Bingen 210–11
Hindemith, Paul 53, 54, 59
Hirstein, William 74
Hobbes, Thomas 127
Hoffer, Charles 96
Holiday, Billie 173
Houlgate, Stephen 131
House, Robert 204
humanness notion 29
Hume, David 15, 41, 69, 127
Huron, David 17, 147
Husserl, Edmund 181

idealism: introduction 91, 125; musical examples 132–3; music philosophy, personal application 250; overview 128–32; summary and thought questions 133–4
image schemata 184
imaginative experiences 63
immediate demonstration of art 27
infectiousness 153
instrumentalism 188, 191
instrumental literature 47
intellectual challenge 63
intellectualism and education 30
intentional consciousness 181
International Music Products Association 256
intervals 155–6
Ives, Charles 174–5, *175*

James, William 188
Joad, C.E.M. 4–5
John Cage Organ Foundation 227–8
Johnson, Mark 184
Jorgensen, Estelle 33, 247
Joyce, James 62
joyful music 176
Juilliard Repertory Project 96–7
Junda, Mary 33
Juslin, Patrik 57, 74, 161, 163

Kania, Andrew 64
Kant, Immanuel: aesthetics and music 66; idealism 128–9; introduction 15, 19; knowledge and music 26; rationalism and empiricism 125; religion and music 19; science and music 15
Karajan, Herbert von 59
Keats, John 241
Kemp, Gary 154
Kepler, Johannes 109
King, B.B. 162
kithara (wooden lyre) 107
Kivy, Peter 57–8, 68, 156, 157
Klein, Peter 25
Klemm, William 16
Kneiter, Gerard 65
knowledge and music: epistemology and 4, 24–6; introduction 7; musical knowledge 26–9; overview 24–9; summary 34–5
Konečni, Vladimir 57–9
Korean musical aesthetics 99
Korsmeyer, Carolyn 221
Krumhansl, Carol 146

Lacey, A.R. 4
Lakoff, George 184
Langer, Susanne 15, 56, 169–70
Laukka, Petri 161
Law of Prägnanz 142
Leibniz, Gottfried 126, 127
Leonhard, Charles 96, 204
lesbian, gay, bisexual, or transgender (LGBT) 33
Levinson, Jerrold 67
Lewis, C.S. 11
liberalism and education 30
liberationism and education 30
Lind, Vicki 34
Liszt, Franz 21, 139
logic 4
Luther, Martin 19, 120–1
Lyotard, Jean-François 226

McAnally, Elizabeth 33
Maccheroni, Anna Maria 32
McClary, Susan 219–20
McDonald, Matthew 175
McKeage, Kathleen 212–13
McKoy, Constance 34
MacLeod, Rebecca 48
McWhinne, Harold 71
Madama Butterfly (Puccini) 159
Madsen, Clifford 62, 70, 71
Mahler, Alma Schindler 212
Mahler, Gustav 212
Mainwaring, James 71
Manuel, Peter 99–100
Marlowe, Christopher 42
Maslow, Abraham 28
Mason, Lowell 31, 191
meaning and value, basis for determining **81**,
    81–93, *82–3*, **84**, *85–9*
Mendelssohn, Felix 211
Merleau-Ponty, Maurice 181–2
metaphysics 4
Metaphysics (Aristotle) 42
Meyer, Leonard 56, 91, 142–4, 148
Michelangelo 39, *40*, 42, 43, *44–5*
Middle Ages 118–21
mirror neurons in music 162–3
Mitchell, Joni 141
Mlodinow, Leonard 15
moment-by-moment experiences 180–1
Montessori, Maria 32
moods, defined 54
morals and beauty 42
Morton, Adam 25
mousike, defined 108
Mozart, Maria Anna 211
Mozart, Wolfgang Amadeus 211
multiple intelligences theory 27–8
music advocacy: defined 255; economic rationales
    260–1; final comments 262–3; introduction 255;
    'music makes you smarter' movement 256–9,
    259; need for 255–6; securing support 260;
    strategies and resources 259–61; summary and
    thought questions 261–2
musical examples: empiricism 132–3; expressionism
    158–60; feminism 214–17, **215**; formalism
    145–6; idealism 132–3; introduction 10;
    praxialism 206–7; rationalism 132–3
musical expectancy 163, 164
musical intelligence 28
musical knowledge 26–9
music as mathematics 108–9
music education, defined 6–7

music education as aesthetic education (MEAE)
    204–5
'music makes you smarter' movement 256–9, *259*
Music Matters (Elliott) 203–5
music philosophy: introduction 3–4, 8–10, 81, 239;
    meaning and value, determination of **81**, 81–93,
    82–3, **84**, *85–9*; music exercises 240–8; need for
    5–7; philosophy, defined 4–5; postmodernism as
    228–31; primary value of music 112; summary
    and thought questions 100–1
music philosophy, personal application: Ancient
    Greeks 249; classical antiquity to Renaissance
    249–50; expressionism 250–1; feminism 253;
    formalism 250; introduction 249; phenomenology
    251–2; postmodernism 253–4; pragmatism
    252; praxialism 252–3; rationalism, empiricism,
    and idealism 250; social philosophy 252;
    symbolism 251
music psychology 7, 16–17, 146
Muxfeldt, Kristina 214–15

National Association for Music Education
    191, 258
National System of Youth and Children's Orchestras
    of Venezuela 197
neuroaesthetics 74–5
Newtonian physics 16
Nietzsche, Friedrich 18, 181, 226–7
non-basic emotions 58
nonconscious emotions 55
Norman, Jessye 216–17
novelty, defined 63
Nusbaum, Emily 73
Nussbaum, Charles 17

object-directedness 172
Octet in F Major (Schubert) 84, *84*
O'Neill, William 30
ontology 4
opinions on beauty 41

Parton, Dolly 83, 242–3
Pascal, Blaise 18
Peirce, Charles Sanders 187
perception and beauty 41
perception and knowledge 25
perception principle 65
Pestalozzi, Johann Heinrich 31
phenomenology: Burrows, David 183; Clifton,
    Thomas 182–3; Dufrenne, Mikel 182; Husserl,
    Edmund 181; introduction 180; Johnson, Mark
    184; Merleau-Ponty, Maurice 181–2; musical
    experiences 180–1; music philosophy, personal

application 251–2; Stubley, Eleanor 183–4; summary and thought questions 184–5
philosophy, defined 4–5
philosophy of religion 18–19
physics and music 18
piano literature 46
Plato (Greek philosopher) 4, 12, 39, 109–10, 116–17
play drive (*spieltrieb*: Schiller) 130; *see also* formal drive, sensuous drive
Plotinus (Roman philosopher) 116–17
Poetics (Aristotle) 42
political philosophy 4
popular music aesthetics 93–5
Porter, Susan 212–13
Possession Theory 171
postmodernism: humanizing experience of 231–3; introduction 93, 226–7; in music 227–8; as music philosophy 228–31; music philosophy, personal application 253–4; summary and thought questions 233–4
pragmatism: Dewey, John 188–90; introduction 92, 187; James, William 188; knowledge and 25–6; music philosophy, personal application 252; Peirce, Charles Sanders 187; summary and thought questions 191–2; utilitarian view of 191
Pratt, Carroll 26, 55–6
praxialism: Alperson, Phillip 202–3, 205–6; Elliott, David 203–5; introduction 92, 201–2; musical examples 206–7; music philosophy, personal application 252–3; Regelski, Thomas 206; summary and thought questions 207
Preference for Prototype Theory (PPT) 72–3, *73*
Prieto, Carlos 53–4
primary (basic) emotions 55
primary value of music 241–8
program music 36, 57, 63, 83, 87, 89, 148, 159, 173, 216
programme music 138–9
proximity strategy 142
psychology and music *see* music psychology
pure music 138–9
Pythagoras (Greek philosopher) 14
Pythagorean theorem 108–9

Quinton, Anthony 4

Ramachandran, R.S. 74
Rasa theory 98–9
rationalism: introduction 91, 125; musical examples 132–3; music philosophy, personal application 250; overview 126–7; summary and thought questions 133–4

rationalistic deductive method 64
reasoning and knowledge 25
Record of Music treatise 99
referentialism 56, 81, 84, 87, 87, 90, 152
Regelski, Thomas 206
Reichenbach, Hans 15
Reid, Louis 67
reification, defined 195
Reimer, Bennett 6, 26, 28, 55, 58, 67, 96–7, 143, 170, 204, 229–30, 258
religion and music: introduction 7; overview 17–21; philosophy of religion 18–19; summary 21
repetitive power of music 196
representative power of music 196
Requiem (Mozart) 83, *83*
rhythmic entrainment 163
Riis, Jacob 12
Ring Model 94
The Rise of Scientific Philosophy (Reichenbach) 15
ritual power of music 196
Robinson, Jenefer 91, 157–8
romanticism 158–9
Romeo and Juliet Fantasy Overture (Tchaikovsky) 88, *88*
Roosevelt, Eleanor 6, 12
Rosenkranz, Karl 42
Rosselio, Antonio 42
Rousseau, Jean-Jacques 127
Russell, Bertrand 12, 15, 125–6, 128

St. Anselm *see* Anselm of Canterbury
St. Augustine of Hippo 117–18
St. Vincent Millay, Edna 41
Sanskrit texts 98–9
Santayana, George 19, 65
Schiller, Friedrich 129–30
Schoenberg, Arnold 160, 194
school music aesthetics 95–8
Schopenhauer, Arthur 26, 56, 131–2
Schubert, Franz 84, *84*
Schultz, Charles M. 241
Schumann, Clara Wieck 211–12
Schumann, Robert 211–12, 214, **215**, 233
Schweitzer, Albert 20
science and music: Ancient Greeks and 112; examples of 14–15; introduction 7; overview 14–17; summary 21
scientific philosophy 14–16
Scruton, Roger 66, 229
Seashore, Carl 48, 71
self-actualization 29
sense of wholeness 172
sensuous-associative 144

sensuous drive (*stofftrieb*: Schiller) 130; see also formal drive, play drive
shared affective motion experience (SAME) 163
Shaw, George Bernard 20, 153
Shona people 99
Shostakovich, Dmitri 28
Shusterman, Richard 95, 190
Silverman, Marissa 204
Silvia, Paul 73
simplicity strategy 142
Sister Wendy 29, 67, 75; Sister Wendy philosophy 231–3
skepticism and knowledge 25
skill, defined 63
Sloboda, John 73
Small, Christopher 201–2
social emotions 55
social justice and CRT (culturally responsive teaching) 33–4
social philosophy: Adorno, Theodor 194–6; Attali, Jacques 196; introduction 92, 194; music philosophy, personal application 252; social context of music 197–8; summary and thought questions 198–9
sociology and music 18
Socrates (Greek philosopher) 12
Sontag, Susan 69
Sparshott, Francis 201–2
Spears, Britney 229
special focus, defined 63
Spencer, Herbert 31
Spinoza, Baruch 126–7
Springsteen, Bruce 172–3
Stapert, Calvin 117
Stauffer, Sandra 204
STEAM (science, technology, engineering, arts, and math) careers 260
STEM (science, technology, engineering, and math) careers 260
Stokes, Dustin 71
Stolnitz, Jerome 65
Strauss, Richard 68, 145, 173–4, *174*
Stravinsky, Igor 53, 194
Strong Experiences with Music (SEM) project 29, 58, 83
Stubley, Eleanor 27, 183–4
style, defined 63
subjective judgments in beauty 42
Sullivan, John 68
Summa Theologiae (Aquinas) 119–20

symbolism: Beardsley, Monroe 171–2; Goodman, Nelson 170–1; introduction 91–2, 169; Langer, Susanne 169–70; music philosophy, personal application 251; Nattiez, Jean-Jacques 172; perspective on 172–5, *174*, *175*; summary and thought questions 176
syntactic evaluation 144
systematic demonstration of science 27

'Take Five' (Desmond) 85, *86*
thrills state 58
Ticheli, Frank 202
Tillich, Paul 19
time-based tensions 155–6
Tolstoy, Leo 39, 42, 62, 153
tonal analogue 169–70
tonal hierarchies 146–7
traditionalism 25
truth and beauty 42
Tudor, David 227

ugliness and beauty 43, *43–5*
unitarianism 229
U.S. Office of Education 96
utilitarian view 191

Vakev, Lauri 32
Västfjäll, Daniel 57, 74
vibrato rates 48
virtuosity, defined 63
visual imagery 163
vocal-choral literature 46
Vonnegut, Kurt 20

Wagner, Richard 139–40
Walker, Robert 229
Warburton, Nigel 145
West-Eastern Divan Orchestra 197–8
Whitehead, Alfred North 64
wholeness, sense of 172
Wilczek, Frank 19
Williams, John 173
wisdom and knowledge 26
Wittgenstein, Ludwig 15
women in music history 210–14
world music aesthetics 98–100

Young, James 26, 94–5

Zappa, Frank 42

Lightning Source UK Ltd.
Milton Keynes UK
UKHW031004060919
349279UK00008B/95/P

9 781138 954519